Marketing

Second Edition

Marketing
Second Edition

DAVID MERCER

BLACKWELL
Business

First published 1992
Second edition 1996
Reprinted 1996, 1998 (twice), 1999, 2000 (twice)

Blackwell Publishers Ltd
108 Cowley Road
Oxford OX4 1JF, UK

Blackwell Publishers Inc
350 Main Street
Malden, Massachusetts 02148, USA

British Library Cataloguing in Publication Data
A CIP catalogue record for this book is available from the British Library

Library of Congress Cataloging in Publication Data
Mercer, David (David Steuart)
Marketing/David Mercer. - 2nd ed.
p. cm.
Includes bibliographical references and index.
ISBN 0-631-19638-2 (pb : alk: paper)
1. Marketing Management. 2. Marketing. I. Title.
HF5415. 13.M395   1996   95-15359
658.8 - dc20   CIP

Commissioning Editor: Richard Burton
Desk Editor: Tony Grahame
Production Controller: Pam Park
Text Designer: Pam Park

Typeset in 11 on 13 pt Baskerville
by Keyword Typesetting Services Ltd.
Printed in Great Britain by The Alden Press, Oxford

This book is printed on acid-free paper

Contents

Acknowledgements

Any book of this size and scope must inevitably draw on the experiences of others. In my case this was not least from those imparted to me in the course of nearly thirty years of practical marketing management. Over that time my ideas were influenced by literally hundreds of managers and professionals with whom I worked. It is difficult, therefore, to select just one or two of these – but I must, and hence my apologies to the vast majority who are not mentioned, yet whose inputs were just as influential.

First, I must acknowledge some of my management mentors: Brian McCabe and Dick Metheringham at Foote Cone & Belding; Eric Williams at Phillips Scott & Turner; John Cahill and Owen Green at BTR; Terry Osborne at IBM. Most important of all, though, were those few exceptional managers who allowed me to develop my own experience: John Elliott and Roland Bligh at Gallahers'; and especially Derek Haslam at IBM.

At the end of the day, though, this is an academic work, and it is to my academic contemporaries and colleagues that I owe the greatest vote of thanks. This legacy goes back to my days as a student, when Paul Samuelson's economics textbook set the standard for production – to which this present edition again aspires – and at the same time drew my into my love–hate relationship with that subject; to Kenneth Galbraith who inspired me to look deeper into that subject and Peter Drucker who showed me that business itself could be just as rewarding in theory. Needless to say, in view of the many references in the main body of the book, Phillip Kotler's body of work, coupled with that of Theodore Levitt, provided the foundations on which later authors, myself included, have built.

My academic ideas, however, were mainly shaped during two periods, the first of which occurred in the late 1970s at the London Business School, when the debates I had with John Stopford and especially with Robin Wensley and Sue Birley were just about the most stimulating of my academic career. No less important, however, have been those of the last four years at the Open University including those with the many tutors, some of whom have been critical readers for this book; but especially my colleagues Harold Carter, Alan Plath, Tony Stapleton, Ian Smith, Richard Mole, David Asch, Leslie de Chernatony and, at Cranfield Business School, Malcolm McDonald.

Finally, I will pay tribute to the course managers who have supported me over this time – Val Page, Glenna White, Sally Brown, Kate Hann, Sarah Avery, Mo Vernon; and my secretaries – Gloria Rippen, Cherry Martin and Karen McCafferty; and, of course, my long-suffering family – and especially my wife Pat – who have invested so much of their overtried patience in this book.

But, above all, it is to Blackwell Publishers that I must pay the greatest tribute; to their editor Tony Graham who turned my chaotic original into the relatively organized prose you now see; to Catherine Meyrick, who had the unenviable task of tracking down many of the illustrations; and, most important of all, to my commissioning editor Richard Burton who persuaded me to write the original book and then managed the four years of its gestation and the further two years for this edition – without his support and boundless enthusiasm it would never have seen the light of day.

Copyright
Acknowledgements

Every attempt has been made to trace copyright holders. The author and publishers would like to apologize in advance for any inadvertent use of copyright material. Acknowledgements are presented in chapter order. Figure 1.1 reproduced from R. Lewis and L. G. Erickson, *Journal of Marketing*, vol. 33, July 1969, p. 12, by permission of the American Marketing Association: figures 1.2 and 14.2 reproduced from P. Kotler, *Marketing Management: Analysis, Planning, Implementation and Control*, 7th edn, © 1991, pp. 17 and 49 – reprinted by permission of Prentice-Hall, Englewood Cliffs, New Jersey; figure 1.3 reproduced from S. Lysonski, *Journal of Marketing*, Winter 1985, p. 27, by permission of the American Marketing Association. Figure 2.1 reproduced from Arnold Mitchell, *The Nine American Lifestyles*, 1983, by permission of the Macmillan Publishing Company and Constance Mitchell, Executrix, Estate of Arnold Mitchell; figure 2.2 reproduced from J. A. Howard and J. N. Sheth, *The Theory of Buyer Behavior*, 1969, by permission of John Wiley & Sons, Inc.; figure 2.3 reproduced from F. E. Webster and Y. Wind, *Organizational Buying Behavior*, © 1972, p. 15 – reprinted by permission of Prentice-Hall, Englewood Cliffs, New Jersey; Tables 3.1 and 3.2 reproduced from G. J. Hooley and C. J. West, *Journal of the Marketing Research Society*, vol. 26, no. 4 (1984); figure 3.1 reproduced by permission of BMRB Limited; Figure 5.1 reprinted by permission of *Harvard Business Review*. An exhibit from 'Strategies for Diversification' by Igor H. Ansoff, September–October 1957. Copyright © 1957 by the President and Fellows of Harvard College; all rights reserved; figure 5.2 adapted by permission from The Boston Consulting Group, Inc., 1986; figure 5.3 reproduced from G. L. Shostack, *Journal of Marketing*, vol. 41, no. 2, 1977, by permission of the American Marketing Association; figure 5.4 reproduced from Rathmell, *Marketing in the Service Sector*, Winthrop, 1974; Table 6.1 reproduced from Saunders and Jobber, *Journal of Marketing Management*, by permission of Academic Press Limited, London; figure 6.1 reproduced from R. Rothwell and P. Gardiner, *Journal of Marketing Management*, vol. 3, no. 3, 1988, by permission of The Dryden Press, Harcourt Brace & Company, Ltd.; figure 6.2 reproduced from B. Twiss, *Managing Technological Innovation*, by permission of Pitman Publishing; figures 6.3, 6.4 and 6.5 reproduced from Booz, Allen & Hamilton Inc., *New Products Management for the 1980s*, 1981; figure 7.1 reproduced from R. M. S. Wilson, in D. Lock and N. Farrow, eds, *The Gower Handbook of Management*,

1 Introduction

Thank you for giving up your time to read what I have to say about marketing. In return, I trust that you will find that it will represent a worthwhile investment of your time as well as offering an interesting (and possibly enlightening) experience.

Marketing is perhaps the most fundamental activity of any commercial organization and an essential discipline even in non-commercial organizations. It is also a fascinating and hugely enjoyable subject.

Preamble

At the beginning of each chapter in this book there will be a short introduction, which summarizes the main themes of the chapter. Needless to say, in this first chapter much of the material is taken up with explaining what the book is about, its biases and, most importantly, how you should use it – together with what you should aim to get out of it. It also offers some words of wisdom about handling advice from experts, including that published in textbooks such as this. Apart from this,

the main focus of the chapter is on getting to grips with exactly what marketing is. What are the definitions of marketing? How does it differ from economics, where the 'market' has now been espoused as a favourite term by politicians as much as by marketers? The chapter comes to the simple, but important, conclusion that the key focus of marketing must be the customer, and the key activity the 'dialogue' between supplier and that customer.

There are some differences between the marketing techniques employed by different types of organizations although the similarities are usually more important. In particular, this chapter explores the important differences between sales-oriented and marketing-oriented organizations – and those between product-based and service-based organizations (including those in the non-profit-making sector). A section on the marketing mix (often described in terms of the '4 Ps' – Product, Price, Place and Promotion) introduces the sets of tools used by marketing to address the needs of the customer and leads on to the specialized chapters in the rest of the book, where these tools are described in more detail.

This book is a comprehensive introduction to marketing. It covers all functions and all types of organization. Indeed, the wide coverage is designed to allow material to be *selected* to meet your specific, individual needs – across a very wide spectrum of organizational situations. It also makes the basic assumption that you may not be currently involved directly in the marketing function itself, and may not previously have had any significant exposure to the theory or practice of the subject. Even so, the coverage is intended to be sufficiently comprehensive to act also as a reference source even in the most demanding of contexts and the book should equip you to meet most practical marketing requirements.

Theory and Practice

The book also allows for those who may be practising managers, and who are learning about the theory of marketing in their spare time. Such practising managers have the great advantage of immersion in a real-life case study – the workings of the organization in which they operate. To tap the power of such a pragmatic approach in the book – which has been developed on the basis of practical experience with many thousands of students who have passed through the Open Business School marketing courses – a wide range of practical exercises has been developed. These exercises are based on continuous reference to a single organization. This organization may be the one in which you are currently working or one which you know about, or simply one that has been well documented as a case study. The exercises are of varying degrees of complexity, from the simplest of questions, which requires only an immediate 'yes or no' answer, through to formulating a complete marketing plan.

In line with its emphasis on practicality, the book will offer the various theories only as tools to be used when applicable: as aids to understanding the customer's real needs, and what may be done to satisfy them. It will critically examine the theories in the context of what they may offer the practising manager. Indeed, it will approach each subject as if you were a practising manager.

In line with this philosophy, the book will, as far as possible, suggest which of these tools might be of most use in a given situation. However, it will stress that there are probably *several* tools which are equally applicable to the situation – each of which offers a different framework for your own individual analysis.

Yoram Wind[1] states that:

> Marketing as a discipline can provide few generalizations, 'principles', or 'laws'. The major contribution of the marketing discipline is in its *approach* to problem identification and solution.

This is a view with which I would concur. The essence of this book is *marketing practice*, and theory is used to provide no more than a useful framework.

Unfortunately, rather less than half a century after the birth of marketing as a widely used practical tool of management, too many marketing theorists appear to be hungering after academic respectability and scientific accuracy; they are beginning to adorn their work with esoteric mathematical approaches, although the subject, as practised, remains just as determinedly 'fuzzy' as it ever was. For a discipline which was once at the leading edge of management theory, there also seems to be a distinct reluctance to invest in new knowledge or ideas. Nigel Piercy[2] makes a very valid point when he says 'there appears to be a temptation . . . to retain familiar and comfortable structures and classifications. These are, in fact, outdated, fragmentary and generally unhelpful in terms of solving management problems – but make it easier to deliver courses and programmes.' This book does *not* shirk its responsibility. It introduces the leading-edge ideas. This may make it that much harder for your lecturer to teach the material – so please thank him or her for the extra work they undertake as a result – but it offers you the best perspective on where marketing is *going*, rather than just on where it has been!

Quinn et al.,[3] in the introduction to their splendidly eclectic handbook on strategy, also make the point that:

---

[1] Y. J. Wind, *Product Policy: Methods and Strategy* (Addison-Wesley, 1982).

[2] Nigel F. Piercy, Marketing and strategy fit together (in spite of what some management educators seem to think!), *Management Decision*, vol. 33, no. 1 (1995).

[3] J. B. Quinn, H. Minzberg and R. M. James, *The Strategy Process* (Prentice-Hall, 1988).

We do not apologize for contradictions among the ideas of leading thinkers. The world is full of contradictions. The real danger lies in using pat solutions to a nuanced reality, not in opening perspectives up to different interpretations. The effective strategist is one who can live with contradictions, learn to appreciate their cues and effects, and reconcile them sufficiently for effective action.

These contradictions will be explained, I hope productively, throughout this book.

In any case, much of marketing practice is pragmatic (that is, based upon what has been shown by experience to work) rather than being what theory would prescribe. Lilien and Kotler[4] report that:

> Marketing people often say that marketing experience is the best teacher, that planning and performing a diversity of marketing activities – selling, pricing, advertising, servicing – create sound judgment about what will work and what will backfire.

Unlike some other authors, I will not pretend that there are grand theories which will magically unlock the inner secrets of the subject and can be applied equally to any marketing situation. Indeed, the most important of contributions to marketing 'theory' have often been practical 'rules of thumb' derived from observation of what really works; these usually turn out to be the most useful guides of all – perhaps precisely because they are honest about their limited ambitions to offer a framework for investigation rather then a predicted solution! Thus, I believe such 'rules of thumb' typically offer the most useful help to practitioners because they are immediately of use in building upon those managers' existing skills and knowledge – whilst clearly highlighting the limitations behind their use. The main reasons for this are

PRACTICAL HELP – 'rules of thumb' are derived directly from practical experience, and aim only to help the reader benefit from that experience. They also have a history of working in practice, which reduces the risk involved in implementing them.

IMMEDIATE (EASE OF) USE – 'rules of thumb' are, and need to be, inherently simple. In general they should be no more than one or two sentences long (or a single diagram) – so that the reader can *immediately* understand what they are saying and can quickly put them into practice.

EXISTING SKILLS AND KNOWLEDGE – 'rules of thumb' build upon the practical skills and knowledge that the manager already possesses, rather than trying to override this, and typically develop a common-sense perspective – while still stimulating the development of real insight – which *empowers the manager to deploy his or her own best judgement.*

[4] G. L. Lilien and P. Kotler, *Marketing Decision Making* (Harper & Row, 1983).

SPECIFIC SOLUTION(S) – 'rules of thumb' relate directly to the unique situation facing the manager, which *only he or she can solve* and to which outsiders can only contribute general ideas, which is why managers have to be empowered to confidently handle the related decision-making.

RECOGNIZED LIMITATIONS – even more important, *users recognize that 'rules of thumb' are not perfect* (as traditional marketing theories often claim to be). They are, justifiably, seen as approximations which will probably help in most (but not all) situations. A realistic awareness of the limitations on what you may do is as important in marketing as recognizing the potential awaiting development.

Such rules offer the most realistic approach to *most* marketing problems; but nobody should expect to apply each and every one of the rules to every situation facing them. They provide, in effect, an extended menu from which the user selects just *those few rules which apply to a specific situation*. This book offers many such rules – though they are too often called theories – to match the many situations which over time face marketers. To do otherwise would be to short-change the reader. Despite the hype generated by those selling simplistic panaceas, which are claimed to have universal applicability, *there are no universal rules in marketing. There are only the best rules of thumb for the specific situation*. That is why it is such an endlessly interesting subject, and why marketing professors are not millionaires!

Coverage

The book attempts to cover almost all of the most important theory, and related practice, in the whole marketing discipline. Where possible, it attempts to supplement this coverage at a deeper level. This is because much of the understanding of marketing comes from an in-depth appreciation of the individual techniques – and the basic customer needs that they address.

As with almost all management education, the theory you learn from this book will not alone make you a qualified marketing manager. For that you will also need relevant practical experience. However, it should give you a good feel for what marketing is about, and help you to talk sensibly and productively to marketers in their own language. Most important of all, though, is that it should provide you with a set of generally applicable tools which you can use in your own work.

SELF-TEST QUESTION 1.1   **?**

At regular intervals through the book I shall ask a series of questions in order to conduct an 'audit' on an organization of your choice. The prime objective in asking these questions will obviously be to consolidate the theory which has just been taught, by requiring you to apply it in practice.

How much effort you put into this depends on you. Some of the questions will be easy to answer. Some may be very difficult because of the way your organization operates. If a question requires a disproportionate amount of work then ignore it or make some reasonable assumptions instead. This 'Audit' is fortunately not a life-and-death exercise.

The questions will not, however, be totally independent. They will gradually build up to give a picture of one aspect of the organization, and ultimately of the whole organization, which may be as valuable to you as the theory you have learnt in the process. At times I shall suggest that you conduct more major exercises, to bring together the material you have collected in your answers to the previous questions, and to give a more formal report on that aspect of the organization. This will eventually lead to the complete marketing plan.

I suggest, therefore, that you write the questions and your answers in a separate exercise book, with a page for each question.

The first questions will be about you:

- Why are you studying this book? (Alternatively, if the book forms part of a taught course, why are you following the course?)
- What are your objectives?
- What do you hope to have achieved by the end of the book (or course)?
- What extra knowledge or skills do you want it to provide you with?

Write down your answers. When you have finished this book come back to these answers and see if the book has achieved not just what I have set out to do but also what you wanted it to do. In marketing the customer – in this case you – is paramount.

It is often quite difficult to put down in words exactly why you are doing something and what your objectives are, but that is one of the generally applicable lessons of marketing. Before you invest considerable time and effort in anything, think through your objectives fully. Here are some of the objectives that students have previously had in studying such material:

- to obtain a qualification
- to understand what made marketing so important to their organization
- to be able to talk to those who carried out the marketing functions
- to be able to work in partnership with those in marketing
- to be able to provide the best customer service
- to add to their set of management tools

(Those of you who are in full-time business education will not, of course, have the 'luxury' of your own organization to study. Fortunately you will, on the other hand, benefit from the support of your marketing lecturer – who will more than compensate for this shortfall. In this situation you may be advised to use specific case studies for each set of 'Audits', although such an approach will not build up to the overall marketing plan. Alternatively, you may be encouraged by your lecturer to use your previous experience (with a previous employer, perhaps in vacation employment) or to use one of the thoroughly documented 'single-case studies'. Whatever the outcome and whatever your choice of approach, the later 'Audits' will continue to refer to 'the organization'.)

Aims and Objectives

The aim of this book is to provide a comprehensive introduction to the theory and practice of marketing, for both non-specialists and newcomers to the discipline.

By the time you have completed the main sections, you should:

- appreciate why marketing is so important for most organizations, and what this means for their operations
- understand the basic principles and main theories of marketing, together with how these may be applied in practice
- recognize the limitations of such theories, and the practical remedies which may help overcome them
- be able to understand the language used by marketing practitioners, and assess the merits of their recommendations
- be able to apply relevant marketing concepts and techniques to the more general, departmental, problems elsewhere in the organization

A Brief History of Marketing

Marketing has been in existence for a number of millennia; ever since people first started to barter the surpluses they had accumulated. For most of that time, though, it has been seen as a peripheral activity; because, in subsistence economies, such surpluses represented a relatively small part of the total.

After the Industrial Revolution made such surpluses more commonplace, the 'marketing' of these became the province of the 'salesman', with his specialized skills.

Jones and Monieson[5] suggest that the first academic discussions of 'marketing' can be traced back to the turn of the century; to, for instance, the E. D. James series of articles in *Mill Supplies* between 1911 and 1914.

However, in the wider sphere of *practical* business management, it was only after 1945 that the newly-fashionable advertising agencies began to redefine the discipline in a way which came close to the modern concept of marketing. The 1950s may be seen as the decade of advertising: the influence of the agencies peaked and their clients appointed advertising managers to control this newly-discovered resource.

Indeed, it was arguably only at the beginning of the 1960s that marketing in its modern form, based upon a customer focus (in particular, making extensive use of market research to investigate customers' needs and wants), emerged on the scale that we now witness. This decade represented the heyday of the 'pure' marketing manager – and, especially, of the few pioneers who became brand managers, at the pinnacle of a new profession. Almost all of these pioneers, however, practised techniques which had been learned by a practical apprenticeship, rather than by the study of classroom theory.

The discipline matured in the 1970s as, led by Philip Kotler's seminal text *Marketing Management*,[6] first published in 1967, the ideas which had developed from practical experience were codified. Marketing became 'routinized' as an increasingly important function of management. Wolf and Smith[7] chart another aspect of marketing's progress during this time: ' . . . the influence of the field waned in the turbulent 1970s when strategic planning ascended. This change forced management to concentrate on reacting to environmental changes and consolidating competitive positions to conserve scarce resources.' These are elements which have now been incorporated into modern marketing.

In the 1980s, however, marketing lost much of its previous self-confidence. Not least in terms of the new ideas being developed, the attention moved to more aggressive techniques with a more immediate payback, including derivatives of those developed by Michael Porter[8] in his *Competitive Strategy*. These derivations, however, conveniently ignored Porter's longer-term perspectives.

[5] B. D. G. Jones and D. D. Monieson, Early development of the philosophy of marketing thought, *Journal of Marketing*, vol. 54 (1990).

[6] P. Kotler, *Marketing Management* (Prentice-Hall, 1st edn, 1967).

[7] J. Wolf and W. R. Smith, Market needs and market changes, *Handbook of Modern Marketing*, ed. V. P. Buell (McGraw-Hill, 2nd edn, 1986).

[8] M. E. Porter, *Competitive Strategy* (The Free Press, 1980).

We can summarize this historic progression diagrammatically:

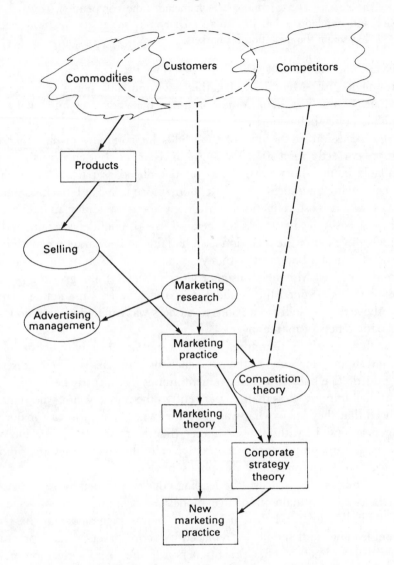

Warren Keegan[9] summarized some of the changes as follows:

By 1980 it was clear that the 'new' concept of marketing was outdated and that the times demanded a strategic concept. The strategic concept of marketing, a major evolution in the history of marketing thought, shifted the focus from the customer or product to the firm's external environment. Knowing everything

[9] W. J. Keegan, *Global Marketing Management* (Prentice-Hall, 4th edn, 1989).

there is to know about the customer is not enough. To succeed, marketers must know the customer in a context which includes the competition, government policy and regulation, and the broader economic, social and political macro forces that shape the evolution of markets.

Somewhat idiosyncratically, Dickson[10] describes this, for instance, as the Five Environments (5E) Mental Model; the 'environments' being own company behaviour, competitor behaviour, consumer behaviour, channel behaviour, and public policy behaviour.

As the recession at the end of the 1980s hit company profits, marketing activity – correctly seen as a long-term investment (but incorrectly seen as expendable in the short-term) – was often reduced as part of organization-wide cost-saving measures. The attention, indeed, moved back to internal activities, where cost reductions – the new focus of senior management – could most easily be made. As the general loss of confidence continued into the 1990s – even after the recession itself had finished – marketing continued to take something of a back seat in many organizations. Even in the traditionally strong area of Fast Moving Consumer Goods (FMCG), the growing power of the retailers undermined the confidence of the supplier's marketing management. Above all, the shift from goods to services was calling into question many of the basic tenets of marketing.

Beneath the surface, therefore, there *was* significant activity at the leading edge; and support for some of the most cherished theories was being discreetly downgraded. The battle for (management) minds had already been won; apart from a small minority (less than 20 per cent) in the public sector who remained convinced that they knew what was good for their clients, the vast majority of managers accepted – without reservation – that the customer's needs and wants had to be paramount; even if – as was typically the case – they then did not know what to do to implement this philosophy!

In academic circles, at least, the leading edge researchers were questioning the viability of the main predictive models – including such basics as the Product Life Cycle[11] and Boston Matrix.[12] It was suggested that these were often misleading, and should be replaced by more practical, and pragmatic, theories which aimed to offer practitioners a framework for decision-making. Thus, when business confidence rebounds, as it inevitably will in the second half of the 1990s, it seems likely that this more practical approach may come to the fore; not unreasonably when, as our own research shows, managers want – above all – practical frameworks to help them take the decisions rather than predictions to usurp their role. It is, therefore, this philosophy – empowering managers to take their own decisions – which permeates much of the thinking in this book.

[10] Peter R. Dickson, *Marketing Management* (Dryden Press, 1994).

[11] D. Mercer, A two decade test of product life cycle theory, *British Journal of Management*, vol. 4 (1993).

[12] J. Scott Armstrong and Roderick J. Brodie, Effects of portfolio planning methods on decision making: experimental; results, *International Journal of Research in Marketing*, vol. 11 (1994).

ACTIVITY 1.1

As we go through the book I shall occasionally ask less rigorous questions which are independent of the organization, and which will not build on one another.

The first of these 'activities' will test your appreciation of the relation between marketing and economics. The question to be answered (without a great deal of research) is:

How would *you* define 'the discipline of the market'?

Is it something remote, impersonal, which does not directly affect your life; one of those grand phrases which you read in the newspapers, but which seem to have no bearing on everyday life? Or do you automatically think of a political explanation, in terms perhaps of the traditional confrontation between right and left? Or do you think of economics – and, possibly, rather esoteric theory? Or is it something which impacts directly upon your business life?

We will return to address this question from the viewpoint of *economics* in chapter 13. For the time being, though, we are trying to establish what is *marketing*?

What is Marketing?

. . . and, as we have seen, despite wide acceptance of the overall concept, marketing is a widely used term which is often very misused and misunderstood – it has come to mean many things to many different people.

ACTIVITY 1.2

To set the context for what follows, by getting you to appreciate your preconceptions or prejudices, the second question is deceptively simple:

What is marketing?

Introduction

What is marketing?

Categories of marketing

Marketing and internal resources

Marketing mix

Selling versus marketing

Product or service

The Essence of Marketing

The definitive answer (or, as it will turn out, *answers*) to the question 'What is marketing?' will occupy several pages. But the essence of what marketing is, even if it is not a complete or definitive description, can be drawn out as follows.

The key aspect of marketing is an attitude of mind. It requires that, in taking 'marketing' decisions, the manager looks at these from the viewpoint of the customer. These decisions will thus be driven by what the customer needs and wants.

Much of what management does is concerned with taking decisions which revolve around how the products or services of the organization can be made to match the customer needs and wants; the definitions which come in the next section allow for this. But the most difficult part of marketing, the key to success, is that of adopting that customer's viewpoint. Tom Peters, the co-author of one of the best-selling management books of all time,[13] puts it more dramatically. He states that if you simply offer your customers the normal courtesies then you will start out ahead of most other organizations.

The next section explores a range of the more complex definitions of marketing. This at first may seem confusing. The intention, though, is to illustrate the spectrum of opinions and by this process to build up a picture of what marketing practice is likely to cover.

Definitions of Marketing?

The classic Western definition, summarized by Philip Kotler[14] is:

> Marketing is human activity directed at satisfying needs and wants through exchange processes.

It is a complex issue, however. Even Kotler, who is one of the acknowledged leaders of marketing theory, has found the subject increasingly complex; for by the seventh edition of the book (1991) his definition was elaborated to:

> Marketing is a social and managerial process by which individuals and groups obtain what they need and want through creating and exchanging products and value with others.

In the UK a very similar definition was given by the Chartered Institute of Marketing:

> Marketing is the management process responsible for identifying, anticipating and satisfying customer requirements profitably.

---

[13] T. J. Peters and R. H. Waterman, *In Search of Excellence* (Harper & Row, 1982).
[14] P. Kotler, *Marketing Management* (Prentice-Hall, 3rd edn, 1976).

Marketing theory, like much business theory, is far from an exact science. There is always scope for different interpretations. For example, Kenichi Ohmae[15] says of Japanese business strategy in general:

What business strategy is about – what distinguishes it from all other kinds of business planning – is, in a word, *competitive* advantage. Without competitors there would be no need for strategy, for the sole purpose of strategic planning is to enable the company to gain, as efficiently as possible, a sustainable edge over its competitors.

To some Western ears this is a very aggressive interpretation, even if it does chime with the widely-accepted views of Michael Porter;[16] it more directly addresses the ideas which engaged marketing theorists at the end of the 1980s, who often claimed that 'The objective of strategic marketing is to achieve sustainable competitive advantage.'[17] It does not directly mention the 'customer' at all. But even here 'competition' implies that the customer is king; since he, and he alone, can decide the *winner* of the competition.

Ohmae's claim is, in any case, an overstatement. Kotler and Fahey[18] make the following important observation:

Japanese marketing strategy, strangely enough, is not based on the discovery of new and fresh marketing principles. Japan's secret is that they thoroughly understand and apply the existing textbook principles. The Japanese came to the United States to study marketing and went home understanding its principles better than most US companies did.

A very different approach to the 'competitive' Japanese view was taken by some writers in the later 1980s, when 'ethics' had become a major subject at a number of leading business schools. Peter Bennett[19] suggests development in this vein:

A *societal marketing orientation* adds an additional consideration to the marketing concept: the impact of a firm's activities on society.

Yet another approach defines it in terms of the 'functions' that marketing incorporates. Thus, for example, Lewis and Erickson[20] illustrate this view by means of a diagram (figure 1.1).

The key element of all marketing is that, unlike almost all other business activities, it is outward-looking; it is firmly centred on the customer. This is sometimes described as the 'outside-in' view. It is described particularly well in these terms by Gareth

---

[15] K. Ohmae, *The Mind of the Strategist* (McGraw-Hill, 1982).

[16] Porter, *Competitive Strategy*.

[17] Robin Wensley, Strategic Marketing: A Review, in *The Marketing Book* (3rd edn), ed. Michael Baker (Butterworth Heinemann, 1994).

[18] P. Kotler and L. Fahey, The world's champion marketers, *The Japanese Journal of Business Strategy*, vol. 3, no. 1 (1982).

[19] P. D. Bennett, *Marketing* (McGraw-Hill, 1988).

[20] R. Lewis and L. G. Erickson, Marketing functions and marketing systems: a synthesis, *Journal of Marketing*, vol. 33 (1969).

Morgan,[21] who requires that the managers involved should adopt the perspective of looking (with the customer's eye-view) from the outside, inwards towards the organization itself. We shall see that these concepts may be applied to almost all types of organization – even to those non-profit-making organizations which have traditionally viewed themselves as apart from normal commercial processes. The needs and wants of the 'customer' (or 'client') should almost always be paramount: the difference – and the difficulty – for such organizations is deciding who their customers (or clients) are, and what are their needs and wants.

Peter Drucker[22] stated the position even more comprehensively:

> Every business can be defined as serving either customers or markets or end users.

Finally, Michael Baker[23] points out one frequent source of confusion, when he states that 'marketing is both a philosophy of business and a business function . . . a state of mind concerning the optimum approach to business, and the activities whereby such ideas are translated into practice . . .'. We have, indeed, seen examples of both in the preceding definitions. He also widens coverage of the activities (though not the viewpoint) even further[24] when he suggests that 'real marketing has four essential features', which he lists as:

1 Start with the customer.
2 A long-run perspective.
3 Full use of all the company's resources.
4 Innovation.

To put all these views in context, our own recent research[25] shows that nearly all organizations (81 per cent of them) at least see marketing in terms of a philosophy which focuses on the needs of the customer. Robertson,[26] for instance, stresses that 'Increasingly, we are recognizing that marketing must be a company wide philosophy . . .'. He goes on, though, to add the important caveat: 'Sometimes it is mainly rhetoric without much substance.'

In terms of practice, again as shown by my own research, nearly all (83 per cent) had a marketing department of one form or another. On the other hand, Robertson would claim that it is increasingly '. . . a process that is conducted across departmental boundaries'.

Nigel Piercy[27] sums up the problem caused by all these different views, in his comment that '. . . we are being told on every side that marketing is the great-

---

[21] G. Morgan, *Riding the Waves of Change*.

[22] P. F. Drucker, *Managing for Results* (Heinemann, 1964).

[23] M. J. Baker, *Marketing Strategy and Management* (Macmillan, 1985).

[24] M. J. Baker, Organizing for planning; marketing, *The Marketing Book*, ed. Michael J. Baker (Heinemann, 1987).

[25] David Mercer, research to be published.

[26] Thomas Robertson, New developments in marketing: a European perspective, *European Management Journal*, vol. 12, no. 4 (December 1994).

[27] Nigel Piercy, *Market Led Strategic Change* (Butterworth Heinemann, 1992).

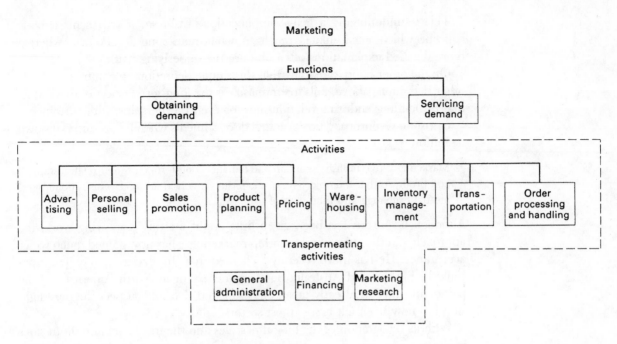

Figure 1.1 Marketing functions and activities.

est thing since sliced bread . . . is something of which we should all have a lot more; is what our international competitors beat us at . . . Unfortunately no one seems to be able to tell us exactly what it is'!

To simplify matters, therefore, I believe the best *practical* metaphor for marketing is a *dialogue*: this is a metaphor I shall develop throughout the book. Like any sales professional who is actually in face-to-face contact with his or her customer, the marketer must communicate the sales points that need to be made, even though it must often be by indirect means such as advertising. More important, though, like any good sales professional, the marketer should spend most of the time *listening* – in this case probably through marketing research: the marketer who listens to his or her customers (and, indeed, understands their viewpoint) is the most effective manager. If you have any doubt, therefore, as to what might be good marketing, simply think of it in the context of this dialogue: would it work face-to-face with the customer?

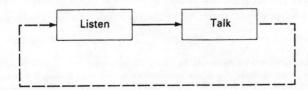

This is undoubtedly a gross simplification. Even so, it represents a basic concept which encapsulates much of what marketing is about – whereas more detailed explanations often obscure the underlying truth.

On the other hand, one thing that this simple definition, in common with the other definitions above, fails to emphasize is the long-term aspect of marketing: that of building enduring relationships (or even partnerships) with customers.

Christian Grönroos,[28] however, led developments when he produced his own definition:

> Marketing is to establish, maintain and enhance long-term customer relationships at a profit, so that the objectives of the parties involved are met. This is done by mutual exchange and fulfilment of promises.

Although Grönroos has been given little credit for this pioneering work, the approach – in the guise of relationship marketing – has now gained much wider acceptance. He has more recently[29] claimed that 'In services marketing, especially in Europe and Australia but to some extent in North America . . . the paradigm shift has already taken place. Indeed, I would suspect the paradigm shift has now been felt across most sectors.'

With its recognition of the long timescales and the involvement of both sides in the process, this offers – I believe – a richer starting point for future developments.

Indeed, successful marketing practice demands this quite specific attitude of mind; but even then it is useful to distinguish two separate levels of approach. Thus, marketing can be seen as simultaneously a *relationship* with the customer, based upon a series of transactions which – over time – should result in mutual benefit, and a parallel *dialogue* between you and the customer(s), which communicates the information necessary to define that 'relationship'.

SELF-TEST QUESTION 1.2

Does your own organization subscribe to any of these views? If not, how would you describe its views? What are the implications of its views for its marketing activities? What do you think its view *should* be?

These general processes may become clearer if I describe the special situation of a salesperson (in a shoe shop, say) making a sale of one product as a result of

---

[28] Ch. Grönroos, Marketing redefined, *Management Decision*, vol. 28, no. 8 (1990).

[29] Christian Grönroos, From marketing mix to relationship marketing: towards a paradigm shift in marketing, *Management Decision*, vol. 32, no. 2 (1994).

one face-to-face contact – the supposedly classical sales situation. Here the 'relationship' is abbreviated to a single transaction, where the product (a pair of shoes) is exchanged for a sum of money, and there are no more elements to that relationship. Accompanying this is the 'dialogue', which in this special case is the conversation between salesperson and customer that builds up to that transaction (the sale/purchase of the pair of shoes). Typically, much of this dialogue is devoted to finding out what the customer needs and wants (what size, what colour, what style etc.) rather then being devoted to persuasion as might traditionally be expected.

In a more general description, this *dialogue* is more complex. More individuals, especially others who may influence the decision to purchase, may enter the process and other media (letters and proposals, or the mass media, such as advertising) may be used. Still, the principle of the two-way dialogue (exploring what the customer wants, even if this is by marketing research rather than face-to-face) is much the same.

Similarly, the single transaction, in evolving to the more general '*relationship*', becomes more complex in two directions. In the first, the elements within it become more diverse. There will be a number of separate transactions involved, not just one. Some of these may be obviously 'physical' in nature; the archetypal product sale. Others, though, may revolve around intangible exchanges, including – most intangibly of all – the corporate/brand image which is needed to reassure the customer. One way in which the description presented in this book departs from most others is that it expects some of these other transactions to flow from the customer, who will not just pay money for the goods – which is traditionally all that is expected of him or her – but will also commit a range of other elements; such as the time and effort involved in buying the product and using it (and perhaps learning to use it), possibly even the purchase of related items to enable the product to be used (or to be used more effectively), a commitment to the supplier (loyalty) etc.

The second aspect is that of time. The traditional single transaction takes no more than the few minutes that the brief dialogue lasts. In the more general model the more complex relationship, extending over multiple transactions, similarly extends over time; and also develops over time. At the most basic level this recognizes that in most markets the customers place repeat purchases with the same supplier; in which process customer loyalty is a major factor. The essence of this on-going relationship is, however, more than this. *It is the investment made by both sides – such that the 'natural state' of the relationship is continuity.* It is only in the exceptional condition, when the relationship breaks down, that it briefly returns to the traditional single transaction mode.

Surprisingly, in view of its importance to both sides, this relationship over time – and the mutual 'investments' associated with maintaining and developing it – is little debated in conventional marketing theory!

These two elements, '*dialogue*' and '*relationship*', are *external elements*. Thus, while they may be defined in an unconventional way, they will be quite recognizable to the most traditionally minded marketer – since they clearly represent marketing links with the outside world, especially with customers. There is, however, a third leg to marketing practice which is the antithesis of traditional marketing – since it is totally *internally* oriented. This is the cross-functional co-ordination of the organization's operations.

Co-ordination

This third element is not considered by, and is by most definitions excluded from, conventional marketing theory. Yet it is seen by many practising managers as the most important aspect of marketing. It should be noted, though, that members of marketing departments – who it might be expected would welcome such an empire-building definition – typically take a much more isolationist view! But for most managers, I repeat, it is this element which is seen as *ensuring that the organization delivers what it has promised. These three legs combine to make up what may be defined as marketing practice.* This compares with the more traditional approach, which has concentrated more mechanistically on a narrower set of discrete topics. Recently these have been most popularly defined as the 4 Ps, which generally fall within the 'dialogue' and 'relationship' sections of my own definition above, but only cover parts of these.

To differentiate the more general, three-legged model, this model is called the '*marketing triad*' (or TRIAD for short – not to be confused, though, with Kenichi Ohmae's 'triad' of *international* markets).

The three key elements of marketing are thus:

DIALOGUE – to establish what are the customer needs and to negotiate suitable solutions to these

RELATIONSHIP – investment in the effective external exchanges necessary to optimize these solutions, in practice, to the mutual benefit of both sides

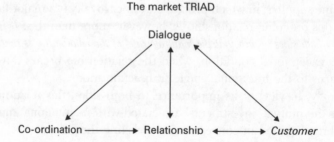

The market TRIAD

CO-ORDINATION – management of internal operational resources across the whole organization in order to deliver this relationship

Marketing and Internal Resources

As we have seen, most marketing theory emphasizes the necessity of starting with the customer/consumer/client, and with his or her needs as the prime focus of all marketing activity. In theory, at least, there is excellent justification for this, as we saw in the earlier section. In practice there may be even greater justification for it, because most organizations are so preoccupied with their internal problems – and it takes a great deal of effort to shift their attention from these.

What, on the other hand, gets lost once the marketer adopts this single-minded concentration on the customer, is the relationship with the organization's internal resources. Much as the organization cannot exist in isolation from its market, neither can marketers exist in splendid isolation from the rest of the organization; although that is often what marketing departments attempt. Marketing's role is, after all, primarily to serve the *organization*, even if its first task may then be to remind the organization that it is also there (secondarily) to serve the customer.

Marketing has to work with those resources that are available, no matter what the market may demand. Indeed, some of the most spectacular failures have arisen from very strong marketing visions, which drove their adherents to commit their organizations beyond any reasonable exposure of their resources. Laker Airways was immensely popular with its customers, but lost hundreds of millions of dollars of its investors' funds. BCCI earned the gratitude of many in the Third World, as the first bank to take notice of their special needs, only to become the subject of even wider opprobrium when it crashed.

The 'expert' approach to marketing

Paradoxically, therefore, the starting point for the expert marketer is, as we will see, the organization itself. The important qualification here is the term 'expert'; it requires considerable expertise to examine these internal requirements without being swamped by them. However, if you can justifiably lay claim to this level of expertise, the process then becomes:

1 *Develop an understanding of what resources the organization has at its disposal.* This requires a considerable degree of sophistication, for the important resources are not those shown on the balance sheet. Above all, it demands an understanding of what the 'product package' is; where this includes all the service, and image, elements as well as the physical ones – and in the widest sense. IBM managed the transition from

punched card tabulators to mainframe computers because even its name embodied the concept that its market was (International) Business Systems. It had the necessary skills (along with the culture), but Exxon, which tried to jump from oil to IT, had not – and failed.

2 *Develop a suitable filter for marketing data.* This is one of the most difficult stages. It requires that the marketer focuses his or her attention, when looking at the outside world, on just those aspects which are relevant to the organization's future. It poses problems of 'marketing myopia' (described in more detail later in the book) whereby the marketer simply does not see changes emerging because they are outside his or her frame of reference (the 'filter'). George Day[30] would describe the correct approach as 'market sensing' – one of the two key capabilities. The other approach is a 'customer linking capability' (comparable with relationship management). George Day stresses that these are especially important for 'bringing external realities to the attention of the organisation'.

On the other hand, a tight focus is very necessary in order for the marketer to be able to handle the mass of data – too much of this will simply swamp the systems (with data overload). More importantly, a tight focus means that every bit of input is transformed so that it is immediately useful to the organization.

3 *Using this 'filter' the marketer can move to find out about the customer.* This is the conventional starting point for marketing theory, which we examined in the previous section. The difference is that the expert marketer conducts this examination in the context of the lessons about the organization's resources which he or she learned in the first two steps. This means that the search for information is 'informed'.

4 *Review the processes to date.* The next step, which requires an extraordinary degree of professional detachment, is to repeat steps 1–3; this time taking into account the lessons learned overall. This may mean that the filter developed in stage 2 has to be modified in the light of what has since been discovered in step 3. This iteration needs to be conducted continuously. It is the step that marks out the really great marketers. It required Ray Kroc to understand that the marketing formula developed by a small hamburger restaurant in the backwoods could be turned into a world-wide McDonald's chain; and Thomas Watson to recognize that a meat-scale manufacturer could eventually become International Business Machines.

5 *Manipulate the organization's resources to achieve the resulting marketing objectives.* Marketing theory, once more, tends to assume that only the resources specifically made available to the marketing department should be taken into account. Expert marketers, on the other hand, recognize that all the resources must be brought into play. Capturing resources which are traditionally the prerogative of other departments is very difficult – and often hazardous to one's career. But it can pay massive dividends.

In this way, the key to successful, but *expert*, marketing is a very close relationship with the rest of the organization. For those less expert, and that is the great majority, the reverse is true! *Thus, the first need for the less expert is to distance yourself from the organization – and that is the posture you should adopt for the next few chapters.*

---

[30] George S. Day, The capabilities of market-driven organizations, *Journal of Marketing*, vol. 58 (October 1994).

Complexity of Interaction and Timescales

Much of marketing theory assumes very simple relationships. This makes the teaching of it easier, but does not prepare you for real life. This is particularly true of the following four main features.

1 *Multiple decision-makers.* In many buying situations there is more than one person involved in the process. This is especially true of those customers in 'industrial marketing', but it can as easily apply to those in consumer goods marketing. Even the purchase of a can of baked beans may need the tacit agreement of the *whole* family; God help anyone who buys beans, no matter how cheap, that the children do not like. Much of marketing theory, though, assumes that the purchasing decision is nicely isolated – taken by the 'buyer' alone.

2 *Multiple factors.* The purchase decision is often bundled together with many other decisions. Thus, the decision on whether to buy baked beans may depend upon whether there is any bread available; the family simply will not countenance beans on anything other than toast! It may depend upon what budget is available, or on what higher priority items have already made a claim to that budget.

3 *Interaction.* Perhaps one of the most unrealistic assumptions is that the buyer takes the purchase decision in isolation from the supplier. In many industrial decisions, as well as in services, the most able purchasers – along with the most perceptive marketers – now employ partnership techniques. *Both* sides are actively involved in the decision-making processes. This is best evidenced by how the Japanese multinationals – and especially Marks & Spencer – work so closely with their suppliers that it is often difficult to know where the boundary line is.

4 *Timescales.* Almost all marketing theory, and most marketing practice, assumes a purchase decision which stands by itself – without any influence from previous experience. This is usually an unduly simplistic viewpoint. Even the purchaser of the can of baked beans has a rich history of exposure to advertising, and personal experience. Yet watch television almost any night and you will see some brand being promoted on a totally different platform from that of a few months ago – the marketers having made the, usually incorrect, assumption that there is no historical effect.

The Structures of Marketing Theory

The previous section defined marketing in global terms. It should not be assumed, however, that there is one vast homogeneous mass of marketing activity, any one bit of which can be interchanged with any other. In practice, there are many differences between the various approaches, and the activities involved, across a wide range of organizations. Indeed, as we saw earlier, the essence of marketing is the specific nature of many of the practical 'rules' which need to be applied to equally specific situations.

On the other hand, one of the first things you should come to appreciate about a genuine, practical marketing approach to problems is that it abhors 'pigeon-holing' any situation neatly into categories. Rather, it prefers to look at the customers' *specific* needs and wants. You will, however, also find that such 'pigeon-holing' is one of the first things that most marketing *theory* actually adopts!

Frameworks are often a valuable aid to organizing ideas. Much of the structure of marketing theory is organized as '*trees*'. Each level is subdivided into a number of sub-levels, and these in turn may be similarly subdivided. To help understand the complexity of these linkages it is often useful to use simple diagrams. This is also a very useful memory aid. This book therefore makes use of such diagrams, but you should recognize that this is a simplification intended to illuminate the ideas rather than to define them.

The danger only arises when this process of pigeon-holing is over-indulged and the categories are allowed to replace the ideas.

The parallel of the family doctor is useful here. When you tell him or her your symptoms, he or she will usually follow a form of tree structure as an aid to diagnosis. If you have a temperature, with a headache, a cough, drowsiness and aching in the limbs, you may have a bout of influenza. If the doctor checks further, however, and finds that you also have a slow pulse and a rash on the upper abdomen you might have typhoid. One moral from this analogy is that the doctor, who has spent a number of years learning how to use these 'trees', applies his or her expert judgement to all the factors observed. The use of 'trees' as a guide to *marketing* diagnosis can be just as valuable; but the whole picture must always be kept in mind.

Organizational Pigeon-holes

In this current context, the pigeon-holes, the categories of 'marketing organization', can be derived from a number of bases; some of which are meaningful in more general terms. In this way, a multidimensional matrix can be built to suit almost any aspect of marketing that you are investigating.

The main dimensions, which have the widest application across the breadth of marketing activities, are as follows.

Product or service

The basic dimension is often thought to relate to the 'product' itself. Is it a tangible product, such as a refrigerator, which is manufactured in a factory by the supplier? Is it an intangible service, such as that of a hairdresser, where the customer has no tangible product to take away in a carrier bag?

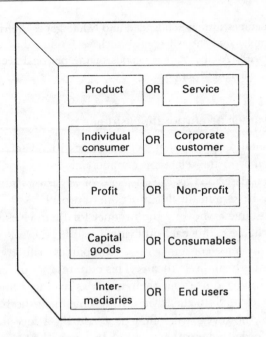

In practice, as we shall see later, there are difficulties in allocating organizations even on this apparently simple dimension. Some products, such as personal computers, have a great deal of 'service' attached to them; the total 'package' of these sometimes being described as the 'extended product'. On the other hand, there are services (even the hairdresser mentioned above) which are dependent upon physical products; the hair-care treatments used are very important, and are clearly physical.

There are differences in the way in which organizations might market a *product*, which will often be promoted on the basis of its physical features, as against a *service*, where promotion may be more associated with the quality of the organization providing it.

In general, however, we shall come to see that the basics of marketing are shared by both sorts of organization (although some of the names used to describe the activities are confusingly different).

Product categories

Even within this overall categorization, marketers often presume that there are significant differences between the various product types. In the general category of consumer goods, for example, there may be:

- FMCG (Fast Moving Consumer Goods), sometimes called 'consumables'. These are the archetypal 'marketed' goods (that is, those goods heavily advertised to build awareness, trial and preference) such as groceries.

- Durables, sometimes further subdivided into 'white goods' (refrigerators and cookers, for example) and 'brown goods' (such as furniture, as well as electrical/electronic devices). As the 'capital' goods of the personal sector, these require more personal selling and support.

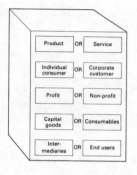

Individual consumer or corporate customer

Just as fundamental a split is that between sales made to individuals – the archetypal consumer in the television commercials – or to organizations. The latter case is often described as *industrial sales* or *business-to-business selling*. Once again, there may be significant differences in approach.

Individual consumers who buy the product for themselves or their families will typically spend less, but each individual will be the sole decision-maker. Their suppliers, the mass-consumer goods companies, will largely have to deal with such consumers by indirect means. This requires that the suppliers listen to the consumers, finding out about their needs as averages and in groups, by market research, and talk to them via advertisements in the mass media.

Industrial sales, however, will often be made by a face-to-face sales call, which can be afforded where the value of the individual sale is higher. The call will be made on someone who merely represents the buying organization and may not even be the only decision-maker. It is the nature (and extended length) of these negotiations, and the technical demands on the sales professionals involved, which frequently offer the most characteristic difference from consumer goods marketing.

On the other hand, as Leslie Rodger[31] says:

> There is no difference in principle between industrial and consumer products marketing. The difference is rather one of emphasis in the way in which the elements of the marketing mix are blended together to meet the particular needs of customers who may be a few specialized purchasers or a mass of consumers. The basic distinction lies in the purpose for which the goods are bought, i.e. goods bought for organizational purposes rather than for personal or family consumption.

Profit or non-profit

One of the divisions which causes the most soul-searching is that between profit-making organizations and non-profit-making sectors such as the National Health Service or voluntary organizations.

The former are easy to deal with. They are, at least in theory, driven by the sole motive of making a profit; and good marketing is an excellent way of increasing the bottom-line (profit) figures.

[31] L. Rodger, The marketing concept, *The Marketing of Industrial Products*, ed. Norman A. Hart (McGraw-Hill, 2nd edn, 1984).

On the other hand, employees of the non-profit sectors frequently have difficulty in seeing how marketing (which is too often associated in the public mind with hard-selling advertisements for fast-moving consumer goods, such as baked beans) is appropriate to their own organization. Exactly how it may be of use will become more obvious as we progress, but at this stage it is necessary to point out that *all* organizations necessarily have links with the outside world; such links are the stuff of marketing. The government department which wishes to influence motorists not to drink and drive will use market research to discover the motivations of those who do, and the most effective means of influencing them. It will then use the mass media to convey those messages – in the process often becoming one of the largest advertisers. But even the smallest charity has to decide who its clients are, and what are their needs, before communicating with them.

Kotler and Andreasen[32] summarize the position as follows:

> Although nonprofit organizations seek to influence exchanges of money for goods and services just like for-profit organizations, what makes them unique is their concentration on exchanges involving non-monetary costs on the one hand and social and psychological perspectives and modified techniques.

However, non-profit organizations are not always as unaware of marketing as some might believe. For instance, Laura Cousins[33] found that in the UK 62 per cent of the non-profit organizations she surveyed claimed to produce a written annual marketing plan; this is in contrast with 57 per cent of for-profit organizations.

Capital goods or consumables

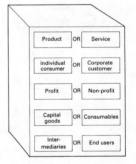

If the product (or indeed the service) represents a major investment, such as a domestic appliance in the home or a new production line in the factory, and has a life measured in years, then it can usually be assumed that the decision-making process will be an extended one – often the province of face-to-face selling, even in consumer markets.

Consumables, cans of beer or typewriter ribbons, on the other hand, will be repeat purchases which may be undertaken almost automatically: the marketer's job will typically be to change these repeat-buying patterns through the messages delivered in the mass media.

Intermediaries or end-users

As we shall see later, many of the marketing processes use intermediaries, such as retailers, to convey the product or service to the end-user or consumer; these

[32] P. Kotler and A. R. Andreasen, *Strategic Marketing for Nonprofit Organizations* (Prentice-Hall, 1987).
[33] L. Cousins, Marketing planning in the public and non-profit sectors, *European Journal of Marketing*, vol. 24, no. 7 (1990).

intermediaries themselves represent a significant proportion of the whole service sector, and they make very different demands on the product or service. They will be – at least according to Western 'capitalist' theory – seeking profit, together with a match to their own marketing needs.

'*High tech*'   Some experts claim that the markets for high technology are rather different, particularly in that they are characterized by rapid change and high uncertainty.

Small firms   It is arguable that small firms are just as susceptible to marketing solutions as large ones. The difference is that they usually do not have the resources or expertise to exploit marketing in its most sophisticated forms and, in any case, would be unlikely to have anything other than a limited impact on their environment. Carson and Cromie[34] say that small firms have a 'distinctive marketing style':

> There is little or no adherence to formal structures and frameworks . . . the marketing style can be described as an 'involved' one which relies heavily on intuitive ideas and decisions and probably most importantly on common sense.

On the other hand, common sense is a very valuable commodity in marketing; and the proprietors in such small businesses are usually much closer to their customers than many marketing managers.

There are other dimensions which may be particularly important to specific sectors; for example, whether or not the sector is largely controlled by government intervention or legislation, as is the ethical pharmaceuticals industry. It should also be apparent, from the five main dimensions, that a five-dimensional matrix is needed to handle all of these; and this will have in excess of 30 categories or pigeon-holes, ranging from the corner grocer, an intermediary who provides highly consumable products to end-users, through to a government department, which is a non-profit organization that uses a wide range of intermediaries itself to provide a service to wide sectors of industry.

Differences in Theory

Fortunately, most of these different categories of organization have more marketing theory and practice in common than that which separates them. Indeed, most of the marketing activities described in this book are widely applicable. Even 'pricing', which should surely have little relevance for non-commercial organizations, turns out to offer them many lessons.

---

[34] D. Carson and S. Cromie, Marketing planning in small enterprises: a model and some empirical evidence, *Journal of Marketing Management*, vol. 5, no. 1 (1989).

At this stage I shall introduce some theoretical material by way of illustration. As with most of the subsequent theory, there is no need to understand the exact details; you should simply get a general impression of what is being laid out. In this case, I am quoting Fern and Brown,[35] who conducted a very thorough search of the literature to establish what various authors have held to be the key differences between two supposedly very different groups (individual consumers and industrial buyers). They record that there are at least 27 different, expert, views of what separates the groups. The conclusion they come to (albeit a controversial one) is that the differences within the groups (between, for example, consumers buying convenience foods and those buying a car) are more important than those between the groups (between, say, a consumer buying a packet of cornflakes and a manager ordering a replacement stock of stationery). Although this is somewhat controversial it is a view which I would at least partially support.

The message is simply that there is probably more theory in common than is often allowed for, even if the names applied to the elements of the theory are different in different industries.

As we saw earlier, one aspect of conventional marketing theory which has come in for some criticism in recent years is its relative neglect of the timescales involved. There has been a tendency, at least in the theory, to concentrate upon the single transaction.

It is argued by some theorists that the reality is that even purchasing of 'consumables' (FMCG, for instance) should be viewed in the context of a whole series of such transactions. In this context, the buyer is not isolated from historical experience, but is well aware of, and possibly dominated by, the habits that he or she has developed over time. This psychological investment in 'brand loyalty' may be high, comparable in influence with the high financial investments involved in some industrial purchases. Certainly, the longevity of the brand life-cycle[36] indicates that there is a high level of investment in the brand itself. This investment is not easily displaced, as conventional marketing theory might hold, by short-term promotional activities in the marketplace.

Most marketing may, therefore, be more realistically viewed in the context of the longer timescales, with relatively high investment levels by purchasers as well as vendors. The definition by Christian Grönroos,[37] quoted earlier, hinted at this aspect of marketing, and this aspect of the subject will be investigated in some detail in later chapters.

---

[35] E. F. Fern and J. R. Brown, The industrial consumer marketing dichotomy: a case of insufficient justification, *Journal of Marketing*, vol. 48 (Spring 1984).

[36] Mercer, A two decade test of product life cycle theory.

[37] Grönroos, Marketing redefined.

SELF-TEST QUESTION 1.3

Which of these categories, if any, does your own organization fall into? How might this determine its specific marketing needs? Does this categorization adequately describe the nature of your organization? If not, why not? (If you have difficulty with the second question because you are in one of the non-profit organizations, then leave it until later.)

The Marketing Mix

Having determined what the customer needs or wants, what can the marketer do to satisfy these requirements?

We can initially consider two aspects to this. The first is the product, or service, itself. This is ultimately what the customer will decide on; and then determine whether it matches his or her needs. The marketer must, therefore, match the 'product' to those needs as closely as possible. This may be accomplished by radically changing the product, or just changing its features or its packaging, or even by describing it in a different way.

The second aspect is the delivery system. The producer must get the product or service to the customer, and even before that he or she must get the message of the product to the prospective purchaser or client.

There are a number of ways in which these separate aspects may be categorized; once again the potentially problematic pigeon-holing tendency of marketing comes into play. Many business schools now use the framework of the 4 Ps (as proposed by E. Jerome McCarthy):[38]

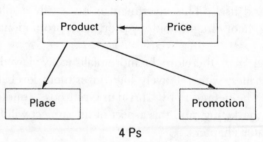

4 Ps

The first two Ps are, in effect, the product-related elements. Perhaps influenced by economics, Price is split off as an element worthy of separate consideration; although this may, in many cases, over-emphasize its importance.

[38] E. J. McCarthy, *Basic Marketing: a Managerial Approach* (Richard D. Irwin, 1981).

The other two Ps are parts of the delivery system: 'Place' is about delivering the physical product or service; Promotion is about delivering the 'sales message'.

ACTIVITY 1.3

Think about some of your own recent purchases (for example, a house, car, video, insurance policy, train tickets, newspaper etc.). For each of these, what was the relative importance of each of the 4 Ps, of the product itself, its price, the place where you bought it and the way in which it was promoted? Rank your estimates of importance in each case from 1 (not important at all) to 5 (very important). What conclusions do you reach about the different purchases, and what does it say about the 4 Ps?

If you are a typical consumer you should find that the factors which played the most important part in each of these decisions will have varied, depending on the nature of the purchasing decision to be made. If you are honest with yourself you may even find that the factors which mattered most were not the ones you might have expected. For example, perhaps price was not the most important: in a house purchase, place might be much more significant. The deciding factor in the purchase of a hi-fi might have been the product characteristics rather than price; or at least, if you are honest, perhaps the product characteristics (including the brand name) as promoted by the supplier might have swung the balance.

It is worth repeating, however, that real life may be (and often is) more complex than the 4 Ps allow for; and, as a result of the over-simplicity inherent in their use, many academics now question the use of the 4 Ps for anything other than a *very* broad framework. Indeed, Christian Grönroos[39] argues that '. . . the Four Ps represent a significant over-simplification of Borden's original work which was a list of 12 elements not intended to be a definition at all'. He argues that McCarthy possibly misunderstood earlier work on the marketing mix.

The over-simplicity of the 4 Ps approach is most obvious in the services sector. Donald Cowell,[40] for instance, suggests two other Ps are needed here: People and Process. Booms and Bitner[41] the addition of a further P: Physical Evidence.

---

[39] Christian Grönroos, From marketing mix to relationship marketing: towards a paradigm shift in marketing, *Management Decision*, vol. 32, no. 2 (1994).

[40] Donald W. Cowell, Marketing for services, in *The Marketing Book*, ed. Michael J. Baker (Butterworth Heinemann, 1994).

[41] B. H. Booms and M. J. Bitner, Marketing strategies and organization structures for service firms, *Marketing of Services*, ed. J. Donnelly and W. R. George (American Marketing Association, 1981).

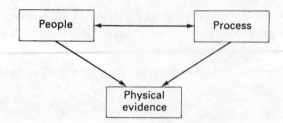

- *People.* People often *are* the service itself. This is probably the most important difference across most of the service sector.
- *Process.* How the service is delivered to the consumer is frequently an important part of the service. In particular, the quality controls which are built in are typically the only guarantee that the service will consistently meet the standards the consumer demands.
- *Physical evidence.* This could, with some justification, be considered to be part of the 'product package' (and, indeed, is discussed in chapter 7). On the other hand, it is so important in the case of services, adding the tangible (the design of the retail outlet and its electronic facilities, say) to the essentially intangible, that it is argued that it should be considered separately by service providers.

Industrial markets

The differences between consumer markets and industrial markets are usually more apparent than real. The balance of the marketing mix is one factor which is likely to be significantly different for each. For example, more emphasis given to direct contact (revolving around face-to-face selling) in industrial markets, as opposed to the indirect techniques (of marketing research and advertising) used in most consumer markets. Those differences which remain arise largely because of the disparity in the costs of contacting the customer personally – and not because of any more basic differences in approach.

Criticism of the 4 Ps Approach

It should be recognized, however, that the 4 Ps offer just one, albeit frequently used, way of approaching marketing. Some pundits may argue for less, as did Albert Trey,[42] who proposed just two factors – the 'offering' (product, price and so on) and 'methods and tools' (such as distribution and promotion). Other writers argue for the need to subdivide these categories further; differentiating, for example, between 'sales' and 'advertising' as forms of 'promotion'.

[42] A. Trey, *Advertising* (Renold Press, 1961).

At the other extreme, Godley,[43] in the days before the simplification offered by the 4 Ps became popular, identified ten major factors in the marketing mix.

Perhaps the most significant criticism of the 4 Ps approach, which you should be aware of, is that it unconsciously emphasizes the inside-out *view (looking from the company outwards), whereas the essence of marketing should be the* outside-in *approach.*[44] Grönroos, again, stresses that 'the marketing mix and its four Ps constitute a *production*-oriented definition'.

Having made these important caveats, the 4 Ps offer a memorable and quite workable guide to the major categories of marketing activity, as well as a framework within which these can be used. It is an approach used in many business schools, and is the one that this book will often adopt.

Even so, you should recognize that, as Malcolm McDonald says[45] in a more general context, 'When the latest fad fails to live up to expectations, it too begins to fade into obscurity, except at management education establishments *where it becomes absorbed into the fabric of teaching.*'

SELF-TEST QUESTION 1.4

Which of the 4 Ps most preoccupies your organization? On the other hand, which do you think its customers might regard as the most important – and why? What might be the implications? How would *you* rank each of the 4 Ps in importance, in the context of your organization's needs and those of its customers – and why?

Selling versus Marketing

'Selling' has long suffered from a tarnished image. It is indeed true that dubious selling practices may occasionally result in a sale if the customer is particularly gullible. But it is arguable that, even then, only good marketing (which encompasses a far wider range of skills, with an almost diametrically opposed motivation) *will lead the customer to buy again from the same company.* Organizations seldom profit from single purchases made by first-time customers. Normally they rely on repeat business to generate the profit that they need.

---

[43] C. G. A. Godley, Overall marketing management, *The Principles and Practice of Management*, ed. E. F. L. Brech (Longman, 1975).

[44] Morgan, *Riding the Waves of Change*.

[45] Malcolm H. B. McDonald, The Changing Face of Marketing, Cranfield School of Management paper, April 1991.

Much of the selling effort of the well organized marketing function will be directed towards keeping down the number of dissatisfied customers. In such organizations, feedback from the market will alert the company to the main reasons why customers do not buy again; such feedback will lead if necessary to an improvement or modification of the product or service. Effective selling is not about half-truths or overrated claims – these practices are almost always counter-productive in the longer term.

This highlights the 'contest' between marketing (or 'market orientation') and selling (or 'product orientation'), which has been a source of some controversy since the 1950s. Many of the criticisms of selling are still valid, since there are many poor salesmen and almost as many poor sales managers. But it is also true to say that the good sales managers and salesmen, particularly those involved in industrial selling (now often called 'sales professionals'), have long recognized and supported the basic tenets of sound marketing.

On the other hand, you should also be aware that the word 'marketing' is often used as an 'honorary' title, adopted by those who are in reality engaged exclusively in pure selling activities. For example, over a number of years the term 'marketing executive was applied to salespeople in general. Even as early as 1964, Peter Drucker[46] observed:

> Not everything that goes by that name deserves it. But a gravedigger remains a gravedigger even when called a 'mortician' – only the cost of the burial goes up. Many a sales manager has been renamed 'marketing vice-president' – and all that happened was that costs and salaries went up.

More recently, the process seems to have gone into reverse. In 1994, *The Economist*[47] reported that Unilever's soap division (Lever Bros.) had abolished the job of marketing director, replacing an old-style marketing department with multi-disciplinary teams – a development which has also been seen in other companies.

The argument has, unfortunately, also become confused by being associated with the use of certain techniques. In particular, 'marketing' has tended to be associated with market research at one end of the spectrum and advertising at the other. This may have some validity in the consumer field, but breaks down in other areas. Thus, for example, in the mainframe divisions of IBM – at the height of that corporation's success – relatively little conventional market research or advertising was undertaken. On the other hand, its salesmen (often heading teams of support personnel) spent months finding out (in far more depth than any market research ever could) exactly what the *individual* customer wanted. Its technical teams then spent as many months building the unique product that was exactly what the customer wanted. It is arguable that

---

[46] Drucker, *Managing for Results*.
[47] Anon., Death of the Brand Manager, *The Economist*, 9 April 1994.

there could be no closer match to perfect marketing; even though everyone involved believed that they were selling, not marketing.

Bower and Garda[48] suggest seven common elements which distinguish marketing-based companies:

1 The use of market share, rather than volume, as the primary measure of marketing success (although if they ignore the cost of acquiring share, profits will be unsatisfactory).
2 The understanding and use of market-segmentation principles.
3 The process for monitoring customer needs, usage and trends, as well as competitive activity – that is, market research.
4 A structure or process for co-ordinating all non-marketing functions toward the achievement of marketing goals.
5 A set of specific marketing goals and targets.
6 A corporate style and culture where marketing plays a key role.
7 A market-based business concept that provides unique value to the customer.

All of these topics will be addressed in the later chapters.

The key point is that 'selling' is inward-looking, *persuading the customer to take what you have got (your product, hence the 'product orientation'). It also implies that product development is detached from the marketplace. Only when the product is ready is there a search for a market, for customers to persuade. On the other hand, 'marketing' is* outward-looking, *trying to match the real requirements of the customer (or 'market', hence the 'market orientation'). The company looks for market opportunities and creates product solutions in response.*

The two approaches are contrasted by Philip Kotler[49] (see figure 1.2). In practice, a mix of both approaches is often used. It is a very poor salesman who does not, albeit instinctively rather than as a matter of theory, use sound marketing principles when questioning a customer to find out what he wants. Equally, it is a fortunate marketer who can produce the new product to match exactly the discovered gap in the market; most new products emerge from non-marketing processes and are only then opportunistically matched to markets.

Customer centred versus organization centred

In the specific context of non-profit organizations, Kotler and Andreasen[50] distinguish 'customer-centred organizations' (those that meet the 'ideals' of marketing), defining them as follows:

A *customer-centred organization* is one that makes every effort to sense, serve, and satisfy the needs and wants of its clients and publics within the constraints of its budget.

[48] M. Bower and R. A. Garda, The role of marketing in management, *Handbook of Modern Marketing*, ed. V. P. Buell (McGraw-Hill, 2nd edn, 1986).
[49] P. Kotler, *Marketing Management* (Prentice-Hall, 7th edn, 1991).
[50] Kotler and Andreasen, *Strategic Marketing for Nonprofit Organizations*.

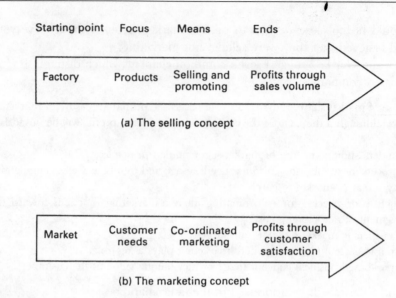

Figure 1.2 The selling and marketing concepts contrasted.

Kotler and Andreasen contrast these with those which are 'organization-centred', in which a number of attitudes exist, including:

1 The organization's offering is seen as inherently desirable.
2 Lack of organizational success is attributed to customer ignorance, lack of motivation, or both.
3 A minor role is afforded market research.
4 Marketing is defined primarily as promotion . . .

Fortunately, as our own research[51] shows, the great majority (more than 80 per cent) of organizations have now learned the central lesson of marketing, and are 'customer-centred'.

SELF-TEST QUESTION 1.5

Who 'sells' and who 'markets' in your organization? Does the organization have a salesforce, and is this involved in the wider aspects of marketing? Does it have a formal marketing department; or is this function handled by another department; or is this a courtesy title given to something that is really the sales department?

---

[51] David Mercer, research to be published.

How do their job functions and objectives differ? How are their activities co-ordinated, if at all? Do you think the position could be improved, and how?

(I shall often be asking you to think about how things might be improved, since this is an excellent way of developing your critical facilities.)

Corporate Strategy

In setting the context for marketing it is important to understand how it fits into the organization's overall corporate strategy. The study of corporate strategy is now usually treated as a separate academic discipline, although it is closely related to the processes of marketing planning. Indeed, Bower and Garda[52] comment:

> We are now coming to see marketing as a business subsystem in itself, encompassing product and market selection, product strategy (the breadth and depth of the product line offered to a given market, as well as the design of each product), pricing policy, channel strategy, advertising and promotion, and after-sales service. Beyond this we are beginning to recognize marketing as an integrative function – a view of serving customers that drives the entire organization's way of doing business and influences decisions along the full range of business activities.

In a very simplified form, the corporate planning process might be represented as shown in the diagram at the top of the next page.

The input into the corporate strategy processes can thus be conveniently separated into two streams. The first, the internal elements (such as production and finance), are those upon which many organizations, and many people within each organization, concentrate their efforts.

The second element comprises the external elements, including 'marketing' in its broadest sense. There are a number of external, environmental influences which can impinge on an organization, such as the prevailing social and economic climate and, more directly, the accompanying legislation.

In any organization which claims to be 'marketing-oriented' the market has to be the starting point for any process of strategic planning. Indeed, the strategic planning process in such organizations usually revolves around the marketing strategy and planning processes. It is for this reason that marketing planning processes are often almost indistinguishable from those of corporate strategy itself.

---

[52] Bower and Garda, The role of marketing in management.

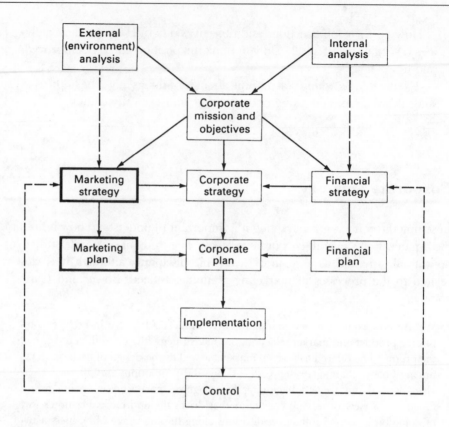

At this stage all that you need to realize is just how intimately the marketing planning process may be tied into the organization's overall strategic processes. This will be explained in more detail in the final chapter.

Before we start to explore the complexities of the whole planning process, however, we shall look at the separate components that are integrated within it. We shall start with the processes (typically revolving around marketing research) which reveal the needs of the customer (and hence of the market), before moving on to the 'product/service' elements, which build up to the offering, which is then tailored to meet those needs, and finally to the promotional techniques used to communicate the messages to that customer:

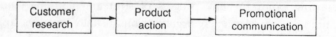

In the simple dialogue model that we looked at earlier these elements can be considered to be first those related to 'listening' (to the customers), before considering what actions are needed, and then 'talking' (to them):

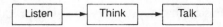

The chapter headings of this book, which broadly follow the above scheme, are (in abbreviated form):

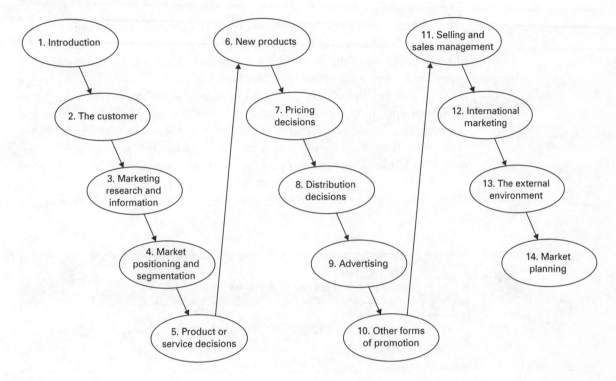

As you can see from this diagram, there is a logic to the sequence of the chapters which should help you build a comprehensive and understandable picture of marketing as a whole. It is also broadly in line with the 4 Ps approach which, after examining customer needs, moves through product decisions to those relating to pricing and promotion. However, you will also see that not all the chapters will be equally applicable to all readers.

Products versus Benefits

In order to provide some context for later chapters, I shall now briefly refer to the 'product' (as well as the service), since it is the demand for this which the marketer is trying to optimize. On the other hand, it is a basic, and oft-quoted, tenet of the sales profession that 'Customers don't buy products . . . they seek to acquire benefits'.

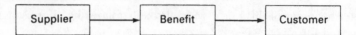

Behind this statement lies a basic principle of successful marketing: when people purchase products they are not motivated in the first instance by the physical attributes of the product, but by the benefits that those attributes offer.

An indication as to what actually (tangibly and intangibly) makes up a product can be found by looking closely at the difference between what customers appear to buy and what they actually want. To take an example – which is a favourite of many marketers – when customers buy a 2 mm drill, what they really want is a 2 mm hole. The drill vendor is in grave danger of losing his business when a better means of making holes is invented – a phenomenon which has led to the demise of many businesses. In the 1960s Theodore Levitt described the problem memorably as 'marketing myopia'.[53]

ACTIVITY 1.4

Why did you or your organization decide to buy this book? What benefits did it promise?

You or your organization presumably bought this book because it implicitly promised to offer certain insights about marketing; perhaps, rather more indirectly, you bought it because (as part of a course) it was a necessary part of obtaining a business qualification. You almost certainly did not invest money in it solely because it was smartly packaged or amusingly written. In other words, you or your organization were seeking specific benefits not limited to the physical materials. If those benefits could be offered to you more efficiently and cheaply by some other product (such as a video course) or by some other training method (such as a residential course) then you would probably switch to one or the other, on the basis of their 'perceived value'. The supplier is selling a physical product (or a service), but the customer is usually buying a set of intangible benefits.

[53] Th. Levitt, Marketing myopia, *Harvard Business Review* (July–August 1960).

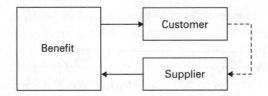

The solution to this problem of perception is for both sides, supplier as well as customer, to look at the product in the same way, through the eyes of the customer.

Even then there are pitfalls. Many sales trainers, for example, teach salesmen not to sell features (the technical aspects of the product) but to sell the benefits (what these mean to the customer). Unfortunately, too many salesmen and sales trainers then happily feel free to decide for themselves just what these 'benefits' are. These supplier-decided 'benefits' may, in reality, be just as much product features as the physical ones. What decides a genuine benefit is that it is the customer who should think of it in those terms.

Product or Service

As with many marketing courses run by business schools, much of this book is based on a framework which derives from the concepts applying most directly to the sale of physical products – more specifically, to consumer goods. There are good reasons for this. One is that describing what happens to physical, tangible products is rather easier than applying the same descriptions to the intangible. Perhaps the most important reason, however, is that *all* students have had some contact with such products, and will appreciate their main characteristics, albeit as consumers rather than as marketers.

I recognize that this approach can sometimes be disconcerting to students who work in the service sector (in particular, to those who work in non-profit-making organizations). Theodore Levitt[54] suggests that 'instead of talking of "goods" and of "services", it is better to talk of "tangibles" and "intangibles"; but the issue is much the same'. It is necessary to restate, therefore, that in many cases where the term 'product' is used in this book the term 'service' (or 'service product') could just as easily replace it. As you will come to appreciate, many of the concepts, as well as many of the specific techniques, will work equally well whether they are directed at products or services. In particular, developing a marketing strategy is much the same for products and services, in that it involves selecting target markets and formulating a marketing mix.

[54] Th. Levitt, Marketing intangible products and product intangibles, *Harvard Business Review* (May–June 1981).

The relatively few exceptions will be highlighted as the book progresses. The main differences, some of which *are* important in terms of the practical details of marketing, will be explored in more depth as part of chapter 7.

As Levitt's article suggests, marketing a physical product is often more concerned with intangible aspects (frequently the 'product service' elements of the total package) than with its physical properties. Charles Revson made a famous comment regarding the business of Revlon Inc.: 'In the factory we make cosmetics. In the store we sell hope.' Arguably, service industry marketing merely approaches the problems from the opposite end of the same spectrum.

In the marketing of 'services', adaptations and adjustments to the basic theory may be required; and the marketing mix may have to be revised to incorporate 'people' resources.

In all sectors of marketing, the customer (together with his needs and wants) is the focus of attention.

Marketing and service cultures

In recent years some service-sector organizations have been at the forefront of marketing – ahead, indeed, of the leaders in other sectors. In general, though, it has to be recognized that much of service-sector management has been antipathetic towards marketing. There have been a number of alternative reasons for this:

- *Lack of tangibility.* As I have already described, the very intangible nature of services makes them less immediately responsive to unsophisticated marketing techniques. It requires a quantum leap in marketing sophistication to apply many of the techniques. As Theodore Levitt[55] says:

   > The most important thing to know about intangible products is that the customers usually don't know what they're getting until they don't get it. Only then do they become aware of what they bargained for; only on dissatisfaction do they dwell. Satisfaction is, as it should be, mute. Its existence is affirmed only by its absence.

[55] Levitt, Marketing intangible products and product intangibles.

- *Lack of 'mass' marketing.* Many service suppliers have a structure based upon a network of relatively small local branches, which are almost autonomous in their face-to-face contact with their customers. There is, apparently, less need for marketing communications; and rarely any central marketing group strong enough to develop them.
- *Lack of direct competition.* Some organizations, such as the high street banks, have not seen their role as having 'customers'. At times they have behaved almost as if they themselves were the customers. (As if those visiting banks, for instance, had to sell themselves before the bank would accept their business.) Such organizations have often been in the fortunate position where the supply of their offering was swamped by considerably more demand than could be met; so that their role was to ration this scarce supply. Some organizations, such as the utilities and local government, enjoy a legal monopoly, since any other solution would be hopelessly inefficient. Finally, many 'non-profit' organizations do not see their role in terms of competition with any other provider.
- *Professional status.* Other groups of service providers have long been organized into professions (lawyers, accountants or dentists, for instance). Their 'profession' therefore is the predominant force, the focus of their 'business' thinking; and, due to its monopoly power, it often effectively removes direct competition in the conventional sense – and with it marketing. (Indeed, several professions have enacted rules which specifically bar their members from almost every form of marketing activity.) In addition, as a justification for their monopoly power (and as a protection from any pressure to weaken this position) these professions impose 'ethical' constraints which act against marketing in the traditional sense.
- *Lack of management.* For a combination of the above reasons, many organizations in the service sector have not stressed the importance of management. Indeed, many of them have de-emphasized it, focusing instead on 'professionalism'. It has only been in relatively recent years that the 'science' of management has been seen to apply to the service sectors in general.

However, the above reasons are mainly self-imposed limitations. They do not relate to any genuine problems inherent in marketing itself.

Non-profit-making organizations

Perhaps the area where there is the greatest difficulty in coming to terms with marketing is that of non-profit organizations. Possibly the main reason for this is that most of marketing theory is described in terms of improving profit performance. This use of profit as the main measure of marketing effectiveness allows for a practical (and measurable) approach in commercial organizations; but it obviously poses major problems for those organizations which cannot measure their performance in such terms.

One resulting problem, therefore, may be that some non-profit organizations simply do not recognize the requirement to meet their customers' needs.

What can replace 'profit' in the non-profit context? The measure most frequently suggested appears to be 'match'. Thus, the non-profit organization seeks, or should seek, to make the best match between use of its resources and the needs of its customers or clients. In this context, marketing is a means of optimizing this 'match', of most productively matching the resources available to provide what the users need and want – exactly as in any commercial operation.

One complication in the case of non-profit organizations may be that there will be several types of 'customer'. There are the 'clients' for the service, as well as those who 'decide' who the 'clients' will be, and the 'donors' of the funds to provide that service. Each of these groups will have a different set of needs and will need to be marketed to separately. As a result there may be multiple objectives; and, in particular, activities may be subject to public scrutiny.

SELF-TEST QUESTION 1.6

To what extent do you consider that your organization's product (or service) range – and the benefits that each product offers – suits the wants of today's customers?

What conclusions can you draw from this information?

Product/Brand Management

At this stage it might be useful to describe one further feature which is often associated with the larger, and most sophisticated, marketing-oriented organizations – that of brand or product management. In theory this need not be a marketing-oriented function; indeed, one might perhaps expect it to be more related to a product-oriented approach, for its focus is on the individual product. On the other hand, as we have seen, many managers see 'marketing' as the function that integrates operations at the level below corporate strategy; with 5 per cent even seeing this as marketing's *most* important role!

Each product (or brand/product group) is the responsibility of one product manager who is personally responsible for co-ordinating all activities to do with that product (from production through to marketing). Wolf and Smith[56] record that:

---

[56] Wolf and Smith, Market needs and market changes.

Early on, it was conceived that the role of the product manager was somewhat like that of a 'little president' or 'little general manager' with bottom line responsibility for the brand managed.

The classical definition of a brand manager thus used to be that he or she was 'to the brand what the managing director was to the company'. More cynically, brand managers have been heard to complain that they carry all the responsibility with none of the authority. Wolf and Smith[57] again report that the position has moderated in recent years:

Although product managers remain enthusiastic champions of their products, their role is now more of making recommendations than making decisions. The product manager may control marketing research, special promotions and minor decisions involving advertising, but major decisions are more likely to be made at higher levels.

In practice there are two main benefits to the brand/product management approach:

- *Cross-functional co-ordination/management.* The most direct, and perhaps the most important, result is that each brand has *all* its activities co-ordinated so that they are optimally managed, in terms of the needs of that *brand*. The more normal, functionally oriented, organization manages the activities in terms of what is optimal for the *function*, which may be counter to the needs of the individual brands. The product manager's central position in relation to other groups is illustrated by Steven Lysonski[58] (figure 1.3).
- *Consumer orientation.* Figure 1.3 also shows that a most important, though indirect, marketing outcome is that the brand manager typically becomes well aware of the consumer's needs and preferences since that brand manager is continually at the focus of all the brand oriented information (much of which originates from consumers). The resulting activities, which will mainly be in the marketing area, thus tend to be more consumer-oriented than in most other management structures (often more so than in other marketing-oriented structures). It is for this reason that 'brand management' often results in better marketing management – and is so closely associated with it.

Category management and cross-functional teams

A development of the brand manager approach – to take account of the growing power of some retailers – has been that of 'category management'. In this context, the manager – who may now focus almost as much on retailer needs as on consumer needs – manages products and activities across the whole

---

[57] Wolf and Smith, Market needs and market changes.
[58] S. Lysonski, A boundary theory investigation of the product manager's role, *Journal of Marketing* (Winter 1985).

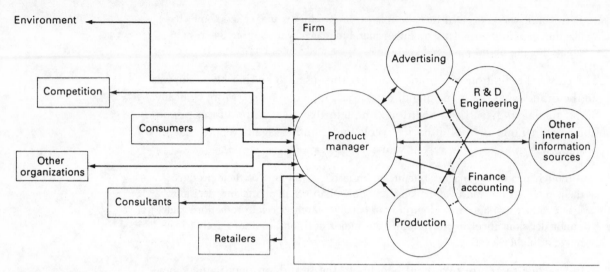

Figure 1.3 Illustration of the product manager's central position.

category which is of interest to the retailer; aiming to optimize the retailer's profits as well as those of the producer.

In further developments, the solitary brand manager has now sometimes been replaced by a *team* – with members from across the various functions – which manages a *network* of relationships with customer organizations. Dickson[59] even claims of such a team that 'it can launch into the task of reaching out, selecting, and managing a whole set of strategic alliances . . .'.

FURTHER READING

Throughout this book I shall suggest other books which will provide further information, should you wish to delve into specific topics. They are those I feel may be of most use to readers in general. The best advice is perhaps to visit a good library (preferably one with a specialized section on marketing), glance through the books on offer and select those which best suit your own needs.

As you will have gathered from the many references to it in this chapter, the most important book in the whole field of marketing is undoubtedly *Marketing Management* by Philip Kotler (Prentice-Hall, 8th edn, 1994). This has influenced a whole generation of marketers, myself included. His book covers much the same material, on a slightly narrower front but often in greater depth about specific topics. It is firmly rooted in the approach of the 1970s, but is none the worse for that, especially where the techniques it describes are now returning to

---

[59] Peter R. Dickson, *Marketing Management* (Dryden Press, 1994).

favour. Although it is directed at marketing specialists, it is well written and easily approachable even by more general readers.

Philip Kotler has also written another, more general marketing book, *Principles of Marketing* (Prentice-Hall, 4th edn, 1989), aimed at a wider audience; but for the general management audience the original *Marketing Management* is still the most suitable. There are many other well-illustrated books, but these do not generally extend the range of material offered by this book, or by Kotler.

The best complement for Kotler was the *Handbook of Modern Marketing*, edited by Victor P. Buell (McGraw-Hill, 1986). With more than 1000 pages, and 80 chapters written by leading experts, it covered most aspects of marketing in considerable, expert, depth. Its price, however, matched this comprehensive coverage. A slightly slimmer (726 pages), but much more affordable, handbook – which is almost as comprehensive, especially in terms of UK coverage – is *The Marketing Book* (3rd edn), edited by Michael J. Baker (Butterworth Heinemann, 1994).

Some books usefully concentrate on marketing in specific 'industry' sectors. Philip Kotler, for instance, collaborated with Alan Andreasen to produce *Strategic Marketing for Nonprofit Organizations* (Prentice-Hall, 1987), offering an excellent introduction to marketing in these organizations. In the specific field of marketing services *The Marketing of Services* by Donald Cowell (2nd edn, Butterworth Heinemann, 1994) gives excellent coverage of the factors which distinguish marketing in this sector.

One academic, Theodore Levitt (Harvard Business School's most famous marketer), has written a number of particularly influential papers. These are gathered together in *The Marketing Imagination* (Free Press, 1986).

For regular contemporary updates to the subject, in 'global' terms, the most useful general periodical is probably *The Harvard Business Review* (as it is in so many fields of management); the very similar *Sloan Management Review* also regularly offers excellent articles, as does *Management Decision*. For a more specialized approach the best vehicle is likely to be the *Journal of Marketing* (the influential marketing periodical of the American Marketing Association), but be warned that this at times describes marketing in very technical terms.

REFERENCES

In addition to the books recommended at the end of each chapter, throughout the text you will also find references to material from other books. At the simplest level these are simply an indication that the fact or idea is derived from the work of that person, but they are also intended as a starting point if you wish to explore that topic further. Where possible, I have given credit to those who have influenced my own thinking. I have not been able to give equal credit to the many more whose work has been subconsciously just as influential. The text is liberally illustrated with quotations. This is partly because, where a reference is made, I have tried to use the original author's own words, without distorting them by my own prejudices. A full reference is given in the first footnote; subsequent references within the same chapter are given in abbreviated form. The first reference can be located by referring to the index.

SUMMARY

The key components of this chapter, which you may wish to revise, have been:

Theory versus practice. Marketing is a particularly practical business 'discipline'. Managers have to be very careful in their use of the many theories on offer.

What is marketing? There are many definitions of marketing, but most of them centre on the customer as the important focus of decision-making and describe the 'dialogue' between the producer and the customer.

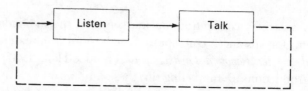

Organizational structures. Marketing varies somewhat, depending upon the different circumstances within which it is practised. The main dimensions or the factors which lead to these differences are:

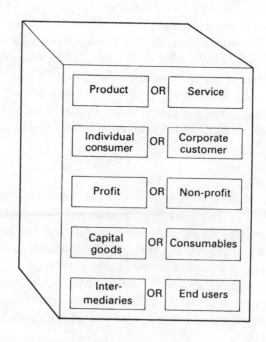

In reality there are very few significant theoretical, or even practical, differences between the various groups; although the balance within the promotional mix may favour more personal selling in the case of industrial goods.

Marketing mix. The various elements of marketing which are employed in marketing campaigns are often described in terms of the 4 Ps:

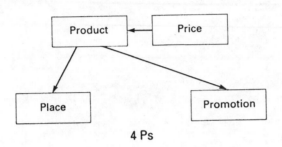

4 Ps

This is a very simplistic framework, however, and can lead to distorted perspectives if adopted too enthusiastically.

Selling versus marketing. Much of the popular stereotype of marketing revolves around the excesses of 'selling', which does not as fully take into account the viewpoint of the customer. Many organizations, however, have yet to adopt the true marketing approach.

Service versus product. There are some genuine differences, in detail, where marketing relates to services rather than products, and these are described in later chapters. There are, however, many more similarities even in the details, and the principles are almost identical.

REVISION QUESTIONS

1 What is the definition of marketing as put forward by the UK's Chartered Institute of Marketing? How does it differ from those of Kenichi Ohmae or Michael Baker? How does it differ from that of Christian Grönroos?

2 When did modern marketing evolve? What came before it? How has it changed in the past two decades?

3 What element distinguishes the 'marketing triad' from more traditional descriptions of marketing? Why?

4 What might be an 'expert' approach to marketing? How, and why, might this differ from an 'inexpert' one?

5 In marketing terms, what are the main differences between individual consumers and corporate customers, and those between purchases of capital goods and consumables?

6 What are the elements of the marketing mix? Into what four categories are they traditionally grouped? What problems does this grouping pose?

7 What differences are there in the case of services, and of non-profit organizations?

8 How is marketing different from selling?

9 How does marketing relate to corporate strategy?

10 How does category management differ from brand management? Why?

2 The Customer

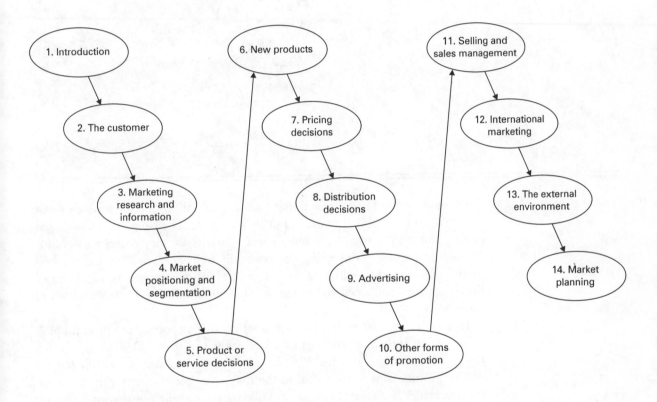

Introduction

Adopting the customer's viewpoint is the essence of sound marketing. The focus of this chapter, therefore, is *that* customer or consumer. In particular, it is about how the customer makes his or her buying decisions; what the processes (awareness, trial and repeat, for instance) and the factors which influence them (traditional or cultural) may be. We also look at the organizational factors in industrial markets, and the diffusion processes (as well as the related elements of brand loyalty and so on) in all markets, as well as specific models of consumer behaviour.

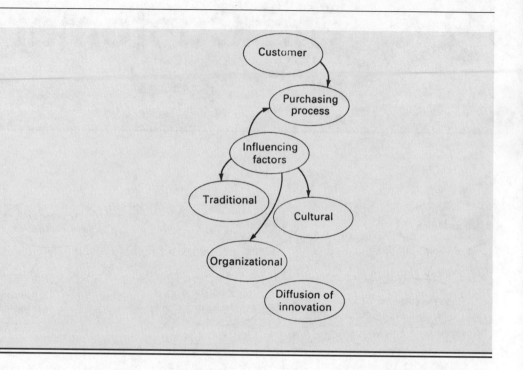

Once more, it has to be stressed that each individual product or service evokes a specific, and possibly unique, response from its set of customers. Indeed, *each buying situation is unique*; a uniqueness which those employing face-to-face selling can exploit – this being the essential strength of such selling – while those in mass markets will have to deal in terms of groups and averages. All of these suppliers will need to recognize what their customers' *specific needs and wants* are.

Inevitably, in this section we will attempt to categorize, or 'pigeon-hole', groups of customers or the factors which influence them. Despite the earlier reservations, such categories – even when they are clearly based on largely artificial distinctions – are useful to the marketer, because they can still serve as a 'reminder list' when he or she is building the specific framework for his or her own brands. Once more, though, do recognize the dangers which are inherent in such simplistic categorizations.

ACTIVITY 2.1

Think back to some of your own recent purchases. Choose several of them, including a consumer durable as well as a repeat purchase food item and some form of service. For each of these purchases *write down* how you came, in the first instance, to purchase that product or service, and then how you came to choose the particular 'brand'. Some questions you might like to consider are:

- How did you decide you needed the product or service?
- Did the stimulus come from within or from outside? Were you persuaded by advertising or social pressures?
- How long did it take you to make the decision?
- Was it an automatic or impulse purchase; or did you give it considerable thought?
- Where did you obtain the information necessary to take the decision? Was it instinctive, or was it from experience, or was it from advertising, or was it from friends?
- How many alternatives did you consider?
- How did you choose between them?
- Was the choice of 'brand' simply a result of it being all that was available, or the best of a very limited range, or did you go out of your way to find a match to exactly what you wanted?
- How important was it that it not only worked, but also suited your 'life-style'?
- Was it the sort of product which your friends would use?

Keep this material until you have completed your next Marketing Audit.

It is possible that you found that the decision-making process was quite varied; ranging from an almost intuitive reaction to shopping for food through, perhaps, to a quite extended process in the case of the consumer durable. The process is, indeed, complex and individual – often uniquely so. Keep this in mind when you read the next section, on the *theory* of how the consumer chooses.

This theory can provide a theoretical framework, and justification, for much of the rest of marketing, particularly in the design of advertising strategies, which agencies sometimes feel needs such legitimization. It has, indeed, become a major focus of research, in the hope that one or more simple models can be found, upon which all subsequent marketing can be based. However, it is, generally speaking, the least useful in terms of practical marketing. It is included in this book because you should be aware that it exists. It may also offer some insight into what motivates your customers.

The Decision-making Process

The first question to ask is: 'How do customers make their decisions?' This is more difficult to answer than one might at first expect. Customers do not come to each buying decision with conveniently blank minds, and then rationally consider the options; even though much of economic theory, and not a negligible proportion of marketing theory, is predicated on such an approach. According to such theory, often the only significant variable to be considered is the price.

In reality, the decision-making process is extended, complex and often confused. Even in the apparently simple case of buying a tin of baked beans, a purchaser in a supermarket, faced by the massed ranks of competing brands, may have a number of factors in mind.

The AIUAPR model

There are a range of alternative models, but of these I believe that of AIUAPR, which most directly links to the steps in the marketing/promotional process, is the most generally useful:

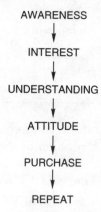

AWARENESS – before anything else can happen the potential customers must become aware that the product or service exists. Thus, the first task must be to gain the attention of the target audience. All the different models are, predictably, agreed on this first step. If the audience never hears the message people will not act on it, no matter how powerful it is.

INTEREST – but it is not sufficient to grab their attention. The message must **interest** them and persuade them that the product or service is relevant to their needs. The content of the message(s) must therefore be meaningful and clearly relevant to that target audience's needs, and this is where **marketing research** can come into its own.

UNDERSTANDING – once an interest is established, the prospective customer must be able to appreciate how well the offering may meet his or her needs, again as revealed by the marketing research. This may be no mean achievement where the copywriter has just fifty words, or ten seconds, to convey everything there is to say about it.

ATTITUDES – but the message must go even further; it has to persuade the reader to adopt a sufficiently positive attitude towards the product or service that he or she will purchase it, albeit as a trial. There is no adequate way of describing how this may be achieved. It is simply down to the **magic of the copywriter's art**, and is based on the strength of the product or service itself.

PURCHASE – all the above stages might happen in a few minutes while the reader is considering the advertisement in the comfort of his or her favourite armchair. The final buying decision, on the other hand, may take place some time later, perhaps weeks later, when the prospective buyer actually tries to find a shop which stocks the product.

REPEAT PURCHASE – but in most cases this first purchase is best viewed as just a trial purchase. Only if the experience is a success for the customer will it be turned into repeat purchases. These repeats, not the single purchase which is the focus of most models, are where the vendor's focus should be, for these are where the profits are generated. The earlier stages are merely a very necessary prerequisite for this!

This is a very simple model, and as such does apply quite generally. Its lessons are that you cannot obtain repeat purchasing without going through the stages of building awareness and then obtaining trial use – which has to be successful. It is a pattern that applies to all *repeat purchase* products and services; to industrial goods just as much as to baked beans. This simple theory is rarely taken any further – not even to look at the series of transactions which such repeat purchasing implies. The consumer's growing experience over a number of such transactions is often the determining factor in the future purchases. All the succeeding transactions are, thus, interdependent – and the overall decision-making process may accordingly be much more complex than most models allow for.

The enhanced AIUAPR model

Accordingly I will, for once, appear to complicate matters! But, fortunately, the additional complexity has a logic to it. In the single dimension which the original model inhabits from top to bottom there is a growing involvement of the customer with the product or service. The '*Enhanced* AIUAPR Model' takes this and adds a further dimension which specifically reflects on one side the attempts by the *vendor* to influence this process – which were implicit in the original model. It shows, however, the way in which the vendor's involvement changes from the most impactful advertising at the start of the process to the highest quality support at the end – a progression which is not fully described in less complex models.

On the other side, though, it also shows the involvement of the *customer* with his or her *peer group* – whose influence is not even hinted at in the original version. The starting point is, in this case, earlier than in the original model.

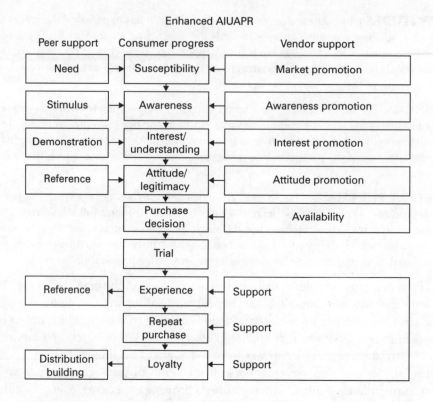

SUSCEPTIBILITY – even before you can build awareness, the consumer's mind has to have been opened up to the concept behind the product or service. In line with the theories we will look at later, this acceptance of a new need may have emerged from the workings of the opinion leaders in the consumer's peer group. On the other hand, this is also the stage where the supplier has to accept some form of market (or segment) building role, often making use of public relations as much as advertising. It should be noted, however, that the seemingly distinct steps often, indeed usually, overlap. Thus, some sections of the population – the opinion leaders say – could be well into the repeat purchasing stage while other sections are only just beginning to perceive the need. Accordingly, promotion and advertising will often have to meet the requirements of a number of stages at the same time – a complex demand which is one reason why very successful advertising campaigns are so rare!

AWARENESS – you have already seen how this works in the original model; though the role of high impact advertising (or prospecting in industrial markets) was there implicit rather than being a formal part of the model, as here. The main difference, though, is that research shows that the stimulus is as likely to come from an opinion leader in the peer group. These offer a hidden, and potentially very powerful, 'sales force' on behalf of the product or service; albeit that they in turn have necessarily been recruited by advertising or by public relations activities (often a neglected medium, which is especially important in reaching this group).

INTEREST/UNDERSTANDING – these two are coupled together, since it is difficult to conceive of one happening without the other being at least in part also involved; though they may offer very different challenges to the advertiser. Again, however, it is members of the peer group, already users, who may be most likely to be able to proffer the 'demonstration' of the product (or the results of the service) to the prospective consumer.

ATTITUDE/LEGITIMACY – although one further stage is added, that of 'legitimacy' (persuading the prospective purchaser that, backed by his or her favourable attitudes, a purchase may be justified), this is merged with the attitude building process; and both may be dependent on the 'reference' support from members of the peer group who are already loyal users, as much as on traditional advertising.

PURCHASE DECISION – this should be, by this stage of the process, almost automatic; and, for once, the consumer is probably alone in making this particular decision. A key element, also featured in the original model but often (wrongly) taken for granted, is that the product or service must be easily *available* for the consumer to achieve that purchase.

EXPERIENCE – one stage ignored by the original model is that which happens when the consumer tries the product or service for the first time. This may, or may not, be a favourable experience; but whichever end of the spectrum it lies it still represents a major discontinuity in the model. At this point the nature of the accompanying processes changes. In the case of the vendor's promotional activities the emphasis switches abruptly from recruitment to support (perhaps still involving advertising, but mainly by conventional support services). This is perhaps best illustrated by the switch from new account selling before to account management afterwards, in face-to-face selling. At the same time the consumer switches from being a recipient of advice to one who can, from experience, give it to his or her peer group. This is, hopefully, of a positive nature, since a bad experience is typically reported to many more peers than a good one!

REPEAT PURCHASE – in this development of the original model this becomes almost a technicality.

LOYALTY – more important is the final step, that of creating a loyal user; based upon successive positive experiences (backed by sound customer support). These loyal users become, in turn, the 'references' for new users (or even the 'opinion leaders' which feature so strongly in this enhanced model).

The Three Pillars

Having made the model necessarily complex – to explain the underlying processes – I will now offer a much more practical, condensed version of it.
This embodies, in much simpler form, most of the essentials of the process. Thus, the central pillar (the consumer's progress) highlights the tentative nature of the first stages as the consumer moves from 'susceptibility' to the actual 'purchase'; and then the no less important subsequent stages as confidence builds into loyalty.

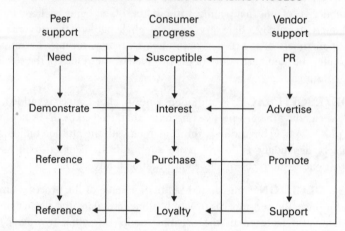

THE THREE PILLARS OF THE PURCHASING PROCESS

The break point, at the time of the first (trial) purchase, is reflected in the vendor's pillar by the switch from promotion to support (though this aspect is rarely emphasized in theory). It is even more obvious in the 'peer' pillar in the switch from 'taker' (of advice) before first purchase to 'giver' (as a loyal referee) after purchase.

Whilst this model is especially useful in providing a framework which most effectively handles the new consumer's progress over time, even it does not really do full justice to the richness of the interaction of the individual consumer with the *whole* community, not just the direct peer group, and the 'inertia' which this may lead to. Added to this is the wealth of (personal and community) experience built up over time, which multiplies the problems of access by the marketer – and often slows down the rate of structural change so that it occurs over the decades measured by the sociologist rather than the months in the marketer's plan.

Evaluation of Alternatives

For most products or services there are likely to be a number of competing brands in the market, ranging from internationally distributed brands, such as Coca-Cola, down to those that can only be obtained in a few local shops. The process of choosing between these can be represented as the result of a number of 'filtering' processes, some of which are under the consumer's control and some under the producer's:

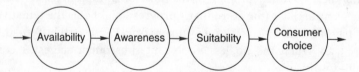

Availability. The first consideration is whether the consumer has access to the product or service. This is mainly under the control of the producers and their distribution chains, which is why producers put so much emphasis on obtaining high levels of distribution. How far the consumer is prepared to venture in search of a difficult-to-obtain product is, of course, dependent upon the characteristics of the market. The tin of beans may have to be on the specific supermarket shelf just when needed. On the other hand, some consumers will wait several months and travel hundreds of miles to see a star-studded show.

Awareness. If the consumer is not aware of the brand it will not be on the shopping list. Again, awareness is to a large degree in the control of the supplier, and reflects the amount spent and the success of the promotional strategy.

Suitability. Not all of the brands will be identical (except in pure commodity markets), at least in terms of how the various suppliers have presented them. Some of them will clearly be more suitable, at least in the consumer's eyes, while some will seem definitely unsuitable. The producer may, for instance, use 'segmentation' (discussed in a later chapter) as a means of targeting the brand on a specific segment of the market. This device matches the brand specification to the needs of that segment, so it is seen to be more suitable – but in the process this probably makes it *less* suitable to buyers in other segments of the market.

Consumer choice. It is perhaps at this stage that the consumer's choice is asserted, to select from the brands that remain after the previous filtering stages. The consumer is not totally at the mercy of the advertiser; and will make his or her choice on the basis of whatever reasons he or she chooses. To the consumer at that time the choice is absolutely rational; the brand best meets his or her perceived needs.

SELF-TEST QUESTION 2.1

What decision-making processes does your organization assume that your customers go through? What decision-making processes do *you* think your customers might go through?

How does this compare with the 3 Pillars? How does it differ at each stage, and why? (Look hard for differences. No model is perfect, and much of the benefit to be derived from the study of marketing comes from the experience of trying to match the framework offered by the theory to the practicality of real life – and often they do not match.) How does it compare with your own experience, which you documented in your last activity (2.1)?

What are the differences between your organization's model and the real-life experiences you described in that activity, and why?

What Factors Specifically Influence Customers?

SELF-TEST QUESTION 2.2

What factors most influence your customers' decisions? Are these factors product-oriented?

It is arguable that in taking their final decision, and indeed throughout the whole process, customers are influenced by a wide range of factors, and not just those relating to the obvious features of the product. Examples of the factors most generally discussed by marketing theorists are:

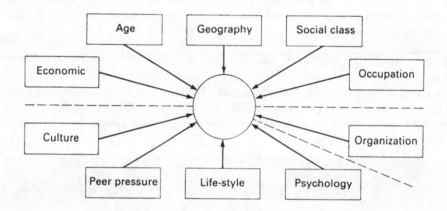

Some of these may represent a direct (measurable) influence on buying decisions. Others are less tangible factors, from which patterns of buying behaviour may only be inferred.

The examples given earlier in this chapter, however, illustrate just how diverse the various influences on consumers may be. Price, the traditionally given basis for choice, is just one factor of many that might apply; it is often a relatively unimportant one. In many markets, even those for industrial goods, intangible factors (which can often be broadly described as the 'image' of the product) may be important. Hence consumer behaviour may be perfectly rational to the consumer, but not to the technically (product) oriented observers!

Attitudinal factors are often seen as the most important. They are the subject of much market research, to ensure that the advertising (for example) conveys exactly the right messages.

Economic factors

For many of the more theoretical marketers, especially those coming from the economic disciplines, the main influence is seen to be economic, particularly in the case of the industrial sale.

The influence of economic factors appears first of all in terms of the economic 'well-being' of the consumers. Put simply, this means that if they receive more money they are likely to spend more money. One of the methods of categorization of consumers, therefore, is by income group.

This behaviour is modified by the overall economic climate. If the climate is optimistic and a boom is under way, the domestic consumer will be likely to spend more money. Sometimes, by means of borrowing, he or she will spend more than he or she earns. The industrialist will also spend more, investing in new capacity to take advantage of the boom.

For many economists and not a few marketing theorists, price is by far the single most important factor. This is the reason for its elevation to become one of the 4 Ps. An even larger group of marketers, on the other hand, would contend that there may be many other factors that, depending on the situation, are even more important.

Age and life-stage

The demands of individuals and families vary over time. William D. Wells and George Gubar[1] identified a number of stages in an adult's life, each of which has characteristic patterns of earning and consumption:

1 *bachelor stage* – young, single people not living at home
2 *newly married couples* – young, no children
3 *full nest I* – youngest child under six
4 *full nest II* – youngest child six or over
5 *full nest III* – older married couples with dependent children
6 *empty nest I* – older married couples, no children living with them
7 *empty nest II* – older married couples, retired, no children living at home
8 *solitary survivor* – in labour force
9 *solitary survivor II* – retired

These stages may have important implications for marketing strategies. Stage 1 individuals, for example, are recreation-oriented, and hence are prospective customers for providers of entertainment. Those in stage 2 have a high joint income and spend it; among them are the yuppies beloved of the suppliers of luxury goods. In stage 3 are the typical first-time house buyers (who at the same time also buy all the other durables and household goods that become part of a home). Those in stages 3 and 4 are often the target of the mass consumer

[1] W. D. Wells and G. Gubar, Life-cycle concepts in marketing research, *Journal of Marketing Research* (November 1966).

advertisers; they represent the archetypal housewife with a family to feed. By stage 5 the pattern of buying may have become more selective as income increases. Those in stages 6 and 7 are once more able to spend on luxuries, although of a different type. Finally, stages 8 and 9 pose different support requirements.

Clearly, each marketer in the consumer field will target those age groups that are most relevant to his or her product or service. Financial service organizations selling insurance, for example, may perhaps tend to ignore stages 1 and 2, in order to concentrate on stage 3.

However, the demography of these age groups is not static, and there are peaks and troughs. Most notable, in recent years, was the 'baby boom' of the 1960s, which was reversed in the 1970s, when there was a comparable drop in birth rates. These changes had significant marketing impacts. Marketers are understandably attracted by a booming market, not least because this allows more opportunities for new brands. A falling market is more difficult to enter, with the existing brands very much on the defensive. Thus, in the 1960s suppliers to the baby market had a field-day, and in the UK the Mothercare retail chain blossomed. By the early 1980s, however, the numbers of babies had fallen by a third or more, and Mothercare's performance looked less dynamic. On the other hand, the boom babies were then reaching their twenties and becoming yuppies, with a consequent benefit to manufacturers of luxury goods for this age group and the builders of 'starter homes'. In the early 1990s, though, marketers were already starting to look to the over-50s, the 'empty nest' stage, for the next big boom in spending.

For the record, some important research work by O'Brien and Ford,[2] in a study that measured product penetration (the percentage of consumers 'using') across a range of 20 typical consumer items, found that, in the UK at least, 'life-stage' (defined in broadly the same age group terms as those above) was the best discriminator of all the factors normally used to classify consumers.

Geography

For some products or services, geographical variations may be quite significant. Much has been made recently of the 'North–South divide' in the UK, but there may also be fundamental differences in taste between regions. For a number of decades the Scots preferred lager to other beers, whereas the English shunned it; this is a pattern that has now been broken (paradoxically by the introduction of Australian lagers). This illustrates the lesson that such factors can change dramatically over time. More prosaically, the North prefers white pickled

[2] S. O'Brien and R. Ford, Can we at last say goodbye to social class?, Paper presented to the 31st Annual Conference of the Market Research Society, 1988.

onions (and shops for such groceries on weekdays), while the South prefers brown ones (and does its shopping over the weekend). The variations are, of course, even greater when the range is expanded to, say, continental Europe.

Much more closely targeted geographical segments have been offered by the MOSAIC and PROFILES systems in the UK. The most widely used, though, is ACORN – A Classification of Residential Neighbourhoods. Based on the range of census data available (including obvious categories such as occupation, household size and composition – together with some unexpected ones, such as mode of travel to work and household facilities), cluster analysis was used to derive 36 categories of neighbourhood types. These were subsequently further reduced to a simpler set of 11 types. These 11 types are now used to map the locations where certain types of people are likely to live in the UK.[3]

		UK Population (%)
A	Modern family housing for manual workers	9.6
B	Modern family housing, higher incomes	7.4
C	Older housing of intermediate status	10.4
D	Very poor-quality older terraced housing	9.2
E	Rural areas	5.8
F	Urban local authority housing	20.6
G	Housing with most overcrowding	2.9
H	Low-income areas with immigrants	4.2
I	Student and high-status non-family areas	4.3
J	Traditional high-status suburbia	19.1
K	Areas of elderly people	6.4

Each of these categories can be subdivided, so that the marketer can target a mailing or door-to-door delivery exactly where it will be most productive. It has perhaps been most effectively used by market researchers who wish to select very specific samples (for mini-test markets, for example), and by the retail trade (for optimizing the siting of retail outlets).

Social class

The traditional 'pigeon-holing' mainstay of much of the advertising industry has been that of social class. This, although it revolves around occupation (usually that of the head of the household), is based on more than just income groups alone.

[3] A. Lunn, Segmenting and constructing markets, *Consumer Market Research Handbook*, ed. R. Worcester and J. Downham (McGraw-Hill, 1986).

It used to be assumed that the upper classes were the first to try new products, which then *trickled down* (the name of the theory) to the lower classes. Historically, there may have been some justification for this. The refrigerator, the washing machine, the car and the telephone were all adopted first by the higher social classes. Recently, however, as affluence has become more widespread, the process has become much less clear. It is now argued that the new 'opinion leaders' come from within the same social class.

The class groupings which have been traditionally used by the advertising agencies[4] are:

		UK Population (%)
AB	Managerial and professional	17
C1	Supervisory and clerical	26
C2	Skilled manual	25
DE	Unskilled manual and unemployed	32

This approach has been reported to be of decreasing value in recent decades. Whereas some four decades ago, when these groupings were first widely used, the numbers in each of the main categories (C, D and E) were reasonably well balanced, today the C group in total (although now usually split to give C1 and C2) forms such a large sector that it dominates the whole classification system and offers less in terms of usable concentration of marketing effort. In addition, increased affluence has meant that consumers have developed tastes that are based on other aspects of their life-styles, and class-related behaviour appears to have decreased in terms of purchasing patterns.

Occupation

The occupation of the individual, or the head of the household, can sometimes significantly affect his or her way of life. This is, once more, less important than when there was the great split between manual (blue-collar) and clerical (white-collar) jobs. Even so, a manager in a high-tech industry may still have a different set of values, on the one hand, from those of a worker on a production line in a declining industry and, on the other, from those of a university teacher.

A number of these measures have now been combined. For instance, SAGACITY analysis,[5] developed by Research Services Ltd, includes life-cycle (in their terminology, life-stage in ours) components split by income (better/worse off) and occupation (white/blue collar).

---

[4] JICNARS National Readership Survey (1989).
[5] Martin Evans, Market Segmentation, in *The Marketing Book*, ed. Michael J. Baker (Butterworth Heinemann, 1994).

SELF-TEST QUESTION 2.3

?

[For those in consumer goods/services only]

Which of these traditional 'predictors' (geography, age, class and so on) applies to your organization's customers or clients? How do they apply? What use can be made of this in concentrating marketing effort?

Culture

The last sections lead to two conclusions. The first is that the overall culture is another, increasingly important, factor. It is most noticeable in terms of nations. The culture of the UK, with its persisting class-consciousness, differs in many ways from that of the USA, with its money-consciousness. The Mediterranean way of life, in the sun, may be quite different from the Nordic, in the cold. But the second conclusion is that cultures change; and much of marketing has yet to recognize the fact.

Within the overall culture there will be smaller *subcultural* groupings, which have their own distinctive values. These are perhaps most obvious in ethnic or religious groupings, which attract their own specialist suppliers. But they may also be as diverse as yuppies in the major financial centres or football hooligans, each of which groups holds a very strong set of cultural values – and each of which may be targeted by specialist marketers, supplying Porsche cars or team colours.

Peer pressure

Within these cultures and subcultures there is a powerful force at work requiring members to conform to the overall value of the group. These 'reference groups' are sometimes referred to as 'membership groups', when the individual is *formally* a member (of, for example, a political party or trade union). Individuals may also have 'aspiration groups' (social cliques, say, such as yuppies) to which they would like to belong. They may also recognize 'dissociative groups' with which they would *not* wish to associate (thus drinkers may go to great lengths to avoid being associated with 'lager louts'). This 'peer pressure' can sometimes be used to great effect by marketers. If they can sway the few 'opinion leaders' in the reference group they will capture the whole group.

Perhaps the most influential 'peer group' is that of the family. Indeed, it is often the family, rather than the individual, that is the focus of the marketer's activities.

Life-style

In the past decade or so, increasing affluence has resulted in spending patterns that may now vary quite considerably, even within the same age and class groups; they now reflect individual life-styles.

A number of life-style classifications have been proposed by researchers, including the following:

AIO (Activities, Interests, Opinions). This approach seeks, via long questionnaires (such as those proposed by Joseph T. Plummer[6]), to measure respondents' positions on a number of dimensions spread across these categories (as well as the more usual demographic groupings). On the basis of their responses, they are then allocated (using sophisticated computer analysis techniques) to the AIO (life-style) groups.

VALS (Value Life-Styles). Arnold Mitchell[7] (of SRI International) has developed similar groupings. He drew up four main categories subdivided into nine life-styles, again based on long questionnaires:

- *need-driven groups* – 'survivors' and 'sustainers'
- *outer-directed groups* – 'belongers', 'emulators' and 'achievers'
- *inner-directed groups* – 'I-am-me', 'experientials' and 'societally conscious'
- *combined outer- and inner-directed groups* – 'integrated'

According to this framework, the outer-directed groups, 'belongers' (conventional, conservative and so on), 'emulators' (ambitious, upwardly mobile and so on) and 'achievers' (leaders who make things happen and so on) account for two-thirds of the US population. Thus *The Times* newspaper, to take a UK example, might expect to target 'achievers', and possibly to address a larger total market segment than *The Guardian*, which might be looking to the 'societally conscious' for its most ardent supporters. Less widely reported is that the VALS typology also suggests that there is a possible progression within the life-styles – from 'survivors' through to 'integrated'. In his book,[7] Arnold Mitchell showed two alternative routes for this progression (figure 2.1).

The framework was updated in 1989, as VALS2 – more directly linked to age and income. TGI, in the UK, analyse life-style on the basis of 246 life-style statements.

Life-styles can apparently even be used by a range of non-profit organizations. One Wisconsin blood centre reportedly turned a deficit of 7000 donors into a surplus of 7000, by concentrating its attentions on people who were affluent, busy and had close-knit families.

---

[6] J. T. Plummer, The concept and application of life-style segmentation, *Journal of Marketing* (January 1974).
[7] A. Mitchell, *The Nine American Lifestyles* (Macmillan, 1983).

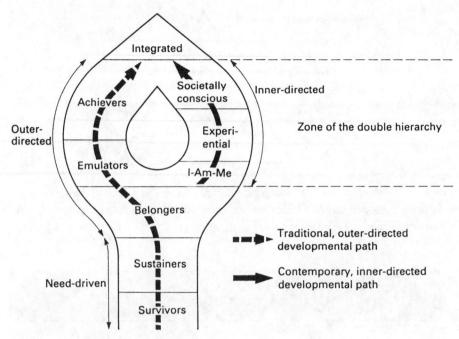

Figure 2.1   The life-style double hierarchy.

Psychological Factors

A number of psychological factors are also proposed; from the widely reported teachings of Freud through to Herzberg's[8] discussion of 'dissatisfiers' (characteristics of a product that will veto its purchase for a given customer) and 'satisfiers' (which will positively persuade the customer to choose that brand).

Maslow's Hierarchy of Needs

In the context of marketing, however, perhaps the most widely quoted approach is that of Abraham Maslow,[9] who developed a hierarchy of 'needs', ranging from the most essential, immediate physical needs to the most luxuriously inessential.

Maslow's contention was that the individual addresses the most urgent needs first, starting with the physiological. But as each is satisfied, and the lower-level physical needs are (at least amongst the affluent) soon satiated, attention switches to the next higher level, resulting ultimately in achievement of the

[8] F. Herzberg, *Work and Nature of Man* (William Collins, 1966).
[9] A. Maslow, *Motivation and Personality* (Harper & Row, 1954).

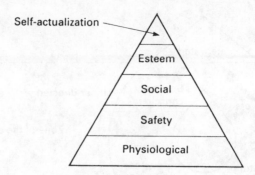

level of self-actualization. It is argued that marketers are increasingly required to address their attentions to the two highest levels; and, even in the near future, almost exclusively to those of self-actualization.

SELF-TEST QUESTION 2.4

Which of these 'cultural' predictors (peer pressure, families, life-style, psychological and so on) applies to the customers or clients of your organization? How important are they? Is their importance growing? How are they used to target your customers or clients?

Cognitive dissonance

There is one more interesting effect on consumer behaviour, to be found immediately after a purchase has been made. This was predicted by Leon Festinger in 1957, as his cognitive dissonance theory, which states that where there were dissonant elements in the original decision to buy (the negative aspects of the product purchased, and the positive elements of the alternatives not purchased) there would, post-purchase, be tension in the consumer's mind. Festinger's prediction was that buyers would read promotional material even more avidly *after* purchase than before in order to justify their decisions and to displace the dissonant elements by concentrating on those aspects of the promotion that stressed the good points of the product purchased. However, later work has not tended to be very supportive. Nevertheless, there is an implication for marketers that they need to recognize the role of their promotion in general and of their advertising in particular in the post-purchase period as well as in the build-up to the sale.

SELF-TEST QUESTION 2.5

?

What allowance (in terms of post-purchase promotion) does your organization make for cognitive dissonance?

Organizational Purchasing

Different pigeon-holes are often applied to the industrial products that are sold to industrial businesses and institutional or government buyers, to be incorporated in their own products, resold or used within their organizations. These buying processes are often categorized, at the most basic level, by the broad product type:

- *basic raw materials* (such as steel, for a car manufacturer). These are usually sold on a contractual basis to a tight specification. Sales are often achieved by competitive pricing, credit terms and delivery reliability.
- *component markets* (such as radiators). These differ from basic materials because of their wider variation. Product quality and reliability become extremely important.
- *capital goods markets* (such as lathes). These are normally dominated by high technical capability on both sides.
- *maintenance, repair and operating goods* (such as detergents for floor cleaning). These are consumable items, usually of low unit value, often sold through distributors.

Derived demand

One clear difference about much of the demand for industrial products or services is that it is a 'derived demand'. The industrial marketer (selling steel, say) may be just as concerned about the demand for the ultimate consumer product (such as the automobile). In recent years this has led to the relationship between some industrial sellers and their customers being more akin to a 'partnership', both sides being in the same boat.

'Joint demand', which is rather different, occurs when the demand for two or more products (or services) is interdependent, normally because they are used together. The demand for razor blades may depend upon the number of razors in use; this is why razors have sometimes been sold as 'loss leaders', to increase demand for the associated blades.

Decision-makers and influencers

In the context of industrial goods marketing, it is perhaps the 'organizational' factors which predominate. There is much theory, and even more opinion, expressed about how the various 'decision-makers' and 'influencers' (those who can only influence, not decide, the final decision) interact. Decisions are frequently taken by groups, rather than individuals, and the official buyer often does not have authority to take the decision.

Robert B. Miller and Stephen E. Heiman,[10] for example, offer a more complex view of industrial buying decisions (particularly in the area of 'complex sales' of capital equipment). They see three levels of decision-making:

- *economic buying influence* – the decision-maker who can authorize the necessary funds for purchase
- *user buying influences* – the people in the buying company who will use the product and will specify what they want to purchase
- *technical buying influence* – the 'experts' (including, typically, the buying department) who can veto the purchase on technical grounds

Webster and Wind,[11] in a similar vein, identify six roles within the 'buying centre':

- *users* – who will actually use the product or service
- *influencers* – particularly technical personnel
- *deciders* – the actual decision-makers
- *approvers* – who formally authorize the decision
- *buyers* – the department with formal authority
- *gatekeepers* – those who have the power to stop the sellers reaching other members of the 'buying centre'

Interaction

One generally ignored aspect of the organizational purchase is its interactive nature, although the International Marketing and Purchasing Group (IMP), a pan-European group of researchers, have investigated it in some detail.

In practice, *both* sides contribute to the purchasing process. It would be foolish to assume that the buyer has a purely passive role. Thus, the discussions and meetings – which may extend over a considerable period – are designed to achieve a 'negotiated' outcome which is satisfactory to both sides. Miller, Heiman and Tuleja[12] hint at this when they say that *both* sides must 'win'

---

[10] R. B. Miller and S. E. Heiman, *Strategic Selling* (Kogan Page, 1989).
[11] F. E. Webster and Y. Wind, *Organizational Buying Behavior* (Prentice-Hall, 1972).
[12] Miller and Heiman, *Strategic Selling*.

(see 'win-win', described in chapter 11). It is also at the heart of 'customer partnership' and 'relationship management' (again described in chapter 11).

SELF-TEST QUESTION 2.6

What organizational factors are important in your marketing to your customers? How are they handled?

Diffusion of Innovation

One particular aspect of consumer behaviour that has attracted considerable interest is that relating to the way new products, or new ideas, are taken up. As Gatignon and Robertson[13] suggest:

> The diffusion process can be characterized in terms of three dimensions; the rate of diffusion, the pattern of diffusion, and the potential penetration level. The *rate* of diffusion reflects the speed at which sales occur over time. The diffusion *pattern* concerns the shape of the diffusion curve . . . Typically, the curve showing only decreasing returns and the S-shaped or sigmoid curve have been represented by exponential and logistic forms, respectively. The *potential penetration level* is a separate dimension indicating the size of the potential market – i.e. the maximum cumulative sales (or adoption) over time.

They also make the point that:

> Marketing actions are important in influencing the speed of diffusion, as well as the process of diffusion by segment. Indeed, in most cases marketing actions are designed to achieve faster penetration, to block competition, and to establish a market franchise. Commitment of sizeable marketing expenditures . . . is likely to result in a diffusion function that is more similar to the exponential curve than to a sigmoid curve . . .

This is just what ambitious new product managers look for in their launches.

A final complication of the consumer decision-making process is that the adoption of new products is not necessarily uniform throughout the population. Everett Rogers,[14] for example, concluded that there were five separate groups

---

[13] H. Gatignon and T. S. Robertson, A propositional inventory for new diffusion research, *Journal of Consumer Research*, vol. 11 (March 1988).
[14] E. M. Rogers, *Diffusion of Innovations* (Free Press, 1962).

of consumers, each of which showed different rates of new product adoption. They were, proceeding from the quickest adopters through to the laggards:

- innovators (2.5 per cent)
- early adopters (13.5 per cent)
- early majority (34 per cent)
- later majority (34 per cent)
- laggards (16 per cent)

The innovators are seen by him to be venturesome, willing to take risks, while the early adopters are the main opinion leaders in their community. This classification suggests that the marketer should perhaps take a particular interest in these two leading groups when a product launch is contemplated.

Usage and Loyalty

From the point of view of many marketers, it is the outcome of all these processes which is most important, and that shows in the customer's response to the 'brand':

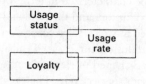

- *Usage status.* Philip Kotler[15] groups 'users' into a number of categories: non-users, ex-users, potential users, first-time users and regular users.
- *Usage rate.* Most important of all, in this context, is usually the *rate* of usage, to which the Pareto 80:20 Rule applies. Kotler's 'heavy users' are likely to be disproportionately important to the brand (typically, 20 per cent of users accounting for 80 per cent of usage – and of suppliers' profit). As a result, suppliers often segment their customers into 'heavy', 'medium' and 'light' users; as far as they can, they target 'heavy users'.
- *Loyalty.* A third dimension, however, is whether the customer is committed to the brand. Philip Kotler,[16] again, defines four patterns of behaviour.

- Hard Core Loyals – who buy the brand all the time.
- Soft Core Loyals – loyal to two or three brands.
- Shifting Loyals – moving from one brand to another.
- Switchers – with no loyalty (possibly 'deal-prone', constantly looking for bargains, or 'vanity prone', looking for something different).

[15] Kotler, *Marketing Management.*
[16] Kotler, *Marketing Management.*

In industrial markets, organizations will regard the 'heavy users' as 'major accounts', to be handled by senior sales personnel and even managers; whereas the 'light users' may be handled by the general salesforce or by a dealer.

Once more, though, life may be much more complex. For example, Andrew Ehrenberg, of the London Business School, says that consumers buy *'portfolios of brands'*. They switch regularly between brands, often simply because they want a change. Thus, 'brand penetration' or 'brand share' reflects only a statistical chance that the majority of customers will buy that brand next time as part of a portfolio of brands they favour! It does not guarantee that they will stay loyal.

Influencing the statistical probabilities facing a consumer choosing from a portfolio of preferred brands, which is required in this context, is a very different role for a brand manager; compared with the – much simpler – one traditionally described, of recruiting and holding dedicated customers. The concept also emphasizes the need for managing continuity – by rules such as the Competitive Saw.

On the other hand, one of the most prominent features of many markets is their overall *stability* or inertia, whichever description you find most useful. Thus, in their essential characteristics they change very slowly, often over decades – sometimes centuries – rather than over months. This stability has two very important implications. The first is that if you are a clear brand leader you are especially well placed in relation to your competitors, and should want to further the inertia which lies behind that stable position. This will, however, still demand a continuing pattern of minor changes, to keep up with the marginal changes in consumer taste (which may be minor to the theorist, but will still be crucial in terms of those consumers' purchasing patterns – markets do not favour the over-complacent!). But these minor investments are a small price to pay for the long-term profits which brand leaders usually enjoy. Only farmhands make a career out of milking cows, and only fools jeopardize the investment contained in an established brand leader!

The second, and more important implication is that if you want to overturn this stability, and change the market (or significantly change your position in it), then you must expect to make massive investments to succeed! Even though stability is the natural state of markets, however, sudden changes can still occur and the environment must be constantly scanned for signs of these.

The Customer Franchise

One of the most positive ways of consolidating the consumer as the most important focus of the organization is to look on this relationship as a prime asset of the business; one that has been built up by a series of marketing investments over the years. As with any other asset, this investment can be expected to bring returns over subsequent years. On the other hand, also like any other asset, it has to be protected and husbanded. This 'asset' is often referred to as the '*customer franchise*'.

At one extreme it may come from the individual relationship developed face to face by the sales professional. At the other it is the cumulative image, held by the consumer, resulting from long exposure to all aspects of the product or service, and especially to a number of advertising and promotional campaigns.

In some markets the customer franchise may be so strong as to be exclusive; in effect it gives the supplier a *monopoly* with those customers. Despite this, Andrew Ehrenberg's work on brand portfolios has shown that consumers may regularly switch brands – for the sake of variety; however, they may still retain an image of the brand, which will swing the balance when their next purchase decision is taken. It may thus still have a value (upon which the advertiser can build) even if the current purchasing decision goes against it. A later decision may, once again, swing in its favour.

The customer franchise is, therefore, a very tangible asset, in terms of its potential effect on sales; even if it is intangible in every other respect. It is based on an *accumulation of impacts over time*. Unfortunately, too many marketers – particularly those in creative departments within advertising agencies – signally fail to recognize the importance, and long-term nature, of this *investment*. They treat each new campaign as if it could, and should, be taken in isolation – no matter how it meshes with previous messages which have been delivered to the consumer. The evidence is that the consumer, on the other hand, does not view the advertising and promotion in such lofty isolation; instead he or she incorporates it into their existing image – to good or bad effect, depending upon how well the new campaign complements the old.

The Consumer Franchise is, to all practical intents, the external alter ego of the brand value. The brand is how the producer typically sees the (internal) investment. The Customer Franchise is the outcome of that internal investment; the counterbalancing entry with the customers.

Most recently, this factor has featured in the emergence of '*relationship market-ing*' in fields other than selling, where (as 'relationship management') it has been developing for some time. According to Grönroos,[17] for example, a key element is *trust*: 'The resources of the seller . . . have to be used in such a manner that the customer's trust . . . in the firm itself is maintained and strengthened.' Even Kotler[18] concedes 'What I think we are witnessing today is a movement away from a focus on exchange . . . toward a focus on building value-lasting relation-ships and marketing networks.'

---

[17] Christian Grönroos, From marketing mix to relationship marketing: towards a paradigm shift in marketing, *Management Decision*, vol. 32, no. 2 (1994).
[18] Philip Kotler, Philip Kotler Explores the New Marketing Paradigm, *Marketing Science Institute Review* (Spring 1992).

Brand Value

In the late 1980s there was a fashion for hostile takeovers of organizations owning major brands, particularly where the book value and the market capitalization did not reflect the real trading value of the brands. This reached a peak with the Nestlé bid of £2.5 billion for Rowntree – a bid of six times Rowntree's reported asset value – and the leveraged buyout of RJR Nabisco for $25 billion. As a result, to make such takeovers that much more difficult, some organizations with especially strong brands wrote a corresponding (goodwill) valuation into their balance sheets. Rank Hovis McDougall, for instance, put a balance sheet value on their brands of £678 million, and Grand Metropolitan one of £588 million.

This practice has since been discouraged by the various accounting bodies; indeed, the Accounting Standards Committee in the UK has called a halt to it.

SELF-TEST QUESTION 2.7

How does the diffusion process work for the new products and ideas deployed by your organization? How does your organization allow for this? How important is customer loyalty to your marketing efforts? What value would you write into the accounts to cover this?

SELF-TEST QUESTION 2.8

The two questions below are the same as those you answered in audit 2.2. Answer them again, in the light of what you have just read.

What factors most influence your customers' decisions? Are these factors product-oriented?

How does your answer differ from that which you gave before you read this section, and why? (This question is asked for two main reasons. First, it should help you appreciate the learning process you are undergoing. The second reason is rather contrary, because it is quite possible that your first answer was more accurate, or at least more practical, since it was not distorted by the 'artificial' models which the theoreticians have now forced on you!)

To what extent does each of the main factors discussed have an impact on your customers:

- economic
- age
- geography
- social class
- occupation

- culture
- peer pressure
- life-style
- psychology
- organization

What factors are important? Which are the most important influences overall? Which factors does your organization believe are most important? Which does it act on?

SELF-TEST QUESTION 2.9

This is the second major exercise. Its brief is deceptively simple: Produce a customer/client profile. All that is required is that you produce a picture of who your customers and clients are, and where they may be found. Needless to say, the exercise is not as simple as it appears, and involves the use of all aspects of marketing which have been described so far. For instance: Who, statistically, are your customers or clients? What does the 80:20 Rule say about their importance to you? Which of the traditional or cultural or organizational factors which are supposed to influence them actually do – and how?

The last question may, as you should realize by now, open up a number of avenues. The important aspect of the exercise, therefore, is that you explore these avenues – though the time you spend on the exercise is for you to judge.

Models of Consumer Behaviour

In this chapter we have looked at a number of factors that may have an impact on behaviour. However, these factors do not act in isolation. The effect is often the result of their combined influence – and also of their interactions.

One of the best known of the explanatory models that have been developed to explain these interactions is the Howard and Sheth Model,[19] the simplified

[19] J. A. Howard and J. N. Sheth, *The Theory of Buyer Behavior* (Wiley, 1969).

version of which is given in figure 2.2. This contains a deal of common sense, although, as is often the case with such models, the rather obscure terminology makes it appear more confusing than it really is. It is divided into four main components.

The *inputs* (stimuli) that the consumer receives from his or her environment are:

- significative – the 'real' (physical) aspects of the product or service (which the consumer will make use of)
- symbolic – the ideas or images attached by the supplier (for example by advertising)
- social – the ideas or images attached to the product or service by 'society' (for example, by reference groups)

The *outputs* are what happens, the consumer's actions, as observable results of the input stimuli.

Between the inputs and outputs are the *constructs*, the processes which the consumer goes through to decide upon his or her actions. Howard and Sheth group these into two areas:

- perceptual – those concerned with obtaining and handling information about the product or service
- learning – the processes of learning that lead to the decision itself

The Engel–Kollatt–Blackwell[20] model, for one further example, follows a slightly more 'mechanistic' approach, but one which is also based on the parameters examined in this chapter.

Such models can help theorists to explain consumer behaviour better, but it can be more difficult to put them to practical use.

Organizational Behaviour

Models have also been produced to explain the complexities of the organizational buying process. The best known of these is probably that of Webster and Wind[21] (figure 2.3). This follows the buying process inwards from the external environment, through the organizational environment, to the 'buying centre' (the group concerned in the buying decision), to the individuals involved and the buying process that they go through. It is useful for illustrating the variables and the complexities which may be involved. Once more, however, it is difficult to relate it to practical decisions.

[20] J. Engel, D. Kollatt and R. Blackwell, *Consumer Behaviour* (Dryden Press, 1978).
[21] Webster and Wind, *Organizational Buying Behavior*.

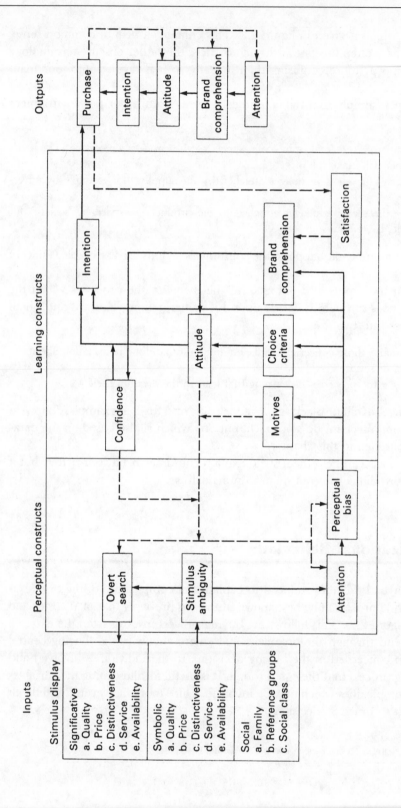

Figure 2.2 A simplified description of the theory of buyer behaviour. Solid lines indicate flow of information; dashed lines indicate feedback effects.

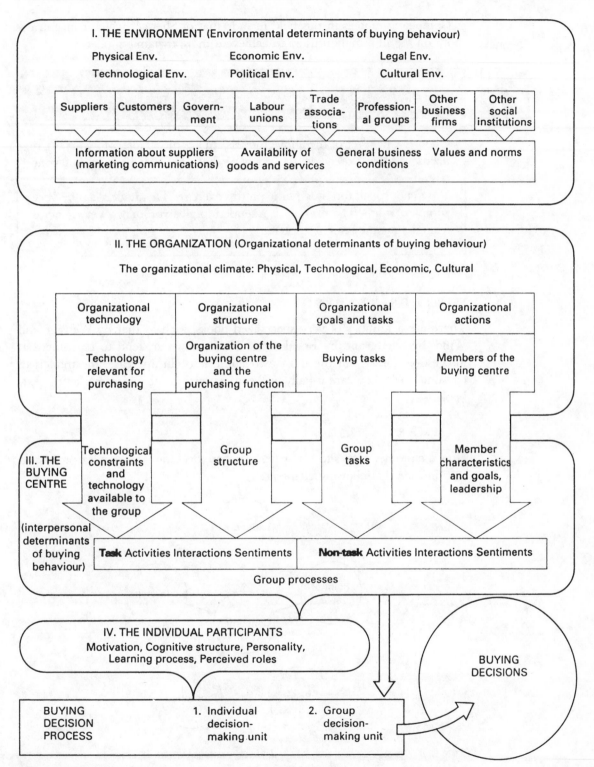

Figure 2.3 A model of organizational buying behaviour.

Competing models in this field include that of Sheth,[22] which concentrates more on the information flows to achieve a more dynamic model.

SELF-TEST QUESTION 2.10

Choose whichever of the above models applies most closely to your organization. How closely does it apply? What does it tell you about your customers?

(Do not spend too much time on this exercise. The models can be very complex to use. The exercise is intended to give you only a very general feel for how they might apply.)

FURTHER READING

There are a number of very specialized books, such as that by Webster and Wind, by Sheth, and by Engel et al. These, however, tend to be somewhat indigestible for all but the most avid enthusiasts. In any case, the models of consumer behaviour are usually well summarized in the major marketing textbooks.

SUMMARY

How a customer comes to his or her purchase decision is a complex process. It may include the following elements:

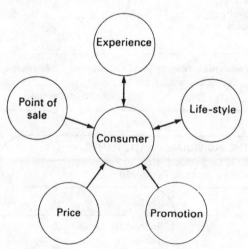

---

[22] J. N. Sheth, A model of industrial buyer behaviour, *Journal of Marketing*, vol. 37 (October 1973).

In the case of repeat purchases, the model can most simply be described as:

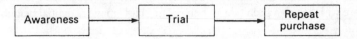

More general factors influencing consumers may be:

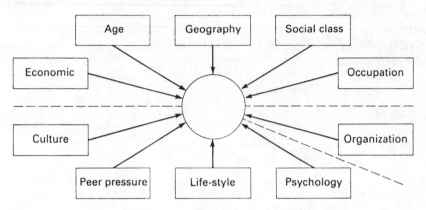

Organizational purchasing is subject to a rather different set of influences, not least because it is usually based on *derived demand*, but also because it is often a group decision, split between:

- decision-makers – economic buying influence and user buying influence
- influencers – technical buying influence

There are other factors which affect *changes*:

- diffusion of innovation
- usage and loyalty – status and rate of use

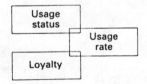

- customer franchise

At a more general theoretical level there are the models of consumer behaviour (Howard and Sheth) and of organizational buying (Webster and Wind).

REVISION QUESTIONS

1 What are the three generally accepted stages of repeat purchasing? How does Philip Kotler's model differ?

2 What specific factors, at the time of purchase, may affect the buying decision?
3 What general factors may affect consumer buying behaviour? How does social class compare with age as a predictor of behaviour? How may residential neighbourhoods be used?
4 What are the two main models of life-style? How do these compare with the various psychological approaches?
5 Who are generally believed to be the two main categories of contributors to the organizational buying process? How do Miller and Heiman expand these categories, and why?
6 What is diffusion of innovation? How does the customer franchise relate to customer usage and loyalty?

3 Marketing Research and Information

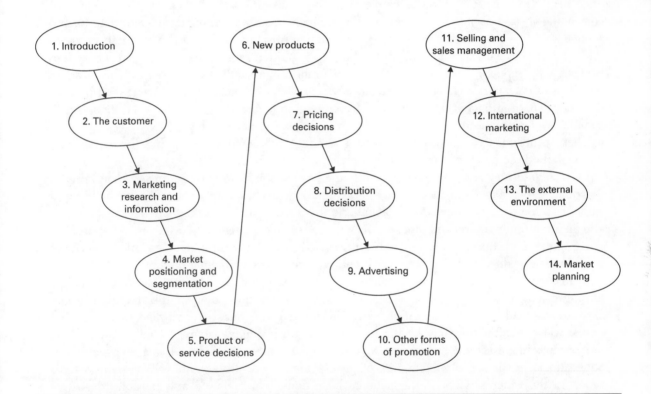

Introduction

This chapter is about marketing research in its very widest sense; often now described as the Marketing Information System (MIS). Much of it, however, is about data which already exists in the organization. Whatever the source of the data, in this book we are primarily looking for information about the customer (and hence about the market, and market research – as it used to be called). This is the 'listening' part of the 'dialogue' which is what marketing as a whole is about. The chapter describes quantitative data (that to which numbers can be put) and qualitative data

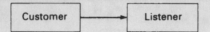

(described by words and, too often, opinions). But the main split of the chapter is between 'internal data' (already collected within the organization – but, in this marketing context, still describing the outside world) and 'external data' (that obtained from external sources, including marketing research as traditionally defined – but which represents only a small part of what is typically available in total).

'Internal data' is probably the richest source of material for any manager, but one which is too often neglected. The most obvious source of quantitative data is the 'performance data' used to control the operations of the organization. Traditionally this is accounting-driven information, and as such it is often incomplete and biased in marketing terms; but, even so it can be a rich source of information (especially about trends in the business). Written reports (particularly, in the current context, sales reports), being largely verbal, are much more difficult to analyse. They lead to problems of data handling, such as data overload and access: managers are so engulfed by data that they cannot find what they want (and hence tend to ignore such sources – even though they contain invaluable information).

These problems are discussed, and the emerging techniques for handling this complexity (particularly those based on computer processing) are evaluated.

Even so, informal 'reports' (usually seen by the participants as interesting conversations) predominate as the manager's main source of data: although they are rarely recognized as such – and without correct handling much of the data is lost. Structuring and 'processing' this data is, therefore, also an important management function. Indeed, 'personal experience' drawn from a vast number of encounters and conversations probably represents the most important 'database' upon which the typical manager draws; yet it is one almost entirely ignored by marketing books.

In many respects the most important management tool for locating external data and then turning it into useful information is 'desk research'. The starting point for this may well be the files already held in the organization – usually unused and dust-covered! The main external source will thereafter probably be the local library, an invaluable source of information in its own right (with directories, which are a prime source of specific data, as well as government publications, which are a good source of general data). The library will, however, also have access to the wider services of the national collections, which should also be able to answer almost any question (provided that it is asked correctly). Other agencies and industry associations, as well as commercial providers, may also be sources for this desk research, the essence of which is a compilation of the relevant pieces (often quite large amounts) already in the public domain.

Marketing research itself represents the pinnacle of the process of data retrieval and analysis. In this case it embodies basic ('primary') research; finding out, at least in the consumer goods area, information about the consumer. In some ways it also represents the definitive skill of marketing since, once the correct information on consumer needs and wants is to hand, the ensuing marketing actions are largely predetermined by it. The real skill in marketing (research) here is in asking the right questions rather than in having the right answers to what may be the wrong propositions. Beyond it lies the actual decision-making process itself, which is described in the later chapters.

Marketing research may be *qualitative*, using individual (in-depth) interviews or discussion (focus) groups to tease out underlying motivations of consumers. On the other hand, the survey based upon doorstep interviews is the archetypal *quantitative* research (although postal and telephone research also have their places, and are now more frequently used). In order to ensure that the information collected by such surveys is not biased, the work needs to be carefully controlled. If the correct sampling procedures are carried out a sample of just a few hundred interviews will tell you almost as much about a population of many millions as a full 'census'.

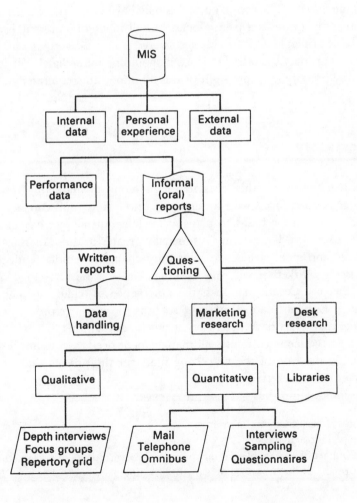

The aspect of marketing which is seen by many managers as being most characteristic is marketing research. Such research is seen, for example, as the main difference between marketing and selling. These managers perhaps overlook some of the breadth of marketing, but their focus on marketing research is justifiable; for such research, whatever form it takes, is the essential starting point for effective marketing. The first part of this chapter will be concerned with establishing how the marketer might go about finding out what consumers really want.

Listening to Your Customers

Marketing research is analogous to listening. Despite the stereotype of the salesman as a blustering huckster, the best sales professionals spend most of their time *listening*. The recent emphasis may have been upon internal processes, and on competition as a prime focus, but all marketing ultimately follows the same basic principle: *before you can offer answers to your customers you must listen to their questions*. This may seem trivial, since it should be immediately obvious; yet far too many practitioners lose sight of this all-important requirement.

Uncertainty

There are, however, other reasons for investing in marketing research. The marketer is often faced with a degree of uncertainty, and can never be quite certain that even the best laid plans will achieve their objectives in exactly the manner expected. Uncertainty is normally greater in those markets which are changing, and greatest in those which are changing rapidly. Unfortunately, a great many markets have been experiencing very rapid change over recent years; the past decade has seen the emergence of 'chaos' as a factor to be managed. Even in mature markets, such as those of car production or shipbuilding, marketers have been caught out by developments.

To help reduce uncertainty, all management needs a constant flow of information. In the case of the marketing manager the process that provides this information is marketing research.

The information thus gathered may cover:

- markets, customers and consumers
- competitive activities
- the impact of environmental factors such as governments or sociocultural changes
- the results of the organization's own marketing activities

In recent years a major emphasis in marketing research has been on reducing its cost, an approach promoted most enthusiastically of all by the market research agencies themselves. It has thus often become a commodity market, with many agencies trying to supply very basic services at the lowest price.

As a result, the more sophisticated techniques, along with much of the quality, are now the province of just a handful of market research agencies. In fact, the best use of marketing research is probably now made by the leading management consultancies – which privately charge large sums for the public lessons of the 1960s.

Marketing Intelligence Systems (MIS)

In recent years, and in particular since the widening availability of computer-ized databases, the process of collecting and distributing marketing information has become systematized. The system that handles these processes in a con-trolled and co-ordinated fashion has come to be called the Marketing Intelligence System (MIS). (This is slightly confusing since the more widely implemented Management Intelligence System, of which the marketing ele-ment is just a part, also goes by the acronym MIS.)

Such a system, however, can be very simple, and is often most effectively used in these simplest of forms. In this context, it is just the systematic collection and organization of the data which are relevant to the needs of the marketer.

First, let us define some of the terminology that marketing researchers (or at least those most exposed to Information Technology) use when they are being 'rigorous':

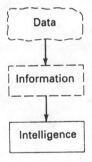

- *Data* are collections of facts; for example, the 'demographic (census)' figures relating to neighbourhoods – although the subject could equally well be measurements of the attitudes of customers.
- *Information* is data which have been selected and ordered with some specific purpose in mind; for example, the overall profile of the neighbourhoods which comprise the catchment area where a superstore chain is considering opening another branch.

- *Intelligence* is the interpretation which is made, following analysis of this information; for example, the resulting profile of the store's likely customers, and its optimal location.

These are important distinctions in theory. Unfortunately most marketers, and even many marketing researchers, use these terms rather loosely; in conversation they are often interchangeable.

The important distinction to be made is that there is a gradation of value in the information as it is processed step by step from its original amorphous form until it becomes a finely honed tool which will help to answer the specific question facing the marketer. Its power as a tool increases as it goes through this process, from raw data to selected prime information to analysed intelligence; but so does the potential bias applied to the data. At the first stage you can make errors of omission, as relevant data are left out (perhaps because they are inconvenient in terms of the end justification wanted). At the second, the errors may be those of commission (seeing things in the information which are not really there, but which you want to be there – much research information is very much like the psychologists' 'Rorschach Blot', in which the viewer can see anything which takes his or her fancy).

As has already been explained, much of this information is already held in most organizations. On the other hand, without an organized Marketing Intelligence System it is often only to be found in a fragmented and unco-ordinated form. It is thus claimed by supporters of MIS approaches that adopting a systems approach to information requirements, which does not have to be computer-based, can provide management with banks of data which are oriented to its particular information needs.

The value of marketing information is having the right information available at the right time. Even so, it is all too easy to be over-ambitious. It is important to be able to control, and hence use, the monster you may be creating; particularly if you choose the computer route.

Perhaps the most important new use of MIS data on the large scale is in 'precision marketing', where the resulting knowledge of small groups of customers (or even of individuals) is used to target promotional efforts very accurately. This is discussed in more detail in chapter 10.

Scanning

Much of market intelligence in general, and of marketing research in particular, is gathered in response to specific stimuli. The information is needed for the development of a new product or a new marketing campaign. Such information is valuable but it is necessarily partial (focusing on one set of questions at one point in time).

A much more powerful approach to MIS is a continuous approach (which, in any case, should automatically happen with internally generated data). This is often described as 'scanning' (or sometimes as 'environmental scanning' or 'environmental analysis', when it covers all the external factors, not just those in the marketing environment). An 'observer' in the organization (usually the marketing manager or, preferably, the whole marketing department) 'scans', or watches, what is happening in the outside world. The most direct input normally comes from trade journals and general business publications; subscriptions to these periodicals represent a sound marketing investment. On the other hand, the most important indirect input comes from the mass media as a whole (television, radio, newspapers and magazines), which give up-to-date information of how society as whole (and specific markets in particular) is developing – in the context of the related news stories.

Scanning is described in more detail in chapter 13.

Internal Sources of Information

The first elements of the information which is available for the marketer relate to the information held within the organization. In the specific environment of this book, they are dealt with in the context of the needs of marketing. It should become clear, however, that the same techniques can apply quite generally to most other areas of management. An engineer looking for historical information on product performance, or an accountant trying to discover what lies behind a certain set of figures, will face much the same task. *Finding and handling information is after all a key aspect of all management* (and is becoming even more important in our increasingly information-based society).

The main internal sources (relevant to marketing needs) are:

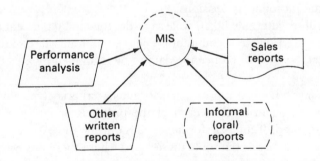

Performance analysis

In most organizations the key data on performance, typically derived from order processing and invoicing, are likely to already be available on its computer databases. These should provide accurate sales data split by product and by region. They should also provide these in a timely manner. In this electronic age it should even be possible to obtain this information on a computer terminal. It should be recognized, however, that such systems are driven by accounting requirements, and in particular by accounting periods; they will often reflect an unbalanced picture until the month-end procedures have been completed.

In the case of non-profit organizations it is just as important to keep track of the clients (recipients, donors, patients, customers and so on), as well as the transactions related to them.

If the computer systems have been designed to cope with the level of detail needed, performance figures should be available down to individual customers or clients. On the other hand, this potentially poses the problem of 'information overload'. There will be so much information, most of it redundant, that it will effectively be useless as a management tool.

There are a number of possible answers to this potential torrent of data:

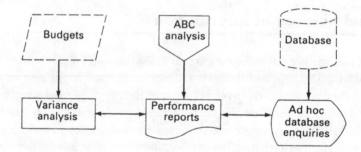

ABC analysis   Typically the reports are sorted in terms of volume (or value) of sales, so that the customers are ranked in order of their sales offtake; with the highest-volume (and hence most 'important') customers at the top of the list and the many low-volume customers at the bottom (since it matters less if they are not taken into account in decisions).

As you will see later, the 80:20 Rule says that the top 20 per cent of customers on such a list are likely to account for 80 per cent of total sales; so this approach can, in effect, be used to reduce the data to be examined by a factor of five.

Variance analysis   In this approach performance criteria (typically budgets or targets) are set, against which each of the products or customers are subsequently monitored. If their performance falls outside the expected range this is highlighted. This means that only those items where there are 'variances' need be reviewed.

However, the variances are only as good as the criteria (usually the budgets) set; and setting these is, in practice, a major task. This is particularly problematical where parameters change with time, so this approach is often only used (if at all) on the 20 per cent of most important items.

Ad hoc database enquiries and reports

If the basic data is suitably organized, on a computer database, it may be possible to access it from terminals. The abstracted data can then be processed from a variety of perspectives. This means that ad hoc reports or enquiries may be easily prepared. Unfortunately, few organizations as yet have their performance data structured in such a way that it can be used for analysis in more than a very limited fashion.

When such information *is* made available via the manager's personal computer it will add an order of magnitude to the productivity of the average personal computer. But this element of designing a Marketing Information System is the province of the experts. In setting up such computer systems it is all too easy to make mistakes which may corrupt the data in the reports. More importantly, corruption of the main files may destroy the validity of the organization's accounting systems.

Despite the above caveats, it remains a fact that most organizations have vast stores of data locked away on their computers – and not just sales data. The computer should also offer data on profit, and on a wide variety of other issues, such as customer returns or product reject levels, which will allow an insight into some of the other dimensions of marketing.

Regrettably, though, many of the key measures may not have been recorded. The data collected by the average system are driven by accounting needs and record only those transactions which result in the actual completion of a sale. It will be a very unusual system if it records details of sales lost, for example because the item wanted was out of stock or did not quite meet the specification required. Such information *may* be available, typically to those taking the orders, but it is usually discarded as soon as it is obvious that a sale is not to be made; yet an analysis of such lost orders can be another invaluable input to marketing planning.

SELF-TEST QUESTION 3.1

What performance reports are regularly produced in your organization? (Sales volume? – by product? by region? by customer? Profit?) Who uses them? How are they used, and what analyses are performed? What other reports could be produced? What would be the benefits of these, and of the existing reports? What other reports do you think should be produced, and why?

Sales Reports

The performance data described above have the great advantage of being numerical: this makes abstraction and manipulation much easier. Much of the remaining data within an organization is, however, available only in verbal form, as memos or reports. From the marketing viewpoint perhaps the most useful of these are the sales reports.

In some respects the reliance on words rather than figures may seem to make the manager's job easier; many, if not most, managers are more at ease with words than numbers. This is something of an illusion, and problems occur in a number of areas.

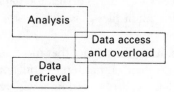

Analysis

Because verbal data are apparently so approachable, there is a tendency to accept them immediately at face value, particularly if the message reinforces the reader's own prejudices. Even if he or she does somehow retain a critical approach, the data are often difficult to analyse: the writers of such reports tend to use the same words to mean different things, and the importance they attach to events often reflects their own enthusiasm.

In addition, collating a number of such reports and distilling these into an overall impression becomes a matter of judgement rather than a simple analysis, and all too often is used to create 'evidence' to bolster the manager's own preconceived ideas.

To a certain extent some of these problems may be corrected by a well designed reporting system or by the use of electronic mail, the structure of which tends to standardize the format and even the language of replies.

Data access and overload

All too often, access to the key data is limited to a few people; the circulation of a memo being rarely to more than half a dozen people – especially from sales personnel in the field (where there are likely to be no carbon copies). The traditional system, then, requires that the recipient (say, the regional sales manager) should recognize the importance of any data and then abstract this to be incorporated in his or her own reports to higher management. The message thus travels hierarchically through the organization, being filtered and distorted at each stage. This inevitably incurs delays. Reporting periods typically increase in length the higher in the organization the message travels. More importantly, it demands that a number of intermediaries recognize the significance of the data. If just one of them chooses to ignore it that data is lost to those in the chain above.

Once again, the increasing use of electronic mail is beginning to have a dramatic effect on the availability of such information, because it is almost as easy to send a memo to a hundred recipients as to one. Indeed, with most such systems, 'standard' distribution lists are available. Even so, there still remains the problem that sales personnel in the field (who should be the main source of MIS data in the marketing context) will probably be the last to be put on such electronic mail systems, and certainly the last to learn how to structure their reports so that they are useful.

Data retrieval

Perhaps the main shortcoming of verbal material is its retrieval. If not filed in the waste-paper basket, memos and reports are consigned to the vagaries of the manager's or department's often outdated filing systems. Indeed, the most useful file in many offices is the 'day file', in which copies of everything being sent out are filed in date order (which means that the area of search can at least be narrowed to a range of dates, if not to the subject). But before even starting such a search, the manager has to remember which document the specific piece of information was included in (always assuming that he or she has kept it). The general problem will not be resolved until all filing is held efficiently on computer. In the shorter term, there are a couple of ways of protecting the key data:

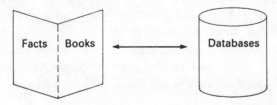

- *Facts books.* One solution is to create a series of 'facts books' which contain all the key data about a particular product, associated with which will be the supporting literature (perhaps in related files), such as reports and competitive brochures. It is sometimes sound practice to circulate to all those involved a summary of the relevant facts book, before the start of the marketing planning process, so that the marketing plans themselves need contain only the planning decisions (and justifications).

- *Computer databases.* Once more, use of a computer database can help. The electronic mail databases by themselves can be useful. Better, though, are the specially developed computer programs for storing and retrieving vast quantities of verbal information. Some of these require the originator to specify the topics covered (often using 'keyword indices'). The best, and most useful, index *every* word in the documents; so that an enquirer on a terminal can ask to be given those documents which mention a given topic anywhere in their contents. Where this may perhaps throw up several hundred references, the search is gradually narrowed by using combinations of words.

Other Written Reports

All of the comments applying to sales reports apply to the rest of the verbal data (memos and reports) which flow around the remainder of the organization. Buried in this mass of data will be facts that will ultimately have an impact on marketing; decisions on new product development, on manufacturing processes and credit policies, for example. The problem, again, is to find and retrieve the relevant data from the mountains of paperwork. It is to be hoped that a move to the correct computerized information systems will help this process. Until then, awareness of such material is more likely to come from personal contacts.

SELF-TEST QUESTION 3.2

How are verbal data, reports and so on (rather than numerical data) acquired by your organization? Are sales personnel required to submit reports – and do they? What happens to these reports, and how useful are they? How are all these data collated and transmitted to management? What are the informal reporting systems? How active, and important, is the grapevine? What plans are there for electronic mail and computer databases? What plans do you think that there should be?

Informal (Oral) Reports

Informal contacts are the staple diet of management. But if it is difficult enough to abstract useful data from written paperwork, it is not usually even considered worthwhile mentioning oral data – yet this probably represents the most important source of data available to any manager. Johansson and Nonaka[1] make the point that 'Japanese-style market research relies heavily on two kinds of information, soft data obtained from visits to dealers and other channel members and hard information about shipments, inventory levels, and retail sales. Japanese managers believe that these data better reflect the behaviour and intentions of flesh-and-blood consumers.'

In any case, every meeting, be it a formally organized meeting of a group or an informal one between two individuals, is potentially rich with useful data.

SELF-TEST QUESTION 3.3

What are the main sources of informal information within your organization? How useful are they? Are there any others which might be developed? What would be your recommendations for new systems?

ACTIVITY 3.1

Over the next working week make notes after every meeting, formal or informal. What happened at the meeting? In particular:

- What was the meeting about?
- Was that what you wanted?
- How much (as a percentage of the time) did you talk and how much did you listen?
- What new information did you learn?
- How did you record that new information, and how did you use it?
- What did you miss?

If you think about it, after most meetings you will realize that there was some question that you failed to ask.

At the end of the week analyse the notes. Ask yourself what is your style in such meetings, and how effective it is, and how it might be improved.

---

[1] K. Johansson and I. Nonaka, Market research in the Japanese way, *Harvard Business Review* (May–June 1987).

External Data

The 'traditional' source of external data for marketing-oriented organizations has been *marketing research*. This is the subject of the succeeding sections.

Even so, the main source of generally available external data is usually that offered by *desk research*. Our research shows that this is used by half of the organizations we surveyed – nearly twice as many as used other sources of data and ten times as many as used doorstep survey research.[2] This type of research is based on 'published' data (in its widest sense), often referred to as 'secondary data' (because it has been generated in response to someone else's questions). Once again, this skill has much wider applicability. *All managers, at some time or other, will need to be able to undertake effective desk research.*

Once the data have been located, their handling follows the same processes as for internal data. It is the 'finding' that is different, and is the key to sound desk research. Parts of the data may, in fact, already be available. It is a common experience of consultants, upon first entering a client's premises, to discover at least one cabinet full of previous reports which have been commissioned and then forgotten. It is worth searching out these invaluable repositories of information in your own organization.

On the other hand, it may be necessary to find these data the hard way, from external sources; and it will certainly be necessary to update the information from the original, external, sources. Some useful sources of data which might be considered in this search are:

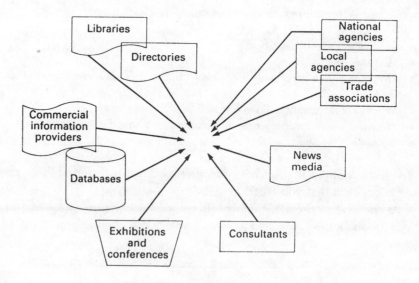

---

[2] D. Mercer, research to be published.

Libraries

The widest-ranging source of published data is usually a library, possibly one within the organization itself, but more usually a public library.

You may be lucky enough, particularly if you are located in a large city, to have an extensive local library, which may meet your needs. Indeed, many libraries (even branch libraries) have a wide selection of non-fiction books which will provide background reading on most subjects, and should not be ignored as a source of data. The reference libraries, which are usually part of the central library, will hold even more.

More important, though, is that these libraries can, and will, obtain books which are not on their shelves. They will typically have a catalogue (usually now held on microfiche or computer) which will list the stock of all their branches. But it doesn't stop there. By way of example I will use the UK to show the range of opportunities but other countries have similar agencies and sources of information. Thus, in the UK the branch library will also have access to the British Library, with its lending section, located at Boston Spa. As a result, if you can find sufficient information to specify the book (usually author, title, publisher and date of publication – although often just the author and title may suffice) it can usually be retrieved. Better still, the service is often free to the enquirer.

On the other hand, much of the published data is located in journals – often specialist periodicals. It is possible that a librarian specializing in information retrieval (or simply in reader enquiries), usually to be found at the central library, may be able to conduct a search for you. Perhaps you will, in any case, know the specific journal you want. Again, it is quite possible that the journal (or a photocopy of the article) can be obtained from the British Library.

News media

The most prevalent, but often unrecognized, source of external data for all managers (and the one which scans with the widest perspective) is that of the news media (especially the national morning newspapers and television news and current affairs programmes). The amount of information that these provide is probably vastly greater than that received from any other single source.

The choice of news media, in particular of newspapers, thus becomes important. The 'quality' papers are likely to be of more value than the tabloids. Ideally, a variety of newspapers should be read to judge the bias that each almost inevitably imparts to even the simplest news item. For example, the reader of *The Times* in the UK (which is now often an ardent supporter of the British Conservative Party) might be well advised sometimes to read *The Guardian* (which is not, and is usually rather radical).

A positive approach to 'news' in general is also necessary. Ideally, there should be some commitment to 'scanning', but an enquiring mind is the next best thing. Reading relevant business journals (such as *The Economist, Business Week, Fortune* and so on) is also informative, as well as entertaining.

> ## SELF-TEST QUESTION 3.4
>
> What are the main sources of external information available to you, and to your organization? What is available in your local library, and what can the library obtain for you? What relevant directories are there? What trade associations and journals provide useful information? What relevant government statistics are there?
>
> How reliable is the information provided by each of these sources? What use is made of them within the organization? What use do you think should be made of them?
>
> Using the resources of your local library (particularly the trade directories and government statistics that it contains), prepare a brief summary of the key statistics relating to the 'industry' in which your organization operates.

Personal Experience

The most important source of information is personal experience. Unfortunately, it is also the most neglected source in terms of management theory in general, and marketing theory in particular.

Beyond this, we have found that the aspect of marketing research our management students find most rewarding is that relating to *personal* research. They want to be able to get the feel of the market personally, rather than just through abstract statistics. Even in this context, however, the key to personal research is questioning – as it is with formal research, which is described later in the chapter. Yet again, you only get the right answers if you ask the right questions.

Questioning

Questioning might seem easy to achieve when you are asking the questions for yourself, but most people simply are not very effective at asking such questions. They ask very specific (closed) questions which tend to narrow discussion; and, in particular, tend to confine the discussion to the areas set by their own personal preferences or prejudices. Much more useful are those (open) questions which allow the person being questioned to adopt a wider view. These questions (of which the simplest – Why? How? What? – are the most powerful) encourage the speaker to say what he or she considers is most important about the topic. The listener can then gain the most benefit from the speaker's knowledge and expertise. Later in the conversation, directive and then closed questions can be used to steer the conversation to the topics of greatest interest to the listener.

Open questions also seem to be the most difficult for a manager to ask; perhaps because they are not so obviously leading directly to the answer that is wanted. But they are the key to unlocking the tongue of the person facing you. If the conversation proceeds with very short replies (and particularly just yes or no), it is likely that you are not using enough open questions; and may be missing the real issues. The more open the question the better. The most powerful question is quite simply 'Why?', often closely followed by 'How?'. In practice, open questions come naturally if the questioner is genuinely interested in finding out what makes the prospect's business tick.

A particular technique, used for example by skilled researchers, is 'laddering'. In this technique, the question 'WHY?' is repeated until the respondent cannot explain any further. It is a powerful technique for finding the underlying motives.

Unfortunately, in most normal discussions (as opposed to its use in research), it is a very aggressive technique and must accordingly be used with great care.

A slightly less stressful and equally successful, if little reported, approach is '*rambling*'. Thus, if the listener simply allows the speaker enough time – and does not interrupt his or her 'rambling' – the answers will emerge. Eden, Jones and Sims[3] report that 'Probably the most obvious method for getting to know about the view a person has of the problem is to give him the time and space to 'ramble' around his subject.' This can be an enormous strain on the listener, for it is difficult not to interrupt. But it works in the same way as interrogation methods, which often depend upon allowing the prisoner to ramble so that they inevitably give away 'too much' of themselves.

Even if managers do ask the correct open questions, they often undermine the progress by stopping the speaker in mid flow. The natural accompaniment to an open question is *silence*. It is, though, a surprisingly aggressive technique, and you should not make it too obvious – it is best just to look very thoughtful. The person you are questioning will eventually feel obliged to talk, and usually what he or she then says is especially enlightening (since he or she too will have had time to consider).

As indicated above, closed questions, typically requiring the answer 'yes' or 'no', have (justifiably) received a bad press. But it is still necessary to use them quite extensively to clarify points. The problem only comes when they are used *instead* of open questions. In many situations by far the most important closed

---

[3] Colin Eden, Sue Jones and David Sims, *Messing About in Problems* (Pergamon, 1983).

questions (and arguably the most important questions of all) are those where you check for agreement. As the discussion progresses, it is imperative that you establish whether or not you are taking the other person with you; or, as is all too often the case, is he or she politely acting out the role of audience to your orator?

Listening

Just as important a skill as questioning is listening. Many managers are too busy trying to put their own view across to hear what is being said in reply; and thus they miss much of the key data in such conversations. Listening implies far more than hearing. It also involves the process of analysing what is heard, to understand it; to make sense of it in general, and then to put it into the intellectual framework of the organizational activities being discussed. Listening is a very active pursuit, not a passive one – or the listener will soon become a sleeper.

It is conventionally reckoned that a good questioner should spend two-thirds of the time listening and only one-third talking. What is important, though, is how you use that time. It is the quality of the listening (which has much to do with how you analyse what you hear) that is as important as the quantity.

Understanding

Thus, hearing, and even listening, is not enough. The key to questioning by managers is understanding. This is a process to which the main contribution must, of course, be made by what the person being questioned says; though it should be noted that this may include what he or she said in a number of previous meetings as well as in the current one. But it will also include all the other evidence you have unearthed. Put it all together and, hopefully, you will be able to complete the jigsaw.

Understanding of informal communications is, therefore, a *cumulative* process which may span several discussions. It is an important skill for managers, yet it is largely ignored by management educators.

RECORDING AND ORGANIZING THE DATA – even before the advent of the Filofax and its electronic equivalents, managers used to carry notebooks in which to write notes on their various meetings and conversations. This is an excellent habit, and forms the basis of the process needed to convert these conversations into a form which is then retrievable. Ideally, such rough notes should then be converted to formal (if brief) reports which then go into the main filing system. It might be more productive, at this stage, to file them every two weeks so that you can begin the process of editing them, and tracking new developments.

PRIORITIZE AND TRACK CHANGE – finally, as with all good marketing research, you should do something with these gems you have been collecting. The first step is to group the ideas. Thereafter, as this internal data will already be quite focused, you will be able to prioritize it so that you can give the most important topics the attention they deserve. Most important, though, query anything which emerges as different from what you might have expected. Why has it changed? It is all too easy to ignore such internal 'weak' signals, but much of management is about dealing with change; and the earlier you recognize that changes are emerging the better.

You will, of course, realize that taking notes and organizing them represent a counsel of perfection! I have rarely met managers who do this; though those who have done so have been amongst the most effective I have known. Most managers carry this data around in their head. They must, therefore, find some other process of carrying out the above instructions. If their head then starts to hurt then perhaps they too should invest in a notebook!

To complement these informal meetings and conversations, which fortuitously provide you with useful 'research' data, you can also use other informal sources. Not least of these is the *grapevine* – the collection of rumours and gossip which permeates most organizations. It frequently acts as a form of hidden neural network for the managers as much as the employees. It is often better informed and more accurate than the formal information channels; so the tighter you can tap into it the better. It is often paralleled by a network of '*fixers*', managers who, perhaps because of their length of service or just their travels throughout the organizations, seem to have contacts everywhere that matter. They know what is happening and what is to come, and in their spare time resolve the cross-departmental problems which others don't even know exist. The thoughts of these individuals should also be grist to your information mill.

The next technique in this section has the simplicity that is the hallmark of the Japanese, and it is their favourite approach:

Walkabout

The power of the Japanese approach to marketing research is no more than going out and about, where the action is on the product or service in question, and experiencing what is happening. In particular, they meet their customers and distributors and talk through, at length, what is important to them.

It has none of the statistical validity which survey research enjoys, and even desk research can often lay claim to. Yet better than anything else it conveys the flavour, the essence, of what is being studied. If you want to understand Toyota you can spend months of desk research reading the hundreds of papers which have been written about its efficiency, or you can spend half a day watching the confident grace with which the workers on its production lines assemble cars; as, decades before, Mr Toyoda himself learned his lessons by similarly spending time, three months in his case, watching American workers going through their, less graceful, routines.

The essence is experience; assimilating what is happening – what is really important to the product or service.

Synthesis and assimilation

You should build an *inner* model of the customers you are dealing with. Using the data you have received you should synthesize a multidimensional picture of them, and then assimilate it into yourself, almost as if absorbing it by osmosis through your skin.

This introduces the final technique in this section on personal research, which (for those managers that can use it) brings together all the research data in the most practical form possible. For many if not most managers the marketing research data remains as so much impersonal data lying on hundreds of pages of tables in dusty files. Just a few managers, however, bring it alive by assimilating it into their everyday view of their business life.

Needless to say, the technique of walkabout is the most useful of all in this process, because it gives the best 'feel' for what the key elements are.

The great benefit of this is that the manager does not have to search through the vast collections of data to know what the customer's reaction would be to any of the several dozen decisions which may be made in a day – that would be unproductively time consuming, and is precisely why the research results gather dust. Instead, he or she can draw upon their inner model to instinctively 'feel' what the customer's response will be. This is a difficult process, especially when there are a number of different customer groups to assimilate in this way but, like the actor, the manager can – after considerable effort – usually achieve success.

Customer simulation   This is a specific version of the technique used by some of the leading management consultancies to bring home to their clients what the customer is likely to think. Teams of managers play the roles of the main groups of consumers (usually families) as they act out a variety of situations relating to the alternative marketing programmes under investigation. Using the same approach on a personal basis is more difficult; you have to get under the skin of the customer – to instinctively feel what he or she feels.

Trial and error

Possibly the most important lesson to be gleaned from the Japanese is the basic need to learn from experience. The performance of a product or service (or of any part of the marketing mix) is carefully monitored; and the reasons for this performance are drawn out. From this experience of actual 'product'/marketing activities they can then change these to improve their performance.

The Japanese make use of this process in two ways which are very different from typical Western approaches:

- *Rapidity of change.* Whereas Western organizations take a long time to launch a 'product', but then expect it to remain largely unchanged over its lifetime, the Japanese launch earlier – often with a less developed 'product' – but then proceed to modify that 'product' many times in its lifetime; so that it gradually approaches the ideal.
- *Seeking experience.* They will often launch a range of 'products' simply to see which will succeed. The market research here is simply letting the consumers choose the winner. It was also a technique used by IBM in its heyday; no less than three PCs (each with a complete distribution system) were launched – of which only the successful variant is remembered.

In summary, then, the most powerful use of information may come from exposing yourself to the richest menu of experiences; and then absorbing these so that subsequent actions may improve incrementally. Robertson,[4] for instance, describes the recent development of 'market sensing': 'This is a broader concept which incorporates traditional marketing research but places the emphasis on *learning* about markets . . . trial and error may sometimes be a preferred mode of discovering new products . . . and it may be necessary to 'live' with consumers to truly appreciate their needs . . .'

Marketing Research

The most generally recognized aspect of marketing (or market) research is that conducted on consumers or customers (usually on a sample, and by professional interviewers). The stereotypical market research interviewer, standing on the street corner, accosting passers-by or walking the streets, clipboard in hand, knocking on closed doors, probably collects only a very small part of the data available to any organization. However, it is particularly important data, since it often provides the only true 'listening' part of the dialogue with the consumer. In the main this is a process undertaken by consumer goods companies. A survey by Hooley and West[5] showed that the widest divergence was in terms of the use of a 'market research agency' (table 3.1). The claimed level of market research in general (including internally handled desk research) was higher than this (approximately twice as high in the case of industrial and service organizations), as their findings of the methods used confirm (table 3.2).

[4] Thomas Robertson, New developments in marketing: a European perspective, *European Management Journal*, vol. 12, no. 4 (December 1994).
[5] G. J. Hooley and C. J. West, The untapped markets for marketing research, *Journal of the Marketing Research Society*, vol. 26, no. 4 (1984).

Table 3.1 The use of market research agency

Does your company employ the services of a market research agency?	All companies (%)	Consumer		Industrial		
		Durables (%)	FMCG (%)	Repeat (%)	Capital (%)	Services (%)
Yes	36.2	37.0 (102)	60.3 (166)	26.8 (74)	25.4 (70)	30.6 (85)
No	63.8	63.0 (99)	39.7 (62)	73.2 (115)	74.6 (117)	69.4 (109)
Number of companies	1690	216	356	351	209	558
No reply	85					

Table 3.2 Method or source of market research employed

Method or source used frequently	All companies (%)	Consumer		Industrial		
		Durables (%)	FMCG (%)	Repeat (%)	Capital (%)	Services (%)
Company records	70.0	72.7 (104)	76.7 (110)	72.6 (104)	67.9 (97)	64.5 (91)
Secondary sources	56.6	57.9 (102)	59.6 (105)	54.7 (97)	55.0 (97)	56.1 (99)
Surveys of consumers	27.9	19.0 (68)	42.1 (151)	20.8 (75)	18.7 (67)	30.3 (109)
Qualitative research	25.6	19.9 (78)	39.0 (152)	19.1 (75)	22.0 (86)	24.7 (96)
Field experiments	18.4	17.1 (93)	25.0 (136)	17.4 (95)	12.0 (65)	17.7 (96)
Surveys of distributors	17.2	23.1 (134)	17.7 (103)	19.9 (116)	13.9 (87)	14.0 (81)
Laboratory experiments	13.1	9.3 (71)	22.8 (174)	12.3 (94)	4.8 (37)	12.0 (92)
Number of replies	1690	216	356	351	209	558
No reply	85					

Despite these lower levels of usage in some fields, marketing research should be seen to be just as important for *all* organizations (since it often represents the only available, and reliable, 'contact' with the consumer or end-user). It is particularly important for non-profit organizations.

It is thus important that you, as a 'manager', understand just what is involved in marketing research, since it gives a profound insight into the whole of the marketing process.

Services and marketing research

In theory, 'services' should be just as susceptible to almost all of the marketing research techniques. In practice, their 'intangibility' makes most marketing research more difficult to conduct. The answers are less certain, because it is more difficult to frame the questions precisely; and the service is often intimately bound up with who delivers it — which makes generalizations less meaningful. In addition, the difficulty in establishing a permanent differentiation (in the absence of patenting, for instance) makes the level of investment tougher to justify.

Donald Cowell[6] comments that:

> The fuzziness and ambiguity of the service concept: the difficulty the customer may have in articulating what benefits are sought from a service . . . and what elements the service should consist of provide a 'researchability' problem for the market researcher. A particular problem is to identify, weight and rank the separate elements, tangible and intangible, that make up a service offer . . . This can mean that in order to determine what a service entity is to a market, a marketer must spend more time and effort on initial marketing research than in product marketing as a tight service specification may be difficult to produce . . .

He adds a balancing advantage, however:

> Some of the differences between services and products in fact offer advantages to the marketing researcher. First the researcher has the opportunity to evaluate services before the sale, after the sale and during the sale (i.e. during the performance of the service) . . . some services are consumed as they are being produced. The performer can thus obtain feedback while the service is being produced and make appropriate adjustments where these are required by the customer . . . Second, direct customer involvement with many services does allow the user to give a direct specification of what service is required to the seller or performer.

Service providers should take marketing research just as seriously; it is just that, as with most aspects of service marketing, they will need to be sophisticated in their use of it.

In practice, marketing research is neglected by many non-profit organizations (with honourable exceptions, such as Mass Observation).

Suppliers of Marketing Research

In any search for suppliers, the starting point is the organizations which offer market research services; for it is a very large, and unusually sophisticated,

---

[6] D. W. Cowell, New service development, *Journal of Marketing Management*, vol. 3, no. 3 (1988).

organization that will have the resources to handle all aspects of its own research – although some do just this. The suppliers can be grouped into three main types, as follows.

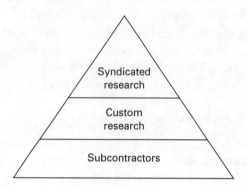

Syndicated research

These suppliers, who usually offer the easiest and quickest service, typically have on-going or *ad hoc* research programmes, the results of which they sell to a number of clients. Some of this can be standard research, such as the A. C. Nielsen store audits which provide information on retail purchases by consumers, or the TGI (Target Group Index) of MRB, which has followed the fortunes of some 5000 brands in the UK for more than 20 years. Shared cost is one advantage of such an approach, but the quality of the research is even more important.

Some research can be *ad hoc*, in that a supplier (often one specializing in the industrial field) sees a topic which it believes will be of interest to a number of companies; it then conducts the research and sells the results 'off-the-shelf'. Finally, some researchers with on-going programmes (especially those conducting opinion polls) will sell 'space' (or, more accurately, interviewer time) on the back of their omnibus surveys; so that one or two simple questions will thus be asked of a large sample at a relatively low cost.

Apart from the ease and speed of obtaining the research information, the great advantage of all these approaches is usually that of cost. Because the overall cost is shared between a number of customers the cost to any one client can be that much lower. It is, thus, quite cheap to ask one or two key – but simple – questions of a large sample. At the other end of the spectrum this allows research (such as store audits) that few individual organizations could afford.

In most cases it is also quick and easy to organize; so that sometimes a few simple questions are asked in this manner as a pilot for more complex studies.

The main areas of syndicated research are as follows:

Retail audits	Panel research
Omnibus surveys	Consultancies

Retail audits   Retail audits are one of the most sophisticated of market research operations, in terms of logistics. The concept, however, is simple. An 'auditor' regularly visits each retail outlet on the panel (which has been recruited randomly). The auditor carries out a physical stock check on the lines being surveyed. The change in stock from the previous visit (combined with the other stock movements, receipt of stock and so on, which are obtained from the store's records) gives the 'consumer sales'.

Such retail audits – for example, those provided by A. C. Nielsen – are generally believed to offer the best results, in terms of accuracy, of the volumes of consumer sales and, in particular, of the value of such sales. These data are the main basis for brand share calculations, as well as for the all-important figures of prices and distribution levels (and also the level of retailers' stocks, which is often very important where 'pipeline filling' in response to promotions is a feature . This information is invaluable to any FMCG company wishing to control its sales through retail outlets.

Panel research   Another approach to accurately measure consumer behaviour (that is, their actions rather than opinions) is by panel. At its best this may approach the accuracy of retail audits (with the added, complementary, advantage that it is categorized in terms of consumer profiles).

The two main approaches are:

- *Home audit.*   The panel member is required to save used wrappers in a special receptacle (hence 'dustbin audit' is sometimes used). Once a week, say, an auditor checks the contents of the receptacle, as well as checking stocks of products in the house and asking the householder a short list of questions. This technique is particularly successful in terms of the recruitment of respondents and their low subsequent attrition rate, and, accordingly, in providing relatively accurate results.
- *Diary method.*   In this case the householder, say, records the required information in a diary, which is collected by the interviewer or (less successfully, but more cheaply) returned by mail.

Both methods have, over long periods, been shown to provide accurate share data.

Most importantly, as compared, for example, with *ad hoc* surveys, these panels can show trend data (and, again, have been shown to do so accurately). They will also show repeat purchasing and brand-switching information, which is almost impossible to obtain using other methods.

Omnibus surveys   These are very similar to ad hoc surveys, except that 'space' on the questionnaire is 'sublet' to different researchers; providing, in effect, their own 'mini-survey'. Such omnibus surveys are often run (covering 2000 respondents per week, say) on the back of on-going research, such as political or opinion polls.

The cost benefits can be significant, since fieldwork forms the major element of most market research costs. Such surveys may also provide a faster turn-around of results, particularly if the survey is conducted by telephone. The 'questionnaire' will, however, need to be short, its questions cannot be complex and the context may be unpredictable (the questions asked by the other researchers cannot be controlled).

Such surveys can also be used to locate individuals belonging to minority groups, so that they can be followed up by conventional 'ad hoc' surveys.

Consultancies   Some large-scale surveys (such as the Taylor Nelson Monitor or MRB's Target Group Index (TGI) in the UK) are run to provide data for the research organization alone. The analysed output, in the form of reports (or computer-readable data) is then sold to a variety of buyers, so recouping the cost of the survey. These surveys may offer a very cost-effective way of building a database of survey information. TGI, for example, monitors some 5000 brands, as well as 200 attitude statements, across 45 000 interviews each year. These data can provide a profile of an individual brand (in terms of its consumer profile, including sophisticated 'life-style' data derived from the attitude statements, as well as readership data and usage of complementary products; and the same data on competitive products) for as little as £20 000 per annum. They are widely used – our research indicates that a third of organizations purchase such data.[7]

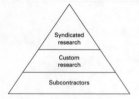

Custom research

Custom research is the staple diet of much of the market research industry. The research organization is commissioned by a client to undertake a specific piece of research. The research company then accepts responsibility for all aspects of the research.

There is usually a quite distinct split between organizations which specialize in the consumer fields, the province of the large 'random' surveys, and those in the industrial field, where research often revolves around extended interviews with individual organizations. Equally, there are clear divisions between those

---

[7] Cowell, *New service development*.

involved in retail audits and those conducting questionnaire surveys on individual consumers; and between those conducting group discussions or in-depth psychological interviews.

Over the past two decades the most important factor in the market for such research has been its *cost*. It has been traded as a *commodity*, and the emphasis has been on cost-cutting. Accompanying this trend has been a reduction in quality, because the methods used have often been 'shaved' to the bare bone to reduce costs – a factor which must be allowed for.

Marketing Research Processes

The eight stages which are most generally followed in the marketing research process are set out in the 'Research Diamond'. Such research projects have a characteristic shape. In broad terms the horizontal dimension indicates the passing of time as the project progresses, and the vertical one the number of people involved at each stage.

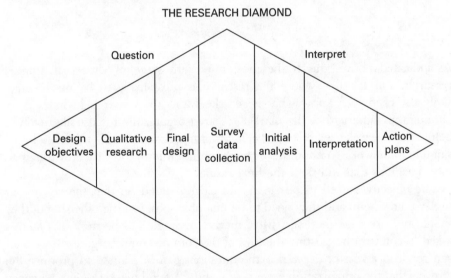

THE RESEARCH DIAMOND

HIDDEN TIME – the main message which emerges from the horizontal progression is that the more obvious elements where you might expect time to be taken, especially those involved in the seemingly complex and relatively lengthy process of data collection, typically only represent a minor part of the overall process. If the research is to be fully productive then the periods at the beginning when it is designed and at the end when it is used as the basis for action plans must be allowed to progress at their own pace. Rushed research is too often wasted research. Sometimes you do need answers very fast, but you must then recognize that, in such a situation, the questions had better be very simple.

THE BULGE IN THE MIDDLE – it is in the middle of the diamond where the main manpower resources are eaten up (and the major costs incurred). But this is usually a matter of relatively menial legwork. Getting the first, design stage right can often reduce this bulge to a more manageable size. Thus, time spent earlier, on design, can often save money, and not infrequently time as well – since the later stages are better planned.

THE CUTTING EDGES – the diagram is well named the 'Research Diamond' since its most important features (albeit the least well recognized) are the cutting edges at the beginning and end. The most important input to research is the design objectives. If you have only a fuzzy idea of what you want out of it at the beginning, you will get a fuzzy set of results at the end.

By far the most important cutting edge, however, is that at the end: the *action* which is generated as a result. Indeed, the focus on that action must begin with the objectives. If the research has no planned actions depending upon it you must question why it is being done. But, above all, you must act on what you eventually find. The Japanese often seem less sophisticated in the research they carry out, but they always *do* something with the results. What is more they usually do something significant. Western marketers are all too prone to look at the many pages of results they receive, find them quite interesting and then file them; they continue their business activities once again, untainted by what they have just read!

Defining the objectives

As indicated above, this is the most important stage of almost all market research, and the one where the research is most likely to be misdirected. Only the client can know what he or she wants the research to investigate; although an expert from the market research organization is usually involved before the research itself takes place, in order to translate the client's ideas into a suitable framework. Without his or her expertise it is all too easy unwittingly to introduce bias that will skew the final results.

The objectives need to be clear, and clearly stated (so that the researcher understands them) and they need to be unambiguous. On the other hand, they should not prejudge the issue. Most market research fails because it is merely asked to confirm the existing theories of the commissioning organization. This can result in errors of *commission* (the questions can be slanted to produce the answers that the organization expects or wants). A good market research agency should, however, detect such bias and remove it. Errors of *omission* (key questions never asked) are more difficult to deal with; this is a problem which few market research organizations would be in a position to detect.

Planning the research

It is at this stage that the initiative passes to the research agency, although the more sophisticated client will still want to remain involved. The design of the research is, indeed, a complex process, and demands the skills of specialist staff. Do-it-yourself research is usually a recipe for disaster, unless those requisite skills are available in-house.

There are many different types of research possible. Just some of them might be:

Observation Watching participants as they undertake some activity, simply to see what happens. The pattern of customer flow in a supermarket is best determined by simply watching it (albeit using sophisticated video recording and computer analysis to make the data more meaningful).

Experimental research This exposes selected participants to different treatments. It may range from testing new products to viewing commercials and measuring responses to them. In theory, this approach may be used to establish experimentally the basic relationships involved. In practice it is more frequently used to select the best solution (of product or advertising concept) from a range of alternatives; or even more pragmatically to check that the one already chosen is acceptable.

The *comparison*, which is the basis of much of experimental research, may be achieved by a number of approaches:

- *Before and after.* The most usual approach is to test the 'subject' before he or she is exposed to the 'stimulus' (typically a product or commercial, or whatever is being tested) and again after exposure to it. The performance of the product or commercial, say, is judged by the change in the 'measurements' taken of the subject (normally in terms of attitudes).
- *Split runs.* In this case, the different stimuli are applied to separate (but statistically equivalent) groups, and the results compared.
- *Difference.* In some tests the objective is simply to see if the subject can tell the difference between the stimuli being presented. The usual method is to present 'triads' (where two are the same and one is different). If the subject cannot tell the difference the results will be random.

Qualitative research This category covers all research which does not produce rigorously validated numerical output. Peter Sampson[8] identifies four main categories:

Individual depth interviews	Repertory grid
Semi-structured interviews	Group interviews

[8] P. Sampson, Qualitative research and motivation research, *Consumer Market Research Handbook*, ed. R. Worcester and J. Downham (McGraw-Hill, 3rd edn, 1986).

Group interviews are especially important, and are dealt with separately in the next section.

Individual depth interviews (or 'intensive' interviews) and *semi-structured interviews*. These can last an hour or more, and can follow a variety of formats; from an almost totally free form (which is so specialized as to be outside normal market research practice) through the non-directive form (where the interviewer, while still in control, allows the respondent to answer in whatever form he or she wants) to the semi-structured (which is much closer to the conventional questionnaire interview, but which still allows the respondent some freedom of expression). The essence of all of these is that the answers are totally open-ended, and have to be analysed by skilled personnel, but the freedom of expression often leads to a less constrained view of their true attitudes.

Repertory (or 'Kelly') Grids. The aim of this technique is to discover what are the key dimensions of the respondents' attitudes towards the matter in hand (usually a product or brand, typically as part of a positioning exercise). By removing interviewer (and questionnaire-designer) bias, while allowing the respondent free rein to his or her own ideas (and indeed 'forcing' this process), it can give a very clear picture of what really motivates respondents. In this individual interview, each respondent is presented with a list of 'stimuli' (which may, for example, be lists of products or brands or statements). Three of the stimuli ('triads', chosen at random) from the list are presented to the respondent at a time. The respondent is asked to choose the two that are most alike (called, rather strangely, the 'emergent pole'). He or she is then asked to say why these two are similar, and why they are different from the third. A number of such interviews (typically 10–50) are conducted and the output analysed (usually by computer) to see which factors can be clustered. This stage of the process (as well as the interview itself) requires considerable skill if the information is to have any worth.

Group research This is often called 'group discussions' or 'focus group research'. It is the most popular form of face-to-face research, used by a fifth of organizations, and by four times as many as use doorstep surveys.[9] A selected, relatively homogeneous, group (usually 6–10 members) of participants is encouraged to discuss the topics that the researchers are investigating. The interviewer ('group leader' or 'moderator'), who has to be skilled in the technique and is often a trained psychologist, carefully leads the discussion, ensuring that all of the group members are able to put forward their views. The interviewer's role is then essentially a passive one, his or her prime concern being to foster group interaction (and, in the terms of William Wells,[8] 'pest control' – including, most importantly, control of any one individual who is dominating the group).

The essence of such group discussions is that the participants can develop their own ideas in an unstructured fashion, interacting with and stimulating others. The whole session is usually captured on a tape recorder or on videotape

---

[9] W. D. Wells, Group interviewing, *Handbook of Marketing Research*, ed. Robert Ferber (McGraw-Hill, 1974).

for later analysis in depth. This often allows insights that are hidden by the preconceived questions posed in conventional surveys.

However, it is increasingly being used as a cheaper and faster alternative for those organizations which cannot afford the full-scale research – and, in line with the move to 'low-cost' research, even for those which can (a feature which William Wells reported as early as 1974). This is arguably better than nothing, but if such use is made the 'researcher' should beware of attributing too much significance to it – in particular to any such 'statistical' outcomes. The sample sizes are usually far too small to allow any statistical conclusions to be drawn, and the conclusions are very dependent upon the researcher's interpretations. You should take heed of the warning of Bellenger et al.[10] that 'there are many charlatans in the business of conducting focus groups, and the marketer must exercise care in selecting the research firm to conduct the interviews'.

Survey research   The most widely-known form of marketing research is that of making use of (questionnaire-based) surveys. On the other hand, our research[11] shows that this is only used – in its traditional doorstep/face-to-face survey form – by a small minority (5 per cent) of organizations. Typically, this form of research may be designed to find out, descriptively, what are the participants' habits, attitudes, wants and so on, simply by asking the respondent a number of questions.

Questionnaire design   The classic device used in survey research is the *questionnaire* (figure 3.1), a printed form on which the interviewer, or the respondent, fills in the answers to a series of questions. These *questions* are the key to the research. They must, therefore, be developed carefully and skilfully. First, they must be *comprehensive*: if a key question is not asked it will not be answered.

Second, they will need to be in a language that the respondent understands, so that the answers will be clear and unambiguous. Many words used by researchers and their clients, even those from their everyday language, may be unfamiliar to the respondents they are testing, particularly where their respondents are less well educated. Even a word such as 'incentive' is only likely to be fully understood by about half the population. Also, if the form of questioning is too complex or too vague it may elicit confused answers.

Finally, *they should not be leading questions*. The most basic fault of much research is that, as a result of bad design, it plays back the answers that the researcher expects (or even wants) to hear. The questions must be neutral, to encourage the respondent to reply truthfully.

---

[10] D. N. Bellenger, K. L. Bernhardt and J. L. Goldstrucker, *Qualitative Research in Marketing* (American Marketing Association, 1976).

[11] D. Mercer, research to be published.

Q24 **Please show how much you agree or disagree with the following statements**
PLEASE TICK ONE BOX FOR EACH

	Agree strongly	Agree slightly	Neither agree nor disagree	Disagree slightly	Disagree strongly	Don't know	
Companies should not give their profits to charity	☐1	☐2	☐3	☐4	☐5	☐6	(57)
Companies should not use their profits to sponsor the arts	☐1	☐2	☐3	☐4	☐5	☐6	(58)
Companies should not use their profits to sponsor sports	☐1	☐2	☐3	☐4	☐5	☐6	(59)

Q25 **Which, if any, of the activities listed below do you do nowadays?**

Q26 **And which, if any, of these do you have close friends who do these nowadays?** TICK AS MANY AS APPLY FOR EACH QUESTION IN THE COLUMN INDICATED

	I do nowadays		Some of my friends do nowadays	
Go to football match	☐1	(60)	☐1	(62)
Drink bitter at a pub	☐2		☐2	
Drink wine in a pub	☐3		☐3	
Read the Sun	☐4		☐4	
Invite people home to a dinner party	☐5		☐5	
Drink malt whisky	☐7		☐6	
Take young children out to eat in a good restaurant	☐6		☐7	
Read the Guardian	☐8		☐8	
Eat at health food restaurants	☐9		☐9	
Use conditioner on my/their hair	☐0		☐0	
Read the Daily Telegraph	☐x		☐x	
Use a deodorant	☐y		☐y	
Buy clothes from Next	☐1	(61)	☐1	(63)
Buy organic food	☐2		☐2	
Watch EastEnders	☐3		☐3	
Go to church	☐4		☐4	
Use hand cream	☐5		☐5	
Do voluntary work	☐6		☐6	
Swim at the swimming pool	☐7		☐7	
Go jogging	☐8		☐8	
Play golf	☐9		☐9	

Q27 **And which two of the following improvements do you think that sports centres generally need to make?** TICK 2 BOXES

Two improvements sports centres need to make		
Wider range of facilities	☐1	(64)
Better standard of facilities	☐2	
Better staff service	☐3	
Lower prices	☐4	
Easier to book facilities	☐5	
More convenient opening times	☐6	
More convenient locations	☐7	
None of these	☐8	

Q28 **When you see advertising on the television, how many would you say are advertisements for something you might be interested in buying?** PLEASE TICK 1 BOX

Nearly all of them	☐1	(65)
Most of them	☐2	
About half	☐3	
Less than half	☐4	
Hardly any	☐5	
None of them	☐6	

Q29 **Have you ever entered a prize draw that came through the post?** PLEASE TICK ONE BOX

Yes	☐1	(66)
No	☐2	
Don't know	☐3	

Q30 **Have you ever bought anything as a result of receiving an offer or circular through the post?** PLEASE TICK ONE BOX

Yes	☐1	(67)
No	☐2	
Don't know	☐3	

Q31 **How often, on average, do you receive in the post at your home advertisements or offers for goods & services that you haven't specifically asked for?** PLEASE TICK ONE BOX

4 or more items a day	☐1	(68)
2–3 items a day	☐2	
one a day	☐3	
one every 2–3 days	☐4	
one every 4–5 days	☐5	
Once a week	☐6	
Less often	☐7	
Never	☐7	

Q32 **How many of these are offers about something you might be interested in buying?** PLEASE TICK ONE BOX

Nearly all of them	☐1	(69)
Most of them	☐2	
About half	☐3	
Less than half	☐4	
Hardly any	☐5	
None of them	☐6	

Figure 3.1 Example of a questionnaire.

To ensure that the questions asked are valid and meaningful, it is sound practice to pilot the questionnaire on a number of respondents, so that potential problems can be debugged before the cost of a full survey is incurred.

The questions to be asked may be of two main types (which you will recognize from the earlier part of the chapter): Open or Closed.

Typical approaches to *closed* questioning are:

1 *Numbers.*
2 *Yes/no.*
3 *Multiple choice.* The basic question can be expanded to cover a number of alternative choices, from which the respondent is asked to select one.
4 *Semantic differentials.* Here the respondent is asked to choose where his or her position lies, on a scale between two bipolar words, or a range of words or numbers ranging across a bipolar position (for example, 'Excellent', 'Good', 'Adequate', 'Poor', 'Inadequate'; or from 5 (powerful) down to 1 (weak).

Collecting the data

At the next stage of the research the army of interviewers descends on the unsuspecting public. There are, however, a number of possible methods of contacting respondents.

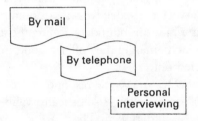

By mail   This is the cheapest solution: hence large overall samples can be used, allowing investigation of small market groups – especially in industrial markets – still within acceptable statistical levels. It is used by a fifth of organizations (four times as many as use doorstep surveys), but in some respects it is the least satisfactory solution. The questions which can be asked are necessarily simpler and the questionnaire shorter; and it must be particularly well designed, to keep the respondent interested and motivated to reply. More fundamentally, the response rates are often so low that their statistical validity may be questioned.

By telephone   In this case the interviewer uses a telephone to contact respondents: more than two-thirds of UK households, for instance, now have a telephone. It is a very fast survey technique, so that results can be available in a matter of hours; hence it is often now used for those opinion polls where time is of the essence. It is also relatively cheap and thus often affordable even in industrial markets.

The interview can last only a short time and the types of questions are limited (particularly since the interviewer cannot check visually that the question is understood).

Personal interviewing This is the traditional (face-to-face) approach to marketing research, and it is still the most versatile. The interviewer is in full control of the interview, and can take account of the respondent's body language as well as his or her words. It is, however, the most expensive and is dependent on the reliability of the interviewer. In the case of some of the more sophisticated techniques it is also dependent on his or her skill. This means that the quality of the supervision provided by the field research agency is critical; this may be a problem now that so many organizations place the emphasis on cost-cutting. Horror stories are told of interviewers making up interviews to avoid going out on cold and rainy days. Fortunately, these instances are few, and the reputable agencies do exert the necessary control over their personnel, usually by having a field manager conduct follow-ups of a subsample.

Samples The basic principle of sampling is that you can obtain a representative picture of a whole 'population', the total group of people or objects being investigated, by looking at a small 'sample' (usually, in this context, only a few hundred). This is a very cost-effective way of obtaining information.

Samples are important in terms of understanding the accuracy which may be placed on the results which emerge; they offer a good indication of the quality of the work being carried out.

To guarantee a known 'accuracy', the respondents to any respectable market research should be chosen to offer a statistically valid sample, so that valid statistical analyses may be undertaken. There are a number of ways in which such a sample may be chosen. The two main approaches are:

Random samples The classically correct method is to select a sample at random. The list of the total 'population' to be sampled is chosen. For consumer research, it is usually the electoral register; although this is not necessarily comprehensive since it excludes those who have chosen not to register, and those who have moved since the last time it was compiled. This list is then used as the basis for selecting the sample; most rigorously by using tables of random numbers, but most simply by selecting every nth name.

A reasonable degree of accuracy may be achieved with samples as low as a few hundred. Occasionally, much larger overall samples (up to 30 000 on the UK National Readership Survey, for example) are used, in order that smaller subsamples may also be accurately observed; thus, in the case of TGI (MRB's Target Group Index), for instance, the need to follow the detailed performance of 5000 brands justifies the overall sample of 45 000 respondents per year.

In the case of a *stratified sample* the original 'population' is 'stratified' (that is, categorized by some parameter – age, for example) and random samples are then drawn from each of these strata. This ensures that there are adequate numbers in each of these subsamples to allow for valid statistical analyses.

The great advantage of random samples is that they are statistically predictable. Apart from any questions as to how comprehensive the original lists are, they cannot be 'skewed' (that is, biased). The major disadvantage is that this process is usually more expensive (and, in any case, the necessary lists may not be available). Accordingly, it may be less frequently used for commercial work (except that based upon mail questionnaires); but it does usually offer a greater degree of guaranteed quality.

Perhaps the easiest solution to understanding the accuracy implicit in various sample sizes is to use a table, such as that provided by John Coulson in his book.[12]

Quota samples   These aim to achieve, at least in theory, an effect similar to random samples, by asking interviewers to recruit respondents to match an agreed quota of subsamples. This is supposed to guarantee that the overall sample is an approximately representative cross-section of the 'population' as a whole. The interviewer, by means of knocking on doors or standing in a busy street, is required for example to select certain numbers of respondents to match specified age and social categories.

This technique clearly may be subject to 'skew', selecting only the more accessible – those who make a habit of visiting their local high street, for example – and excluding the more elusive elements of the population. It is also difficult to apply rigorous statistical tests to the data. Quota sampling is significantly cheaper than using random samples, and so it is the approach most frequently chosen for commercial research. Despite its apparent theoretical shortcomings it often works well.

Analysing the results

The statistical data thus collected can be analysed in a wide variety of ways (as can that which is already available in the results emerging from desk research – in particular, those from performance data). Increasingly, analysts use the massive computing power now available to cut through the superficial results. The mathematics of these various techniques is beyond the scope of this book; the practical skill needed is that of finding the best expert to implement them and knowing how much reliance to put on his or her judgement. Some examples of the techniques now used include:

Multiple regression analysis   This mathematical analysis is one form of a number of '*multivariate*' analyses using complex and sophisticated statistical

---

[12] J. Coulson, Field research – sample design, questionnaire design, interviewing methods, *Handbook of Modern Marketing*, ed. V. P. Buell (McGraw-Hill, 2nd edn, 1986).

(computerized) methods, which attempt to determine the structure of relationships where there are more than two factors involved.

Factor analysis   This is another multivariate technique, which is used to group together 'related' variables (by the detection of related patterns in the data, usually concerned with buying behaviour). It is primarily a tool used in 'data reduction', to reduce a large number of possible variables to a smaller, aggregated or summarized, number which can be handled more easily.

Cluster analysis   On the other hand, factors can be found, by this *set* of methods (rather than by a single technique), which strongly differentiate, for example, certain customer groups from others; so that the 'cluster' is isolated from other clusters, while being internally cohesive. This is best demonstrated graphically:

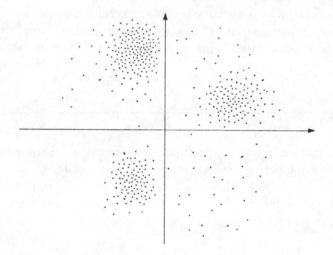

The 'clusters' are represented by higher densities of points (individuals on the above 'scatter diagram') in the space (the two dimensions) being mapped. Cluster analysis seeks to define the boundaries of these more dense regions. In the words of Punj and Stewart:[13] 'it is designed to identify groups and entities (people, markets, organizations) that share certain common characteristics (attitudes, purchase properties, media habits etc.) . . . segmentation research becomes a grouping task'.

There are a variety of software packages which offer such analyses. One of the best known and most powerful is SPSS (Statistical Package for the Social Sciences), which has traditionally been run on a mainframe, although a personal computer version is now available.

[13] G. Punj and D. W. Stewart, Cluster analysis in marketing research: review and suggestions for application, *Journal of Marketing Research*, vol. 20 (May 1983).

In his book, Arthur Meidan[14] comprehensively lists (and graphically shows the relationships between) the main quantitative techniques used across the whole of marketing.

Reporting the findings

The final stage is to disseminate the results to all who need to know them. This process may require more effort, and be more important, than the simple clerical task that it superficially seems to be. For one thing, one needs to understand who would find the results useful; indeed, important results may have relevance to managers throughout the organization.

Equally importantly, the 'language' of the report may need to be 'translated' for these different audiences: very few of these managers will understand the terminology of market research (or, rather more importantly, its limitations).

This poses some problems. It is inevitably a process of simplification, and may accordingly result in the loss or alteration of some meaning. The favourite approach (at least in presentation to top management) seems to be that the dry statistics (which have probably already been considerably simplified) are illustrated by verbatim quotes from individual respondents. William Wells[15] describes the advantage (in the context of focus groups, but the comments apply more widely):

> Instead of mysterious symbols and dull tables, there are direct quotations in which believable people give their views at length and in their own words. For many clients this is the texture of the world.

The particular danger here is that senior management unversed in market research skills will merely remember the most striking comments (particularly the ones that reinforce their existing prejudices) rather than the boring statistics. Ideally, the results presented to each audience should be tailored to their particular needs.

This stage of research is quintessentially a communication process (indeed, a sales process), where the recipients of the information will usually need to be persuaded to make use of it. This will in part be by the mandatory report. On the other hand, perhaps the best approach (and one favoured by many marketing research agencies when they present the results to their clients) is a formal face-to-face, usually group, presentation.

---

[14] A. Meidan, Quantitative methods in marketing, *The Marketing Book*, ed. M. J. Baker (Heinemann, 1987).
[15] Wells, Group interviewing.

What market research does your organization undertake? Who commissions it? What types of research are undertaken? Why is it undertaken? How successful is it, in terms of achieving its objectives? What other research do you think should be undertaken, and why?

SELF-TEST QUESTION 3.6

To consolidate what you have learnt so far, you should now undertake your first major piece of work: doing the desk research, collecting the best available background material, as the basis for preparing a 'facts book' on your organization.

At this stage all you should do is to collect various items of general information, which is easily available from the main sources identified in the preceding sections. The most obvious items might be:

- performance data – the internal sales and profit figures, for example
- library material – whatever is available in your local library, or the central reference library
- industry sources – including journals and directories
- other internal reports – from individual sales reports through to the annual report
- market research – information from whatever research is available

The amount of material that you collect at this stage will depend on what is easily available, particularly on whether you have access to key internal information and whether your local library has information on your industry. It will also depend on the amount of time that you are able to devote to it.

Industrial Marketing Research

Marketing research in the area of industrial goods is usually less involved with survey research. On the one hand, the output of statistics about the 'average customer' may be less useful, as each customer's needs often have to be considered separately (the value of their business justifies this, and the contact with the salesperson makes it a possibility). On the other hand, the difficulty and cost of conducting such survey research on industrial customers is much higher. For one thing, the 'lists' (which define the 'sampling frames', the population from which the sample is drawn) are often not available, or are inaccurate and incomplete. The result is that desk research is even more prevalent – and even more important – than in consumer research. It is often conducted by 'experts' (typically outside agencies) rather than by the individual manager.

Much of the survey work which is done tends to revolve around in-depth (unstructured) interviews with relatively few respondents. In any case, the total population, the 'universe', may be just a few hundred organizations. The interviews are usually conducted by 'experts' on senior managers, and the views of the 'organization' sought rather than those of the individual.

Mail and telephone surveys are often used for larger surveys since the cost of face-to-face interviewing is usually prohibitive. Response rates may be poor, however: figures of as low as 20 per cent are quoted as being typical.

Fractures and Marketing Research

One final note concerns areas where marketing research may *not* be particularly helpful. When there is a major discontinuity in the overall environment, described by Gareth Morgan[16] as a 'fracture', this changes all the factors to such an extent that market research may be largely useless.

In this situation most marketing research is meaningless since it essentially measures the historical position, unearthing data on what has gone before. The discontinuity means that the future is decoupled from the past – it means the future will be different. Even consumer research will be largely valueless when this happens, since the consumers asked their opinions will not know enough of the new developments to answer the questions accurately, but will base their answers (incorrectly) on their existing perspective – and this will, again, not offer the researcher a valid view of the future.

John Stopford[17] makes the point that the really significant new products have not emerged from incremental (and marketing researched) changes, but have been genuine innovations. Perhaps more important, for the readers of this book, is his associated comment that the organizations which have survived such fractures (that is, major changes in their environment) have been the ones

---

[16] G. Morgan, *Riding the Waves of Change* (Jossey-Bass, 1988).
[17] J. Stopford, personal communication (1989).

which have thrown out their standard operating procedures manuals – and the sooner they did this the better they fared. This may say relatively little about marketing research, but it says a great deal about the value of outdated theory as compared with practical flexibility in coping with change!

Fortunately, for most managers, such innovations are very rare,[18] though they have recently preoccupied some theorists. Notwithstanding the comments of these theoreticians, some of whom have even suggested that the possibility of these discontinuities undermines the value of marketing research as a whole, obtaining the best possible information about the outside world is still the key to the great part of successful marketing. The more you understand about the environment in general, and customers in particular, the more effective your marketing is likely to be.

FURTHER READING

As may be apparent from the number of references made to it in this chapter, the most informative book on marketing research in general is *The Consumer Market Research Handbook*, edited by Robert Worcester and John Downham (McGraw-Hill, 3rd edn, 1986). It also has chapters which provide an insight, from a rather different perspective, into other aspects of marketing. As with almost all worthwhile books on marketing research, however, it is written (albeit often quite entertainingly) at a technical level which may be daunting to those not already experienced in the subject matter. Those books which deal with the more specific techniques usually prove to be even more esoteric.

SUMMARY

The key components of this chapter, which you may wish to revise, have been:

MIS (Marketing Information System).   The overall system (computerized or manual) which holds the organization's information on 'external' factors (although much of this still comes indirectly, from internal sources).

Internal/external.   Indeed, much of the data is already available from within the organization, but some may have to be found from external sources.

Quantitative/qualitative.   The image of 'marketing research' brings to mind quantitative (numerical) data, and there is a considerable amount of this within the organization as well as outside it. However, much of the data is qualitative (usually verbal), and this requires different methods of processing.

---

[18] D. S. Mercer, A two decade test of product life cycle theory, *The British Journal of Management*, September 1992.

Internal data. This is usually the richest source of material. It can be divided into:

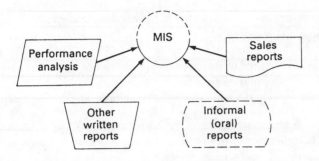

Data handling. This leads to the problem of handling such data:

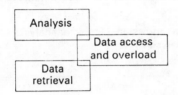

Computerized databases and electronic mail may offer some solutions to these problems.

External data/desk research. This is probably the most important set of techniques (for use by all managers) used in locating and handling external data. The main sources (after that already held in internal files) will usually be:

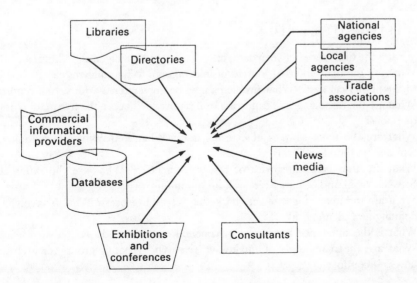

Marketing research. This is the pinnacle of the whole process. Asking the right questions and listening to the consumer's answers is the key to effective marketing:

- observation/experimental research – specific techniques typically used to measure special marketing activities
- individual depth interviews/repertory (or Kelly) Grids – sophisticated interviewing techniques (unstructured or structured, requiring skilled researchers) used to expose underlying attitudes and motivations
- focus groups – group discussions which also indicate underlying motivations

Surveys. Doorstep interviews represent the (theoretical) backbone of consumer marketing research. The elements to be considered are questionnaire design, data collection techniques and control, and sample design.

Analysis. Many techniques are available to turn the data into more useful information, including:

Multiple regression analysis	Factor analysis
Cluster analysis	Conjoint analysis

Reporting the findings. Finally, it is essential to report the findings in the most suitable form, so that they can actually be used by the management involved.

REVISION QUESTIONS

1 What is the difference between data, information and intelligence? What is an MIS?
2 What are the main internal sources of information? What analyses can be applied to the numerical data? What problems may be encountered with verbal reports?
3 What are the three stages of capturing oral reports? What are the five main types of questions?
4 What are the main sources of external data? What sources of information can typically be found in libraries?
5 What are the main categories of research agencies? What are the differences between retail audits, panel research and omnibus surveys?
6 What are the main stages of the marketing research process? What is involved in defining and planning it?
7 What is the difference between experimental research and qualitative research? What are the main tools of qualitative research? What is group research and how is it conducted?

8 What are the most important aspects of questionnaire design? What techniques may be used on questionnaires in order to categorize answers? What is the difference between multiple choice and semantic differentials questions?

9 How may marketing research data be collected? What are the advantages of each method? What are the differences between random and quota samples?

10 What are the four main mathematical methods of analysis? What is each used for?

11 What should you look for when you use marketing research reports?

4 Market Positioning and Segmentation

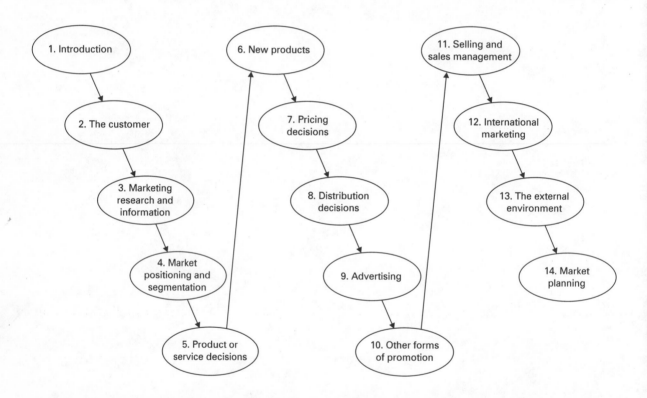

Introduction

The interface between the consumer and the supplier is the 'market'. The 'position' chosen in that market, by the supplier, for the product or service – against the 'map' of consumer needs – should define all of the marketing actions thereafter. Whether decided formally or by default, it is at the heart of marketing.

The initial stage, however, may be to 'segment' the market itself; to which to concentrate the organization's resources – to gain control ov However, the segment has to be viable; and sophisticated marketing re the 'segmentation'.

Positioning, or targeting, then places the product or service in the against the competitors, on the 'dimensions' which are most critical to users.

The focus for this activity is often a 'brand', and the alternative branding policies are inve gated. Branding, combined with positioning, usually offers the most sophisticated and powerful application of marketing principles.

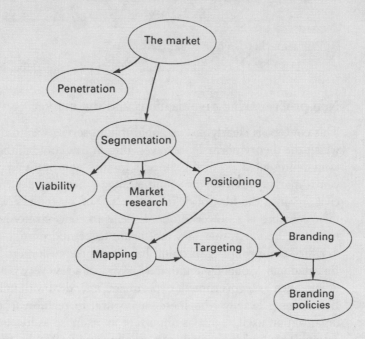

What is a Market?

To a producer or service provider, the most practical feature of a market is that it is 'where' the product or service is sold or delivered – and the profits generated. On the other hand, it can be defined in terms of the product or service (where the 'market' describes all the buyers and sellers for that product or service – the automobile market, the money market, and so on) and this is the framework favoured by many economists. It can also be defined geographically or demographically.

The key for a marketer, however, should be that the market is always defined in terms of the *customer*. Philip Kotler[1] sees *buyers* (actual and potential) as constituting the *market*, whereas *sellers* constitute the *industry*, and he defines it as follows:

> A market consists of all the potential customers sharing a particular need or want who might be willing and able to engage in exchange to satisfy that need or want.

SELF-TEST QUESTION 4.1

What market is your organization in?

Non-profit-making organizations and the market

This concept is clearly just as applicable to services as to the products around which the theory normally revolves. But, in this context, the term 'market' can even represent a powerful concept in the 'non-profit' sectors. Although the word 'market' itself might sound strange emerging, say, from the mouths of civil servants, the idea of defining the 'set' of 'customers' who are the focus of their activities is a powerful one. It helps to concentrate their attention, externally, on the needs that they are meant to be addressing.

Every non-profit organization has clients or 'customers'. Some, such as the International Monetary Fund, may have just a few very powerful clients; while others, such as a government department, may deal with millions of individuals. But defining exactly who these clients are, in relation to the activities of the organization itself, is just as important an exercise as for a commercial organization. This 'market', albeit not usually complicated by the same competitive overtones as its commercial equivalents, is ultimately just as powerful a force on a non-profit organization.

Who is the Market?

The market is, thus, the group of customers. However, in many practical respects it is still defined in the short term by the suppliers. They say, in effect, what is to be supplied to whom, and hence where the initial boundaries are to be set. After all, the consumer cannot make his or her wishes known if there is no suitable product on offer; and this lack of short-term feedback became a

---

[1] P. Kotler, *Marketing Management* (Prentice-Hall, 8th edn, 1994).

major long-term problem for the planned (command) economies of eastern Europe – hence one of the reasons there for western market capitalism.

In the long run it is the customers, however, who will decide what the market really is – by their buying patterns. They set the boundaries, and by their purchases choose what products or services will remain in the market.

The inevitable outcome is that to understand the market, the producer must understand the customer: hence my concentration on market research in chapter 3 – it provides the cornerstone for effective marketing.

Remember that the basis of sound marketing practice is the ability to identify with the customer or client – to be able to adopt the consumer's viewpoint.

SELF-TEST QUESTION 4.2

Who are your organization's customers or clients, and how does this define your market?

Is this different from your answer in audit 4.1?

Channels

One complication is that the producer may not sell direct to the end-user, but may be forced to sell through distribution channels, which act as intermediaries. This may be as true of services as of products: Commercial Union and the Prudential need their brokers to act as intermediaries. Even in the non-profit sector the universities, which are independent of government, have a major impact on the delivery of its higher education policy.

The 'producer' thus has consumers who are unseen, and customers, those in the distribution chain, who are met face to face. As we shall see later, these customers have different needs from the consumers; and, although they are conventionally seen as part of the same market, these marked differences have to be allowed for.

SELF-TEST QUESTION 4.3

What are the differences in market requirements posed by your organization's customers in the distribution channels, as opposed to the end-users?

In setting its strategies, how does your organization cope with these differences?

Market Boundaries

We have seen, in earlier chapters, that consumers – of both products and services – can be grouped on the basis of a number of factors. Their position against these factors, which may be different for each market, 'maps' the true boundaries of that market; and the market is defined by the consumers' view of it, and in their 'language'.

On the other hand, producers, especially those without marketing expertise, tend to have much more 'physical' ideas of where markets lie. They want to be able to go and 'touch' them; and often feel somewhat uncomfortable when trying to deal with what they see as an ephemeral 'life-style'. Despite all the very sound marketing theory, therefore, the practical definitions of markets tend to revolve around the following factors:

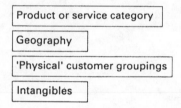

- *Product or service category.*   This sets out what is bought, as defined in the 'physical' terms of the producer. To reverse Leo McGinneva's example, often quoted by marketing theorists, the product is the 2 mm drill, not the 2 mm hole that the end-user wants to make.
- *Geography.*   Where the product or service is sold or delivered is another clearly understood concept.
- *'Physical' customer groupings.*   Producers do recognize obvious groupings of customers. In industrial markets, for example, suppliers of medical diagnostics recognize that hospitals have different needs from those of corporate health centres.
- *Intangibles.*   The only intangible which is widely recognized, and then only as differentiating commercial markets, is price; although even then many, if not most, marketers would treat price as if it was fully tangible. Thus there is often seen to be a 'cheap' market, often described rather patronizingly as 'down market' (which also carries some class connotations) as opposed to a 'quality' market.

You need to recognize that this myopia exists, because it is highly prevalent. Even committed marketers still talk about the market for replacement drills; a much easier concept to handle than that of selling the potential for holes. But, even so, you also need to recognize that it is ultimately the customer who decides 'where' your market will be.

In the light of what you have now read, where does your organization draw the boundaries of its markets? How would you modify these, to make its marketing more effective?

Customers, Prospects and Penetration

Taking this myopia one stage further, producers or service providers mainly see markets in terms of where they themselves are in these markets. This means that they often look at them specifically in terms of their own existing customers and potential customers:

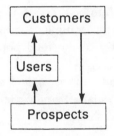

Customers. In commercial markets it might seem an easy task to define who your customers are; they are simply the buyers of your brand. But the dividing line is often not quite so clear. Where do those lie who have now switched to another brand? Where do you put very loyal users who have most recently bought another brand just for a temporary change? How do you categorize a consumer of a particular durable, when their last purchase might have been half a decade ago? In the public sector, the boundaries may be even more blurred; unemployment benefit is paid to those out of work, but is intended just as much to support their dependants.

Users. Sometimes users are not quite the same as purchasers. It may be the children in the family who actually consume the cornflakes; and they will usually make their brand preferences very well known, even if it is only because they want to collect the free gifts in the packets. The difference is most noticeable in the case of newspapers and magazines, where readership figures (the number of those who read a given issue, as determined by market research surveys) can be much higher than those for circulation (the number of copies actually sold, from special audits of the publishers' own accounts).

Prospects. The term 'prospects' is most often used in face-to-face selling, 'potential customers' often being used in mass markets, but the meaning is the same; those individuals in the market who are not the organization's customers. Again, however, the boundaries are not quite so clear. Are lapsed customers to be included? Is everyone in the market a prospect, or should only those who are likely to buy the particular brand be included? The concept of 'prospects' may sometimes be just as applicable in the public sector. A government will undertake extensive advertising campaigns because as few as 50 per cent of those entitled to family benefits actually claim them. The government is here attempting to convert prospects into customers.

In practice, however, these are seen as broad categories, so the fine distinctions questioned above do not normally pose critical limitations. The important fact is that some of the individuals in the market buy the producer's brand and some do not. The measure of this difference is often given by brand *penetration.*

Penetration

This is the proportion (percentage) of individuals in the *market* who are users of the specific (brand) product or service, as determined by the numbers who claim in response to market research to be users. In the non-profit sector it can often be used just as effectively as, for example, a measure of the number of clients receiving help as a proportion of the total population who might need the service.

The measure of 'penetration', however, does not allow for the rate of usage or purchase by different individuals. The most commonly used measure, therefore, is market share or brand share.

Brand (or market) share

This is the share of overall *market sales* taken by each brand. In the consumer field, this is usually measured by audit research on panels of retail outlets, such as that undertaken by A. C. Nielsen; hence it represents consumer purchases and not necessarily usage – although the distinction is usually not important. In the industrial field it is usually a 'guesstimate' based on research of a limited number of customers; although in some fields government departments audit total output.

Once more there are complications. The share can be quoted in terms of volume (the brand has a 10 per cent share of the total *number* of units sold) or in terms of *value* (at the same time the brand took 15 per cent of the total money being paid out for such products, since it was a higher priced brand). This difference can sometimes be dramatic. Amstrad claimed at one time to have achieved the same market share as IBM, which was then the market leader in the PC market. But this was in terms of volume – in terms of value Amstrad had less than a third of IBM's share, and was actually in fourth or fifth place.

The results of Andrew Ehrenberg's research have complicated matters further. He shows that – unlike the traditional view that customers buy just *one* brand – they actually buy a '*portfolio*' of brands. Their brand loyalty is, therefore, measured in terms of the share of overall purchases over time, within that portfolio, held by the brand in question!

The measure of share, and the concept of prospects, are important because they delineate the extra business that a producer can reasonably look for, and where he or she might obtain it. On the other hand, the evidence in many markets is that most business comes from repeat purchasing by existing customers.

SELF-TEST QUESTION 4.5

What problems, if any, are there in defining who are your organization's users or prospects? How does your organization resolve these problems?

Approximately what 'penetration' of users or clients does your organization achieve (to the nearest 10 per cent, say)? Are there significant groups still to be addressed?

Approximately what market share does it hold in terms of volume and of value?

The Pareto, 80:20, Effect

We identified, above, the fact that there may be heavy and light users, the former being that much more important to the producer.

At the end of the nineteenth century, Pareto noted that the bulk of the wealth of Italy was in the hands of 10 per cent of the population. This principle has since been adopted by management in general, and enshrined as a very valuable 'rule of thumb', the 80:20 Rule, which can be applied to a wide range of situations, in mass consumer markets as well as industrial ones. Indeed, this is possibly the *most* useful of all the 'rules of thumb'.

It applies to groupings of customers; in the industrial sales field the top 20 per cent of customers will often account for 80 per cent of sales. It also applies to groupings of products, where there is an extended product list; the best-selling 20 per cent of products will often take 80 per cent of the volume or value of overall sales.

The importance of the principle is that it highlights the need for most producers, often against their natural inclinations, to concentrate their efforts on the most important customers and products.

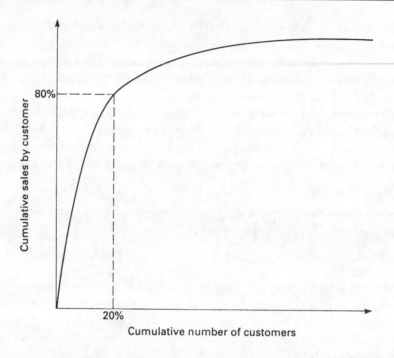

SELF-TEST QUESTION 4.6

Who are the five most important customers or clients (or groups of these) of your organization? Approximately what proportion of its business (or activity) do they account for? What special steps does your organization take to reflect the importance of these customers?

What steps does your organization take to review which are unprofitable customers, and what actions does it then take?

What proportion of its sales are accounted for by the five best-selling brands, and what strategies recognize the importance of these?

What procedures are in place to discontinue low-selling products or services?

Market Segments

As we have seen, producers tend to define markets quite broadly, in terms of the physical characteristics which are important to themselves. The result is that these larger markets often contain groups of customers with quite different needs and wants, each of which represents a different 'segment', with different characteristics in terms of its consumers. This process is called 'segmentation'; or sometimes 'target marketing', because the supplier carefully targets a specific group of customers.

If we look at the personal computer market we may see how segmentation works.

ACTIVITY 4.1

How would you define the personal computer market?
   Within this overall market what segments, separate groupings of customers, can you think of?

This overall market is often loosely defined in terms of being that for self-contained, stand-alone, computers which are used by one person. However, a number of alternative criteria may be employed. 'Segments' within this market can be defined in terms of the physical hardware. Those based on the Intel range of 'chips', and following the conventions originally chosen by IBM for its PC, form the 'IBM compatible market' or segment, depending on how you define each of these terms. There are other segments, however, one based on the Motorola 68000 series of chips and yet another on the PowerPC range, while another is almost exclusively the province of Apple.

Personal computers can also be defined in terms of use. There are those in the home, used mainly for games, and those used as integral parts of other systems, such as some retail systems or process control applications. Mainly, though, they are used in office systems – but even here their use can be further segmented. There are the basic work-horses (the main IBM compatible market), but there are also 'desktop-publishing' systems, a segment very effectively exploited by Apple. Then there is the multi-media approach being developed by Compaq, amongst others.

There is also segmentation by price and quality. The early IBM PC clones, for example, were clearly aimed at a market which could not afford the IBM and Compaq machines, which were then up to ten times the price.

The value of discovering such separate segments, each with rather different characteristics, is that they allow producers to offer products that address the needs of just *one* segment, and hence are not in direct competition with the overall market leaders.

While IBM and Compaq still offer a comprehensive range, with almost universal applicability, unbranded clones specifically target the price-sensitive segment. Despite their aggressive posturing, these are actually avoiding head-on confrontation with IBM and Compaq – and by concentrating on the specific segment, they can offer users in that segment a better match to their needs.

Once again, although the concept of segmentation is classically described in terms of products, it can be just as applicable to services. In the PC market, there are dealers who provide support for the smaller organizations and those who specialize in supporting the large multinationals – each a totally different segment of the overall market.

Segmentation can even be a powerful concept in the non-profit sector, although it tends to be a device for focusing resources rather than dealing with competition. Thus, for example, there may be seen to be a number of possible segment of the 'unemployed'. Each of these 'segments' has different characteristics and offers correspondingly different opportunities for government action.

Segmentation

In one sense, 'segmentation' is a *strategy* used by vendors to concentrate, and thus optimize, the use of their resources within an overall market. In another sense, it is also that group of *techniques* which are used by these vendors for segmenting the market.

One focus for segmentation may be that of consumer behaviour. In this context, the factors that we discussed earlier – the influences on the consumer – provide one set of starting points. These are often grouped as follows:

* geographical – region, urban or rural, etc.
* demographic – age, sex, marital status, etc.
* socio-economic – income, social class, occupation, etc.
* psychological – attitudes, life-styles, culture, etc.

Philip Kotler[2] distinguishes between two major approaches:

* consumer (inherent) characteristics
  - geographical
  - demographic
  - psychographic
* consumer (product-related) responses
  - occasions (when used)
  - benefits
  - usage (including heavy or light)
  - attitudes (including loyalty)

[2] Kotler, *Marketing Management*.

The first of these categories reflects 'who buys'. The second, on the other hand, is generally based on 'what is bought'. If the emphasis is on the supplier's viewpoint, which it often is, this can be expanded to include elements of the 4 Ps:

- price
- distribution channels
- physical characteristics of product or service
- packaging

However, these patterns are probably unrelated to the customers' own perceptions. The customer may genuinely believe, like a supplier, that a disinfectant bought in a plastic bottle from a supermarket belongs to a different segment of the market than one in a glass bottle bought from a pharmacy. On the other hand, the consumer may actually be making the choice on totally different grounds: that it offers specially gentle protection for the baby in the family, say. It behoves a supplier to know what the true reasons are, not least because the promotional message often determines what the product is in the eyes of the consumer.

Most recently, in a related vein, there has been some emphasis on *competitive* positions as one determinant of segmentation; you choose to fight on the ground where you have the greatest competitive *advantage*.

The characteristics that are important to a specific market may, however, be much more closely defined. The aim of much market research is to identify what are the *exact* characteristics which are the most important (conscious or subconscious) delineators of buying behaviour. It is then these specific characteristics which are the most powerful tools for segmentation.

In practice, the picture may be much more complex; with the truly meaningful segments hidden from the supplier – being based, for example, on intangible benefits which only the consumer sees, or based on natural consumer groupings which emerge from much more deep-seated social processes. In some consumer markets it may need the use of significant amounts of research, using the 'factor analysis' and 'cluster analysis' techniques mentioned in the last chapter, on marketing research, just to surface these hidden characteristics and to start to identify what the key segments are.

'Intangibles' represent the type of characteristic most often used in the segmentation of consumer markets (services as well as products). Those used in industrial markets may be more directly related to the product or service characteristics (for example, powerful single-use cleaners rather than general cleaners), or at least to product usage characteristics (cleaners to be used on floors rather than on upholstery); but also to 'customer set' characteristics (cleaners to be used in workshops in heavy industry, rather than in operating theatres in hospitals).

Segmentation by benefit

The use of generalized factors as the basis for segmentation has its limitations. It is much more productive to relate segmentation to the specific characteristics of the market for the product or service. Different customers, or groups of customers, look for different combinations of benefits; and it is these groupings of benefits which then define the segments. It is these differences which the producers can use to target their brands – or the public service providers their offerings – on the segment, and to position them where they most clearly meet the needs of the consumers in that segment.

Walters and Knee[3] show very clearly how segmentation is applied by one UK fashion retailing chain, in terms of a different outlet for each segment (Evans for larger sizes, Dorothy Perkins for the 'Young').

Referring back to the earlier example, in order to meet the needs of the 'desktop-publishing' market, Apple provided graphics-oriented hardware and software – which offered the benefit of very easy 'typesetting' to users in the ordinary office environment – and told them about it with particularly effective commercials on television. Atari, on the other hand, offered very sophisticated screen-handling hardware; which is ideal for the fast-moving images demanded by computer games.

Segmentation by consumption profile

In recent times, a number of research agencies have started to characterize consumer segments in terms of the buying choices of the consumers in them. Thus, they are characterized by their purchases of a range of key products and, in particular, by the range of media read and television programmes watched. The data for this may be provided in some depth by MRB's TGI survey, or in less (but still adequate) depth by less wide-ranging surveys. Whatever the set of key products chosen, the profile as described in terms of the bundle of brands purchased is supposed to be more meaningful to marketers than the relatively esoteric categories offered by life-styles.

In a simpler variation on this theme, Raaij and Verhallen[4] suggest that the most feasible level for segmenting markets is what they call the 'domain-specific' level, which focuses on behaviour at the level of the product and is based on class of usage (including usage situation, frequency of use and substitution behaviour).

---

[3] D. Walters and D. Knee, Competitive strategies in retailing, *Long Range Planning*, vol. 22, no. 6 (1989).
[4] W. Fred Van Raaij and Theo M. M. Verhallen, Domain-specific market segmentation, *European Journal of Marketing*, vol. 28, no. 10 (1994).

SELF-TEST QUESTION 4.7

What are the benefits of the products or services that your organization provides for its customers or clients? Are there different groups (or clusters) of customers who have the same responses to these as one another, but different from other groups?

What segments do you think your organization may be addressing? Do you think they are the right ones? How does the organization use this segmentation?

Segment Viability

There is a pure, customer-oriented, marketing reason behind segmentation. By designing products or services which are narrowly targeted on the needs of one specific segment, it may be possible to offer them the best match to their needs. In practice, however, producers usually target segments rather than the overall market because this allows them to concentrate their *resources* on a limited group of consumers, so that the brand can be made to dominate that segment – and gain the benefits of segment leader.

In the public sector, greater efficiency may be the justification for such concentration; but in the commercial world, the ultimate objective is, of course, to make a profit. To be viable, a segment has generally to meet a number of broad criteria:

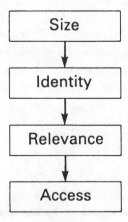

Size

The first question to be asked is simply whether the segment is substantial enough to justify attention; will there be enough volume generated to provide an adequate profit? As segmentation is a process, at least in the short term, that is largely under the control of the producer, it might be possible to find an increasing number of ever smaller segments which could be targeted separately. In general, however, it is best to choose the *smallest* number of segments, and hence the largest average size, which still allows the resources to be concentrated and head-on competition with the market leaders avoided.

In part, the viable size will be defined in terms of the producer's cost structures. The car market is heavily segmented, with Ford targeting a wide range of separate segments, but even the smallest of these (sharing the same assembly line as others) has to be worth some tens of thousands of cars a year simply to earn its place on that assembly line. On the other hand, Aston Martin, with its custom hand-building, can very effectively target a segment which is worth just a few hundred cars a year.

Identity

The segment has to have characteristics which will enable it to be separately identified (and measured by market research) by both the producers and the consumers. In the car market there is, for example, an identifiable segment for small cars – against which Renault targets the Clio, Peugeot the 205, and so on.

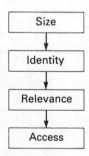

Relevance

The basis for segmentation must be relevant to the important characteristics of the product or service – it must be 'actionable'. For example, the type of pet owned will be highly relevant in the pet food market, but will rarely be so in the car market.

While this may seem obvious, much marketing is still undertaken (mistakenly) on the basis of overall population characteristics rather than those directly relating to the specific product or service. Thus, for example, in many markets the tacit segmentation has been made in terms of social class: yet the major manufacturers' segmentation of the car market, to give one example, no longer follows these lines.

Access

Finally, the producer must be able to gain access to the segment that has been found. If tapping that segment is too difficult, and accordingly too expensive, it clearly will not be viable. Let us say, for the sake of argument, that there might be a small segment of the general low-priced car market which could be met by a small manufacturer using hand-building techniques. If the consumers within the segment were, however, diffused evenly throughout the population the producer might face difficulties on two levels. The first would be in obtaining national distribution on the low volumes. Setting up a separate dealership network, to provide the maintenance facilities, would be almost impossible (even some of the smaller existing manufacturers, such as Peugeot and Fiat, have incomplete networks). The second would be finding the means of delivering the promotional message to these potential buyers.

All of these criteria are equally applicable to the segmentation available in the non-profit sector, and if they can be met segmentation is a very effective marketing device. It can allow even the smaller organizations to obtain leading positions in their respective segments ('niche' marketing) and gain some of the control this offers. *It is worth repeating that the most productive bases for segmentation are those which relate to the consumers' own groupings in the market*, and not to artificially imposed producers' segments. In any case, it must be remembered that segmentation is concerned only with dividing *customers or prospects* (and not products or services) into the segments to which they belong.

Segmentation Methods and Practical Segmentation

In order to achieve a genuine consumer-based segmentation. Richard Johnson[5] suggests that three 'technical' problems need to be addressed:

1 To construct a product space, a geometric representation of consumers' perceptions of products or brands in a category.
2 To obtain a density distribution by positioning consumers' ideal points in the same space.
3 To construct a model which predicts preferences of groups of consumers towards new or modified products.

In practice, segmentation is so very clearly bound up with the market research programmes described in chapter 3 that it often almost becomes one element of this aspect of marketing activity.

---

[5] R. M. Johnson, Market segmentation: a strategic management tool, *Journal of Marketing Research*, vol. 8 (1971).

To discover, and use, these 'natural segments' requires a number of steps:

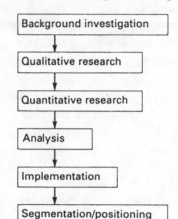

Market research

The basis for almost all effective segmentation must be sound market research.

Background investigation.   The first stage is to undertake the desk research which will best inform the researcher, and the marketer, as to what the most productive segments are likely to be. This essential stage will lead to the 'hypotheses' to be tested, but it must not be the only one used to define the segments. At each stage, the marketer must be prepared to abandon any preconceptions or prejudices, in the light of actual data about the customer's view of such segments.

Qualitative research.   It is vital, in particular, that all the characteristics which are important to the consumer are measured; and that these are described in terms that are meaningful to him or her. The 'language' which is used by these consumers should be first investigated in the group discussions that are frequently used to pilot major research projects – and that are best conducted by psychologists who are trained to recognize the important nuances. However, other techniques can also be used. One particularly effective one is that of 'repertory grids' or 'Kelly Grids'.

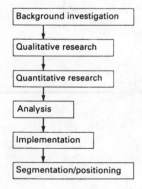

It is this research that discovers the 'dimensions' that are important to the consumers (and which are described in their language), from which the later strategies will be developed.

Quantitative research.   Frequently making use of 'semantic differentials' based upon the dimensions (the key descriptive words) revealed by the qualitative research, this research will usually attempt to measure attitudes to the brand (and to its competitors). This work may also, perhaps, extend to the consumer's 'ideal brand'. The validity of such 'idealizations' is often questioned, since they are artificial conceptualizations which are not easy for the consumer to handle; and the results can be ambiguous. Robin Wensley[6] reported that very *different* clusters had been

[6] Robin Wensley, Strategic marketing: a review, in *The Marketing Book*, ed. Michael J. Baker (Butterworth Heinemann, 1994).

found for *each* year of one segmentation tracking study – and that, as a result, the management involved had chosen to fix on those set by the first year, and then to only *track* the changes to these! In practice, though, the concept (of the ideal) usually appears to work well; especially when the questions are carefully phrased and are specific (and are 'mapped' on the specific dimensions involved in the positioning exercise).

Analysis

This stage is critical, and is now almost invariably dependent upon the use of considerable computing power to undertake the complex analyses involved. Some form of 'factor analysis' is usually used to separate out those variables that are highly correlated, and hence are almost interchangeable in the consumers' eyes.

The news that these variables are related is often very enlightening to the suppliers. In some pioneering work undertaken in the 1960s, the 'strength' of pipe tobacco was seen to be related mainly to the 'darkness' of the tobacco (rather than to the actual strength which the manufacturers were – without great success – trying to reduce). This allowed Gallahers to reposition its main brand (Condor) to appear milder, simply by making the colour lighter.

Only when this factor analysis is complete is 'cluster analysis' used to create a specified number of maximally different clusters, or segments, of consumers. The number of such clusters specified is that which can reasonably be handled in marketing terms (but which still adequately describes the significantly different segments in the market). Each of these clusters of consumers is then homogeneous within itself, but as different from other clusters as possible. The typical outcome will be a set of prioritized position maps, preferably limited to the six to eight most important dimensions.

Implementation

These clusters (typically no more than half a dozen in number) then need to be described in terms of the key characteristics which differentiate them. In the case of Condor pipe tobacco, for example, the factors which differentiated the cluster on which it was targeted included the colour of the product and the colour of the pack (which was seen as almost as important), but – crucially – it also included 'psychographic' elements (in this case the consumers saw themselves as significantly more mature than other pipe smokers).

Then, and only then, can the supplier's products (and the competitors) be mapped onto these dimensions, and the product 'positioning' exercise begun, so that the target segments are optimally addressed.

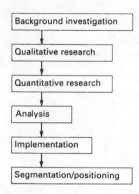

Background investigation

↓

Qualitative research

↓

Quantitative research

↓

Analysis

↓

Implementation

↓

Segmentation/positioning

Segmentation/positioning

The marketer must then pore over these 'maps' to decide exactly what his or her 'battle plans' should be, taking into account the available resources as well as the competitive and consumer positioning on the 'map'. Which will the target groups be? Which will the chosen segments be? Where will the products or services be repositioned (if this is needed) to compete most effectively and/or to be most attractive to consumers? *This is probably the most important set of decisions that any marketer has to make, and from it most other decisions should emerge naturally. The intellectual effort which needs to be committed to this process cannot, therefore, be underestimated.*

The complexity of this whole process does mean that marketer and researcher must work closely together. They must each have a sound appreciation of what the other is doing and – most importantly – confidence in the other's ability to handle the complexities. It is a time- and resource-consuming process, but the benefits to be derived far more than outweigh this. For example, Tony Lunn[7] reports (on the basis of a major unpublished review of market structure projects from several European subsidiaries of a multinational corporation) that:

> In all cases examined in the review, marketing men volunteered the information that the benefits more than justified the time and expenditure involved. In some cases the findings were held to have contributed to substantial gains in market share, in others to arresting decline in share in the light of fierce competition.

ACTIVITY 4.2

Identify a small segment of the 'market' which your organization has not yet exploited. Then, using the four criteria given above, decide whether that segment is viable in terms of bringing in enough income to justify the effort and costs involved.

SELF-TEST QUESTION 4.8

Examine, as far as the information you have at your command will allow, the segments in which your organization has chosen to operate. Are all of these viable in terms of the above factors – if not, why not?

[7] T. Lunn, Segmenting and constructing markets, *Consumer Market Research Handbook*, ed. R. Worcester and J. Downham (McGraw-Hill, 3rd edn, 1986).

Product (or Service) 'Positioning'

There can be some confusion between 'segmentation' and 'positioning', and indeed the two processes often overlap. The key difference is that the former applies to the market, to the customers (or occasionally 'products') who are clustered into the 'natural' segments which occur in that market; while the latter relates to the product or service, and to what the supplier can do with these 'products' to best 'position' them against these segments.

A further complication is that 'positioning' can sometimes be divorced from 'segmentation' in that the supplier can choose dimensions on which to position the brand that are not derived from research, but are of his or her own choosing. Indeed, such positioning can be applied (to differentiate a brand, for instance) even when segmentation is not found to be viable. Further confusion can arise when the process is associated with 'product differentiation' – the practical 'positioning' of products or services so that they are recognizably different from their competitors – as measured in terms of their positions on the 'product space', the 'map' of competitive brand positions against the dimensions which matter to the consumer.

As we have already seen, the most effective 'segmentation' of a market is usually based on sets of characteristics that are specific to that market. The spread of users across these characteristics may, however, differ quite significantly:

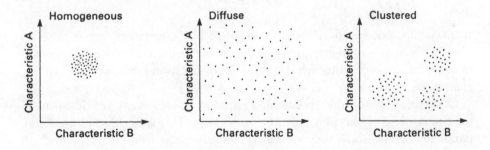

Both the homogeneous example, where all the users have similar, closely grouped, preferences (for example, a commodity such as sugar), and the diffused example (where they have requirements evenly spread across the spectrum) tend to specify treatment of the market as one single entity (but for very different reasons); and segmentation is not relevant – unless competitors in a diffused market have left part of it uncovered.

It is in the 'clustered' market – which is often encountered in practice – where segmentation can be most successfully used. Ideally, the marketer would choose

... exactly in the centre of the cluster that he or she is aiming

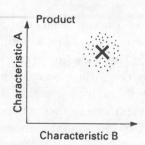

...ther approach, though, where the clusters may be too small to justify a segmentation policy (or the marketer simply wants to have a more general product/brand which can be correspondingly larger) is to launch the product or service so that it is equidistant from several clusters that the marketer wishes to serve:

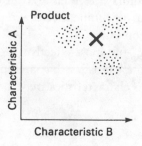

It may, thus, not exactly match the needs of any one group, but is close to meeting those of several groups. However, such 'positioning' may be vulnerable to attack from a competitor who positions his or her brand exactly on one of the clusters.

Conventionally, product positioning ('product space') maps are drawn with their axes dividing the plot into four quadrants. This is because most of the parameters upon which they are based typically range from 'high' to 'low' or from '+' to '−' (with the 'average' or zero position in the centre). This is best shown by the typical example shown at the top of the page opposite. On this, the value of each product's (or service's) sales (or 'uptake'), as well as that of each cluster of consumers, is conventionally represented by the *area* of the related circle.

In this case there are just two clusters of consumers, one buying mainly on the basis of price (and accepting the lower quality that this policy entails) and one on the basis of quality (and prepared to pay extra). Against these segments there are just two main brands (A and B), each associated with a cluster or segment. There is also a smaller brand (C), associated with cluster 1, offering an even higher quality alternative, but at an even higher price.

Real-life product positioning maps will, of course, be more complex, involving a number of such dimensions; and they will be drawn with less certainty as to where the boundaries might lie. But they do offer a very immediate picture of where potential may lie, and which products or services are best placed to tap it.

They also offer a sound basis for 're-positioning' existing products (or launching a complementary new product), so that they better match the requirements of the specific 'clusters' on which they are targeted. In the above example, Brand C might be content to remain a 'niche' product. Alternatively, the positioning map shows that if it were reduced in price slightly (and were backed by sufficient promotion) it might become a very competitive contender for Brand A's market share.

It is, of course, possible – at least in theory – to use promotion to move the consumer ideal closer to the brand rather than the other way around; and this technique is much favoured by 'conviction marketers' (discussed in some detail in chapter 9). Equally, the launch of a really innovative new product (such as the compact disc audio player) may change the dimensions of the whole market. Such approaches, however, while very effective indeed when they succeed, are very difficult to achieve.

Positioning over time

So far we have been discussing the 'positions' at one point in time – the 'current' position. However, if the positioning research is carried out regularly, over time, the map can also show that these positions are changing, hopefully in line with the strategy:

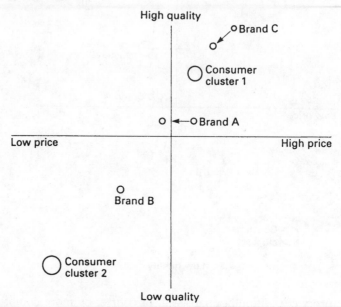

Here we can see that Brand C has only moved slightly (in line with strategy), but in so doing it has improved its competitive position significantly (helped by the fact that Brand A's competitive response, also reducing price, has moved it *away* from the ideal).

The Cadillac Division of General Motors may provide an example of an organization failing to track such market changes over time. Even when it finally revamped its range, in 1985, its slimmed-down models actually seemed to move away from where the core of its market was; this move offered Ford's Lincoln-Mercury Division, which continued to produce larger cars, a major competitive advantage. Tracking changes in position is thus a very powerful marketing tool.

Position drift

Positioning over time is a very important task for any brand owner. Let us take the example of a very simplified positioning map, covering some possible elements behind a set of product/service strategies.

You will remember that this map of positions should be used to position the brand as close to the ideal as is possible for the segment(s) you wish to address (and hopefully dominate). The problem is that this shows only a static picture. Over time 'position drift' can significantly change the picture. This may come about for three main reasons:

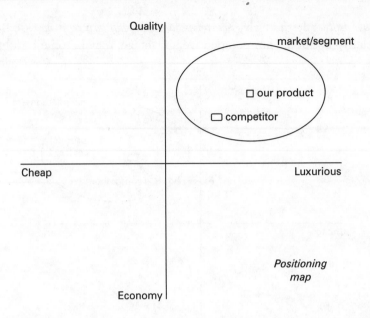

Positioning map

Consumer drift   *As consumer tastes change the segment (cluster) which contains them will shift its position.* Its centre of gravity will move – and its size may change as consumers switch to other, perhaps newer, segments.

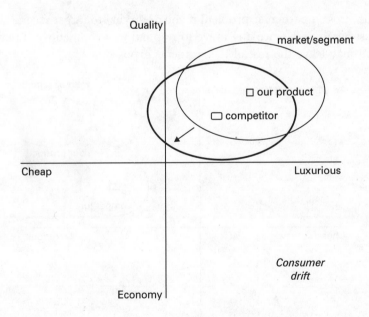

Consumer drift

The position of your brand *relative* to the ideal position, within this cluster, will reflect this drift.

Competitor drift Alternatively, *your competitors may shift their positions* – so that your own relative position, your competitive advantage, may become less than optimal.

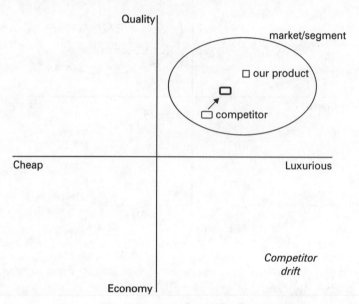

This may pose a particular problem if you are trying to target several segments with just one brand, since any move to respond to a competitive threat in one segment may leave the rest of the segments exposed.

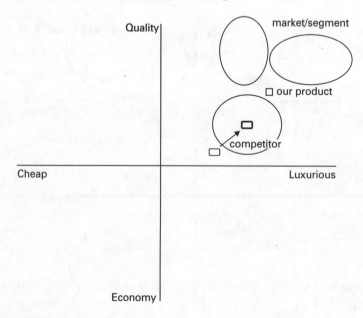

Ego drift   Perhaps the most prevalent drift of all, however, occurs where 'brand managers' (or their advertising agencies) *gratuitously reposition their own brand in a less optimal location*. This is usually justified on the basis that consumers are bored with the existing messages, and an exciting new approach is needed. The real reason often is that members of the management team, frequently persuaded by an agency creative team itching to make their own distinctive mark, are themselves bored.

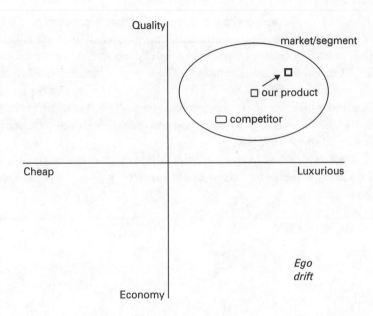

The biggest problem caused by drift, of any of these types, is that it usually occurs so slowly that it is not noticed by the brand manager – in the timescales that he or she works to, the changes are imperceptible. De Chernatony and Daniels[8] emphasize the point, in the context of brand management: 'An overt reliance on the brand team's perceptions could lead to an inwardly focused orientation . . . could leave the brand unprepared for the changed environment.' It is for this reason that brand positioning maps must be updated regularly, and the changes plotted as accurately as possible – so that the trajectory of any drift may be determined, and corrected.

It is likely, therefore, that most product/service packages will need to be redeveloped, from time to time, to compensate for this drift.

---

[8] Leslie De Chernatony and Kevin Daniels, Developing a more effective brand positioning, *Journal of Brand Management*, vol. 1, no. 6 (1994).

SELF-TEST QUESTION 4.9

What are the main dimensions against which your organization's products or services are positioned? Do they include price and quality? Do they cover more sophisticated, more complex factors (such as image).

Draw the positioning diagrams (two for each product or service, using the four main dimensions that apply to each of these) for each of the main products or services (four products or services should suffice). On each diagram show where (in your opinion or, if available, where research indicates) your own product or service is positioned, as well as the positions of its main competitors and the ideal position as seen by the consumers (or the various ideal positions if there are several clusters of consumers).

What does this tell you about the strength of each 'brand' in relation to its competitors? How could the 'brand' be repositioned to improve its competitive position?

Repositioning

Peter Doyle[9] gives a useful list of the alternative approaches to repositioning in general:

1 Real Repositioning – by making physical changes to the product or service.
2 Psychological Repositioning – changing the consumer's beliefs about it.
3 Competitive Repositioning – undermining the competitor's position.
4 Reweighting Values – persuading consumers to attach different weights to key values.
5 Neglected Values – introducing new choice criteria.
6 Changing Preferences – persuading buyers to change their views.
7 Augment the Brand – adding value in some way.

Above all, though, these repositioning actions must be taken in the light of the specific positioning requirements identified as a result of the actions described earlier in this chapter.

---

[9] Peter Doyle, *Marketing Management & Strategy* (Prentice Hall, 1994).

Possible Approaches to Segmentation

Clearly, there may be a wide range of detailed actions which are suggested by the outcome of a segmentation analysis. In overall terms, though, there are four main strategies which may be adopted:

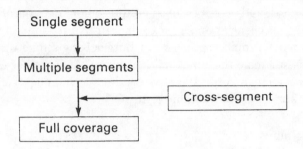

Single segment

The simplest response – often the case where limited funds are available – is to concentrate on one segment, and position the product firmly within that segment (sometimes described as 'niche' marketing). This is a very effective form of marketing, especially for the smaller organization, since it concentrates resources into a very sharply focused campaign. It is perhaps more risky, since there may be a greater likelihood of the 'niche' disappearing than of the whole market being subject to catastrophic change. On the other hand, it is considerably less risky than spreading resources too thinly across a number of segments.

Mass Customization   In recent years two trends have combined to allow for ever narrower segments or niches:

- increasing variety demanded – consumers have come to demand more variety from their suppliers, so that their 'exact' needs are catered for; as against accepting a more uniform product (even if this means that a higher price has to be paid by the consumer)
- flexible manufacturing methods – delivering a much greater variety of products without reducing productivity to any significant extent; though it should be noted that Toyota, in trying to push the process to the ultimate, has now found limits to productivity – and has rediscovered the 80:20 Rule![10]

The outcome has been that even some 'mass marketers' can now provide individually customized products (at least to some degree). With the use of

---

[10] B. Joseph Pine II, Bart Victor and Andrew C. Boynton, Making mass customization work, *Harvard Business Review* (September–October 1993).

'precision marketing' techniques, described in chapter 10, the supplier is now able to 'talk to' and deliver a 'product' specifically designed for an individual. Robertson[11] nicely sums up this trend when he says: 'Segments are becoming more and more discrete and the ultimate is a segment of one.' He describes this process as 'micro-marketing'. Philip Kotler,[12] however, reserves the same term for 'a geographically-based group of customers who have their own distinctive requirements . . .', and describes 'mass-customization' in terms of 'segments-of-one' giving the excellent example – excellent in that it shows how other firms might easily deploy a similar strategy – of Burger King setting up salad bars so that *customers* can create their own tailored menu. At the other extreme, however, there was a move in the 1980s to 'head-on positioning' – challenging the main competitor on *exactly* the same terms.

Multiple segments

A more complex response is to address several major segments with one brand, or to launch several brands each targeted against different segments. This latter strategy is adopted, for example, by Nestlé, which has brands to meet the 'ground coffee', 'continental' and 'decaffeinated' segments, as well as the main brand itself which – in line with the former strategy – spans a number of segments.

This technique may also be adopted by an organization which ultimately intends to achieve full coverage, but is approaching this by invading the market, segment by segment.

Cross-segment

Most suppliers resolutely ignore the segments and pattern their marketing on other factors. This is almost invariably the case in the more bureaucratic responses of the public sector, which are based on the demands of the 'delivery systems' rather than on the needs of the clients. But, in the commercial field, this often represents a successful strategy. For example, a company may specialize in a particular type of product which covers a number of segments, with a band of devoted supporters who recognize the specialized expertise embodied. This is a particularly prevalent, and successful, strategy in the industrial area. A more sophisticated approach would be based upon deliberately targeting across segments which have similar characteristics (such as similar production technologies).

---

[11] Thomas Robertson, New developments in marketing: a European perspective, *European Management Journal*, vol. 12, no. 4 (December 1994).

[12] Philip Kotler, Reconceptualizing marketing: an interview with Philip Kotler, *European Management Journal*, vol. 12, no. 4 (December 1994).

Full coverage ('mass marketing')

Full coverage, limited to those organizations that can afford the strategy – and with the intention of addressing the whole market – can take two forms:

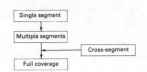

- *Undifferentiated.*   A few organizations attempt to address a whole market (including its segments) with a single product or non-segmented range. Coca-Cola is arguably such a company.
- *Differentiated.*   Where the organization covers the market with a range of products or services (under the one brand) which are more or less individually targeted at segments, the coverage may to some extent be differentiated. IBM, for example, covers almost the whole range of computer products and services, but with individual products aimed at each segment.

The most sophisticated approach would match the pattern to the stage of development of the market. In a new market, typically being developed by one supplier, just one brand is launched to cover the whole market. As the market develops, and competitors enter (usually targeting specific segments in order to obtain a foothold), the major supplier may move to pre-empt this competitive segmentation by launching its own new brands targeted at the most vulnerable segments. On the other hand, a competitor seeking to enter a market may initially target a particularly vulnerable segment, and then use this as a base from which to grow incrementally by taking in more segments.

Horizontal and vertical industrial markets

At a much less sophisticated level, some markets for industrial products are described as 'horizontal' or 'vertical'. 'Horizontal' markets are those in which use of the product or service stretches across a wide range of industries. Thus, the use of 'word-processing' or 'spreadsheet' software is general, across most businesses. 'Vertical' markets are those in which use of the product or service is strictly limited to a single industry (or a limited number of industries). Software designed to support dairy herd management, for example, has a very narrow ('vertical') market – that of dairy farmers.

Niches

A specialized, and indeed extreme, version of segmentation is that of creating 'niches', as practised by some organizations in the retail sector. In this form the 'niche' (the segment) chosen is barely viable for one 'supplier'. The organization then sets out to capture this segment (and possibly to expand it), confident in the knowledge that no competitor will subsequently be able to follow profitably. The danger, as was discovered by 'Sock Shop' for instance, is that competitors based in other segments may still be able to draw sales from the niche market and – in the process – reduce the viability of the niche operation itself.

Counter-segmentation

Segmentation has been a very popular strategic marketing device in recent years. There is an argument, therefore, that it may have been taken too far in some areas. The response could, accordingly, be to consolidate several segments: launching a brand (or repositioning a brand or integrating several existing brands) to cover several segments. This may allow economies of scale, without major reductions in benefits; it may, on balance, increase competitive advantage. This process has been called 'counter-segmentation'. Although it may only rarely apply, it should not be forgotten in the enthusiastic rush to segment.

SELF-TEST QUESTION 4.10

Which of these segmentation policies, if any, does your organization follow?

Differentiation and Branding

Another technique, which is more normally considered under 'product' or 'product strategy', is 'product differentiation'. Usually seen as specifically applicable to commercial organizations, it is used to give products unique identities to distinguish them from their competitors (in particular, between competitors in the same market from the same company).

The epitome of this process is 'branding'. The product is given a 'character', an 'image', almost like a personality. This is based first of all on a name (the brand), but then almost as much on the other factors affecting image – the packaging and, in particular, advertising. This all attempts to make the brand its own separate market, or at least its own segment (so that shoppers buy Heinz Baked Beans rather than ordinary baked beans). This sometimes succeeds to the extent that brands (such as Kleenex, Hoover and Biro) become generic.

Trevor Watkins[13] specifies branding in the following terms:

---

[13] T. Watkins. *The Economics of the Brand: A Marketing Analysis* (McGraw-Hill, 1986).

The firm's strategy is to make its products different from its competitors in such a way that customers can be convinced that they are superior. This can be done by making the physical product different or by making the way in which the customer perceives the product different, i.e. by psychological or emotional differences. These factors can be achieved by packaging differences, by having a range of sizes, shapes, qualities etc., by gimmicks, by after-sales service provision or perhaps most importantly by promotional activity – usually linked to at least one of the other differences. In monopolistic competition promotion is very often *the* main form of competition. The main aim of media advertising or 'above the line' promotion is to create a definite and distinct brand image.

De Chernatony and McDonald[14] list no less than eight different types of brands: 'Brand as a'

Sign of Ownership – who is paying for the promotion of the brand

Differentiating Device – as above

Functional Device – to communicate capability

Symbolic Device – allowing consumers to express themselves

Risk Reducer – insurance for the purchaser

Shorthand Device – encapsulating all the information about the product

Legal Device

Strategic Device

They personally subscribe to the last of these approaches – stressing the strategic importance of brand equity.

In recent practice, branding is also being applied to non-profit activities. Saxton,[15] though, suggests that the form of this may be rather different: 'Beliefs lie at the heart of what makes charities different and, for this reason, it is logical to use them as the source of the charity's brand.' In any case it is usually not for competitive reasons (although 'competition' between charities can sometimes be as cut-throat as any in the commercial sector) but as a means of improving awareness of what is available, and of differentiating between alternative offerings designed for different segments. It has even reached the stage where government departments, such as the DTI, have adopted expensively created 'logos'.

---

[14] Leslie De Chernatony and Malcolm H. B. McDonald, *Creating Powerful Brands* (Butterworth Heinemann, 1992).

[15] Joe Saxton, A strong charity brand comes from strong beliefs and values, *Journal of Brand Management*, vol. 2, no. 4 (1995).

Brand Monopoly

In economic terms the 'brand' is, in effect, a device to create a 'monopoly' – or at least some form of 'imperfect competition' – so that the brand owner can obtain some of the benefits which accrue to a monopoly, particularly those related to decreased price competition; as De Chernatony and McDonald[16] stress, 'Brands are able to sustain a price premium . . . since consumers perceive relevant added values.' In this context, most 'branding' is established by promotional means. However, there is also a legal dimension, for it is essential that the brand names and trademarks are protected by all means available. The monopoly may also be extended, or even created, by patents and intellectual property (or copyright, as it used to be called in a narrower context).

As an aside, it is worth noting that from the consumer's point of view, however, the effect of powerful brands, rather than disadvantaging them, may actually be – according to Reibstein and Farris[19] – to 'make it easier for the customer to find the product, but also increase the level of inter-store competition'.

In all these contexts, retailers' 'own label' brands can be just as powerful. The 'brand', whatever its derivation, is a very important investment for any organization. Coca-Cola, for instance, has a turnover in the United Kingdom alone of £500 million[17] and RHM (Rank Hovis McDougall), for example, value their international brands at anything up to twenty times their annual earnings! Baxter,[18] though, suggests that 'such a document [a brand valuation] will remind the critical reader of the Emperor's New Clothes. Every one of each year's figures must usually be a very dubious guess.'

SELF-TEST QUESTION 4.11

Does your organization 'brand' any of its products or services? If so, how does it achieve this (for example, by advertising or packaging) and how does it make use of this branding?

[16] Leslie De Chernatony and Malcolm H. B. McDonald, *Creating Powerful Brands* (Butterworth Heinemann, 1992).
[17] Alan Mitchell, Britain's biggest brands, *Marketing* (10 June 1993).
[18] W. T. Baxter, Asset values goodwill and brand names, ACCA occasional research paper, no. 14 (1993)
[19] David Reibstein and Paul Farris, Do marketing expenditures to gain distribution cost the customer?, *European Management Journal*, vol. 13, no. 1 (March 1995).

Branding Policies

There are a number of possible policies:

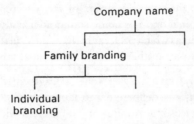

- *Company name.* Often, especially in the industrial sector, it is just the company's name which is promoted (leading to one of the most powerful statements of 'branding'; hence the well-known – though now out-dated – saying 'No-one ever got fired for buying IBM').
- *Family branding.* In this case a very strong brand name (or company name) is made the vehicle for a range of products (for example, Mercedes or Black & Decker) or even a range of subsidiary brands (such as Cadbury's Dairy Milk, Cadbury's Flake or Cadbury's Wispa).
- *Individual branding.* Each brand has a separate name (such as Seven-Up or McDonald's), which may even compete against other brands from the same company (for example, Persil, Omo and Surf are all owned by Unilever).

Derived brands

A recent development has been that the supplier of a key component, used by a number of suppliers of the end-product, may wish to guarantee its own position by promoting that component as a brand in its own right. The most frequently quoted example is Intel (in the PC market, with the slogan 'Intel Inside'), but the sweetener Aspartame used much the same approach (to lock in the soft drinks manufacturers who represented a major market for the product).

In terms of existing products, brands may be developed in a number of ways:

Brand extension. The existing strong brand name can be used as a vehicle for new or modified products; for example, after many years of running just one brand, Coca-Cola launched 'Diet Coke' and 'Cherry Coke'. Procter & Gamble (P & G), in particular, has made regular use of this device, extending its strongest brand names (such as Fairy Soap) into new markets (the very successful Fairy Liquid, and more recently Fairy Automatic). According to David Aaker: 'Each year from 1977 to 1984, 120 to 175 totally new brands were introduced into America's supermarkets. In each of these years, approximately 40 percent of the new brands were actually brand extensions.'

Interestingly, P & G – arguably the biggest brand owner of all – seems to have even tried to bring together separate families, by using a shared *component* ('Excel'), across these.

On the other hand, Quelch and Kenny[20] argue that this process may now have gone too far. They say that it can weaken the 'line logic', since more and more lines can lead to oversegmentation, and this dilutes brand loyalty. Our own research,[21] however, shows that almost half the products holding the top three places in new markets *were* brand extensions; though more than three-quarters of these were, indeed, in new markets closely related to the original one – echoing sound advice also given by Sharp:[22] 'Use brand extensions for products which preferably share those features of the original brand which were an important part of the original's differential advantage.'

Multibrands. Alternatively, in a market that is fragmented amongst a number of brands, a supplier can choose deliberately to launch totally new brands in apparent competition with its own existing strong brand (and often with identical product characteristics); this is done simply to soak up some of the share of the market which will in any case go to minor brands. The rationale is that having 3 out of 12 brands in such a market will give a greater overall share than having 1 out of 10 (even if much of the share of these new brands is taken from the existing one). In its most extreme manifestation, a supplier pioneering a new market which it believes will be particularly attractive may choose immediately to launch a second brand in competition with its first, in order to pre-empt others entering the market. As Roberts and McDonald[23] point out:

> Individual brand names naturally allow greater flexibility by permitting a variety of different products, of differing quality, to be sold without confusing the consumer's perception of what business the company is in or diluting higher quality products.

Once again, Procter & Gamble is a leading exponent of this philosophy, running as many as ten detergent brands in the US market. It should be noted that, at the end of the 1980s, P & G was represented in 39 product categories and was number one in 22 of these,[24] so it must be doing something right! This also increases the total number of 'facings' it receives on supermarket shelves. Sara Lee, on the other hand, uses it to keep the very different parts of the business separate – from Sara Lee cakes through Kiwi polishes to L'Eggs pantyhose. In the hotel business, Marriott uses the name Fairfield Inns for its budget chain (and Ramada uses Rodeway for its own cheaper hotels).

Cannibalism

This is a particular problem of a 'multibrand' approach, in which the new brand takes business away from an established one which the organization also owns. This may be acceptable (indeed to be expected) if there is a net

[20]John A. Quelch and David Kenny, Extended profits not product lines, *Harvard Business Review* (September–October 1994).

[21] David Mercer, A two decade test of product life cycle theory, *British Journal of Management*, vol. 4 (1993).

[22] Byron M. Sharp, Managing brand extension, *Journal of Consumer Marketing*, vol. 10, no. 3 (1993).

[23] C. J. Roberts and G. M. McDonald, Alternative naming strategies: family versus individual brand names, *Management Decision*, vol. 26, no. 6 (1989).

[24] Rita Mårtinson, The role of brands in European marketing, *Journal of Brand Management, vol. 2, no. 4 (1995).*

gain overall. Alternatively, it may be the price the organization is willing to pay for shifting its position in the market; the new product being one stage in this process.

> **SELF-TEST QUESTION 4.12**
>
> Which of these branding policies, if any, does your organization use?

Own brands and generics

With the emergence of strong retailers there has also emerged the 'own brand', the retailer's own branded product (or service). Where the retailer has a particularly strong identity (such as Marks & Spencer in clothing) this 'own brand' may be able to compete against even the strongest brand leaders, and may dominate those markets which are not otherwise strongly branded.

The degree of penetration by own brands, however, varies considerably from country to country. For example, it is high in the UK (estimated at 37% share),[25] about the European average in France (16%) and relatively low in Germany (7%).

There was a fear that such 'own brands' might displace all other brands (as they have done in Marks & Spencer outlets) and indeed the Henley Centre[26] reported in 1993 that 56 per cent of consumers thought retailers' own label products were usually better value for money, but the evidence is that – at least in supermarkets and 'department' stores – consumers generally expect to see on display something over 50 per cent (and preferably over 60 per cent) of brands other than those of the retailer. Indeed, even the strongest own brands in the UK rarely achieve better than third place in the overall market.[27] Therefore the strongest independent brands (such as Kellogg's and Heinz), which have maintained their marketing investments, should continue to flourish. More than 50 per cent of UK FMCG brand leaders have held their position for more than two decades, although it is arguable that those which have switched their budgets to 'buy space' in the retailers may be more exposed. The Henley Centre,[28] again, reported that 54 per cent of consumers thought it best to

[25] Harri Laaksonen and Jonathan Reynolds, Own brands in food retailing across Europe, *Journal of Brand Management*, vol. 2, no. 1 (1994).
[26] Henley Centre for Forecasting, Metamorphosis in marketing, *Marketing Business* (July–August 1993).
[27] D. Mercer, A two decade test of product life cycle theory, *British Journal of Management*, vol. 4 (1993).
[28] Henley Centre for Forecasting, Metamorphosis in marketing, *Marketing Business* (July–August 1993).

buy major brands; a figure which was, interestingly, a distinct improvement on the 1981 figure (37 per cent).

The strength of the retailers has, perhaps, been seen more in the pressure they have been able to exert on the owners of even the strongest brands (and in particular on the owners of the weaker third and fourth brands). Relationship marketing, which is described in more depth in the later chapter on selling, has been applied most often to meet the wishes of such large customers (and indeed has been demanded by them as recognition of their buying power). Some of the more active marketers have now also switched to *'category marketing'* – in which they take into account *all* the needs of a retailer in a product category rather than more narrowly focusing on their own brand. This is, in many respects, an extension of relationship marketing, discussed in more detail in the chapter on Selling. It offers some opportunities for suppliers. Whoever first 'defines' the category (to their own advantage) may put themselves in a winning position.[29] On the other hand, it is demanding of resources, tailoring marketing to each retailer, and it poses a threat in that retailers use it to cut price on brand leaders – attracting customers into the store – but promoting their own brand alongside!

At the same time, probably as an outgrowth of consumerism, 'generic' (that is, effectively unbranded goods) have also emerged. These make a positive virtue of saving the cost of almost all marketing activities; emphasizing the lack of advertising and, especially, the plain packaging (which is, however, often simply a vehicle for a different kind of image). It would appear that the penetration of such generic products peaked in the early 1980s, and most consumers still seem to be looking for the qualities that the conventional brand provides. As Harris and Strong[30] comment, 'for generics to continue to attract the consumer, they will need to be positioned by the retailer as a sensible value alternative and backed by the retailer's guarantee of acceptable and consistent quality'.

Differentiation of Services

In the case of services, in particular (but not exclusively), marketers may have difficulty in differentiating their own offering from those of their competitors. The service company can add 'innovative features' to distinguish its offering (where the primary service package is identical for all suppliers in the market). Unfortunately, such 'service innovations' are relatively easy to copy. Perhaps

[29] Alan Mitchell, Turned on by category marketing, *Marketing Week* (7 April 1995).
[30] B. F. Harris and R. A. Strong, Marketing strategies in the age of generics, *Journal of Marketing* (Fall 1985).

the most frequent, and effective, means of such differentiation is, once more, branding; or a similar 'intangible' benefit which cannot be copied so easily.

FURTHER READING

Despite its importance, this topic is relatively poorly served by the literature; even the main marketing textbooks vary in their coverage (although Kotler, as usual, is the best of these). The *Consumer Market Research Handbook* (3rd edn), edited by Robert Worcester and John Downham (McGraw-Hill) also gives sound coverage.

Probably the best detailed coverage, at times in considerable technical detail but clearly explained, is included in Yoram Wind's book *Product Policy: Concepts, Methods, and Strategy* (Addison-Wesley, 1982).

SUMMARY

There are a number of ways of defining markets, but for a marketer the key definition is in terms of who is the customer. Even so, there are different categories:

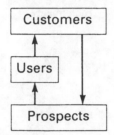

This leads to the concepts of penetration and brand (market) share.

Within markets there may be *segments*, which a producer may target to optimize use of scarce resources. The viability of these segments depends upon:

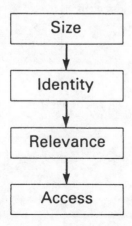

The use of these segments requires a number of activities to take place:

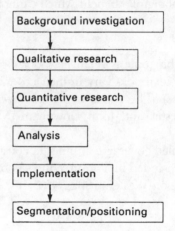

A major aid to positioning is offered by maps based on the critical dimensions, for example:

Approaches may include:

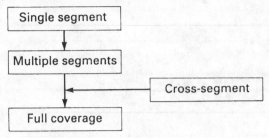

and horizontal or vertical industrial markets.

The most powerful marketing device for differentiation is that of *branding*,

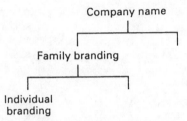

which may in effect create a near *monopoly*. Branding policies may be based on:
These may be developed further by brand extensions and multibrands, but this
may be limited by cannibalism.

'Own label' brands are becoming increasingly important, but usually at third
or lower place in the marketplace.

REVISION QUESTIONS

1 What is the basic element, in marketing terms, of a market? What are the differences
   between customers, users and prospects? What is the difference between penetration
   and brand share?
2 What are the tests for viability which should be applied to segments within a market?
3 What steps may be involved in practical segmentation?
4 In the process of segmentation, what marketing research techniques may be used,
   and how?
5 What are the differences between segmentation, market targeting and brand positioning; and how does each work?
6 How may maps be best used to aid positioning?
7 What segmentation strategies may be employed? Where does niche marketing fit in?
   How may industrial marketing differ?
8 What benefits may be obtained by branding? How may this create a near monopoly?
9 What branding strategies may be employed? How may brands be extended?

5 Product or Service Decisions

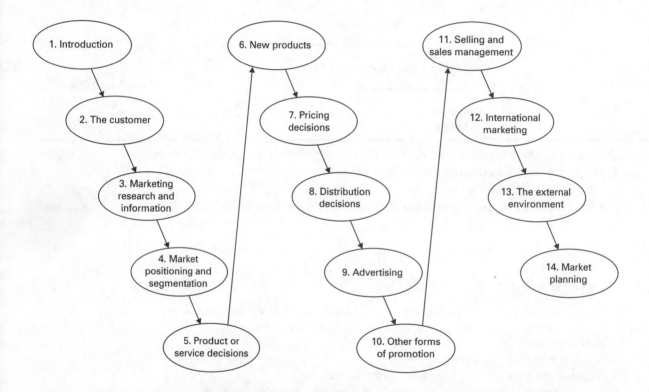

1. Introduction

2. The customer

3. Marketing research and information

4. Market positioning and segmentation

5. Product or service decisions

6. New products

7. Pricing decisions

8. Distribution decisions

9. Advertising

10. Other forms of promotion

11. Selling and sales management

12. International marketing

13. The external environment

14. Market planning

Introduction

The focus of suppliers' activities is the product or service that is offered. While all other aspects of marketing have their part to play, it is the product or service itself that ultimately matters to the consumer. By defining the product/service offer (which, in its extended form, will involve most of the 4 Ps), the supplier defines almost all of the marketing mix.

The strongest, most influential, theories of marketing have been developed in this area. The Ansoff Matrix, covering degrees of diversification, is one example. The most important and pervasive – in theory if not in practice – is, however, that of the Product Life Cycle (PLC). A significant amount of other marketing theory relates to the PLC, and hence the theory behind it is crucial; if, as this chapter shows, often fundamentally flawed in terms of practical applicability. The Competitive Saw, and its developments, may offer better guidance for 'mature' stable products and services. The other main element of theory is the Boston Matrix, which is also very influential – and again also potentially flawed in practical use. Despite their attractive simplicity, these theories typically have only specialized applications.

Beyond this theory, the product specification is developed, particularly in the area of quality. The last part of the chapter extends this, in some detail, to meet the specific needs of the service sector in general, and of non-profit organizations in particular.

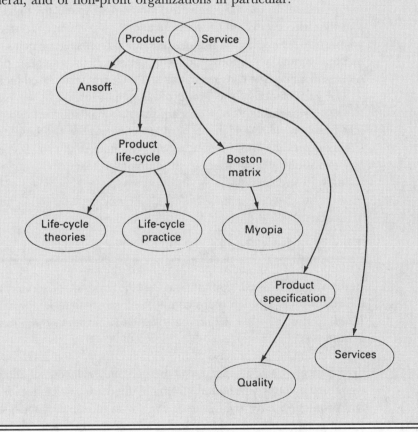

So far we have considered that part of marketing which deals with the processes of finding out what the customer wants; arguably this is the most important element of marketing – and the one which is most often neglected. But knowing about customer wants is not sufficient in itself, and so we now turn our attention to the responses of the producer or supplier.

It is worth reiterating that the 4 Ps (Product, Price, Place and Promotion) simply provide a convenient framework. But whatever the framework, *the most important contribution to the overall marketing mix will almost certainly be the product or service itself*. Cooper's research,[1] across more than 1000 new product projects, shows that a unique, superior product is the most important success factor; and our own research[2] lists physical advantages as one of the key factors for success in gaining the brand leadership. A good product might sell even if the promotion is mediocre. A bad product will rarely obtain repeat sales, no matter how brilliant the promotion is. Unilever developed a toothpaste dispenser which was able to add stripes to the paste coming out of the neck of the tube. In the USA this feature was emphasized using the slogan 'Looks like fun, cleans like crazy'. It was a smash hit, but repeat sales were dismal – because the 'fun' only justified one purchase. In the UK, however, the company sold the product on the basis that the stripe contained the flouride and was an essential component – it is still going strong. Despite the feelings of some advertising agencies, and the echoes in popular myth, a good product or service is the essential prerequisite to a successful marketing campaign; this fact is clearly recognized by most managers.

The importance of the product was demonstrated in the early days of the market for portable PCs. Compaq, then a small start-up company, and IBM met head on. It should have been no contest. Yet the customers judged the Compaq product to be better, albeit only marginally so, and eventually IBM had to withdraw its product from the market, leaving Compaq to go on from strength to strength.

The 'Product Package'

At this stage it is worth pointing out that the product (or service) as perceived by the customer is a much more complex construct than is normally allowed for. *Indeed, the most important specification of that product or service is the 'positioning' described in chapter 5.*

For example, in the case of branded products, such as Heinz Baked Beans, the physical product itself is submerged under layers of image, not to say emotional involvement built up from childhood, to which decades of advertising and promotion have contributed. Even with industrial goods, such as computers, it is often the intangibles which are most important. Hence IBM's philosophy of 'customer service'.

This overall combination of product, packaging and service is often referred to as the 'extended product'.

[1] Robert G. Cooper, New products: the factors that drive success, *International Marketing Review*, vol. 11, no. 1 (1994).
[2] David Mercer, Winning the brand leadership by uncompetitive means, *British Academy of Management* (September 1992).

Confusion may sometimes be caused by taking too sophisticated a view of superficial answers by consumers. As Gardner and Levy[3] point out:

> ... the reasons people usually give for using a product are inclined to be either strongly rationalized or related to the product's most obvious purposes... When such goals as these are taken at their face value, and considered to be the end of the matter, they lead up many blind alleys. The belief that people are fretting over these minute differences... results, sometimes, in a shrill focus on product merits beyond all proportion and sensible differentiation.

This is the reason why the more sophisticated research techniques (such as repertory grids) have been developed to explore the consumer's hidden motivations.

The 'Product Audit'

For existing products or services, the starting point is to decide exactly what you have. As Drucker[4] says:

> The best way to come to grips with one's business knowledge is to look at the things the business has done well, and the things it apparently does poorly. This is particularly revealing if other apparently well-managed and competent businesses have had the opposite experience.

This is not as obvious as it might at first seem. Even the 'physical' features of the brand may need to be reviewed; and the facts book added to, because those managers (possibly including the brand manager) who have become used to seeing the brand perform – in the way it has always performed – may have forgotten what other features it may potentially have.

SELF-TEST QUESTION 5.1

Prepare a short description of the important features of your organization's main products or services, together with the technology that lies behind them.

Are there other features, or aspects of the technology, which are not currently important but which might be useful in future?

[3] B. B. Gardner and S. J. Levy, The product and the brand, *Harvard Business Review* (March–April 1955).
[4] P. F. Drucker, *Managing for Results* (Heinemann, 1964).

The main feature of a product audit, though, is to look at the products or services in terms of what the customer sees in them. The brand which counts is the one that the *customer* sees. Some of the factors which may need to be examined in this review or audit might be:

- What is the market segment that this 'brand' addresses?
- Who are the existing customers?
- Who are the prospective customers?
- What benefits are these customers and prospective customers seeking?
- How does the product or service match up to these customer needs and wants?
- How does it compare with competitive products?

You will later find that there are other, more detailed and sophisticated questions that will also need to be examined. But, for the moment, the basic question, 'How does the customer view the brand?' is a good starting point.

SELF-TEST QUESTION 5.2

Now conduct the second part of your product audit and answer the list of questions above in terms of your organization's main brands.

These questions could be addressed in the form of a *benefit analysis*. This is a more rigorous analysis of the benefits that the product(s) offers, in terms of what the customer needs and wants. In sales-oriented organizations it is often described as *feature/benefit* analysis; though this too frequently substitutes a mechanistic, product-oriented set of supplier-determined 'benefits' to match the chosen list of product 'features'.

The list of customer benefits must, therefore, be very carefully compiled, preferably using sophisticated market research, to see it from the customer's viewpoint. The list also needs to be clearly *prioritized*, to be ranked in order of what the customer considers most important: otherwise the temptation is for the supplier to concentrate on the items where the organization can excel, regardless of the fact that these are relatively unimportant to the customer. On the other hand, the *differential benefits* which the supplier can offer, as against the competitive offerings, may be very important; particularly if most of the other important benefits are offered by all brands – and do not differentiate between brands in the market. Equally, *the benefits offered by the organization itself* should not be ignored; it is often these 'service' and support elements, rather than the product, which are the final influence on the customer's buying decision.

Product (or Service) Strategy

The 'product' strategy, the route by which to reach your long-term product objectives, will need to be developed specifically for each product or service. But, in general, there are said to be four basic product strategies for growth in volume and profit (which is what shareholders conventionally demand):

- market penetration
- product development
- market extension
- diversification

These were originally described by Igor Ansoff;[5] and were subsequently developed as the well-known 'Ansoff Matrix':

		Product	
		Present	New
Mission (market)	Present	Market penetration	Product development
	New	Market development	Diversification

Market penetration

The most frequently used strategy is to take the existing product (or service) in the existing market and try to obtain improved 'penetration' (or, more accurately, an increased share) of that market. There are two ways in which this can be achieved:

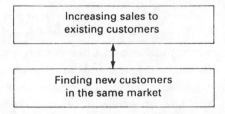

In general, the first strategy means persuading users to use more. This may be achieved by motivating them to use the product on more occasions, perhaps

[5] I. Ansoff, Strategies for diversification, *Harvard Business Review* (September–October 1957).

by replacing an indirect competitor; for example, inducing a household to eat beans on toast an extra time each week, instead of fish fingers. It may, on the other hand, simply be to persuade them to use the product more often without any need to take business from competitors; Unilever used Timotei to promote the more regular shampooing of hair. Possibly it may be that they use more each time: promotions offering '30 per cent more free' may have, as one objective, the intention of persuading customers to get into the habit of using more.

The second strategy almost invariably relates to taking business directly from competitors, increasing both penetration and market share.

Product (or service) development

This involves a relatively major modification of the product or service, such as quality, style, performance, variety and so on. Returning to our example of the car market, the provision of 'high-performance' versions of the existing models can be used to extend the ranges to cover additional customers. Similarly, adding sausages to tinned baked beans will possibly cause some existing users to increase their usage, but may also attract new users.

To be most effective, such developments should extend the 'product' into a new segment, or to a new competitive position in relation to the clusters of consumers.

Market extension

This depends upon finding new uses for the existing product or service, thereby taking it into entirely new markets – as Apple did in persuading customers to use its PCs for desktop publishing. Alternatively, this may be achieved by moving into other countries; in this context, most export operations can be viewed as 'market extensions'.

Diversification

This quantum leap to a new product and a new market involves more risk, and is more normally undertaken by organizations which find themselves in markets that have limited, often declining, potential. One obvious example is that of the tobacco companies which have diversified – often at considerable cost – into areas as diverse as cosmetics and engineering. However, it can be a positive move to extend the application of existing expertise; for example, Amstrad diversified from consumer electronics to home computing and thence to business computing. But beware of diversification which is undertaken simply because the grass looks greener in the new market.

Heinz, for instance, has steadily (and successfully) extended beyond its '57 varieties' core business (which revolved around baked beans and soups). Its 'Weight Watchers' brand is now worth more than $300 million in the US. But it should be noted that, in common with many other similarly successful diversifications, this was built on a logical extension of the company's existing strengths.

The Ansoff Matrix

As already mentioned, these four basic product strategies are often shown in a modified version of the 'Ansoff Matrix'[6] (figure 5.1). The four alternatives are simply the logical combinations of the two available 'positioning variables' (products and markets).

A number of such matrices (but with different characteristics/dimensions/ variables) are used in this book, since this is one of the favourite graphical devices adopted by marketing academics. All they are intended to convey, however, is a useful visual representation of the four categories to be obtained by splitting each of two groups of variables (or 'characteristics' or 'dimensions') into two further categories – giving four possible permutations. The resulting 'pigeon-hole' matrix just shows these four resulting combinations.

In this context, the matrix illustrates, in particular, that the element of risk increases the further the strategy moves away from known quantities – the existing product and the existing market. Thus, product development

Mission \ Product	Present	New
Present	Market penetration	Product development
New	Market development	Diversification

Figure 5.1 The Ansoff Matrix.

[6] Ansoff, Strategies for diversification.

(requiring, in effect, a new product) and market extension (a new market) typically involve a greater risk than 'penetration'; and diversification (both new product and new market) generally carries the greatest risk of all. In his original work, which did not use the matrix form, Igor Ansoff stressed:

> The diversification strategy stands apart from the other three. While the latter are usually followed with the same technical, financial, and merchandising resources which are used for the original product line, diversification usually requires new skills, new techniques, and new facilities. As a result it almost invariably leads to physical and organizational changes in the structure of the business which represent a distinct break with past business experience.

For this reason, amongst others, most marketing activity revolves around penetration; the Ansoff Matrix, despite its fame, is usually of limited value – although it does always offer a useful reminder of the options which are open.

In a similar vein to the original Ansoff Matrix, Peter Drucker[7] has identified three kinds of opportunities:

Additive
Breakthrough
Complementary

- *Additive.* The 'additive opportunity more fully exploits already existing resources'. In Ansoff's terms, it is the new product in an existing market or the existing product in a new market. As Drucker says, 'it does not change the character of the business'.
- *Breakthrough.* This typically 'changes the fundamental economic characteristics and capacity of the business'. It is the high-risk extreme of diversification, of which Ansoff in effect warns. This warning (which lay at the heart of Ansoff's categorization) has, however, largely been ignored by subsequent teachers.
- *Complementary.* This is a category not separately explored by Ansoff (although, in practice, it could possibly lie in either of the two development quadrants, but is most likely to lie in that of diversification). As Drucker says, 'The complementary opportunity will change the structure of the business. It offers something new which, when combined with the present business, results in a new total larger than the parts.' But he also emphasizes that it 'always carries considerable risk'.

---

[7] Drucker, *Managing for Results.*

SELF-TEST QUESTION 5.3

Using the Ansoff Matrix, plot what product (or service) and market strategies your organization is following.

What strategies do you think it ideally ought to follow? What are your reasons for your suggestions?

The 'Product' Life-cycle

The 'life-cycle' has long been a very important element of marketing theory. You should be aware, though, that its supposed universal applicability is largely a myth, albeit an important one, which you will need to appreciate before you can dismiss it! Its 'intuitive appeal' is based on the analogy of natural (human) lives. It, thus, suggests that any product or service moves through identifiable stages, each of which is related to the passage of time (as the product or service grows older) and each of which has different characteristics:

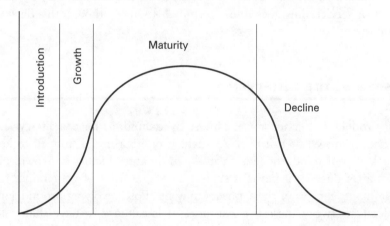

Introductory stage

At this first stage of a product's life, the supplier can choose from strategies which range from 'penetration', where the supplier invests to gain the maximum share of a new market, through to 'skimming', where the maximum short-term profit is derived from the 'innovation'. In either case the main task is to create awareness of the brand. In general the 'pioneer' which invests in a new market can expect to retain the highest market share – usually double the share of later entrants, even over the longer term.

Growth stage

As a result of awareness having been largely established, and in the light of growing competition, the emphasis at this stage may well be on promotion of the 'brand'; that is, establishing the correct attitudes to the product. Promotion is still heavy, and suppliers often have to make further, substantial investments. In recent years, another feature of this phase has been the battle for distribution.

Maturity

No product or service can grow forever; eventually all the significant, potential uses will have been developed. The sales curve will flatten, and it will have reached maturity. *The majority of products or services currently in the marketplace are at this stage*, and much of the theory and practice of marketing revolves around this 'steady state'; building groups of loyal users, and attracting those of competitors.

Decline stage

Eventually the whole market may decline or other newer products may be introduced which are themselves a substitute for the established product. The product or service thus goes into a terminal decline – though this decline can last for years.

Lessons of the Life-cycle

Every product or service must, almost by definition, have a life-cycle. It is launched, it grows, then it dies. As such, it offers a useful 'model' to keep at the back of your mind. Indeed, if you are in the introductory or growth phases, or in that of decline, it perhaps should be at the front of your mind; for the predominant features of these phases may be those revolving around such life and death. Between these two extremes, it is salutary to have that vision of mortality on front of you.

The most important aspect of product life-cycles (PLC) is, however, that to all practical intents and purposes they often do not exist! In most markets the majority of the major (dominant) brands have held their position for at least two decades. The dominant product life-cycle, that of the brand leaders which almost monopolize many markets, is therefore one of continuity![8]

---

[8] D. Mercer, A two decade test of product life cycle theory, *British Journal of Management*, vol. 4 (1993).

In their much respected criticism of the product life-cycle, Dhalla and Yuspeh[9] state:

> . . . clearly, the PLC is a dependent variable which is determined by market actions; it is not an independent variable to which companies should adapt their marketing programs. Marketing management itself can alter the shape and duration of a brand's life cycle.

Thus, the life-cycle may be useful as a description, but not as a predictor; and usually it should be firmly under the control of the marketer! *The important point is that in many, if not most, markets the product or brand life-cycle is significantly longer than the planning cycle of the organizations involved. It thus offers little of practical value for most marketers.*[10] Even if the PLC exists for them, their plans will be based just upon that piece of the curve where they currently reside (most probably in the 'mature' stage); and their view of that part of it will almost certainly be 'linear', and will not encompass the whole range from growth to decline.

I have included the above section on the Product Life Cycle despite the fact that – as you no doubt detected – I think that it has little value in practice. Indeed, I believe that its use may be positively dangerous for many organizations since it tempts managers of successful, mature brands to prematurely anticipate their move into decline. *But it is probably the most widely known, and taught and respected, piece of marketing theory!* It is imperative, therefore, that you appreciate the problems that its use, in any form, might pose.

How, then, might you manage change? At one extreme, seeing fractures in advance, or even recognizing their implications after they have occurred, is very difficult. This is best handled by '*scanning*', described in the later chapter (13) on the 'External Environment'. Responding to them once they have been detected is perhaps best ensured by undertaking the most effective possible marketing – better than that of other organizations which might also attempt to take advantage of the fracture – and, most important of all, reacting much faster than these competitors.

The Competitive Saw

Handling the less dramatic changes which regularly occur in the *stable* market – and are the staple diet of most marketers – is a different matter. These are dealt with especially poorly by the PLC. The technique which has accordingly been

[9] Nariman K. Dhalla and Sonia Yuspeh, Forget the product life cycle concept, *Harvard Business Review* (January–February 1976).

[10] D. Mercer, A two decade test of product life cycle theory.

developed, as a positive alternative to ineffective use of the PLC in this ('Mature') range, is called the '*Competitive Saw*';[11]

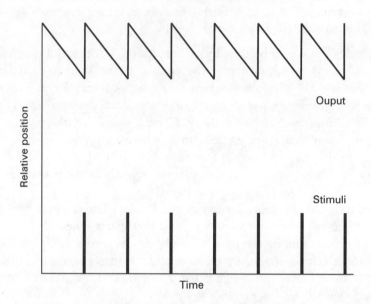

THE COMPETITIVE SAW

The principles involved are very simple, as indicated by the chart above. The first is quite simply that every 'stimulus' (every investment, be it an advertising or promotional campaign or a new feature added to the 'product') results, after a short delay, in a rapid improvement in 'output', raising the product or service's position (typically directly in terms of its competitive position, and indirectly in terms of sales levels). The second principle is that this advantage is then steadily diluted as competitors invest in their own activities, and the performance level (the competitive advantage or sales) slowly drops until the next stimulus is applied. Because of the competitive aspect and because it largely removes variations due to seasonality etc., the measurements are usually in terms of relative share (though absolute figures may also be used).

This is a very simplified model of what actually happens, though something approaching it can be observed in practice (in the way that, for instance, advertising agencies routinely track the impact of advertising campaigns on awareness levels), which is not the case with the Product Life Cycle which it replaces. Despite its simplicity, it offers a number of significant benefits:

INTIMATIONS OF MORTALITY – it very effectively replaces the one important function of the Product Life Cycle, that of reminding managers that there will be no

---

[11] D. Mercer, Death of the product life cycle, *ADMAP* (September 1993).

future if they do not look after their brands, and continue to invest in them – but it does this more directly and practically, without the major drawbacks inherent in the PLC model.

TIMESCALING – on much the same theme, it is an ever-present reminder that you cannot neglect your brands, or stop investing in them, for too long – especially during the very extended 'maturity' phase of a successful brand.

LINKAGE OF INPUTS AND OUTPUTS – it encourages, and provides a framework for, managers to actively plan what inputs are needed, when, and what the outputs will be; and what the efficiency of conversion of inputs to outputs is.

SURFACING OF INVESTMENT – it makes very clear the need for, and the results of, investment policies on brands.

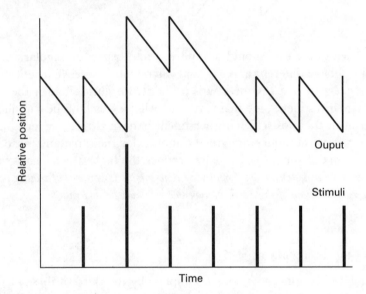

This becomes even more clear in the '*Stepped Saw*'.

The '*Stepped Saw*' looks at the effect of *major* inputs, major investments (such as new products or significantly increased promotional spending). These may have the effect of raising the average level of the 'saw teeth'; though, as shown above, later neglect (or a comparably strong competitive response) can just as easily result in a step down to a lower average level.

As the '*Stepped Saw*' illustration shows, there are two elements to performance. One is the average level; averaged over the short timescales that normally are reported on by the Competitive Saw. This is strategically most important since it shows longer-term trends (a slowly decreasing average might be hidden by the variations in the short-term saw). The other is the pattern of the saw itself, the time intervals and the performance variation per cycle, which determines the tactical approach.

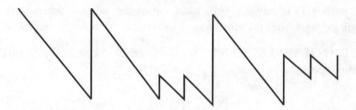

The idea of the saw should not lull you into expecting regularity. Different stimuli will have different impacts, and will be more or less efficient, so the saw will be a jagged one. As the saw is primarily an illustration of the impact of short-term investments, the main criterion will be which of the stimuli available will result in the most efficient investment pattern (which, advertising or new features say, will produce the greatest impact for the same amount of money), though a mix of stimuli will usually produce the highest efficiency overall.

The three main lessons of the Competitive Saw are the importance of relative performance, the time-related nature of this, and the investments which lie underneath.

Marketing depreciation

Adopting the long-term perspective implied by the third of these observations reveals another important implication. Thus, following the implied principle of the fixed asset, the shorter-term sawtooth *maintenance* pattern can be overlaid on a gradually declining trend in performance; this is notionally equivalent to *depreciation* in financial accounting.[12] Thus, over time there may be a slow drift away from the ideal position – as the customers' needs and wants change and/or competitive positioning improves. Your own response to this may take two forms. The first, and perhaps the most effective, is that of '*dynamic repositioning*'. The need for change is regularly tracked and the brand's position readjusted – in much the same way that an autopilot's feedback mechanisms ensure that an airliner follows the correct flightpath. The emphasis here is on the dynamic approach to (current) change – where most of marketing theory revolves around decisions based upon static (historic) positions. If such

[12] D. Mercer, Death of the product life cycle.

dynamic repositioning is not possible, perhaps because the necessary product changes come in discrete steps, then periodic readjustments may be needed. This is where the concept of *depreciation* is especially valuable. Thus, it allows the build-up of reserves to cover the significant costs of such repositioning exercises.

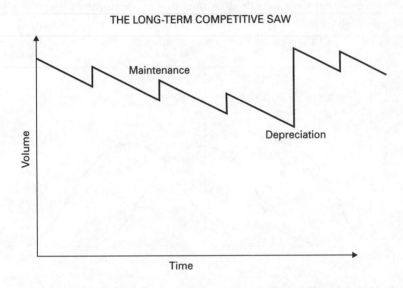

THE LONG-TERM COMPETITIVE SAW

The investment in a successful brand needs to be maintained both in the short term, by regular marketing programmes funded from annual budgets, and in the longer term, by less frequent major investments (in repositioning and relaunching) which require reserves provided by a depreciation fund – Marketing Depreciation.

Encouraged by PLC theory, which seems to emphasize the futility of long-term investment, the long-term asset investment aspect of brand performance is largely ignored by traditional marketing theory. We believe that, on the contrary, it should represent the main element of marketing strategy – and (in view of the dangers it poses for the unwary) the PLC should be dropped from the marketer's vocabulary!

Indeed, our own research[13] has shown that, at least among those organizations where the brand leadership of an FMCG market has been won or lost, the relative commitment of the management and the relative levels of investment were the two key characteristics (rating 4.2 on a scale from 1 to 5); compared with, for instance, price which was rated as the least important factor (with a rating of 2.5).

[13] David Mercer, Winning the brand leadership by uncompetitive means, *British Academy of Management* (September 1992).

Product Portfolios

Most organizations have more than one product or service, and many operate in several markets. In the context of the product life-cycle this theoretically confers the advantage that the various products, the 'product portfolio', can be managed so that they are not all at the same phase in their life-cycle; indeed, ideally, so that they are evenly spread throughout it. This allows for the most efficient use of both cash and manpower resources.

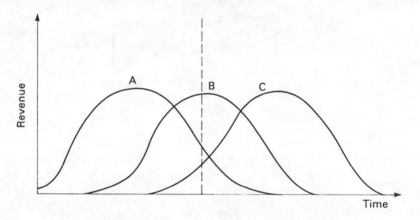

This simple example shows some of the benefits that can be obtained from a well-managed product portfolio. The current investment in C, which is in the growth phase, is covered by the profits being generated by the earlier product, B, which is at maturity. This had earlier been funded by A, the decline of which is now being balanced by the newer products.

An organization looking for growth can introduce new products or services which it hopes will be bigger sellers than those which they succeed. Perhaps an easier, and more likely, route is to introduce more products or services, of equal size, than are being lost – thus increasing the size of the portfolio, and with it the volume of sales.

On the other hand, if this expansion is undertaken too rapidly many of these brands – at the beginning of their life-cycles – will be hungrily demanding investment; and even the earliest of them will be unlikely to generate profits fast enough to support the numbers of later launches. Therefore, the producer will have to find a source of funds until his investments pay off.

The Boston Matrix

As a visual tool for managing portfolios, the Boston Consulting Group, a leading management consultancy, developed its well-known matrix. For each product or service the *area* of the circle represents the value of its sales. The Boston Matrix thus offers a very useful 'map' of the organization's product (or service) strengths and weaknesses (at least in terms of current profitability) as well as the likely cash flows.

The need which prompted this idea was, indeed, that of managing cash flow. It was reasoned that one of the main indicators of cash generation was relative market share, and one which pointed to cash usage was that of market growth rate.

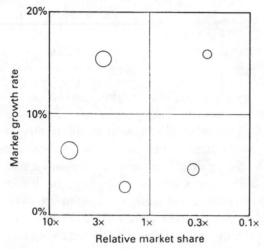

Relative market share

This indicates likely cash generation, because the higher the share the more cash will be generated. As a result of 'economies of scale' (a basic assumption of the Boston Matrix), it is assumed that these earnings will grow faster the higher the share. The exact measure is the brand's share relative to its largest competitor. Thus, if the brand had a share of 20 per cent, and the largest competitor had the same, the ratio would be 1:1. If the largest competitor had a share of 60 per cent, however, the ratio would be 1:3, implying that the organization's brand was in a relatively weak position. If the largest competitor only had a share of 5 per cent, the ratio would be 4:1, implying that the brand owned was in a relatively strong position, which might be reflected in profits and cash flow. If you are using this technique in practice, it should be noted that this scale is logarithmic, not linear.

On the other hand, exactly what is a high relative share is a matter of some debate. The best evidence[14] is that the most stable position (at least in FMCG

[14] D. Mercer, Death of the product life cycle.

markets) is for the brand leader to have a share double that of the second brand, and treble that of the third. Brand leaders in this position tend to be very stable – and profitable; this is the Rule of 123.

The reason for choosing relative market share, rather than just profits, is that it carries more information than just cash flow. It shows where the brand is positioned against its main competitors, and indicates where it might be likely to go in the future. It can also show what type of marketing activities might be expected to be effective.

Market growth rate

Rapidly growing brands, in rapidly growing markets, are what organizations strive for; but, as we have seen, the penalty is that they are usually net cash users – they require investment. The reason for this is often because the growth is being 'bought' by the high investment, in the reasonable expectation that a high market share will eventually turn into a sound investment in future profits. The theory behind the matrix assumes, therefore, that a higher growth rate is indicative of accompanying demands on investment. The cut-off point is usually chosen as 10 per cent per annum. Determining this cut-off point, the rate above which the growth is deemed to be significant (and likely to lead to extra demands on cash), is a critical requirement of the technique; it is one that, again, makes the use of the Boston Matrix problematical in some product areas. What is more, the evidence,[15] from FMCG markets at least, is that the most typical pattern is of very low growth, less than 1 per cent per annum. This is outside the range normally considered in Boston Matrix work, which may make application of this form of analysis unworkable in many markets.

Where it can be applied, however, the market growth rate says more about the brand position than just its cash flow. It is a good indicator of that market's strength, of its future potential (of its 'maturity' in terms of the market life-cycle), and also of its attractiveness to future competitors.

The development of the theory is that, in common with other four-quadrant matrices (such as the Ansoff Matrix, which we have already met), products or services lying in each of the quadrants will behave differently, and require different marketing strategies. As is often the case with such techniques, however, the quadrants have since been given rather exotic names (presumably to improve their memorability – though in practice causing considerable confusion):

[15] D. Mercer, A two decade test of product life cycle theory.

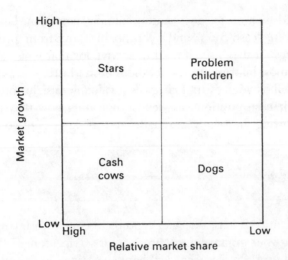

- *Stars* (high market share, high market growth rate). These are probably relatively new products in the growth phase. Because they have high market shares, however, they may be generating sufficient gross profits to cover their current investment needs. Usually the predominant strategy is to grow them to the next stage, the 'cash cow', where the most profit is made.
- *Cash cow* (high market share, low market growth rate). Here the brand has maintained its high share, and hence cash generation capabilities, but the market lifecycle has now moved to maturity and the growth is slow (as we have seen, conventionally below 10 per cent per annum), if at all. Investment is not required to any significant extent, because there is little need to recruit new customers and almost no demand for new plant. A 'cash cow' is, therefore, the main generator of cash, of the profit which will cover the on-going investment in new products.
- *Problem child* (often called the 'question mark' – low market share, high market growth rate). This is a product, typically a recently launched one, which has not yet built its market share. As it does not yet have the share to deliver reasonable profits, it will almost certainly be a net user of cash; possibly substantially so. Such 'problem children' are often where most of the cash flow generated by the 'cash cows' transfers to, but the organization hopes that this will be a good investment; the market is attractive and the 'problem child' could eventually become a winner, as one of its future 'cash cows'.
- *Dog* (low market share, low market growth rate). A product here has little or no prospects. It may not yet be making a loss, unless it is demanding a disproportionate use of overheads, but it will probably do so in the not too distant future. Hence it too should have its future regularly reviewed, so that it can be discontinued as soon as it becomes a burden.

A basic, but hidden, assumption behind the Boston Matrix is the product lifecycle. Thus, following the PLC, successful products will steadily process around the quadrants in anti-clockwise fashion; starting as 'problem children', then moving through 'stars' to 'cash cows', where hopefully they will dwell for some time, and then on to 'dogs' and eventually extinction. Unsuccessful ones will never become 'cash cows', and will probably move from 'problem children' directly to 'dogs', if they are allowed to survive for that long.

One of the most informative uses of the Boston Matrix is to plot competitors' positions as well as your own. This gives a valuable insight into their position (especially their cash position), as well as indicating how they may behave in future and showing the relative strengths and weaknesses of your own brands.

SELF-TEST QUESTION 5.4

Can you identify at least one 'star', 'problem child', 'cash cow' and 'dog' from among your organization's product (or service) range? Plot them on a Boston Matrix. Predict what will happen to each in five years' time.

Now apply the same principles to all the major products of your organization (or at least, say, the top products). How well balanced does the 'portfolio' look? What does this imply for future development of the organization? What changes are needed to ensure a more stable future growth?

Criticism of the Boston Matrix approach

As originally practised by the Boston Consulting Group, the matrix was undoubtedly a useful tool, in those few situations where it could be applied, for graphically illustrating cash flows. If used with this degree of sophistication its use would still be valid. However, later practitioners have tended to over-simplify its messages. In particular, the later application of the names ('problem children', 'stars', 'cash cows' and 'dogs') has tended to overshadow all else – and is often what most students, and practitioners, remember.

This is unfortunate, since such simplistic use contains at least two major problems:

● *Minority applicability.* The cash flow techniques are only applicable to a very limited number of markets (where growth is relatively high, and a definite pattern of product life-cycles can be observed, such as that of ethical pharmaceuticals). In most markets, its use may give misleading results.

Morrison and Wensley[16] succinctly sum the issue up as '. . . the Boston Box was a technique for a season rather than one "for all seasons".'

---

[16] Alan Morrison and Robin Wensley, Boxing up or boxed in: a short history of the Boston Consulting Group Share/Growth Matrix, *Journal of Marketing Management*, vol. 7 (1991).

- *Milking cash cows.* Perhaps the worst implication of the later developments is that the (brand leader) cash cows should be milked to fund new brands. This is not what research into the FMCG markets[17] has shown to be the case. The brand leader's position is the one, above all, to be defended, not least since brands in this position will probably outperform any number of newly launched brands. Such brand leaders will, of course, generate large cash flows; but they should not be 'milked' to such an extent that their position is jeopardized. In any case, the chance of the new brands achieving similar brand leadership may be slim – certainly far less than the popular perception of the Boston Matrix would imply.

As with most marketing techniques there are a number of alternative offerings vying with the Boston Matrix; although this appears to be the most widely used (or at least most widely taught – and then probably *not* used). The next most widely reported technique is that developed by McKinsey and General Electric – a three-cell by three-cell matrix, using the dimensions of 'industry attractiveness' and 'business strengths'. This approaches some of the same issues as the Boston Matrix, but from a different direction and in a more complex way (which may be why it is used less, or is at least less widely taught).

On the basis of a survey of more than 1000 subjects, Armstrong and Brodie[18] conclude: 'detrimental effects of the BCG Matrix (in misleading decision makers) outweigh possible gains (e.g. additional insights, adding structure to chaos) that might be produced when firms use the matrix as a diagnostic aid'.

Boston Consulting Group's Advantage Matrix

The Boston Consulting Group subsequently developed another, much less widely reported, matrix which approached the 'economies of scale' decision rather more directly. This is their 'Advantage Matrix' (figure 5.2), which takes as its 'axes' the two contrasting 'alternatives', 'economies of scale' (here shown as 'potential size of advantage') against 'differentiation' (here shown as 'number of approaches to achieving advantage'). In essence, the former category covers the approach described in the preceding section, while the latter represents the approach (described by Michael Porter,[19] for instance, as well as in chapter 13 of this book) of 'differentiating' products so that they do not compete head-on with their competitors. The result is the four quadrants shown in figure 5.2.

- *Volume business.* In this case there are considerable economies of scale, but few opportunities for differentiation. This is the classic situation in which organizations

[17] D. Mercer, A two decade test of product life cycle theory.

[18] Scott J. Armstrong and Roderick J. Brodie, Effect of portfolio planning methods on decision making: experimental results, *Journal of Research in Marketing*, vol. 11 (1994).

[19] M. E. Porter, *Competitive Strategy* (Free Press, 1980).

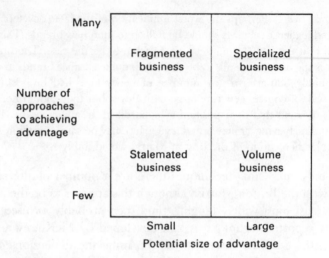

Figure 5.2 The Boston Consulting Group's Advantage Matrix.

strive for economies of scale by becoming the volume, and hence cost, leader. Examples are volume cars and consumer electronics.

- *Stalemated business.* Here there is the opportunity neither for differentiation nor for economies of scale; examples are textiles and shipbuilding. The main means of competition, therefore, has been reducing the 'factor costs' (mainly those of labour) by moving to locations where these costs are lower, even to different countries in the developing world.
- *Specialized business.* These businesses gain benefits from both economies of scale and differentiation (often characterized by experience effects in their own, differentiated, segment); examples being branded foods and cosmetics. The main strategies are focus and segment leadership.
- *Fragmented business.* These organizations also gain benefit from differentiation, particularly in the services sector, but little from economies of scale; examples being restaurants and job-shop engineering. Competition may be minimized by innovatory differentiation.

Apart from the fact that it has not suffered as badly at the hands of later popularizers, the particular advantage of this matrix is that it highlights the assumptions that are hidden in the Boston Matrix. It may also give a better feel for the optimum strategy and the likely profits, but it does not give any feel for the cash flow, which was the main feature of the original matrix.

The strategies that can be developed on the basis of this matrix are illustrated by Rowe et al.[20]

[20] A. J. Rowe, R. O. Mason, K. E. Dickel and N. H. Snyder, *Strategic Management: A Methodological Approach* (Addison-Wesley, 3rd edn, 1989).

ACTIVITY 5.1

Company A	Stars	Problem children
	○ ○	○ ○
	Cash cows	**Dogs**
	○ ○	○ ○

Company B	Stars	Problem children
	Cash cows	**Dogs**
	○ ○ ○ ○ ○ ○ ○ ○	

The Boston Matrices for two organizations are shown above. Each has eight products. In the case of company A they are evenly spread around all four quadrants. In the case of company B they are concentrated only in the 'cash cow' quadrant.

Which organization do you think is better placed?

Inherent Dangers

Having now completed our description of two of the most elegant and widely-taught marketing techniques, the Ansoff and Boston Matrices, it is worth issuing a further warning.

Marketing techniques should be the servants of the marketer. They should be used as an aid to the creative decision-making processes, and can never be a substitute for them. Although they may frequently offer helpful insights, they almost never offer definitive answers in themselves.

There is sometimes a desire to look for simple solutions to what are usually complex marketing problems; and, in particular, to look for solutions which incorporate the expertise of acknowledged masters in the field. These desires are not infrequently stimulated by the service providers who offer such marketing panaceas.

The temptations for the marketer can be severe when the techniques are as elegant, and in their own way powerful, as those we have just looked at. Indeed, they do frequently offer a *very* valuable insight (into the issues of portfolio planning, for example).

In all cases, however, the wise marketer will recognize that such techniques usually offer just one perspective on the problem. The marketer should always consider other perspectives; which are almost invariably available – even the Boston Consulting Group has several. In any case, as we have seen, each of these tools typically has a limited range of situations in which it may be appropriately applied.

Malcolm McDonald[21] summarizes the position when he says 'not only are most of the tools and techniques themselves inherently complex (and therefore misunderstood and misused) but no one tool on its own is adequate in dealing with the complexity of marketing'.

The experienced marketer will approach each new situation afresh. In many ways a blank sheet of paper is the most powerful analytical tool. Only when all the options have been examined should it be decided which of the specific tools available, if any, is most suitable. That marketer will then use these chosen tools in the most appropriate manner, as part of the overall approach. *There is no one tool that offers a universal answer to all marketing problems.* Undue attention to any one individual tool can distract the marketer from the range of other factors which may apply. The myopia this can cause is particularly well illustrated by the dangers inherent in ill-informed use of the Boston Matrix. The apparent implication of its four-quadrant form is that there should be balance of products or services across all four quadrants; and that is, indeed, the main message that it is intended to convey. Thus, money must be diverted from 'cash cows' to fund the 'stars' of the future, since 'cash cows' will inevitably decline to become 'dogs'. There is an almost mesmeric inevitability about the whole process. It focuses attention, and funding, on to the 'stars'. It presumes, and almost demands, that 'cash cows' will turn into 'dogs'.

The reality is that it is only the 'cash cows' that are really important – all the other elements are supporting actors. It is a foolish vendor who diverts funds from a 'cash cow' when these are needed to extend the life of that 'product'. Although it is necessary to recognize a 'dog' when it appears (at least before it bites you) it would be foolish in the extreme to create one in order to balance up the picture. The vendor, who has most of his (or her) products in the 'cash cow' quadrant, should consider himself (or herself) fortunate indeed, and an excellent marketer; although he or she might also consider creating a few 'stars' as an insurance policy against unexpected future developments and, perhaps, to add some extra growth.

Returning to activity 5.1, the chances are that 80 per cent of you would have chosen company A, because of the evenly balanced spread of products. Even the 20 per cent of you that chose company B would have probably felt nervous about that choice. Yet, as you should now realize, the clear choice has to be company B. Think of it in terms of the eight 'cash cows'. Which two would you want to downgrade to become only 'stars', which to problem children – and which would you want to destroy by making them 'dogs'? Of course, the question over-

[21] Malcolm H. B. McDonald, Strategic marketing planning: a state of the art review, *Marketing Intelligence and Planning*, vol. 10, no. 4 (1992).

simplified the position. It did not specify the size of the brands (a 'star' the same size as a 'cash cow' might be preferable, since it will presumably grow).

The real lesson is that the Boston Matrix is useful as a tool to do a certain job. It should, for example, remind the owners of company B to invest in some new products, so that they may become 'stars' and then 'cash cows', to underwrite an uncertain future. On the other hand, it should not distract attention from the much more important task of maintaining the 'cash cows' so that they *do not* turn into 'dogs'; and the money stripped out to fund new developments should never be at the expense of the future of those existing 'cash cows'.

Igor Ansoff,[22] almost alone amongst writers of textbooks, issues this warning about the need to understand what is being measured:

> . . . before the BCG matrix is used, it is essential to make sure that the future prospects are adequately measured by volume growth and the firm's relative competitive position by its relative market share. When the conditions are right, the BCG has the advantage of simplicity . . .

Marketing Myopia

One of the most important marketing papers ever written was that on 'Marketing Myopia' by Theodore Levitt.[23] Some commentators have even gone as far as to suggest that its publication marked the beginning of the modern marketing movement in general. Its theme was that the vision of most organizations was constricted in terms of what they, too narrowly, saw as the business they were in. It exhorted CEOs to re-examine their corporate vision, and redefine their markets in terms of wider perspectives.

It was successful in its impact because it was, as with all of Levitt's work, essentially practical and pragmatic. Organizations found that they had been missing opportunities which were plain to see once they adopted the wider view. The impact of the paper was indeed dramatic. The oil companies (which represented one of his main examples in the paper) redefined their business as energy rather than just petroleum; although Shell, which embarked upon an investment programme in nuclear power, subsequently regretted this course of action – even good ideas can sometimes lead to unforeseen, and costly, problems.

Indeed, this point can also be used to illustrate the dangers inherent in any 'management fashion'. Peter Spillard[24] comments, rather critically, that:

> Following the lead given by Levitt in his over-popular writings on myopia of one kind or another, marketers faced with market shifts have been only too ready to

[22] H. I. Ansoff, *Implanting Strategic Management* (Prentice-Hall, 1984).

[23] T. Levitt, Marketing myopia, *Harvard Business Review* (July–August 1960).

[24] P. Spillard, Ansoff revisited: logic, commitment and strategies for change, *The Marketing Digest*, ed. M. J. Thomas and N. E. Waite (Heinemann, 1988).

respond by chasing them uncontrollably wherever they might lead. They have ascribed objectives to their organizations *in toto* which they probably would not have espoused had they thought about them carefully.

In the wider context, though, Levitt's concept of myopia is invaluable. Even now, too much of marketing is constricted by the narrow vision of marketers using just the few tools they have bothered to learn. The world is a large place and it cannot be limited by a few crude rules-of-thumb – no matter how expert, or charismatic, their inventors!

SELF-TEST QUESTION 5.5

This will be a rather unfair set of questions; but it does reflect the problems caused by the apparent strength of the PLC and Boston Matrix theories.

Look at your answers to the previous two audits (5.3 and 5.4). In the light of the last two sections (which indicated uncritical application of these theories) how would you now change your answers? What does this say about the influence of management theory?

In the light of this new 'realism', what would you now propose for your organization?

Product (or Service) Mix

There are other dimensions on which the 'product' portfolio, 'the *product mix*', can be balanced. Classically, the two most important are:

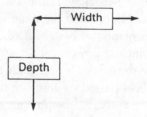

- *Width.* The number of different (independent and distinct) 'product' lines carried; this is a measure of the number of different *markets* addressed. Thus, Unilever has a very wide range of product types (covering Birds Eye frozen foods as well as Persil detergent) but Coca-Cola for many years had a very narrow range (based on just the one product).

- *Depth.* This refers to the total number of products carried, across all the product lines, and thus relates to the market *segments* addressed. These may be very simply defined segments; where a range of pack sizes (from 'trial size' to 'jumbo economy') can address the differing value needs of consumers. Alternatively, they may be carefully targeted brands, such as Unilever uses in the detergent market, precisely aimed at different segments of a very large market.

The balance of the product mix also concerns the *volumes* achieved by the different lines. What may appear to be a wide and deep portfolio may be an illusion if just one product within it produces 90 per cent of the total sales. The same is true, and is more frequently found, in relation to profit. A sound product portfolio (or product mix) will show a balanced profit contribution from a number of lines (although, as predicted by the Pareto 80:20 Rule, it will be likely even then that a minority of products will contribute most of the profit).

The other major overall 'product' decision will therefore be on portfolio size, 'product line' width and depth. How many items are to be carried, in what markets and segments? If too few lines are carried then sales opportunities will be missed. By adding a variation on an existing line, a different pack size for example, additional sales will be created; and the additional revenue created will be greater than the additional costs, so that these extra sales will generate extra profit. On the other hand, there is a tendency for product lines to grow in size, to the point at which some products in the list will actually make a loss.

There are, therefore, two types of product mix decision to be taken in this context:

- line stretching – additional items need to be added to tap potentially profitable extra business
- line rationalization – items need to be removed, to reduce costs and improve profitability

SELF-TEST QUESTION 5.6

What is the width and what is the depth of your organization's product line?
Does it need to be stretched or rationalized, and if so, how?

The Product Plan

It is at this stage, having decided upon the 'position' of the brand (which in real life represents a variety of decisions covering a rich mix of attributes, tangible and intangible) as well as the 'product' and portfolio combinations, that the product plan should be prepared in order to document the strategy and proposed implementation deriving from these ideas. Many managers see marketing's most important contribution to be that of integrating the different activities of the organization (internally just as much as externally). Bringing together a product plan is a classical example of this integrative process.

I do not propose to detail the formal process at this stage, since it is a variation (containing rather fewer elements) of the marketing plan, which is described in some detail in chapter 14. It is important to note, however, that the product plan should be brought together at this earlier stage, and incorporated in the overall marketing plan later; all the separate elements of that overall plan (promotion and pricing plans as well) are usually best developed separately, before being finally combined.

SELF-TEST QUESTION 5.7

Now for another major exercise. Although it will not necessarily follow the detailed format of a formal product plan, you should now bring together the various elements that make up the product/service strategy, which you have started to develop in the context of the theories and techniques explored in the last two chapters.

First you need to collect the answers you have given to the questions about the market, including:

- What is the market?
- Is it segmented, and how are you (or will you be) targeting the chosen segments?
- What is your (brand) positioning strategy? How does this need to change to match the latest circumstances?
- How well is the product or service branded? Does this need attention?

Then you should bring together the product or service strategies you explored, using Ansoff, PLC, Boston Matrix and Advantage Matrix.

How useful have these techniques proved to be in the case of your product or service? Is there any marketing myopia to be found? What is, or should be, the specification? What implications are there for quality?

Packaging

In its most basic sense, packaging is simply necessary to deliver a product to the consumer in sound condition. This requirement may demand a bottle for a shampoo, or a box with moulded shock-absorbing padding to protect delicate electronic goods. The requirement here is purely technical; the container has to be designed to be most efficient at containing and protecting the product. This requirement most obviously predominates in the fibre-board 'shipping outers' or 'cases' which are used to protect the product, or to hold numbers of packs, during delivery to retailers. Even here, though, the 'case' is increasingly being used as a vehicle for advertising just in case a customer might see it and be swayed by the message printed on it.

In recent years, particularly as 'self-service' has become a predominant feature in most distribution chains, the packaging of a product has become a major element of the promotion of that product. It is often the supplier's only opportunity, at the point of sale, to present the benefits of the product to the potential consumer who has picked it up to evaluate its potential value. Packaging requirements, therefore, include:

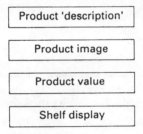

Product 'description'

Product image

Product value

Shelf display

- *Product 'description'.*   The pack must convey to the potential consumer not just what the product is, but what it does in terms of the benefits it offers – the promotional message. This may be conveyed by the words, but for the most impact the graphics and overall design are usually chosen to deliver the main, initial messages. The potential buyer is expected to read these messages in a few brief seconds, and probably at a distance of three feet or more.
- *Product image.*   It must also at least match the required image; so that the boxes for expensive chocolates look expensive in themselves – so much so that one almost hates the waste of throwing the packaging away.
- *Product value.*   The pack is often designed to make its contents look more than they really are. Those apparently 'artistic' designs, for example those which feature 'cut-outs' for use as handles, are frequently chosen to give a bigger outline without using extra product; in the hole for the 'handle' the supplier is selling 'air'.
- *Shelf display.*   Alternatively, the pack may be designed to make the most of the shelf space available; so this may even mean making the pack as compact as possible, so that more may be placed on the shelf. 'Stackability', so that the shelf can take several layers of product, is another possible pack feature.

These are all promotionally-based design decisions. It should never be forgotten, though, that the formal pack description, typically on the label, must conform to any legislative standards for the product category, particularly in terms of the list of ingredients.

It should also be noted that some packaging represents an important element of the physical product itself. Thus, it delivers pharmaceuticals in tamper-proof and child-proof containers for dispensing exact quantities; and occasionally with built-in applicators, such as inhalers. Built-in handles allow 'giant economy' packs to be carried, albeit with difficulty. The package also delivers the aerosol spray of the hair product or deodorant; and, again, it adds the stripe to toothpaste.

SELF-TEST QUESTION 5.8

How does your own organization's 'packaging' match up against the product description, product image, product value and shelf display headings? What changes would you suggest?

Services

At the beginning of this book, I confidently stated that much of marketing activity could be just as easily applied to services as to tangible products – with just the word 'service' inserted instead of 'product'. This clearly poses most difficulty when it comes to the element of 'product' itself. Packaging, for example, does not appear to be relevant to services; although the very handsomely produced printed portfolios which now accompany the purchase of some services (from a financial service to a holiday) indicate that many service providers find that even this element has a role to play.

Service Categories

'Service', though, is a very general classification, which covers a spectrum of activities, ranging from services that support products to pure services that stand by themselves:

- *Services related to a physical product.*   The more complex products, such as computers, demand sophisticated support services. In cases such as these, service elements are ultimately as important (and as costly) as the physical product itself; although, typically, customers still continue to think in terms of the physical product as being the dominant element.

- *Services with a product attached.* On the other hand, some services (which are clearly seen as such by consumers) revolve around products. The home security service is based upon physical intruder alarms and smoke detectors, for example, but many householders will be happy to pay for a consultant to design and fit them; and they will expect a large part of the cost to be accounted for by the 'people' cost (design and fitting) associated with the service.
- *Pure services.* Then, of course, there are some services which can reasonably be described as 'pure'; consultancies are one obvious example.

A widely reproduced diagram by Shostack[25] clearly illustrates the spectrum of product/service mixes (figure 5.3). Within these overall categories there are other dimensions which may also be used to categorize services:

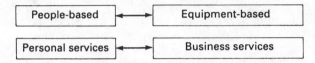

Each of these dimensions has implications for the related 'product'.

A further dimension which can be applied to services is that of *when* the service is supplied:

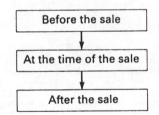

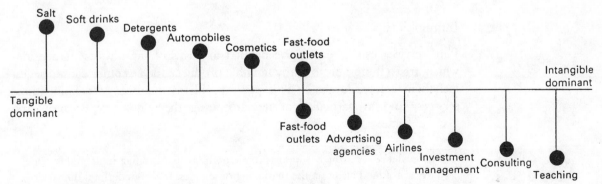

Figure 5.3 The spectrum of products and services.

[25] G. L. Shostack, Breaking free from product marketing, *Journal of Marketing*, vol. 41, no. 2 (1977).

- *Before the sale.*   Some products (such as fitted kitchens) require a substantial investment of service support *before* the sale can be made. Thus, for example, designs may need to be prepared, technical advice proffered or quotations submitted (and, on the larger scale, tenders drawn up).
- *At the time of the sale.*   This usually represents the service that the distribution chain offers, and the added value that this represents. It may be related to the physical product; for example, stockholding so that the product is immediately available. On the other hand, it may once more relate to technical advice.
- *After the sale.*   This element relates to after-sales support, which is traditionally seen as the main element of (product) service support.

SELF-TEST QUESTION 5.9 (for service providers only)

Using the categories listed above (and any others which may be relevant) categorize your organization's services.

Distinctive Features of Services

There are some distinctions which may apply to services, as opposed to products:

Intangibility	Inseparability
Variability	Perishability

Intangibility

Pure services usually cannot be defined in terms of the physical dimensions which are so important to many tangible products; the customer cannot see or feel them before purchase. This poses problems in terms of defining these services, and in particular of demonstrating their 'quality'. Rushton and Carson[26] state:

> The evidence ... strongly supports the hypothesis that product intangibility does have a profound effect on the marketing of services. It also underlines the lack of

[26] A. M. Rushton and D. J. Carson, The marketing of services: managing the managers, *European Journal of Marketing*, vol. 23, no. 8 (1989).

guidance for service marketers in tackling problems, and capitalising on the opportunities, created by having a product which is predominantly intangible ... The lack of knowledge and control is reflected in inadequate and sometimes inappropriate use of generalised tools of marketing such as conservative and often unsuitable pricing policies, and promotional methods and messages which are confused and which frequently focus on the fringe areas of the product package simply because they are tangible.

Indeed, the customer for many services has to buy them 'on trust', since they cannot be inspected before use. This also means that service consumers are often 'loyal' to the service which they have found justifies their trust. The competitive suppliers' investment in overcoming that loyalty may be correspondingly higher than in product markets, where trial use is more easily obtainable. The result is often that, as indicated in the quotation above, the few 'tangible' elements that are associated with the service become especially important:

| People |
| Place |

| Promotion |
| Branding |

People.   People are often the most tangible evidence of quality, from the face-to-face salesman selling financial services in the customer's home to the counter clerk in the travel agency. In many fields the service *is* the people, and in others the people are often the critical element in its successful delivery. In the hotel and catering trades it is people who make the difference between the good and the bad – and yet, paradoxically, they are traditionally grossly underpaid.

Place.   Where there are local centres for delivering the service (bank branches or travel agents, for example), the premises themselves become a means of demonstrating the quality of the service.

Promotion.   The image of the service, carried by all the promotional material, may well become the main ingredient after people.

Branding.   Above all, suppliers of services have considerable difficulty in differentiating their 'product' from all others. Even if they do manage to find a unique feature, it is likely to be copied rapidly. As a result, the larger service suppliers tend to rely on 'branding', typically using the company name.

Intangibility	Inseparability
Variability	Perishability

Inseparability

Generally speaking, production and consumption of services are inseparable; the 'sale' occurs before both (but frequently only just before). This means that distribution usually has to be direct – the service cannot be stocked by a distribution chain. Rathmell[27] graphically illustrates the difference (figure 5.4).

The purchaser of a 'good' has that 'product' in his or her *ownership*, to use as he or she pleases, in perpetuity. The purchaser of a service, on the other hand, only receives the direct benefit at the time it is taking place (although the indirect benefits of, say, a haircut may last longer). Comparison is, therefore, more dependent on the memory of previous transactions.

This also means, according to Grönroos,[28] that there is a need for marketing activities throughout the whole purchase process, or customers may be lost at a number of stages.

Intangibility	Inseparability
Variability	Perishability

Variability

Sometimes referred to in this context as 'heterogeneity', variability occurs largely as a result of the 'people' content, but also because the service is usually produced and consumed at the same time. A hi-fi system or a television can be guaranteed exactly to match the specifications each time one comes off the production line, whereas a service often depends upon who is actually providing it and under what conditions. A performance of *Antony and Cleopatra* at

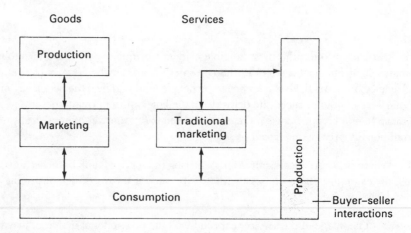

Figure 5.4 The relationship between production, marketing and consumption; for products versus services.

[27] J. M. Rathmell, *Marketing in the Service Sector* (Winthrop, 1974).
[28] C. Grönroos, Designing a long range strategy for services, *Long Range Planning* (April 1980).

London's National Theatre, starring Anthony Hopkins and Judi Dench, has a very different feel from the same play produced by a local amateur dramatic society.

The most important implication is that services require much higher levels, and standards, of management to ensure that the service actually being provided matches the specification; and, indeed, many service-based industries have a higher ratio of managers to employees.

Training also has an important part to play. Japan Air Lines, for instance, give their cabin crew longer etiquette and politeness training than any other airline – and it shows (not least because they now sell their training package to those other airlines).

Perishability

Intangibility	Inseparability
Variability	Perishability

As mentioned above, most services are produced and consumed at the same point, and are totally perishable. The service may be available over time, but if the 'time-slot' is not available, or is not sold, the lost revenue can never be recouped (whereas a product held in stock can always be sold later). Surprisingly, then, 'stock' control becomes even more important for a service provider.

SELF-TEST QUESTION 5.10 (for service providers only)

Which of these features of services are most important to your organization's operations, and why?

How do these problems affect the performance of your own organization?

What strategies are in place to reduce, or compensate for, these problems?

What changes would you suggest?

?

The elements of variability, perishability and people pose problems for productivity, since there are bound to be periods of lower volume when the staff are under-utilized. This is mainly dealt with by scheduling staff to overlap at peak times (or by split shifts, as in the hotel and catering industry, to give the same effect). Use of part-timers, called in at peak periods, or seasonal staff is another approach. A further possibility is to use job flexibility, so that peak-time employees in one function can be redeployed into another (which is not time-sensitive) when not needed in the off-peak; for example, line managers in the hotel and catering industry are often forced to help with the serving at peak times.

Core Services

In many service sectors, a 'package' of services is offered. Within this package there will often be a range of core services, such as the provision of a bedroom for a hotel client, which the customer must use. But there will often be a range of optional services, such as the restaurant or leisure facilities, on which the hotel may hope to make an extra profit (and indeed often hopes to make most of the profit – the core services only recovering the basic overheads). The balance of the various elements of the package, and their management, is therefore a major aspect of marketing in these industries.

Social Marketing

Some marketing, almost always originating in the non-profit sector, is quite deliberately targeted at changing the behaviour of its target audience, without selling any accompanying product or service. Examples have been the various attempts to stop cigarette-smoking or to increase donations to charities. Kotler and Andreasen[29] define this as follows:

> *Social behaviour marketing* is the design, implementation and control of programs designed to ultimately influence individual behaviour in ways that the marketer believes are in the individual's or society's interests.

FURTHER READING

'Product' strategy (particularly that relating to life-cycles and the Boston Matrix) is the life-blood of general marketing textbooks; although their coverage is usually uncritical. The books listed at the end of chapter 1 are, therefore, likely to be the best source of such material for managers in general – although much of it will duplicate what is in this chapter.

In terms of 'service marketing', Donald Cowell's *The Marketing of Services* (2nd edn, Butterworth Heinemann, 1994) provides a comprehensive coverage of the most important differences which are experienced in this field of marketing.

---

[29] P. Kotler and A. R. Andreasen, *Strategic Marketing for Nonprofit Organizations* (Prentice-Hall, 3rd edn, 1987).

SUMMARY

The product or service as seen by the consumer may be much more than the 'physical' core 'product'; hence reference to the 'product package'. The *product audit* is used to explore what this package comprises.

The Ansoff Matrix is one device for looking at the four main growth strategies:

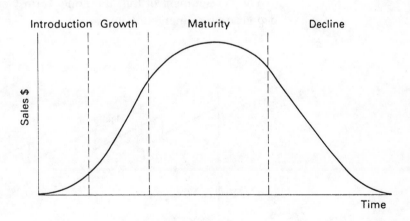

		Product	
		Present	New
Mission (market)	Present	Market penetration	Product development
	New	Market development	Diversification

There is, however, an increase in *risk* as one moves from the known (market penetration) to the totally unknown (diversification).

The most widely quoted, and hence important, theory is that of the *Product Life Cycle (PLC)*, which says that the stages a product (or service) goes through in its inevitable life-cycle are important factors in its performance:

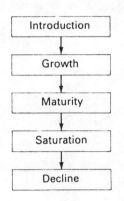

Introduction

Growth

Maturity

Saturation

Decline

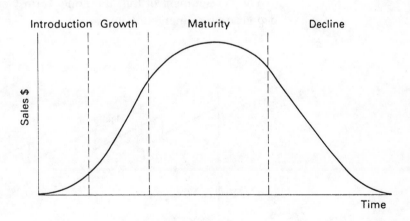

Despite the popularity of the PLC as a theory, most brands are in the maturity phase. PLC theory may, therefore, hold relatively little value for most marketers, except that it offers a useful reminder of potential brand mortality. A more useful concept for stable products and services is therefore that of the Competitive Saw.

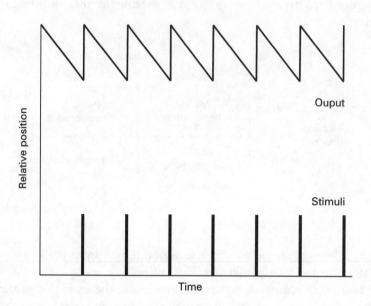

THE COMPETITIVE SAW

The development of this, the Long-Term Competitive Saw, also allows for depreciation of marketing investment.

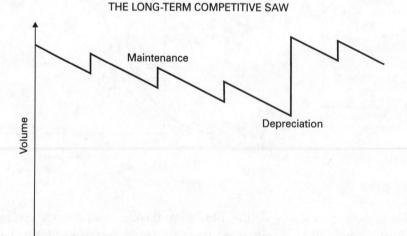

THE LONG-TERM COMPETITIVE SAW

The other popular theoretical tool is the *Boston Matrix*. It is most popularly simplified, and its four quadrants given the following names:

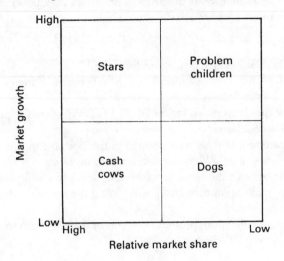

Due to its assumption of a significant PLC and economies of scale, it too may have less relevance than its popularizers might advocate; and the popular names listed above may well be misleading, and lead to inappropriate strategies. In any case, use of the Boston Matrix requires a sound understanding of the complex interrelationship between its *market growth rate* and *relative share*.

Economies of scale, and in particular *learning effects*, were explored by the Boston Consulting Group; they were the basis for its other matrix, the *Advantage Matrix*.

The product or service mix can have both width and depth; it may need line stretching or line rationalization.

Packaging may be as much influenced by promotional factors as by any need to protect the product.

Services, ranging from those which are related to products through to pure services, have distinctive features:

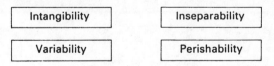

In particular, they are dependent upon people, which means that more, and higher, standards of management are needed. The intangibility means that the associated physical elements (particularly the premises) may be used for promotion; strong branding is usually important.

REVISION QUESTIONS

1 How do you determine what the product or service package comprises?
2 What is the Ansoff Matrix? How is it used, and what risk is involved?
3 What are the stages of the Product Life Cycle (PLC)? What strategy is employed at each stage?
4 How does the Competitive Saw differ from the PLC?
5 How does the Long-Term Competitive Saw reflect marketing depreciations?
6 What is the Boston Matrix? How is it used?
7 What are the problems posed for use of the PLC? What are the problems posed by use of the Boston Matrix?
8 How are economies of scale incorporated in the Boston Advantage Matrix? From where might they arise? What else is taken into account?
9 How can you achieve the requisite width and depth in the product mix?
10 What are the main approaches to quality? What are the main differences between them?
11 How do services differ from products in terms of their key characteristics? How are these differences dealt with?

6 New Products

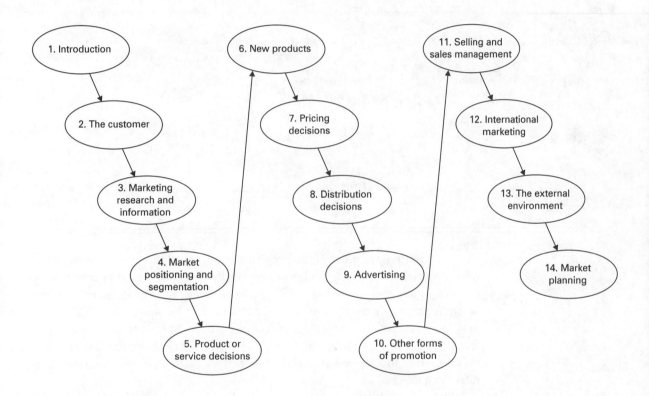

Introduction

In theory at least, the first stage in developing new products or services is to undertake a 'gap analysis', to establish what the new offering will need to provide. This need may well be best met by a 'feature modification' of an existing product or service; most 'new product development' is, in fact, incremental development of existing brands rather than totally new offerings.

Following the usual (Western) approach, a new development has first to be judged against corporate needs, and then against the product factors which the organization can handle. The 'creative' steps of developing new products are also described, as are the subsequent screening and testing stages, to ensure that the – very real – risk is minimized.

Major caveats are, firstly, that brand stability implies there should be more emphasis on the further development of existing brands than on totally new ones – contrary to conventional teaching – and, secondly, that the Japanese approach is to launch many more 'new products' without following any of the stages of testing described here.

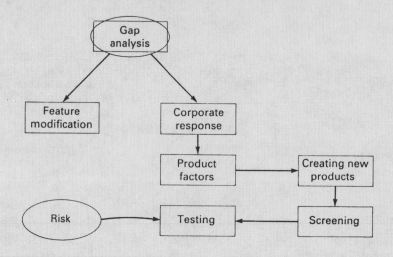

The one common element of life-cycle theory and portfolio management that is uncontroversial – indeed, is almost universally accepted – is that products or services which remain *unchanged* will sooner or later die. The consumers' tastes or circumstances may change, or the product may be superseded. The inevitable outcome is that any organization that plans to be around for more than a few years has to move into the area of 'new product development', even if it is only to redevelop its existing product or service, so that its life-cycle is indefinitely extended.

Indeed, it should be noted that the most successful new product development typically revolves around the revitalization of existing products. Launches of totally new products generate the drama, but the profit is more likely to come from the more mundane relaunches. Rothwell and Gardiner[1] illustrate the point in figure 6.1.

In this chapter, as elsewhere in this book, the term 'product' includes services and non-profit activities. In the service sector, just as in the manufacturing sector, there is a continuing need to develop the offerings that are made to customers or clients, even though there is normally much less activity in terms of new product development to be observed in the service sector.

---

[1] R. Rothwell and P. Gardiner, Re-innovation and robust designs: producer and user benefits, *Journal of Marketing Management*, vol. 3, no. 3 (1988).

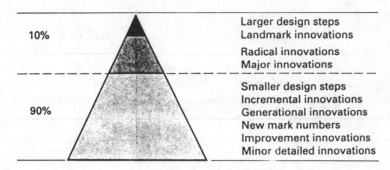

Figure 6.1 Levels of technical change.

Gap Analysis

The need for totally new products or, perhaps more realistically, for additions to existing lines, may have emerged from the portfolio analyses, in particular from the use of the Boston Matrix (see chapter 5). The gaps in the projected cash flow demonstrated by that exercise could have provided sufficient stimulation. More probably, that need will have emerged from the regular process of following trends in the requirements of consumers. At some point a gap will have emerged between what the existing products offer the consumer and what the consumer demands. That gap has to be filled if the organization is to survive and grow.

To locate such a gap in the market the technique of gap analysis can be used. In figure 6.2 the thick descending line shows what the profits are forecast to be for the organization as a whole. The rising dotted line shows where the organization (in particular its shareholders) *wants* those profits to be. The shaded area between these two lines represents what is called the planning gap: this shows what is needed of new activities in general and of new products in particular.

The planning gap may be divided into four main elements:

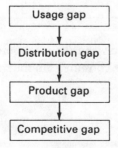

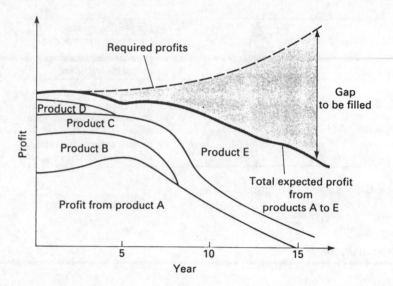

Figure 6.2 Gap analysis – showing the shortfall between required profit and the contribution to be expected from existing products and markets.

The relationship between these is best illustrated diagrammatically:

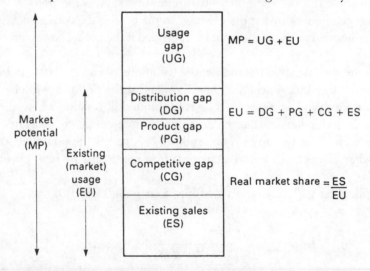

Usage Gap This is the gap between the total potential for the market and the actual current usage by all the consumers in the market. Clearly two figures are needed for this calculation:

- market potential
- existing usage

Market potential The most difficult estimate to make is probably that of the total potential available to the whole market, including all segments covered by all competitive brands. It is often achieved by determining the maximum potential individual usage, and extrapolating this by the maximum number of potential consumers. This is inevitably a judgement rather than a scientific extrapolation, but some of the macro-forecasting techniques, which will be discussed in chapter 15, may assist in making this 'guesstimate' more soundly based.

The maximum number of consumers available will usually be determined by market research, but it may sometimes be calculated from demographic data or government statistics. Ultimately there will, of course, be limitations on the number of consumers. The cosmetics market, for example, is currently limited to most women and girls over the age of 12. But it also needs to be considered whether the boundaries will not shift in the future. Not so long ago the lower age boundary was something over 16 years. Who is to say that men will not at some time in the future also take up cosmetics? After all, they have in recent years taken up the use of perfume, albeit suitably camouflaged as 'aftershave'.

For guidance one can look to the numbers of consumers using similar products. Those wishing to sell the newly-developed compact disc must have paid great attention to the existing sales of record and cassette decks. Alternatively, one can look to what has happened in other countries. It is often suggested that Europe follows patterns set in the USA, but after a time-lag of a decade or so. The increased affluence of all the major western economies means that such a lag can now be much shorter.

The maximum potential individual usage, or at least the maximum attainable average usage (there will always be a spread of usage across a range of customers), will usually be determined from market research figures. It is important, however, to consider what lies behind such usage. One consumer panel produced some very high averages when one of the panel members decided to feed her flock of turkeys on a specific brand of porridge oats: the resulting dramatic increase in usage was not, though, included in the final results.

Existing usage The existing usage by consumers makes up the total current market, from which market shares, for example, are calculated. It is usually derived from marketing research, most accurately from panel research such as that undertaken by A. C. Nielsen but also from *ad hoc* work. Sometimes it may be available from figures collected by government departments or industry bodies; however, these are often based on categories which may make sense in bureaucratic terms but are less helpful in marketing terms.

The *usage gap* is thus:

$$\text{usage gap} = \text{market potential} - \text{existing usage}$$

This is an important calculation to make. Many, if not most marketers accept the *existing* market size, suitably projected over the timescales of their forecasts, as the boundary for their expansion plans. Although this is often the most realistic assumption, it may sometimes impose an unnecessary limitation on their horizons. The original market for video-recorders was limited to the professional users who could afford the high prices involved. It was only after some time that the technology was extended to the mass market.

In the public sector, where the service providers usually enjoy a 'monopoly', the usage gap will probably be the most important factor in the development of the activities; although, as we shall shortly see, the product gap should not be ignored. But persuading more 'consumers' to take up family benefits, for example, will probably be more important to the relevant government department than opening more local offices.

The usage gap is most important for the brand leaders. If any of these has a significant share of the whole market, say in excess of 30 per cent, it may become worthwhile for the firm to invest in expanding the total market. The same option is not generally open to the minor players, although they may still be able to target profitably specific offerings as market extensions – as Amstrad and Compaq did in their original extensions to the PC market.

All other 'gaps' relate to the difference between the organization's existing sales (its market share) and the total sales of the market as a whole. This difference is the share held by competitors. These 'gaps' will, therefore, relate to competitive activity.

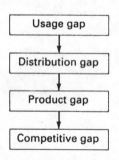

Distribution gap

The second level of 'gap' is that posed by the limits on the distribution of the product or service. If it is limited to certain geographical regions, as some draught beers are, it cannot expect to make sales in other regions. At the other end of the spectrum, the multinationals may take this to the extremes of globalization. Equally, if the product is limited to certain outlets, just as some categories of widely-advertised drugs are limited by law to pharmacies, then other outlets will not be able to sell them. A more likely outcome is that, not being the market leader, a brand will find its overall percentage of distribution limited. The remedy for this is simply to maximize distribution.

Unfortunately, maximizing distribution is not quite as easy as it sounds, except for the obvious market leaders. It is true that additional salesforce effort, backed by suitable sales promotional activities, should be able to increase distribution somewhat, although there will still have to be some balance between the benefits to be gained and the costs to be incurred. But the prime barrier to distribution will probably be the resistance of the distribution chains to stocking anything other than the bestsellers. This can partially be overcome in the short term by offering better terms and higher margins, so that the distributors make more on each sale. But the distributors have long since learned that their biggest profits come from concentrating on the main brands. They, above all, live by the 80:20 Rule.

Product gap

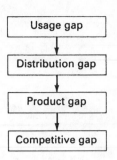

The product gap, which could also be described as the segment or positioning gap, represents that part of the market from which the individual organization is excluded because of product or service characteristics. This may have come about because the market has been segmented and the organization does not have offerings in some segments, or it may be because the positioning of its offering effectively excludes it from certain groups of potential consumers, because there are competitive offerings much better placed in relation to these groups.

This segmentation may well be the result of deliberate policy. As we have already seen, segmentation and positioning are very powerful marketing techniques; but the trade-off, to be set against the improved focus, is that some parts of the market may effectively be put beyond reach. On the other hand, it may frequently be by default; the organization has not thought about its positioning, and has simply let its offerings drift to where they now are.

The product gap is probably the main element of the planning gap in which the organization can have a productive input; hence the emphasis on the importance of correct positioning in chapter 4.

Competitive gap

What is left represents the gap resulting from your competitive performance. This competitive gap is the share of business achieved among similar products, sold in the same market segment, and with similar distribution patterns – or at least, in any comparison, after such effects have been discounted. Needless to say, it is not a factor in the case of the monopoly provision of services by the public sector.

The competitive gap represents the effects of factors such as price and promotion, both the absolute level and the effectiveness of its messages. It is what marketing is popularly supposed to be about. But, as we have already seen, the product or service itself will still be the prime focus of marketing activity.

Gap analysis is a tool to help you examine as thoroughly and objectively as possible your current marketing position and the strategies which you could follow, to improve them in line with overall company strategies. It is very likely to direct you to fresh product or market strategies, and to the need to develop new and improved products.

Market Gap Analysis

In the type of analysis described above, gaps in the product range are looked for. Another perspective (essentially taking the 'product gap' to its logical conclusion) is to look for gaps in the *market* (in a variation on 'product positioning', and using the multidimensional 'mapping' described in chapter 4) which the company could profitably address, regardless of where its current products stand.

Many marketers would, indeed, question the worth of the theoretical gap analysis described earlier. Instead, they would immediately start proactively to pursue a search for a competitive advantage, say.

SELF-TEST QUESTION 6.1

Carry out a gap analysis on your organization's ranges of products or services.

What total gap is there in future profit projections? (In the non-profit sector, what gap is there in the future provision of services for clients?)

Does this come from overall usage, distribution, 'product' or competitive position?

What do you think needs to be done to rectify this gap?

Beyond the Trends

Even the widening of perspective described in the previous section does not, however, cover the major developments in markets which result in quantum leaps, which overturn the long-standing positions in those markets. These brilliant innovations, IBM's development and marketing of the 360 range of computers, which established its dominant position, or Henry Ford's invention of the assembly line, typically cannot be deduced from extrapolation of existing trends (and will often fly in the face of them, to become the subject of derision from more sensible experts).

Indeed, even after the idea has emerged, it often cannot be adequately explored by market research, since the respondents, the general public, have no understanding (based upon previous experience) of what it may mean. Educating the customer is frequently the first objective of such product or service launches.

For instance, as described by Carol Kennedy,[2] even after 3M's laboratory technician, Spencer Silver, had discovered the glue now used on 'Post-It Notes'

---

[2] C. Kennedy, Planning global strategies for 3M, *Long Range Planning*, vol. 21, no. 1 (1988).

and his colleague, Arthur Fry, had made the intellectual leap of applying this to the 'Notes' themselves:

> Conventional test marketing still failed, however, until the two executives took a hand. Enthusiasts themselves for the product, they realized its potential indispensability would only be appreciated if it got physically into the hands of potential customers. They gave away wads of little notepads to secretaries, receptionists, bank clerks and businessmen, saying 'Here, try this', and watched people becoming literally addicted to the product.

The role of the product champion, the executive who drives the development of the product (often against the odds), is frequently a critical element of new product success.

These dramatically innovative new 'products' have had major impacts in a number of markets. Their influence, in these markets, has been vastly greater than that of the evolving products or services: 'supernovas' outshining the 'stars'. What is more, as we have seen, they follow few of the rules of conventional marketing. Even market research is of little use in the basic decisions (although it still is of considerable use in helping to determine the exact details of the launch). The main requirement is for faith in the new development. The most successful organizations try to create the sort of environment in which such creativity is nurtured. They also foster the attitude of mind which will quickly recognize the merits of such outstanding innovations.

As a result of the lack of conventional marketing input to these important new developments, a number of practitioners, as well as some academics, have recently tended to play down the importance of conventional marketing. That is a mistake. With the distorting benefit of hindsight, we tend to notice the few major developments. We do not see the many hundreds of failures, which were just as sincerely believed in by their creators.

Booz, Allen and Hamilton's 1981 research[3] measured the proportions as follows:

NEW TO THE WORLD PRODUCTS (entirely new markets) – 10%

NEW PRODUCT LINES (new products in existing markets) – 20%

ADDITIONS TO EXISTING LINES – 26%

IMPROVEMENTS IN/REVISIONS TO EXISTING PRODUCTS – 26%

REPOSITIONING (existing products in new segments/markets) – 7%

COST REDUCTIONS (similar performance at lower cost) – 11%

[3] Booz, Allen and Hamilton Inc., *New Products Management for the 1980s* (1981).

Booz, Allen and Hamilton also show the role of these new products graphically (figure 6.3).

Above all, it should be remembered that, despite the glamour of the new product process, it is the plodding (steadily regenerated) 'cash cow' which continues to dominate even the 'development' process in most markets.

Product Modification

In practice, most 'new' products are modified existing ones. How many times have you seen a television commercial that tells you 'New Brand X now has added Y!'? Such changes are incremental, often barely even that, and follow

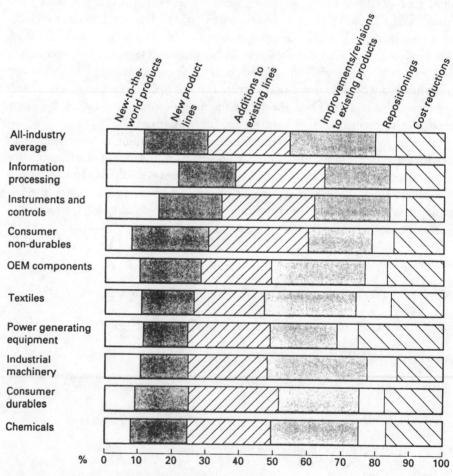

Figure 6.3   Product introductions by industry.

somewhat different rules from genuine new products. Typical modifications may include:

> Feature modification

> Quality modification

> Style modification

> Image modification

- *Feature modification.* Sometimes called 'functional modification', this approach makes changes (usually minor ones) to what the product or service does. Manufacturers of compact disc players added 'programming' and remote control to these basic devices – to make them marginally more attractive to users (but a margin that gave them a competitive advantage).

  Frequently, the main element of the modification will simply be a change in packaging. It may, though, be expanded into the major message needed to rejuvenate a jaded advertising campaign.
- *Quality modification.* As consumers grow more discriminating, many suppliers (often led by their Japanese competitors) have gradually increased the quality of the basic product. This may be more difficult to convey to consumers, particularly if the product already has a bad image. However, it can be very powerful if successful – as the Jaguar Car Company demonstrated in the 1980s and Rover did in the 1990s.
- *Style modification.* This is perhaps the most frequent modification, at least in style-conscious industries (which covers a very wide range, from Coca-Cola through to IBM PCs). An 'old-fashioned' product may be unsaleable in some markets, although it may find a niche in more conservative ones.
- *Image modification.* This may also be associated with style modification (or 'perceived quality' changes), but in essence the product or service itself remains unchanged; and some image modifications may actually stress this (Ovaltine and Bovril in the 1980s, for example). 'Image modification' concentrates on changing the 'non-product attributes' so that consumers feel that the 'total package' has changed. Image is often the most important element of that package.

SELF-TEST QUESTION 6.2

What product or service modifications has your organization undertaken recently? How were these planned and developed? How did this compare with the process used for new products?

How much development effort is expended upon such modifications, as compared with that on totally new products?

How much of the overall business is accounted for by 'brands' regularly modified in this way? How much by recently (within the last five years, say) launched new products?

What 'product' modification plans does your organization make? What should it do?

Corporate Response

Assuming that the gap analysis has shown the need for a specific new product or service, or for some marketing activity to improve performance in some other area, the next stage will be to determine whether such a product or service, or activities, can be 'profitably' developed.

The first consideration will be how it 'meshes' with the existing activities undertaken by the organization. The context for this examination should be that of the formal 'corporate strategy'; the statement of where the organization has decided it is going.

Some of the 'internal', corporate, factors which may, therefore, need to be taken into account in the further investigations will be:

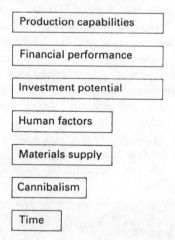

Production capabilities

Financial performance

Investment potential

Human factors

Materials supply

Cannibalism

Time

Production capabilities

Whether the new product or service can actually be produced will depend upon what is available within the organization. Adding extra demand on to equipment which is already being run close to full capacity may either place impossible demands on production or lead to a disproportionately large investment.

The existing plant may in any case be unsuitable, or simply be located in the wrong place. One furniture plant, picturesquely situated in the centre of an old town, was tripled in capacity – at considerable cost – only for it to be discovered that the bridge across the river, which was the plant's only possible entrance and exit, could only handle double the original output. As a result, a third of the expensive new capacity was forced to remain idle.

The limitations on services might at first sight appear to be less serious; although expansion of local branch premises, if needed, may not be a trivial matter. But the constraints imposed by the availability of human resources, especially those involving specialist skills, may prove to be just as severe.

Financial performance

Financial performance is, in large part, what the Boston Matrix is about. The question to be asked is whether the organization can afford the proposed changes. This is not just a matter of potential profits, but of cash flow. The extra investments in stock and debtors, let alone in plant or promotion, may be too much for a strained cash flow or departmental budget to support.

Investment potential

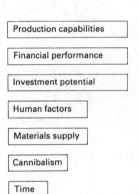

The Boston Matrix relates to cash generation for investment, from internal cash flows. This represents the usual form of investment for most larger organizations; the stock market has declined in importance as a primary source of investment funds. On the other hand, in some situations external finance (now more usually obtained from banks rather than the stock market) will be needed. The standing of the organization with the financial community then becomes an important factor.

This phenomenon is particularly problematic for those medium-sized businesses which are still too small to challenge the major players effectively, but which have grown to have overheads which mean that they can no longer survive as small 'niche' players. New product policy is particularly important in this situation, as are mergers and acquisitions – which may (at least in theory, but not always in practice) offer a more immediate solution.

Human factors

The availability of manpower may also be a factor, and will become an increasingly important one with the demographic changes which are taking place. The chances are that new developments will require skilled personnel, and they might be difficult to recruit. It may just be possible for the existing workforce to be retrained, but this would mean that the marketing plans may have to take the organization's training capabilities into account.

Production capabilities

Financial performance

Investment potential

Human factors

Materials supply

Cannibalism

Time

Materials supply

The availability of raw materials or components, or subcontracted services, may be critical. Producers increasingly depend on outside suppliers for the greater part of the final product or service that they are assembling. Even the insurance broker depends upon the underwriters who will do business with him or her, and the fast food outlet will have a whole range of suppliers – from the wholesale butchers who provide the meat to the employment agencies which constantly cope with the high staff turnover. If suppliers are scarce, or erratic, they will pose major problems.

Cannibalism

One often neglected factor is how much of the new brand's business will come from those of existing brands. Such 'cannibalism'[4] must be taken into account where there is any degree of overlap; and if the organization is building on its strengths there often will be (and should be) significant overlap.

Time

One of the factors often overlooked in any process of innovation is just how long it may take. For instance, IBM may now be able to develop a new feature for an existing product and bring it to the market in a few months, but developing and testing even the simplest complete mainframe is likely to take between three and five years; and bringing in a new technology (a new 'generation' of computers) is likely to need a development period nearer to a decade.

SELF-TEST QUESTION 6.3

Think back to some recent 'products' launched by your organization. How did they match the 'production' capabilities, financial performance, human factors and 'materials' supply?

If some of the 'products' did not match all of these requirements, why do you think they were launched? Should they have been?

---

[4] R. A. Kerin, M. G. Harvey and Rothe, Cannibalism and new product development, *Business Horizons* (October 1978).

Marketing Response

At a more detailed level, the 'mesh' with the existing marketing factors will need to be considered:

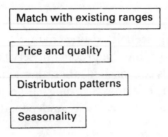

Match with existing ranges

Price and quality

Distribution patterns

Seasonality

Match with existing ranges

'New products' will be easier to sell if they complement the existing ranges. Then they will be able to build on existing distribution patterns, and may even be able to capitalize upon existing awareness and favourable consumer attitudes. The 'new products' may possibly help sell more of the existing ones, because they make the range more comprehensive. A range of slimming foods will benefit from new additions; these offer a wider choice for the consumer, who may have become bored by the narrower selection previously available. They may also obtain a larger display ('facings') at the point of sale, up to the point beyond which the retailer will not stock additional packs.

Price and quality

There has to be at least a rough comparability with the existing products or services, in terms of consumer perceptions of what price (and quality) range the organization lies in. This is particularly true of introducing a cheaper product into a high-quality range. The buyers of the existing range may see this as reflecting a reduction in quality of their normal products; and this may have a disastrous effect overall. It may not even help the new product, for consumers in general may assume that, in line with the price, quality has been abandoned. In the 1970s, following a merger, the then very successful range of Rover cars was drowned in the overall mediocrity of the rest of the British Leyland range – without any noticeable increase in sales of the cheaper ranges.

At the other extreme, adding a higher-priced product to a cheap range will probably not be a successful strategy either; for the obvious reason that it is out of line with the overall strategy, and is unlikely to meet the needs of the existing customers who are, presumably, interested in price. Both the Fine Fare supermarket chain and Fortnum & Mason in the UK were at one time owned by Garfield Weston. He, wisely, did not publicize this link, for the simple reason that it probably would have damaged the sales of both.

| Match with existing ranges |
| Price and quality |
| Distribution patterns |
| Seasonality |

Distribution patterns

Clearly, as we have already seen, if existing channels of distribution can be used then costs will be minimized and the product or service will be built on existing strengths. If new channels are needed, then development of these may pose significant costs, and will lead to a learning curve in the handling of those channels, a factor which is not necessarily understood by management.

Seasonality

The ideal organizational trading pattern is an even one, with no seasonal variation, so that resources may be most efficiently utilized without the unproductive problems posed by having to meet peaks and troughs of sales. A new product or service will, therefore, ideally not be seasonal; or, even better, be one which complements existing seasonal patterns – making its peak sales when the others are in a trough, and vice versa. It was reportedly for this reason that, many years ago, Walls decided to complement its range of ice creams, with its summer peaks, by starting a sausage business, with its peaks in winter.

SELF-TEST QUESTION 6.4

Return to the 'products' you considered in audit 6.3. How did these match up in terms of the match with existing range(s), price and quality, distribution patterns and seasonality?

Again, if some of the 'products' did not match all of these marketing factors, why do you think they were launched? Should they have been?

Innovation is important (indeed essential) to the future of most organizations. However, it must be kept in context. Tom Peters and Robert H. Waterman Jr's[5] well-known exhortation still offers sound advice:

> Stick to the knitting... While there were a few exceptions, the odds for excellent performance seem strongly to favor those companies that stay reasonably close to the businesses they know.

[5] T. J. Peters and R. H. Waterman Jr, *In Search of Excellence* (Harper and Row, 1982).

'Focus', as it is now more fashionably known, is a sound policy. More important, perhaps, is a keen awareness that the future usually also depends on the existing products (albeit so – incrementally – changed over time that they would be unrecognizable to today's customers!).

In this context it is worth nothing that Robert Cooper's research,[6] among 140 companies in Canada, identified five new product strategy scenarios:

- *Technologically driven strategy* (26.2 per cent of firms). A strategy based on technological sophistication, but lacking marketing orientation and product fit/focus. New products ended up in unattractive, low-synergy markets with 'Moderate results: high impact on firm, but low success rate . . .'
- *Balanced, focused strategy* (15.6 per cent of firms). This *winning strategy* featured a balance between technological sophistication, orientation and innovation and a strong marketing orientation. The programme was highly focused, and new products were targeted at very attractive markets. 'By far the strongest performance . . .'
- *Technologically deficient strategy* (15.6 per cent of firms). A 'non-strategy': weak technology, with low technological synergy, yet involving new markets, and new market needs. 'Very poor results . . .'
- *Low budget, conservative strategy* (23.8 per cent of firms). A low level of R&D spending, involving 'me-too' products, but with a 'stay-close-to-home' approach – high technological synergy, and high product fit/focus. A safe, efficient but undramatic programme. 'Moderate results: good success rate and profitability, but low impact . . .'
- *High budget, diverse strategy* (18.9 per cent of firms). A high level of R&D spending, but poorly targeted; new (highly competitive) markets to the firm; no programme focus. 'Very poor results . . .'

The ideal approach, as they identify, is that well-planned one which nicely balances all these factors (which is, in its own way, the strategy towards which this book is building). On the other hand, the authors do seem to dismiss the 'conservative approach' too glibly. This may not have the 'impact' (glamour?) of the other, but if you do not yet know the well-planned, balanced route, better stay where you are until you can find it!

Creating New Products

In the 1960s and 1970s, when marketing was a relatively young profession, it was often claimed that the best new products were bound to be those which were specifically created to meet the needs of the marketplace. This was clearly spelled out by Professor Corey of the Harvard Business School:[7]

[6] R. E. Cooper, Overall corporate strategies for new product programs, *Industrial Marketing*, vol. 14 (1985).
[7] E. R. Corey, *Industrial Marketing, Cases and Concepts* (Prentice-Hall, 1976).

... the form of a product is a variable, not a given, in developing market strategy. Products are developed and planned to serve markets.

Ideally, such products originated with the market researcher discovering unsatisfied wants. It is still held to be true that new product ideas, once they have emerged, should be rigorously tested against the needs of the market, before the organization's full resources are committed.

However, marketing practice has since shown that the really creative ideas can rarely be turned on like a tap, to meet the market researcher's specifications. They come, instead, from every direction, sometimes emerging from the least likely of places. They may come from technical developments in the laboratories (according to one story, the Sony Walkman was created by an engineer for his own fun), they may come from the salesforce, or they may come from practice in other countries or other industries. *It turns out that the secret of finding new products is not to be able to specify them but simply to be able to* recognize *them.*

This means, then, that the managers of new products must be constantly scanning the sources available to them, particularly the literature, to find these new ideas. The need is, therefore, for an open mind: the Sony Walkman was eventually shown to Akio Morita, Sony's chairman, who had the very good sense to back its commercial development. The NIH (Not Invented Here) syndrome is the worst enemy of new product development.

Peter Doyle[8] makes the very sensible point that:

> Perhaps the most common means of building an outstanding brand is being first into a market.

He adds the very important footnote, however:

> This does not mean being technologically first, but rather being first in the mind of the consumer. IBM, Kleenex, Casio and McDonald's did not invent their respective products, but they were first to build major brands out of them and bring them into the mass market.

Customers

By far the greatest sources of new product ideas are customers. After all, they are the users of the product or service; and the new uses they make of it, or the changes in specification they demand, are both the most potent forces on the product development process and its richest source of ideas.

This customer 'information' will normally be received from the salesforce (or even through correspondence). This may be in the form of descriptions of what the customer is actually doing with the 'product' (which may indicate new uses for it), or requests from the customer for specific new products or services.

[8] P. Doyle, Building successful brands: the strategic options, *Journal of Marketing Management*, vol. 5, no. 1 (1989).

Eric Von Hippel's research[9] (into the rather specialized area of innovation in the scientific instruments market) reported that:

> ... in 81 per cent of all the innovation cases studied, we found that it was the user who perceived that an advance in instrumentation was required; amended the instrument; built a prototype; improved the prototype's value by applying it; and diffused detailed information on the value of the invention ...

Von Hippel found that the pattern was repeated in the process equipment industry, but it was not universal (two of his students found that the reverse was true in parts of the polymers industry, where it would have been difficult for users to undertake the development). He continued to make a plea for separating 'all users' into 'routine users' and 'innovative users', with extra effort devoted to the latter (in view of their importance for product innovation).

Innovative imitation

Theodore Levitt[10] points out that, despite the rhetoric, most so-called innovation in the field of product development is actually imitation:

> ... by far the greatest flow of newness is not innovation at all. Rather it is *imitation*. A simple look around us will, I think, quickly show that imitation is not only more abundant than innovation, but actually a much more prevalent road to growth and profits. IBM got into computers as an imitator; Texas Instruments into transistors as an imitator; Holiday Inns into motels as an imitator ... In fact, imitation is endemic. Innovation is scarce.

Peter Drucker[11] also explains the advantages of this principle:

> Like being 'Fustest with the Mostest', creative imitation is a strategy aimed at market or industry dominance. But it is much less risky. By the time the creative imitator moves, the market has been established and the new venture has been accepted. Indeed there is usually more demand for it than the original innovator can easily supply. The market segmentations are known or at least knowable. By then, too, market research can find out what customers buy, how they buy, what constitutes value for them, and so on. Most of the uncertainties that abound when the first innovator appears have been dispelled or can at least be analyzed and studied.

What they do *not* add is that the Japanese are perhaps the most successful exponents of this technique. For instance, as reported by Pascale and Athos,[12] Matsushita deliberately adopts a policy of 'followership'. This has most clearly been demonstrated by the company's domination of the video-

---

[9] E. A. Von Hippel, Users as innovators, *Technology Review* (1978).

[10] T. Levitt, *The Marketing Imagination* (Free Press, 1983).

[11] P. F. Drucker, *Innovation and Entrepreneurship* (Heinemann, 1985).

[12] R. T. Pascale and A. G. Athos, *The Art of Japanese Management* (Simon and Schuster, 1981).

recorder market using its VHS format (together with its Panasonic and RCA brands) to displace the original (arguably more technically innovative) Betamax brand, pioneered by Sony; so that Matsushita now has more than two-thirds of this market.

Sony learned an important lesson in defence from this experience. Only six months after it launched its revolutionary palm-sized camcorder, Matsushita launched an even lighter look-alike. Within weeks, on this later occasion, Sony hit back by launching two new models; one even lighter still and the other with new features. It was able to do this because it had invested in *parallel development* – it had been developing the next generation of product even while it was still introducing the previous one.

Kotler and Fahey[13] provide the wider picture:

> Succinctly stated, Japanese marketing revolves around the management of product market evolution. They manage not only the product life cycle of individual products, but the evolution of a complex of product lines and items. They carefully choose and sequence the markets they enter, the products they produce, and the marketing tactics they adopt.

An alternative approach, still based upon 'imitation', is to find (by market research) what are the major problems associated with existing products in a market, and then develop a product that resolves these (or at least resolves those which are seen by consumers as having the highest priority). However, this approach will not work against the majority of brand leaders, since they can – and should – easily change their own product to counter the new entrant.

SELF-TEST QUESTION 6.5

How does your organization search out ideas for new products or services?

More specifically, think back to one of your company's recent launches (or, better still, hunt out any internal news items about one). Where, from the evidence, do you think the 'product' idea came from?

Having found an idea, how does your organization assess the viability of the new product(s) or service(s)?

With the benefit of hindsight (i.e. what you have learned so far in this module), how would you change or adapt your organization's procedures?

[13] P. Kotler and L. Fahey, The world's champion marketers: the Japanese, *Journal of Business Strategy*, vol. 3, no. 1 (1982).

The Product Development Process

For the purposes of this chapter, the complete development process can be conveniently split into a number of stages:

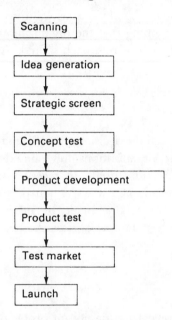

The importance of formalizing the process is highlighted by Booz, Allen and Hamilton's comment[14] that: 'According to our survey results, companies that have successfully launched new products are more likely to have had a formal new product process in place for a longer period of time.'

The first two of the above activities, 'scanning' and 'idea generation', have already been described. The others are outlined below.

Strategic screen

Much of the subsequent process comprises steps which are designed to minimize the risk. Indeed, the very next stage is that of the initial screening of these ideas. The contexts for this screening process are the corporate and marketing strategies. We examined the requirements imposed by these in some detail at the beginning of this chapter. The potential new 'products' which have been found are now simply matched against these requirements. This can be handled as a two-stage process.

[14] Booz, Allen and Hamilton Inc., *New Products Management for the 1980s* (1981).

Qualitative screen

This simply involves qualitative study of the ideas: to examine, at the broadest level, whether they are in conflict with the overall corporate or marketing strategies. This need not demand major effort, since the key characteristics of the new 'product' will usually be obvious, as will those of the relevant parts of the strategies – always assuming that the organization takes notice of its own planning documents. A match or mismatch should, thus, be fairly obvious.

Make or buy

This is also the stage at which the decision either to 'make' or to 'buy-in' is likely to be taken. Traditionally, organizations only offered the products or services which they themselves 'manufactured'. In recent years, on the other hand, many organizations have adopted a wider perspective, and have marketed products (either in part or totally) made by other organizations, because those other organizations had the special expertise necessary or simply because their costs were lower.

Financial analysis

If the qualitative screen reveals no significant problems, the acid test – at this early stage – is to forecast the financial performance of the new brand. The best way to achieve this is to prepare a dummy profit and loss statement, together with the associated balance sheet and the traditional further analyses such as cash flow. With the advent of spreadsheets on personal computers this should now be a relatively simple process; especially if a standard 'skeleton' is already available.

The great potential benefit of such spreadsheets, but one which is rarely capitalized upon, is the ability to carry out 'What if?' tests very easily. This means that there should no longer be any excuse for not examining all of the alternatives.

This carefully controlled approach has generally been successful in the West, where there may be heavy penalties, to brand or corporate image in particular, in backing failures. In Japan, however, the reverse is often true. Rather than screening out potential failures, *many* new products may be launched (as many as 1000 new soft drinks a year, for example). This process, called 'product churning', apparently works well in Japan, because their corporations develop new products in half to a third of the time, and at a quarter to a tenth of the cost, of their Western counterparts. In addition, the Japanese public has been persuaded to accept, indeed to want, new developments at this break-neck pace.

Concept test

Research has shown that more than 80 per cent of new product ideas fail. The proportion which never make it into development is probably at least as high so that, overall, possibly less than 5 per cent of new product ideas are successful. It is important, therefore, that the 95 per cent of failures are culled as early as possible, before large sums are invested in them.

The most widely quoted, and indeed definitive, research has been that conducted by Booz, Allen and Hamilton.[15] Figure 6.4 shows the 'mortality' rate at various stages of the new product process. This shows that, in 1981, only one in

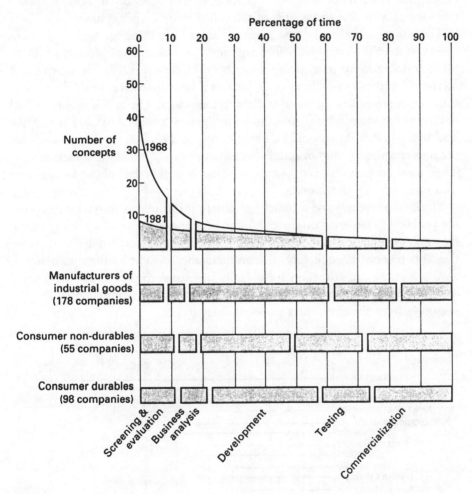

Figure 6.4 The mortality rate at various stages of the new product process.

[15] Booz, Allen and Hamilton Inc., *New Products Management for the 1980s* (1981).

seven new product ideas resulted in a successful new product introduction. It is perhaps even more interesting that this was a dramatic improvement on their equivalent survey of 1968, when the success rate was only one in 58.

It appears that this dramatic improvement may have come about because of the improvement in screening procedures at the earliest stage of the new product process – an improvement which may, in part, have been stimulated by that earlier report. Indeed, in the later report they note that the success rate of new products once launched had not varied (at 65 per cent). Beyond this, their research showed a number of factors contributing to the success of new products (figure 6.5). They also found a significant 'learning curve' ('experience effect'), where each doubling of the number of new products introduced apparently led to a decline in the cost of introduction by 29 per cent.

The 'concept test' is the first true consumer filter to be applied. At least in theory, it should be applied before any significant amount of product development is undertaken; particularly as such development can be very expensive (perhaps hundreds of millions of dollars for a new pharmaceutical). The test is usually undertaken by conventional market research. The aim is simply to find out from consumers what their attitudes to the new 'product' would be; and (the acid test) whether they would be likely to buy it. This is easier said than done, because consumers will not usually be able to draw upon existing experiences. They have enough difficulty communicating how they feel about brands that they have actually purchased.

Market researchers use a battery of different techniques to try to overcome the problem. They may produce dummy versions of the product. More often, they may produce a rough commercial, perhaps just in 'story-board' form, since this also reflects the difficulty of conveying the concept to the consumers – always a major consideration for a really innovative product. The better finished the vehicle used to carry the concept, the more representative are the responses from the consumers involved likely to be.

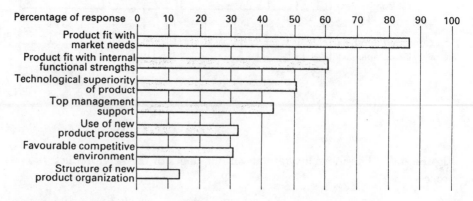

Figure 6.5   Factors contributing to the success of new products.

Despite the lack of precision in any of these techniques, they are useful in weeding out products or services which have little chance of success. This is potentially very valuable since their creators, who have probably fought many hard battles to reach even this stage, usually can no longer be considered to be objective.

Product development

Having a viable concept is one thing, but having a developed product is quite another. Between the two may lie a number of years and millions of dollars of research expenditure. Such development should, ideally, be driven by the product parameters which were determined by the earlier market research (and, in particular, by the outcome of the concept tests). The reality, though, is that product development is often more of a creative art rather than a scientific certainty; and what emerges may only be the best possible approximation to what is needed. Indeed, it is probably true to say that the majority of new products are developed (on the basis of creative inspiration) *before* any market research is undertaken; and the subsequent market research is only carried out to test their viability (and probably to 'justify' their launch).

Devendra Sahal[16] makes the point, however, that:

> To begin with, it is apparent that innovations depend upon a multitude of causes rather than any one single factor at the exclusion of all others. Thus success in innovative activity critically depends upon pursuing several small-scale scientific and technical experiments at the same time. In essence variety in innovative activity is best stabilized through variety in R&D activity.

On the other hand, the most important change to the product development process over recent years, led by the Japanese, has been *speed*. As Ralph Gomory[17] explains:

> One cannot overestimate the importance of getting through each turn of the [development] cycle more quickly than a competitor. It takes only a few turns for the company with the shortest cycle time to build up a commanding lead.

Japanese corporations have reportedly achieved this on the back of a highly-trained workforce, a willingness to build from off-the-shelf components and very close relationships with their suppliers; as well as by approaches such as joint development teams and parallel development. But whatever the reasons, this competitive advantage poses a major challenge to their Western counterparts.

[16] D. Sahal, Invention, innovation, and economic evolution, *Technological Forecasting and Social Change*, vol. 23 (1983).
[17] R. E. Gomory, From the 'Ladder of science' to the product development cycle, *Harvard Business Review* (November–December 1989).

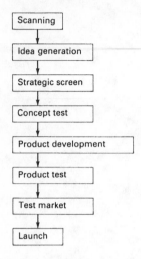

It is worth noting that many organizations in the service sector do not have the equivalent of new product development departments. This may be understandable in view of the less tangible and more transitory nature of their 'products'. It may, however, also represent an inherent weakness in their marketing armoury; it leaves them very exposed to the developments being explored by their more sophisticated competitors, who are learning *all* the lessons of conventional marketing.

Product test

With luck, a workable new product or service will be delivered by the product development team. However, there still remains the investment to be made in the launch itself. To reduce the risk, a further round of testing is normally undertaken. This takes the new product or service and tests it on potential consumers, in much the same way as the concept was tested earlier. The testing may, however, be more detailed now; the output of this research can be used to modify the 'product' itself to best match the consumers' needs.

Test market

The test market ideally aims to duplicate *everything* – promotion and distribution as well as 'product' – on a smaller scale. The technique replicates, typically in one area, what is planned to occur in a national launch; and the results are very carefully monitored, so that they can be extrapolated to projected national results. The 'area' may be any one of the following:

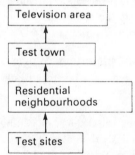

A number of decisions have to be taken about any test market:

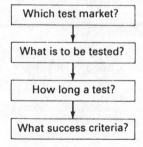

The decision so far has revolved around a simple go or no-go decision; and this, together with the reduction of risk, is normally the main justification for the expense of test markets. At the same time, however, such test markets can be used to test specific elements of a new product's marketing mix; possibly the version of the product itself, the promotional message and media spend, the distribution channels and the price. In this case, several 'matched' test markets (usually small ones) may be used, each testing different marketing mixes.

Clearly, all test markets provide additional information in advance of a launch and may ensure that the launch is successful: it is reported that, even at such a late stage, half the products entering test markets do not justify a subsequent national launch. However, all test markets do suffer from a number of disadvantages:

Replicability.   Even the largest test market is not totally representative of the national market, and the smaller ones may introduce gross distortions. Test market results therefore have to be treated with reservations, in exactly the same way as other market research.

Effectiveness.   In many cases the major part of the investment has already been made (in development and in plant, for example) before the 'product' is ready to be test marketed. Therefore, the reduction in risk may be minimal; and not worth the delays involved.

Competitor warning.   All test markets give competitors advance warning of your intentions, and the time to react. They may even be able to go national with their own product before your own test is complete. They may also interfere with your test, by changing their promotional activities (usually by massively increasing them) to the extent that your results are meaningless.

Cost.   Although the main objective of test markets is to reduce the amount of investment put at risk, they may still involve significant costs.

Risk

It has to be recognized that the development and launch of almost any new product or service carry a considerable element of risk. Indeed, in view of the on-going dominance of the existing brands,[18] it has to be questioned whether the risk involved in most major launches is justifiable. In a survey of 700 consumer and industrial companies, Booz, Allen and Hamilton[19] reported an average new product success rate (after launch) of 65 per cent, although it had to be noted that only 10 per cent of these were totally new products and only 20 per cent new product lines – but these two, highest risk, categories also dominated the 'most successful' new product list (accounting for 60 per cent).

New product development has therefore to be something of a numbers game. A large number of ideas have to be created and developed for even one to emerge. There is safety in numbers; which once more confers an advantage to the larger organizations.

Risk versus time

Most of the stages of testing, which are the key parts of the new 'product' process, are designed to reduce risk – to ensure that the product or service will be a success. However, all of them take time.

In some markets, such as fashion businesses for example, time is a luxury which is not available. The greatest risk here is not having the 'product' available at the right time, and ahead of the competitors. These markets consequently obtain less benefit from the more sophisticated new product processes, and typically do not make use of them at all.

When to enter a market with a new product should, in any case, be a conscious decision. In relation to competitors there are two main alternatives:

- *Pioneer.*   Being first into a market carries considerable risks. On the other hand, the first brand is likely to gain a major, leading and on-going, share of that market in the long term. Pioneering is often the province of the smaller organizations, on a small scale, since their investment can be that much less than that of the majors.

On the other hand, Macrae[20] suggests that one way of entering global markets is that of brand seeding, which is by 'cultivating a brand's myth/fashion among opinion leaders and subsequently transferring these added values to mass markets . . .'. Amongst the examples he cites are Häagen Dazs and Weight Watchers.

- *Latecomer.*   This offers the reverse strategy. The risk is minimized since the pioneer has already demonstrated the viability of the market. On the other hand, the related reward, that of becoming the market leader, may also be missed. The solution to this, as practised by IBM for instance, may be to move into a market

---

[18] David Mercer, A two decade test of product life cycle theory, *British Journal of Management*, vol. 4 (1993).

[19] Booz, Allen and Hamilton Inc., *New Products Management for the 1980s* (1981).

[20] Chris Macrae, Brand benchmarking applied to global branding processes, *Journal of Brand Management*, vol. 1, no. 4 (1994).

as soon as it is proven, and then to invest heavily to wrest leadership from the pioneer before it becomes impregnable. This is not a cheap solution, since all the development work has to be undertaken anyway, and the battle for the command of the new market may be very expensive. Even then it may not succeed, as IBM found when Compaq consolidated its position in the portable PC market (and went on to successfully assault the desktop PC market as well).

To a certain extent this discussion has now been overtaken by events. Japanese corporations have led the way in reducing development time dramatically, and even to halving it in the very mature car industry. To quote George Stalk[21] of the Boston Consulting Group:

> The effects of this time-based advantage are devastating; quite simply, American companies are losing leadership of technology and innovation... Unless U.S. companies reduce their product development and introduction cycles from 36–48 months to 12–18 months, Japanese manufacturers will easily out-innovate and outperform them.

Thus, according to Rothwell[22] at least, 'the ability to control product development speed can be seen as an important core competence'. Paradoxically, Stalk[23] has now described the *problems* caused to Japanese industry by organizations, in their droves, focusing on time as the main – and indeed only – competitive advantage. As he now says – with a rather more marketing flavoured approach – 'Strategy is and always has been a moving target . . . but, regardless of the form it takes, it will remain rooted in a company's ability to connect its customers and its employees in as rapidly interacting and closely knit relationship as possible.'

Accordingly, the choice to pioneer or to follow no longer exists in a number of industries. *The only way for an organization even to survive may be to shorten development times below those of its competitors.*

Product Replacement

One form of 'new product launch' which is little discussed, but is probably the most prevalent – and hence most important – of all, is that of replacement of one product by a new one; usually this is an 'improved' version. The risk levels may be much reduced, since there is an existing user base to underwrite sales (as long as the new product doesn't alienate them – as 'New Coca-Cola' did in the US and 'New Persil' did in the UK). Such an introduction will be complicated by the fact that, at least for some time, there will be two forms of the product in

[21] G. Stalk Jr, Time – the next source of competitive advantage, *Harvard Business Review* (July–August 1988).
[22] Roy Rothwell, Towards fifth generation innovatory processes, *International Marketing Review*, vol. 11, no. 1 (1994).
[23] George Stalk Jr and Alan M. Webber, Japan's dark side of time, *Harvard Business Review* (July–August 1993).

the pipeline. Some firms may opt for a straight cut-over: one day the old product will be coming off the production line, and the next day the new product. Most will favour parallel running for a period of time, even if only because this is forced upon them by their distribution chains. This ensures that the new really does, eventually, replace the old; and it occasionally, as with Coca-Cola, may reveal that both can be profitably run together.

Saunders and Jobber's research[24] shows the length of the average 'parallel running' (table 6.1).

Table 6.1 Time period of parallel marketing

Time period	%
1 week	0
1 month	14
3 months	42
1 year	30
Longer	14

SELF-TEST QUESTION 6.6

Describe the stages your organization goes through in its new product or service launches. It will probably help to concentrate on one or two of the latest launches.

Does it follow all of the stages described above? If not all the stages, which does it follow? Why does it not follow the others?

What improvements might you suggest to your organization in future new product launches?

SELF-TEST QUESTION 6.7

We now come to the next major exercise, that of producing the full product (or service) strategy, including the elements of new product development. This consists of two parts.

[24] J. Saunders and D. Jobber, An exploratory study of the management of product replacement, *Journal of Marketing Management*, vol. 3, no. 3 (1988).

You should already have done most of the work of the first part when you produced the outline product plan of audit 5.7.

In the first part you should spell out the objectives of the strategy: where you would like to see the products or services in three years' time. Where should they be positioned? In what segments? What should be the port-folio, and how should the various life-cycles (if any) be dealt with? What branding policies will be followed? What will be the penetration and brand share targets? What new products or services are needed to fill any gaps?

In the second part you should follow these objectives through into a positive strategy – a plan that states how these objectives should be attained over the three years. Some of the topics which might be addressed across both parts are:

- segmentation (viability)
- positioning
- branding
- portfolio (Ansoff Matrix, Boston Matrix)
- product mix
- service strategy
- new products (launches, development programme)

Non-profit 'New Products'

With many of the commercial pressures removed, and probably with no com-petitive challenges in sight, one might ask why this sophisticated new product process should apply, for example, to the public sector. The answer is that most, if not all, of the elements are just as applicable in the context of making sure that the 'product' is the best possible match to the clients' needs – and that it is the most productive use of resources.

FURTHER READING

Once more, the general theory of 'new product development' (from the market-ing perspective) is covered mainly by the standard textbooks. However, some specific topics are the 'creative' theory behind the handling of new product ideas; for which Edward de Bono, in his book *Lateral Thinking* (Ward Lock Education, 1970), offers a stimulating approach.

The overall topic is also covered, in some technical detail by Yoram Wind in *Product Policy; Concepts, Methods, and Strategy* (Addison-Wesley, 1982).

SUMMARY

The theory of new products (which is traditionally also what new services are called) starts with a *gap analysis* which looks to the following:

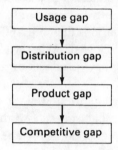

In practice, much organizational development effort is – correctly – devoted to modification of *existing successful products or services*, by:

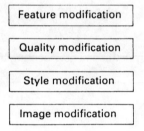

Potential new products need to be screened against a number of *strategic dimensions*:

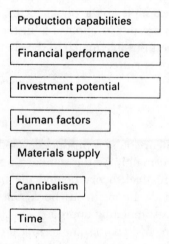

Market factors also need to be considered:

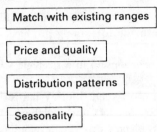

Match with existing ranges

Price and quality

Distribution patterns

Seasonality

Sources for generating *new product ideas* include: customers and innovative imitation.

In the Western approach, the product development process is then supposed to follow a number of formal steps:

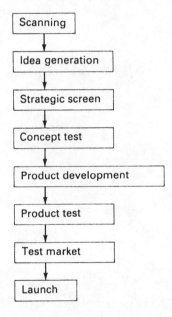

Scanning

Idea generation

Strategic screen

Concept test

Product development

Product test

Test market

Launch

A test market may take place in a television area, a test town or just a residential neighbourhood. In industrial markets in particular, it may be restricted to test sites. All of these pose problems of effectiveness and cost, while possibly offering competitors advance warning.

It is worth remembering the major caveats mentioned at the beginning of this chapter:

1 Brand stability implies that there should be more emphasis on the further development of existing brands than on totally new ones, contrary to conventional teaching.
2 The Japanese approach is to launch many 'new products' without following any of the stages of testing described here.

REVISION QUESTIONS

1 What are the elements of gap analysis? How are they related to each other?
2 What modifications can be made to existing products or services? Why are such modifications important?
3 What dimensions may be incorporated in a strategic screen? Why is each of these important?
4 What market factors need to be screened for? What is the relevance of each?
5 What practical sources of new product are available?
6 What are the various stages of new product development? What happens at each stage?
7 What types of test market may be employed? What are the advantages and disadvantages of each?
8 How do some Japanese product development processes differ from those in the West?

7 Pricing Decisions

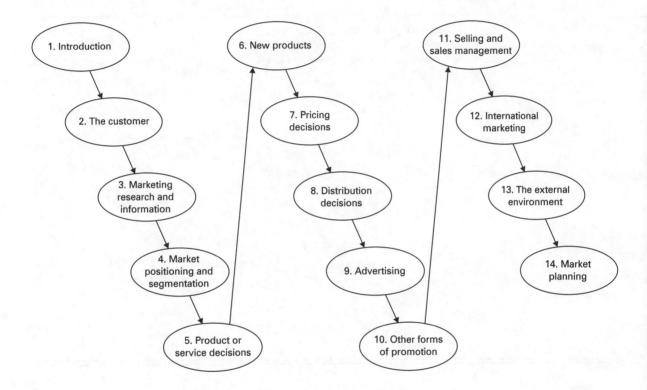

1. Introduction
2. The customer
3. Marketing research and information
4. Market positioning and segmentation
5. Product or service decisions
6. New products
7. Pricing decisions
8. Distribution decisions
9. Advertising
10. Other forms of promotion
11. Selling and sales management
12. International marketing
13. The external environment
14. Market planning

Introduction

The traditional theory of pricing, that of supply versus demand, is developed from economics. As such it offers a useful intellectual framework for the consideration of pricing issues. Unfortunately, most of the parameters needed to apply this theory cannot normally be measured in practice; and customer needs and market factors tend to dominate the more 'practical' marketing theory.

New product pricing, whether to 'skim' profits or to 'penetrate' the market, is a particular form of pricing which poses rather different challenges.

However, much of this chapter is taken up with a description of the various practical pricing policies adopted: from cost-plus and market-based strategies to selective ones. Discounts are also investigated as well as, in some detail, competitive pricing.

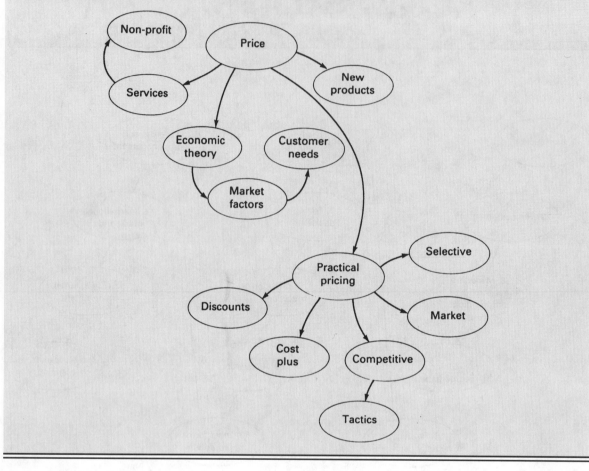

Probably the single most important decision in marketing is that of price. This is partly because price may have an impact on sales volumes. If the price is too high, and the market is competitive, sales may be correspondingly reduced. Indeed, many economists would see price as the main determinant of sales volume. On the other hand, many of the more sophisticated marketers have found ways to reduce the impact of price.

In practice, the main reason for the importance of price is that it is one of the three main variables which determine the profit. Thus, the profit per unit is equal to the price less the total cost of producing that unit:

$$\text{profit} = \text{price} - \text{cost}$$

The third factor is the volume of sales, since the organization's net profit is equal to the number of 'units' sold multiplied by the net profit obtained on each of those units. At this level the mathematics are very simple – but also very important.

A sensitivity analysis conducted by Marn and Rosiello,[1] across nearly 2500 companies, showed that a 1 per cent improvement in price resulted in an 11 per cent increase in operating profit; where a 1 per cent improvement in cost only gave an 8 per cent increase in profit.

Thus, the higher the price can be raised, always assuming that unit costs and sales volume do not change, the greater the profit the organization makes; and many of the most powerful marketing techniques have, therefore, been designed to maximize the price which can be achieved. In practice, the calculation of profit is much more complicated than this simple explanation allows for. The long-term problems caused for the large Australian corporations by that country's relatively loose definitions of accounting have been evidenced by the massive insolvencies that have resulted when reality has caught up with theory. Yet the basic principle still holds – even if it is not necessarily easy to implement!

SELF-TEST QUESTION 9.1

How does your organization set its prices?

If your organization is in the non-profit sector, how does it ration the resources amongst the competing demands, which, in a commercial market, is normally supposed to be a function of the price mechanisms?

Service prices

Most pricing theory talks in terms of products, but for services the potential complication is added that some service providers tend to have different terms for price (admission, tuition, cover charge, interest, fee, and so on). However, the result is exactly the same. The consumer has to pay a price, and the mechanisms for fixing that price are much the same, although there may be some marginal differences, such as:

- negotiation – in view of the variability of the service being offered, there may be more scope for individual negotiation

---

1 Michael V. Marn and Robert L. Rosiello, Managing price, gaining profit, *Harvard Business Review* (September–October 1992).

- discounts – owing to the 'perishability' of the service, there may be incentives to use it at unpopular times (off-peak train fares, matinée prices for theatres, and so on)
- quality – higher pricing, to demonstrate quality (which is usually much more intangible in a service) may be more prevalent

Price and non-profit organizations

Price is an element of the marketing mix which seems, at least on first inspection, largely irrelevant to non-profit organizations. Even so, there are a number of such organizations which (while having charitable status and, accordingly, not being allowed to make a profit) still charge for their services. It is frequently the case that the term 'surplus' is interchangeable in these organizations with profit; and they behave in exactly the same way as profit-making organizations.

However, there remain a large number of organizations (typically in the government sector) where no money changes hands. There simply is no price. Allocation of the service to the consumer is by other means, such as need (determined by a doctor, for example) or queueing (such as in hospital waiting lists). Many aspects of pricing are, therefore, not fully applicable. On the other hand, some of the principles can still be applied if 'price' is replaced by the 'perceived value' to the consumer (discussed later in this chapter). Thus, the consumer still puts a value (often a high value) on the service, and this can be dealt with much as 'price' itself. Certainly, if the service providers are to best match their consumers' needs they should have a good appreciation of the value the consumers put on the service.

As Kotler and Andreasen[2] point out, however, there may be other 'costs' that some of these 'consumers' might be asked to pay, including:

- 'sacrifices of old ideas, values or views of the world'
- 'sacrifices of old patterns of behaviour'
- 'sacrifices of time and energy'

Supply and Demand

Much of the theory of pricing has derived from that of economics. The basic idea, according to such theories, is that 'demand' will be different at each price which might possibly be chosen. In one of the leading economics textbooks, Begg[3] defines it thus:

> *Demand* is the quantity of a good [which] buyers wish to purchase at each conceivable price.

[2] P. Kotler and A. Andreasen, *Strategic Marketing for Nonprofit Organizations* (Prentice-Hall, 3rd edn, 1987).
[3] D. Begg, S. Fischer and R. Dornbusch, *Economics* (McGraw-Hill, 2nd edn, 1987).

Demand is normally, but not always, assumed to fall as price increases. Thus, a *demand curve*, showing the demand at each price, can be drawn:

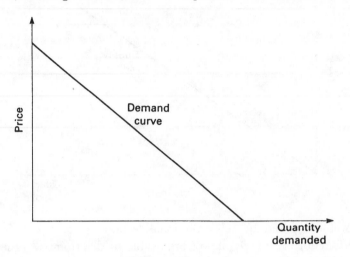

For convenience, the demand curve (with demand increasing as price falls) is here shown as a straight line, but it could follow other paths; and, indeed, is most often shown as a smooth curve which is concave towards the origin, reflecting a constant price elasticity of demand (described below), since demand is normally expected to be inversely proportional to price (that is, the higher the price the less the demand).

Much of economics was, and still is, traditionally taught on the basis of graphical representation, and the graphical approach does make the theory easier to appreciate. In recent years, particularly with the wider availability of personal computers and the presumed increase in numeracy, this approach has been complemented by the equivalent mathematical representation – in this case as the *demand function*. For an explanation, if you are a mathematics aficionado, consult an economics textbook, such as that written by Richard Lipsey.[4] Similar concepts apply to *supply*. Again, Begg's[5] definition, not surprisingly, is:

> Supply is the quantity of a good [which] sellers wish to sell at each conceivable price.

Not unreasonably, supply is expected to increase as price increases (the reverse of demand), giving the *supply curve*. The supply line is conventionally assumed to be straight.

[4] R. G. Lipsey, *An Introduction to Positive Economics* (Weidenfeld and Nicolson, 6th edn, 1983).
[5] Begg, Fischer and Dornbusch, *Economics*.

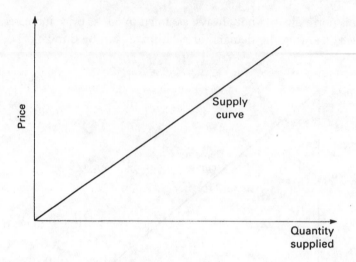

The problem posed by this traditional 'economic' approach is that the 'demand function' is usually almost impossible to determine. As the eminent economist W. J. Baumol[6] said:

> We have seen, then, how difficult it is to find actual demand relationships in practice. These problems are, to a large extent, a consequence of the very peculiarity of the demand function concept itself – the fact that it represents the answers to a set of purely hypothetical questions and that information is taken to pertain simultaneously to the same moment of time.

Equilibrium price

However, if we assume that the function *is* known, and if the two curves (of demand and supply) are superimposed, we have:

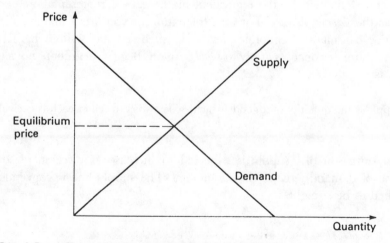

[6] W. J. Baumol, *Economic Theory and Operations Analysis* (Prentice-Hall, 3rd edn, 1972).

This is the conventional graphical representation of the *theory of supply and demand*.

At the *equilibrium price*, the quantity demanded by consumers matches the quantity supplied by sellers; there will be nothing left to sell, nor will there be any shortage – and it is said that the market has 'cleared'. This is the price which will, therefore, be set by the market. Begg's[7] definition is:

> The equilibrium price clears the market ... It is the price at which the quantity supplied equals the quantity demanded.

In economics, therefore, the basis of price is this balance between supply and demand; and price itself is most often seen as the prime determinant of both supply and demand.

The body of this theory was largely developed in the nineteenth century, when the economic wealth of nations was still developing. At that time most of the markets were still almost pure commodity markets, supplying basic essentials, which were undifferentiated; and the consumers' choice was accordingly based on price alone. Their purchasing strategy was to use their very limited funds to obtain the maximum amounts of these basic essentials. This simple approach may still work in commodity markets, where professional buyers purchase identical commodities solely on the basis of price.

In addition, as Webster and Wind[8] point out:

> This price-minimizing model from the theory of the firm, or microeconomics, also assumes that the buyer has near perfect information about the alternatives available to him in the market. It further assumes that competing brands are reasonably close substitutes.

They also take the model rather further, when they extend it in terms of a *lowest total cost model* which:

> ... is essentially an elaboration on the minimum price model [above] in which additional costs (other than initial purchase price) are recognized as significant. This model assumes a goal of profit-maximization and a very well informed buyer. It adjusts initial purchase price to reflect additional costs of the product-in-use ...

This is the 'rational' model used to justify many capital goods purchases.

In recent years, however, the majority of the inhabitants of the developed nations have moved into a period of 'affluence', and the basis for their purchasing patterns, and the associated economics, have changed. One view of this was particularly well described by J. K. Galbraith.[9] In essence, this new view of economics is that most purchasers are no longer restricted to buying

[7] Begg, Fischer and Dornbusch, *Economics*.
[8] F. E. Webster Jr and Y. Wind, *Organizational Buying Behaviour* (Prentice-Hall, 1972).
[9] J. K. Galbraith, *The Affluent Society* (Hamish Hamilton, 1958).

essentials, but can indulge in luxuries. The suppliers of these differentiate them, to the extent that some suppliers can achieve almost monopoly powers over their markets. The resulting price theory is, therefore, much more complex. It is in this area of business that most marketing activities take place; and here there may be more truth in what Kenneth Galbraith says, despite his criticisms of marketing, than in the teachings of some of the neo-classical economists.

Price elasticity of demand

The degree to which demand is sensitive to price is called *price elasticity of demand*. This is often shortened to 'elasticity of demand', although strictly this is incorrect, since economists recognize that demand may also depend on other factors, such as income. Again, Begg[10] gives the classical definition:

> The *price elasticity of demand* is the percentage change in the quantity of a good demanded divided by the corresponding percentage change in its price.

or

$$\text{price elasticity of demand} = \frac{\text{change of demand (per cent)}}{\text{change of price (per cent)}}$$

This simply recognizes that some products or services are more sensitive to price than others. In the commodities market, for example, the demand for your product will be very dependent upon the price you ask; and if you foolishly set the price above that which prevails in the market, you will be very unlikely indeed to sell anything, for the buyers well know that they can buy exactly the same goods elsewhere at lower prices. The demand, or even sometimes price itself, is said to be *elastic*; although purists would once more object, for the reasons mentioned earlier.

At the other end of the spectrum there are those products demand for which is very insensitive in terms of price. Thus, for example, Apple so differentiated its original PCs that they had a virtual monopoly of their segment and could set almost whatever price the company wanted, within limits. Again at the risk of offending the purists, this is often called 'inelastic demand'.

The reason why Apple was still somewhat constrained in its pricing is that, in theory, depending upon the relative prices there can often be switches of demand between various segments or even between markets. Thus if the price of one good (say, the Apple computer) rises too high, some of its buyers will switch to an alternative good (say, an IBM computer), even though this is not a perfect substitute. This is called the *cross price elasticity of demand*:

[10] Begg, Fischer and Dornbusch, *Economics*.

The cross price elasticity of demand for good (i) with respect to changes in the price of good (j) is the percentage change in the quantity of good (i) divided by the corresponding change in the price of good (j).[10]

The point to note here is that a 'good' in this context is any similar product in one market or segment i. The 'good' j is a product in another segment (j). Thankfully, Begg shortens the term to 'cross elasticity of demand'; yet again despite the risk of offending the purists.

Real Demand

For most markets that now exist, however, a more practical demand curve might look rather different from this classical model:

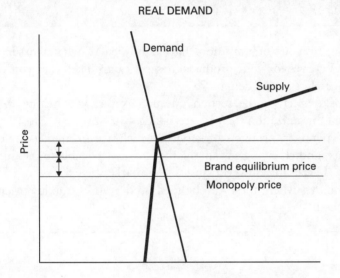

REAL DEMAND

Thus, the typical *demand* 'curve' of most products or services is much steeper than traditionally assumed. In essence the demand is relatively inelastic (with respect to price). At the same time the *supply* 'curve' is very elastic above the entry price (the price at which the market becomes attractive to new entrants). Below this point, however, it is inelastic. In other words new entrants require a given price level before they will make the investment necessary to enter. Above it they will produce in ever larger quantities, but below it they will not even consider production.

In recognition of this '*entry*' level price, the existing tenants will (or at least should, according to this theory) maintain the actual price in the market some-what below this level. The amount of this 'discount' can be described as the '*competitive insurance*', since it represents their uncertainty as to what is the exact entry level.

Contrary to much of economic theory, the evidence suggests that (except for those protected by patents) the monopoly price will often be lower still; it represents the '*monopoly insurance*' the monopoly-holder is willing to pay in order to avoid the monopoly being taken away (directly by competitive activity or indirectly by government regulation).

The problem is that these models describe price activity in only one context – that where only price counts, and 'commodity' prices obtain. On the other hand, when the operators within a market decide that its products or services should be treated as commodities, and be priced accordingly, then something like this holds. Fortunately, this applies to only a small minority of markets.

SELF-TEST QUESTION 7.2

Do you, or your organization, have any idea of what the supply and demand curves for your products or services are like? Can you measure the price elasticity of demand?

If the answer to the second question is yes, you belong to a very fortunate organization (or you are faking your answers). Most organizations depend on products or services which are in markets that are so complex, and changing so rapidly, that it is not possible to measure these factors. There are, however, just a few markets (such as those for basic commodities) where these can be measured – and 'scientific pricing' can be applied.

Factors Influencing Price

The above theory assumes 'perfect markets', in which all consumers and suppliers come equipped with perfect knowledge of all the prices available, for products (commodities) which are identical to each other. In addition, the market always clears; that is, all the demand is exactly matched by supply, and vice versa. This may be true of a few money markets, and the pure commodity markets; although even in these cases other factors are often also at work.

As suggested earlier, it clearly is *not* true of most markets in which marketers are plying their trade. Indeed, it is almost impossible, by definition, for a marketer to have any effect in a 'perfect market'. In economics this unwelcome intrusion of real life is the subject of extensions to the basic theory, to cover 'monopolies and imperfect competition', for example; these extensions are generally rather esoteric.

Even so, an understanding of the basic theories of supply and demand does offer the marketer a useful insight into some of the key factors which may affect the prices that he or she is able to obtain. In particular, the concept of 'elasticity of demand' is one which is widely discussed, and does have a major role to play in pricing decisions. In some markets, such as the car market, where a long sales history is available and the behaviour of the participants has been reasonably consistent and rational, it may even be possible to use 'regression analysis' to establish what the curves of supply and demand actually are. As always, though, this is a historical process; and the future behaviour may not be so consistent.

Estimation of the demand curve and 'price elasticity'

Three main ways of measuring the demand curve (and the related price elasticity of demand) are suggested by theorists:

- *Statistical analysis of historical data.* This, at least in theory, uses historical data to 'plot' the curve. Unfortunately there are very few situations in which this can be carried out directly since there are too many variables in the normal complex market situation – and the 'environmental' factors, in particular, change over time. Even the use of 'regression analysis', as mentioned above, may not be able to remove the effects of those other factors.
- *Survey research.* It might seem that market research should be able to find out what consumers would buy at various prices, allowing the curve to be plotted. In practice, as it turns out, the results from such research are generally so inaccurate that the curves cannot be plotted with any certainty.
- *Experiment.* The one successful device is to test prices, in a test market. For many manufacturers this may be of questionable value: the costs of the test are significant, and the price effect measured may be relevant for just a short time. Retailers, with the luxury of many branches, are much better placed to run such trials.

The practical reality is that these techniques are rarely used.

SELF-TEST QUESTION 7.3

What are the most important factors which influence the prices that your organization can obtain?

Let us, therefore, now look at the factors which can influence 'elasticity of demand', and thus affect price. The main factors can be grouped into those which are almost totally under the control of the organization and those which are out of its control, or can only be partially controlled:

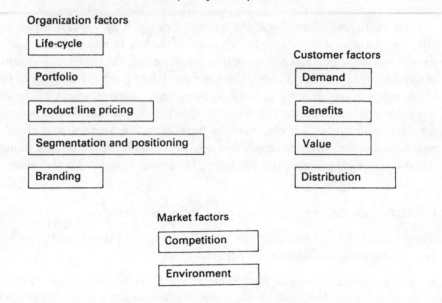

Organization-controlled Factors

Even in a very competitive market, at least some of the factors affecting prices may be under the direct control of the organizations involved.

Product life-cycle

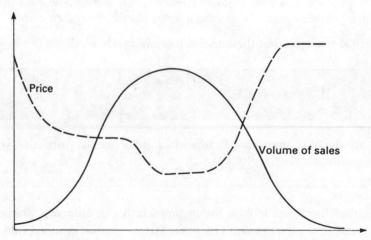

We saw earlier that the stage of the life-cycle through which the 'product' is currently passing may in *theory* have an impact on price. At the 'introduction' it may be set high to capitalize on its uniqueness ('skimming'), as the first video-recorders were. This high price may be carried through to 'maturity' or later; taking 'skimming' to its logical conclusion – as a 'niche player', such as Bang & Olufsen, might do. More probably, as we shall see later in this chapter, the price might be reduced to maximize 'penetration'. It is only at the end of 'maturity', when the market moves into 'saturation', that, according to this theory, price competition should break out in earnest. Even then, as products go into decline, prices should rise again as they are 'milked'.

The theory also requires that, to be under the control of the organization, the 'product' has a life-cycle which is separate from that of the overall market; and that only happens if the organization develops a segment, or 'niche', of its own – which is discussed below. *Overall then, the PLC is usually not a particularly useful guide to pricing policy.*

Services life-cycles For 'non-profit' services the life-cycle is also important, in that the perceived value of the service will vary in much the same way over the life-cycle (and service producers need to recognize this). The concept of 'product' portfolio may also be used, based on value, to ensure that the 'offering' to consumers balances the *range* of their needs. For example, a national health service may need to maintain support for a wide range of services, including some 'old-fashioned' treatments (which patients still demand), at the same time as bringing in new and exciting services.

Portfolio

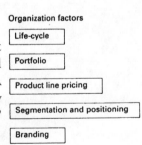

Organization factors

Life-cycle

Portfolio

Product line pricing

Segmentation and positioning

Branding

If, as is likely, the organization has a portfolio of products, it can follow different pricing policies on each; balancing these against each other, so that the overall impact is optimized. In any case, such pricing may be forced upon it. A 'problem child' may fail to become a 'star'; and if it is not to be immediately discontinued, its price will probably need to be raised so that it can be 'milked' to retrieve some profit cover from the situation.

Looking at the portfolio in more general terms, it may even be possible to run two or more very similar brands with different pricing policies. Thus one brand can be in the mainstream of the market and at a reasonably high price, as is Unilever's Persil detergent, while another is quite specifically targeted at a lower price to cover those consumers who are particularly price conscious – as Unilever's 'Square Deal Surf' very obviously was for a number of years.

The portfolio approach is a powerful one, not least because it can 'underwrite' any attempts to set a high-price policy by differentiation, balancing the risk of such experiments against the security offered by the brand remaining in the lower price position. Such a higher-price policy often succeeds, not infrequently against the expectations of most of those involved. *The portfolio approach, however, is only available to those who have the financial resources, and the position in the market, to make it worthwhile.*

Organization factors

Life-cycle

Portfolio

Product line pricing

Segmentation and positioning

Branding

Product line pricing

Another variation may be that the pricing of one product or service has an impact upon others supplied by the organization:

- *Interrelated demand.* The price of one product may affect the demand for another. They may be complementary (for example, the computer and the software that runs on it), so that an increase in one part of the 'package' results in demand for both falling. They could, however, be alternatives; as already mentioned, Procter & Gamble have a range of detergents, and increasing the price of one may switch demand to another.
- *Interrelated costs.* Sometimes the products use the same facilities (the same car assembly line may produce a range of models) or may be derivations of the same process (so that petrol and heating oil are different 'fractions' of crude oil, and one cannot be produced without the other). In these circumstances, changing sales volumes can obviously have knock-on effects on other costs.

Pricing strategies under these circumstances can be complex, and are usually a matter of judgement.

Segmentation and product positioning

The 'classical' techniques for obtaining higher prices are those of positioning and segmentation. By creating a distinct segment which the brand can dominate, the producer hopes that the price can be controlled. Indeed, unlike some of the more theoretical approaches, experience shows that this can often be achieved in practice (Apple, with its own special 'niche', was able to stand out against the cut-throat pricing which infected the rest of the PC market).

Most of the techniques involved were covered, in some detail, in chapter 4. All that need be said at this stage is that a prime benefit of such segmentation and positioning is the reduction in price pressures. *If price competition is severe, therefore, the first action should be to see if segmentation can offer a degree of protection.*

Creating a brand 'monopoly'

As already explained, most of the economic thinking which lies behind the theory of price elasticity of demand revolves around 'perfect competition' (which, in the economic context, usually means exclusively price-based competition). On the other hand, it can be argued that one of the main objectives of the marketer is to create a monopoly for the brands that he or she manages.

The ideal outcome would be that the brand was so differentiated from its competitors that the customer would not choose these other brands, even if the first choice brand was not available. The marketer wants to see the consumer enter the supermarket determined to buy Heinz Baked Beans, not just a suitable variety of ordinary baked beans.

A variation of this process, in the industrial purchasing sector, is described by Webster and Wind:[11]

> The constrained choice model concentrates on the fact that most supplier selection decisions involve choosing from a limited set of potential vendors. Potential suppliers in this set are 'in' while all other potential suppliers are 'out'. Constraints on the set of possible suppliers can be imposed by any member of the buying organization which has the necessary power ... The source loyalty model assumes that inertia is the major determinant of buying behaviour and stresses habitual behaviour.

Another element (which sometimes leads to the constrained choice model) is that of 'perceived risk'. As Cyert and March[12] explain:

> The perceived risk model emphasizes the buyer's uncertainty as he evaluates alternative courses of action ... buyers are motivated by a desire to reduce the amount of perceived risk in the buying situation to some acceptable level, which is not necessarily zero.

Something approaching this view surely led to the famous motto 'Nobody ever got fired for buying IBM'.

Regulation

In some circumstances, such as those which used to be enjoyed by the power and telephone utilities, the organization holds a near-absolute monopoly, and can set its own prices. Paradoxically, there is evidence that such monopolists often choose to set *lower* prices, to expand the market and preserve their monopoly position (at least from the threat of regulation).

Indeed, regulation, including self-regulation, is a factor which has a significant impact on the pricing policies employed by many organizations – and perhaps also, down the line, in those other organizations whose demand derives from them.

[11] Webster and Wind, *Organizational Buying Behaviour*.
[12] R. M. Cyert and J. G. March, *A Behavioral Theory of the Firm* (Prentice-Hall, 1963).

Customer Factors

The major determinant of prices, of course, will be what the consumer is prepared to pay, which is in turn related to a number of other factors:

Customer factors

Demand

Benefits

Value

Distribution

Customer demand

Following from the earlier economic theory, and assuming a steady supply – as is often the case – variations in customer demand should result in changes in price. This is most obvious in the commodity markets, such as that in oil: for example, consumers reduced their demand for oil to such an extent following the massive 1973 price rises that there was eventually a glut and prices were forced down again. It is also evident in other markets, such as that for housing, which have alternating periods of boom or bust, often seasonally related. Holiday markets are closely tied to the seasons, in particular to the school holidays, and the prices reflect this. The railways operate a similar approach, but on a daily basis, with high 'rush-hour' prices, but 'off-peak' bargains.

In the non-profit sector, such surges in demand may be controlled, at least to some extent, by allowing queues to lengthen (as happens for cosmetic surgery).

Customer benefits

The more important or desirable the benefits, the more the consumer will be prepared to pay. Thus, as we have seen, there is the basic 'commodity price' which would be paid for any product of an identical type, assuming that there was perfect competition. Beyond this there is the 'premium price' which consumers will pay for the additional benefits they believe the specific brand will give them. This emphasizes, yet again, the importance of understanding which are the most important benefits in the eyes of the consumer since these are the very ones which will justify a premium price.

Customer factors

Demand

Benefits

Value

Distribution

Customer value

These benefits are conceptualized as the 'value' that the customer sees in the product and, in theory, there should be a balance between this and the price asked.

This 'perceived value' can then be matched against the price on offer, to see whether the purchase is worth making. This theory does at least recognize that different buyers, or groups of buyers, may have different motivations. The Volvo buyer probably places a higher value on personal safety than does the buyer of a Porsche; and it is likely that the latter will consider that the car's value as a status symbol is not to be ignored, in comparison with, for example, that of a similarly specified Japanese car.

In this 'model' the *rational* consumer is seen to weigh up all the benefits and determine what they are worth. This idea also lies behind the economists' theories of supply and demand. It is assumed that each 'consumption bundle', which may be made up of a number of different goods, offers the consumer a specific value of *utility*. Different combinations of goods may offer the consumer the same amount of utility, so that a line can be drawn on a graph, linking these points of equal utility. This is called an *indifference curve*, since the consumer is believed to be indifferent between any of these choices – they are all equally attractive. Few workable indifference curves have been produced, and it is not normally a viable basis for pricing.

Paradoxically, price itself is often seen as a measure of quality: the higher the price the higher the quality is presumed to be. As Erickson and Johansson's research[13] showed:

> The price–quality relationship appears to be operating in a reciprocal manner. Higher priced cars are perceived to possess (unwarranted) high quality. High quality cars are likewise perceived to be higher priced than they actually are.

[13] G. M. Erickson and J. K. Johansson, The role of price in multi-attribute product evaluations, *Journal of Consumer Research*, vol. 12 (1985).

The theoretical balance of 'perceived value' and price can also be used to apply this element of the 4 Ps to non-profit organizations. In these cases the 'perceived value' may be used instead of 'price'. Thus, the hospital consultants, who have a degree of control over the disposition of clinical resources (and as a result, over the queues) in a state health service could (and perhaps should) take into account the patients' 'perceived value' of the various treatments, rather than just their own view of the medical needs. In the light of this it might, for example, be found that increasing the proportion of resources devoted to minor surgery (rather than that dealing with life-threatening ailments) would increase the overall 'satisfaction' of the patients as a whole. Without asking the patients (which is a central concept of marketing) which choice they would make, at least in terms of 'perceived value', it is difficult to see how their total 'satisfaction' could be maximized.

If we return to the earlier factors, which we have already discussed, we may see how this 'perceived value' works for non-profit organizations. In terms of the life-cycle, for example, a product's perceived value may vary with its 'age'; a newly-launched social service may be seen as more valuable (perhaps because it will be tapping a backlog of clients with the most need) than it will be late in its life-cycle, when alternatives will probably have been developed. A portfolio of offerings may also be used, but this time to present the community as a whole with the best possible perceived value, balancing those little-used services which (while they may have high value for each of the individuals involved) may be seen as marginal by the community. Segmentation or positioning, in particular, is an especially valuable technique for ensuring that the 'perceived value' offered to groups is maximized.

The position of 'social marketing' is inevitably more complex. William Novell[14] comments that:

> ... the complex objectives of social marketers usually compel them to focus on price reduction. That is they seek primarily to reduce the monetary, psychic, energy, and time costs incurred by consumers when engaging in desired social behaviour ... much of the time, the social marketer cannot manipulate price and simply tries to convince the target market that the practical benefits outweigh the barriers, or costs.

Customer factors

Demand

Benefits

Value

Distribution

Price and the distribution channel

In many situations the producer simply *cannot* determine the final price to the end-user or consumer. The intermediaries in the distribution channel will apply their own pricing strategies, which may be totally unrelated to those of the producer – and may even be contradictory. Thus the distributor may even choose to absorb any price increases which the producer imposes. IBM

[14] W. D. Novell, Newbusiness or social marketing, *Handbook of Modern Marketing*, ed. V. P. Buell (McGraw-Hill, 2nd edn, 1986).

found itself with a price war on its hands in the PC market, not because that was what IBM wanted – indeed, it was totally in contradiction to IBM's policies – but because that was what its dealers chose to do. On the other hand, the distributor may equally ignore a price decrease which the producer has introduced (to improve penetration of the product, say) to increase his own profit, again with the result that the consumer sees no difference.

SELF-TEST QUESTION 7.5

What are the major benefits which your organization's customers balance against price?

What is the perceived value of its main products or services? Is this significantly higher then the actual prices, and if so, why?

Market Factors

The other factors in the market may also have an important impact, and may often be the ultimate determinant of prices:

> Competition

> Environment

Competition

Apart from the competence of the supplier, in terms of the ability to match price to the consumers' 'perceived value', the major factor affecting price is probably competition. What the direct competitors, in particular, charge for their comparable products is bound to be taken into consideration by the consumers if not by the producers.

The framework for the analysis of and response to competition, in general as well as price terms, will be covered in chapter 13, which explains that there are means of managing competition, even price competition, so that its impact on profits may be minimized.

Another response to price competition, therefore, should be to examine if there are ways of 'managing' it to reduce its impact, and to signal to competitors that your response is not aggressive.

Direct competition may be rare in the non-profit sectors, but indirect competition is not, and many of the same techniques can be applied. If, say, you are trying to attract people to keep-fit classes you may have to persuade them that the 'value' of these is greater than that of an alternative, which may be a session of bingo.

Competition

Environment

Environment

The wider environment can also have its impact. Whether the economy is booming or in recession may have a direct impact on what consumers can afford to spend; although in recent years this effect often seems to have been very selective, mainly hitting those supplying capital goods to industry, while consumer sales, to those still in work, have (except in the greatest depths of recession) continued to rise.

Then despite governments' suggestions to the contrary, there are also all the various aspects of legislation which constrain freedom to move prices. At the very least, there is often the veiled threat of interest from those agencies that are responsible for monitoring 'fair trading' and monopolies hanging over those who are especially effective in managing their price competition. The possibility of such regulatory intervention should never be discounted.

SELF-TEST QUESTION 7.6

Are the markets of your organization price-competitive?

What actions has your organization taken to manage such competitive price activity? What actions do you think it should take?

What legislation affects its prices? What future regulations might apply?

Geographical pricing

Where transport costs are important, and particularly where there are widely-separated populations (as there are in the USA), then geographical location may become a factor in pricing. There are a range of strategies to cope with this:

- uniform pricing – the same price is offered at all locations, regardless of delivery costs. This is the most widely-applied policy in consumer goods markets; not least because it is easiest to apply, in terms of the paperwork created.
- FOB (free on board) – the cost of all transport is charged to the customer (this is more likely to be found in industrial markets).

- zone pricing – the price is different for each geographical region, or 'zone', to incorporate the average transport costs incurred in shipping to that region.

There are, of course, other possible regional pricing policies. Not least of these are regional variations to allow for the strengths of local, regional, competitors.

Pricing 'New Products'

The time when an organization is most free to determine the price of its products or services is when they are launched. Once the price has been set, so has a precedent. In the event of any future changes consumers will not only have the competitive prices as a comparison, but they will also have the previous prices as a *very* direct point of reference. This makes it very difficult to make substantial changes to the prices of existing products or services. Consumer reactions may be severe if they think they are being taken advantage of.

The new product may be entering an existing market. If this is the case then price will be just one of the positioning variables. On this basis, the price will be carefully calculated to position the brand exactly where it will make the most impact – and profit. At a less sophisticated level, perhaps, the producer of a new brand will decide which of the existing price ranges – cheap or expensive – the product or service should address. A supplier entering a mass consumer market can simply go to the local supermarket, or specialty store, and see what prices are already accepted. In industrial markets it may be much more difficult to obtain competitive prices, even where published price lists are available, since these are often only the starting point for negotiations which result in heavy discounts.

In the case of a totally new product or service, the pricing exercise will be that much more difficult; for there are no precedents to indicate how the consumer might behave, and this is an area where market research is notoriously inaccurate. In the end it will have to be a judgement decision, as to what 'perceived value' the consumer will put on the offering.

Strategy

Within these pricing limits, however, there are two main approaches possible for a new product, and to a lesser extent for an existing one:

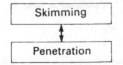

Skimming

One approach is to set the initial price high, to 'skim' as much profit as possible, even in the early stages of the product life-cycle. This is particularly applicable to new products which, at least for some time, have a monopoly of the market because the competitors have not yet emerged, and is a pattern often seen in the *introduction* of new technology. The price is then reduced, possibly in stages, gradually to expand demand, until it reaches a competitive level just before the competitors enter the market. This is a fine judgement, though; and it is interesting to note that in the case of video-recorders it was the late-comers, with competitive prices, who actually swept the board.

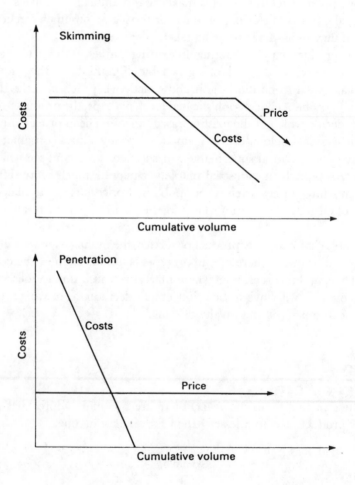

The rationale behind skimming (sometimes called 'rapid payback') is normally quite simply that of maximizing profit. But there may occasionally be another motive – that of maximizing the image of 'quality'. This is a policy which holds in consumer markets such as the upper end of the perfume trade: for example, sales of Chanel Number 5 would probably not increase dramatically if the price was reduced. But it can just as easily apply in industrial markets. It is the foolish consultant who asks for a low price, because the client will probably think that the quality is comparably low.

As indicated above, the danger of a skimming policy is that a high price encourages other manufacturers to enter the market, because they see that sales revenue can quickly cover the expense of developing a rival product. Even if your prices are not exorbitant you may still need, therefore, to plan for a steady reduction in price as competitors appear and you recover some of your launch costs. Such a price reduction will normally be helped by economies of scale.

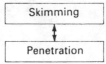

Penetration policy

On the other hand, a manufacturer could choose the opposite tactic by adopting a penetration pricing policy; and, indeed, this has been the very successful policy behind the move of Japanese corporations into a number of existing markets. Here an initial low price might make it less attractive for would-be competitors to imitate innovations, particularly where the technology is expensive; and it encourages more customers to buy the product soon after its introduction, which hastens the growth of demand and earlier economies of scale. The main value of this policy is that it helps to secure a relatively large market share, and to increase turnover, while reducing unit costs – so that the price domination can be maintained and extended. Its major disadvantage lies in lost opportunities for higher profit margins.

Under this broad category, however, there are a number of more specific policies:

- *Maximizing brand/product share.* This justification is sometimes made in terms of maximizing sales growth; particularly in new markets where competitive activity is less evident.
- *Maximizing current revenue.* The assumption is that higher sales automatically lead to higher profits, although in practice most products are more sensitive, in terms of profit, to price than to volume.
- *Survival.* For some organizations, maximizing revenue by price-cutting may be seen as the only way to survive. This is the philosophy of despair.

The circumstances generally favouring the skimming and penetration policies are summarized below:

Skimming	Penetration
Prices are likely to be inelastic	Prices are likely to be elastic
The product or service is new and unique	Competitors are likely to enter the market quickly
There are distinct segments	There are no distinct segments
Quality is important	Products will be undifferentiated
Competitive costs are unknown	Economies of scale apply

SELF-TEST QUESTION 7.7

For which products or services has your organization adopted a skimming policy?

For which products or services has your organization adopted a penetration policy?

What were the results in each case? Were the decisions correct? What would your own recommendations have been, and why?

Practical Pricing Policies

The problem is that very little of the pricing theory which has been described has any great value in practical pricing. As Alfred Oxenfeldt[15] says:

> The current pricing literature has produced few new insights or exciting approaches that would interest most businessmen enough to change their present methods. Those executives who follow the business literature have no doubt broadened their viewpoint and become more explicit and systematic about their pricing decisions; however, few, if any, actually employ new and different goals, concepts or techniques ... Most authors deal with pricing problems uni-dimensionally, whereas most businessmen must generally deal with price as one element in a multidimensional marketing program.

[15] A. R. Oxenfeldt, The differential method of pricing, *European Journal of Marketing*, vol. 13, no. 4 (1979).

In fact, practical pricing can be reduced to just one key decision!

PRICING ROULETTE – the first, and most important,
decision for any manager in
pricing his or her Product/Service Package is the simple one
– is it in a market which is based on commodity prices –

If the products or services are treated as commodities,
and if prices reflect this,
then you MUST do the same in order to survive, even in the short term.

If, as is usually the case, the market is not commodity based,
you MUST adopt price maximization rules.

Pricing is either commodity-based or not!

Much the same as Russian Roulette is played with a revolver, suppliers often play Pricing Roulette with the market. The odds are a little bit better – our research indicates that only a tenth of markets indulge in commodity pricing (where there is one live round out of six in the revolver). The end effect may be much the same, however, if your spin of the chamber lands you on a commodity-based market – it is often tantamount to commercial suicide!

If the products or services are treated as commodities, and if prices reflect this, then you MUST do the same in order to survive, even in the short term. You have no pricing choice. You must hope that the situation changes at some time in the future, when you can make a reasonable profit, but in the short term you can only reduce costs to staunch the bleeding.

Fortunately, as mentioned above, 90 per cent of the markets are not commodity based. You can heave a sigh of relief that you have survived the test and get on with the marketing described in the rest of this book.

So if, as is usually the case, the market is not commodity based, your should adopt price maximization rules. This is one of the very few situations in marketing where there are no grey areas, no spectrum of options. Beware though! One of the great temptations in marketing, to which many succumb, is to think that a significantly lower price will improve your position. *The odds show (9:1, as we saw above) that this is likely to be a mistake* – price-cutting may switch the whole market to commodity-pricing (so that everyone loses, especially the initiator).

This is not to say that a drive for reduced costs, which is typically initiated by commodity-pricing, should be abandoned. There must always be an awareness that commodity-pricing may one day emerge into your market, even if this would be suicidal for all involved. The organization has (while making its investments in the future), therefore, to develop a cost structure which will enable it to survive even this eventuality – and in the meantime it will reap even higher levels of profit.

For the great majority of markets suppliers can, happily for them, count on achieving more than the base commodity price. The difference is known as the '*price premium*'; this is a simple concept, but a useful one – not least because it acts as an antidote against the very strong temptation to indulge in price-cutting.

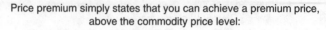

Price premium simply states that you can achieve a premium price, above the commodity price level:

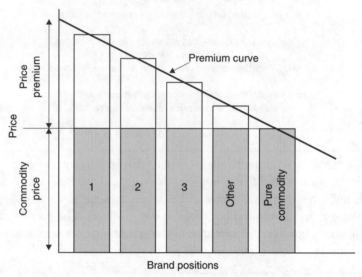

This diagram above also indicates that, in general, the brand leaders are progressively placed to achieve such premiums (though they may choose to trade this off against higher volumes of sales).

The premium may be justified by a variety of factors, including those such as image, quality, differentiation positioning etc., which have already been discussed. The exact reason for the premium is not important, it will vary from situation to situation. What is crucial is that you recognize it as a possibility, *and work to maximize it*. The evidence[16] is that around a quarter (24 per cent) of organizations already successfully follow a strategy of setting premium (or even luxury) prices. Perhaps more – of those who are not caught in commodity markets – ought to follow their example, and earn more profit for very little extra effort!

'Marlboro Friday', when Philip Morris was forced to cut the price of its leading brand, is often quoted[17] as one piece of evidence that premium pricing has become more difficult to achieve. On the other hand, it could just as easily be seen as one further mistake by a once strong marketing organization which had lost its way – not least because some of its more influential non-executive directors came from organizations which did not commit themselves to the

[16] D. Mercer, research to be published.

[17] Thomas Robertson, New developments in marketing: a European perspective, *European Management Journal*, vol. 12, no. 4 (1994).

marketing philosophy in the same way – and no longer had confidence in its own marketing abilities.

If you avoid the pitfall of commodity-pricing, along with that of the many 'guaranteed' techniques of pricing offered by academics and consultants, most pricing then turns out to be relatively simple. This is because most products or services are either existing 'products' with a known track record, or are new products entering markets where there already are similar products with known track records.

Thus, despite the theory described earlier, prices are most often set by one of a number of more pragmatic 'rules of thumb':

Cost plus

The starting point for most pricing exercises is an examination of the cost of the product or service. In practice, such 'cost plus' pricing is probably the most common initial approach. Indeed, in something like a quarter of organizations (26 per cent[18]) this is also the finishing point! This may be understandable where the price list contains hundreds of items; although, under those circumstances, it is highly debatable whether the 'cost' for each item represents anything more than an estimate.

Paradoxically, 'cost plus' pricing seems to suggest that inefficiency (which would lead to a higher unit cost) should be rewarded.

The one area in which cost plus pricing is possibly justifiable is where the supplier has a long-term relationship, almost a partnership, with a customer (often the government). In these circumstances it is sometimes agreed that a certain level of profit (as a percentage of cost) is acceptable. But even here there

[18] D. Mercer, research to be published.

has to be a question as to the efficiency of such a pricing policy, for the customer as well as for the supplier, since profit is supposed to be the main incentive. The legal actions taken by government to recover unwarranted profits made by some defence contractors operating under these pricing policies seem to argue for some dissatisfaction.

Exactly what 'cost' should be chosen is a matter of debate; few producers actually conduct such a debate, and often select as their 'cost' – by default – the first figure thrown up by their accounting system. Choosing what cost to apply and, more importantly, understanding the assumptions which lie behind it is an art; it is one in which many marketers are unskilled.

The most critical element in this process is often the most arbitrary – that of the allocation of overheads. The process of 'absorption' of overheads (whereby indirect overheads are allocated, on the basis of 'judgement', to production departments and then, combined with direct overheads, 'absorbed' into the individual product costs, often on the basis of labour content) is summarized nicely by Wilson[19] (figure 7.1). It can be seen how many stages require 'judgements' as to where overheads are to be allocated.

As we saw earlier, 'marginal costs' (which avoid the problem of overhead allocation) may well be the most favoured approach for new products, but may leave gaps in terms of overhead recovery as the older products die. A judgement also has to be made as to the period over which any initial investment is to be recovered.

Oxenfeldt and Kelly[20] list a number of 'fundamental errors committed by business executives in setting price':

1. The tendency to think in terms of averages ... it ignores the particular and unusual circumstances under which the price move occurs and which call for the use of *marginal* or incremental costs ... the assumption that all customers behave in the same way ...

2. The reluctance to 'let bygones be bygones' ... letting irrevocable and irretrievable past expenditures enter into the cost computations underlying price decisions ... The vital concept to apply here is *sunk* costs. These are outlays already made that cannot be revoked and about which nothing can be done. Such costs must be ignored ...

3. The tendency to ignore alternatives ... businesspeople frequently charge out these elements on the basis of what was paid for them in the past (book costs) rather than what they would yield in alternative use. The concept of *opportunity* costs has been developed to help highlight the constant need to think in terms of alternatives when arriving at the decision.

---

[19] R. M. S. Wilson, Cost accounting, *The Gower Handbook of Management*, ed. D. Lock and N. Farrow (Gower, 1983).

[20] A. R. Oxenfeldt and A. O. Kelly, Pricing consumer products and services, *Handbook of Modern Marketing*, ed. V. P. Buell (McGraw-Hill, 2nd edn, 1986).

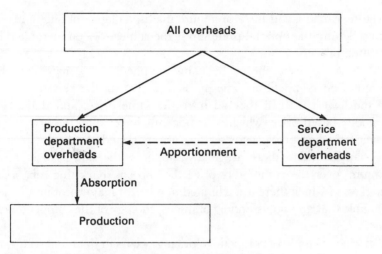

Figure 7.1   Overhead apportionment and absorption.

4. The tendency to emphasize cost considerations over demand considerations ... This tendency reaches its pinnacle in *cost plus pricing* where demand considerations are simply ignored.

Competitive pricing

The other popular approach – used again by around a quarter (27 per cent[21]) of organizations – and the most usual form of pricing, based on evidence from the market – is that where product prices are determined by reference to the prices of competitive products. This may well be realistic when the product is a follower rather than a market leader.

A sound appreciation of competitive actions, especially prices, is necessary for the most effective strategies to be formulated. The most effective marketing manager will, however, try to develop an *understanding* of the various competitive positions – based on an appreciation of the customer's needs. A market leader should take advantage of the power that position offers, and a niche marketer should be able to use that uniqueness of positioning to gain some control over prices.

In a 'brand monopoly' the marketer may have a significant degree of control over prices. On the other hand, in a commodity market no control at all may be available. Once more, the marketer has to make a judgement as to the 'price elasticity of demand' (in this case in the context of competitors' prices).

The position is usually more complex than participants allow for. Products or services, and in particular brands, are rarely identical. Each will have its special features, presumably developed by its management to meet some market need.

[21] D. Mercer, research to be published.

Therefore, each may justify a premium, that is, a degree of differentiation in its pricing. Setting the optimal premium is the subject of considerable skill – and not a little bravery.

The 'easy' answer, chosen by many suppliers, is to match or preferably undercut their competitors. The problem is that all the participants can only have the lowest price if they all have the same price; and that is usually a commodity-based price, which is significantly lower than the price that should be achieved when products or services are marketed effectively.

In markets where there are many suppliers, the skill is in knowing what 'premium' over the commodity price the chosen 'marketing mix' will justify. In markets in which there are a limited number of major products or services it is arguable that an understanding of the psychology of the competitors is just as important.

A specific example of competitive pricing occurs in the retail sector, in which 'loss-leader pricing' is sometimes employed. The prices of certain lines are deliberately set low – perhaps even making a loss, the line then becoming a 'loss leader' – to attract customers into the store. The intention is that these customers will then also buy other lines, on which the real profit will be made. You should note that the practice may be invalidated by customers who realize what is happening, and ethical objections have resulted in the 'loss leader' approach being made illegal in certain US states.

Target pricing

In this case, the intention is not just to obtain a 'profit' over costs, but to obtain a reasonable 'return on investment' (ROI). Therefore, the price has to be based on both the variable costs (as in 'cost plus') and the capital employed (related to the sales value).

As Russ and Kirkpatrick[22] state, 'The process of trying to consider investment decisions and pricing decisions simultaneously is a very complex one, requiring accurate information ...'

It is not surprising that this is one of the less popular policies, except where it is used, often in a theoretical rather than practical context, as part of (usually a justification for) a large capital investment programme.

| Cost plus pricing |
| Target pricing |
| Historical pricing |
| Range pricing |
| Competitive pricing |
| Market-based pricing |
| Selective pricing |

Historical pricing

One normal extension of cost plus pricing is to base today's prices on yesterday's. The annual round of price increases, for example, is based on last year's price uplifted by something approximating to the increase in the cost of living, or the true increase in costs – whichever is the higher.

[22] F. Russ and C. A. Kirkpatrick, *Marketing* (Little Brown and Co., 1982).

Range pricing

The pricing for a given product may be decided by the range within which it fits. There may thus appear to be an inevitable logic, derived from the rest of the range. A 300 gram pack, for example, is expected to have a price somewhere close to the median of the 200 gram and 400 gram packs. A premium price on a member of a cut-price range would pose questions; and, at the other extreme, a cut-price entry into a luxury range might do severe damage to the quality image of that range.

A more specific example of range pricing comes from retailing, where it is often called 'price lining'. In this case there are a limited number of pre-determined price points, and all items in a given price category are given a specific price, say $9.99. This also illustrates the 'psychological' aspect of choosing certain price points on the basis that customers will read $9.99 as $9, rather than the $10 it much more nearly is!

Market-based pricing

This is classically what marketing theory would require. As discussed earlier, it is sometimes called 'perceived value pricing', because the price to be charged needs to match the value that the customer perceives the product or service to offer.

Clearly it is near ideal, because it is likely to be optimal in terms of obtaining the maximum premium on the commodity price; and very few suppliers price too high, with the great majority pricing too low. Indeed, although just over a quarter (27 per cent) of organizations say they are committed to a strategy of pricing based on perceived value, only 15 per cent implement this when it comes to the process of pricing itself.

This is also the ideal price in that it matches the 'position' of the product to the customer's perceptions. Particularly in the luxury goods markets, the price is an element of the overall 'description' of the product, and one which is seen as reflecting its quality. There are many examples of new luxury products which have performed badly until the price has been increased in line with the quality expected.

The problem is, of course, determining just what is the perceived value; or, more basically, finding out what price consumers will be willing to pay. Even in the mass consumer markets, where extensive research is undertaken, establishing optimal prices is difficult. It is not possible to ask market research respondents how much they would be willing to pay, because such research has almost invariably given wildly optimistic results.

There is one situation in which the price is obvious, described by Kent Monroe[23] as 'customary pricing', which 'excludes all price alternatives except

| Cost plus pricing |
| Target pricing |
| Historical pricing |
| Range pricing |
| Competitive pricing |
| Market-based pricing |
| Selective pricing |

---

[23] K. B. Monroe, Buyer's subjective perceptions of price, *Journal of Marketing Research.* vol. 10 (1973).

a simple price point. The traditional example has been the five-cent candy bar or package of gum.' The supplier's choice here is the 'quantity' to offer against this fixed price – and 'price changes' become incremental 'size changes'.

At the end of the day, most pricing still comes down to management skill – and courage.

Price positioning   In addition to a determination of where the 'market' price lies, a further decision needs to be taken, that of where the brand price is to be positioned in relation to the market price.

Quality pricing.   Some organizations make a conscious decision to deliberately price above the market average. This price is intended to demonstrate the quality, or even the luxury, of the product or service. Rolls-Royce is the example quoted most often, but Hilton Hotels, Sony and many of the cosmetic and perfume houses follow the same policy. James Myers[24] demonstrates this nicely in terms of the related demand curve (figure 7.2).

Although the initial reduction in price will – as usual – result in increased sales, beyond a critical point any further reduction in price here will lead to a *reduction in sales* (as the curve bends back upon itself). For this reason it is arguable that the problems encountered by the Cadillac division of General Motors were actually exacerbated by the price cuts which were made to try to restore its competitive position.

Cut pricing.   The organizations with the most obvious price positioning are those deliberately choosing to price below the market; since such cut prices are often the main

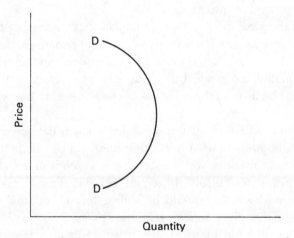

Figure 7.2   Luxury demand curve.

[24] J. Myers, *Marketing* (McGraw-Hill, 1986).

element of their marketing mix. Bic ballpoints, Amstrad computers and the Virgin airline have all been exponents of this approach.

Alfred Oxenfeldt[25] makes the important point that:

> Most firms can command a premium from *some* customers. They might want to deal with only those customers; on the other hand their numbers might be so few as to preclude that possibility. *Price setters will usually err badly if they base their price demands on the evaluations of the average or typical customer.*

Selective pricing

Some suppliers apply different prices for the same product or service:

Category pricing

Customer group pricing

Peak pricing

Service level pricing

- *Category pricing.* The supplier aims to cover the range of price categories (possibly all the way from cheap to expensive) with a 'range' of 'brands' based on the same 'product' (repackaged, and possibly with some minor changes). This was particularly obvious when Unilever in the UK marketed 'Square Deal Surf' as price leader alongside 'Persil'. It may be less obvious when suppliers run high-priced brands while at the same time offering low-priced 'own brands'.
- *Customer group pricing.* The ability of various groups to pay prices may be met by having different categories of prices: entrance fees and fares are often lower for students and senior citizens.
- *Peak pricing.* The price is matched to the demand: high prices are demanded at peak times (the 'rush hours' for transport, or the evening performances for theatres), but lower prices at 'off-peak' times (to redistribute the resource demands by offering incentives to those who can make use of the services off-peak).
- *Service level pricing.* The level of service chosen may determine the price. At its simplest, the buyer may pay for immediate availability rather than having to queue (or may pay more for the guarantee of a seat, by patronizing the first-class section of a train). This may be extended to levels of 'delivery'; the product may be available immediately, and gift wrapped, in an expensive store – or it may arrive some weeks later by post from a cheap mail-order house. There may also be levels of 'quality' in delivery; for instance, seats in different parts of a theatre may have differing levels of access to the performance, although the basic 'product' may be identical.

The last three of these are particularly prevalent in the service industries, where the supplier is in direct contact with the customer.

Above all, *the main temptation to avoid is the assumption that price is the most important variable in the marketing mix.* Sometimes it may be, and you will obviously need to recognize that. But in *most* situations it is not, and in many it may be a very minor consideration. Under these 'typical' circumstances it is important to attend to the other elements of the marketing mix first, and then deal with price in this context.

[25] Oxenfeldt, The differential method of pricing.

SELF-TEST QUESTION 7.8

Which of these pragmatic approaches to pricing (cost plus, historical pricing, range pricing, competitive pricing, and market-based pricing) does your organization use?

For each of these approaches, which has been used:

- How successful has it proved to be?
- How easy is it to set prices by this rule of thumb?
- How acceptable to consumers are the resulting prices?
- What profits does it generate?
- Does it match the specific needs and culture of the organization?

Discounts

Having set the overall price, the supplier then has the option of offering different prices (usually on the basis of a discount) to cover different circumstances. The types of discount most often offered are:

- trade discounts
- quantity discounts
- cash discounts
- allowances
- seasonal discounts
- promotional pricing
- individual pricing
- optional features
- product bundling
- psychological pricing

- *Trade discounts.*   Members of the supplier's distribution chain (retailers and wholesalers, for example) will demand payment for their services. Trade discounts are covered in more detail in chapter 8.
- *Quantity discounts.*   Those who offer to buy larger quantities of the product or service (again typically as part of the distribution chain, but also the larger industrial buyers) are frequently given incentives. In consumer markets this is more often achieved by larger pack sizes (or by banding together smaller packs) as 'family or economy' packs. It is often deemed more cost-effective to offer extra product ('30 per cent extra free' or '13 for the price of 12') instead of reducing price because the extra product represents only a marginal increase in cost to the supplier – and may push the user into using more (and even finding new uses).
- *Cash discounts.*   Where credit is offered, it is sometimes decided to offer an incentive for cash payment or for prompt payment (to persuade customers to pay their bills on the due date, although too often they take the discount anyway and still pay late).

- *Allowances.* In the durable goods market suppliers often attempt to persuade consumers to buy a new piece of equipment by offering allowances against trade-in of their old one. Generally speaking, these are simply hidden discounts targeted at a group of existing 'competitive' users.
- *Seasonal discounts.* Suppliers to markets which are highly seasonal (such as the holiday market) will often price their product or service to match the demand, with the highest prices at peak demand.
- *Promotional pricing.* Suppliers may, from time to time, wish to use a price discount as a specific promotional device. This is discussed at more length in chapter 10.
- *Individual pricing.* Under certain circumstances, it may be possible for a customer, even in a consumer market, to negotiate a special price; such haggling is the essence of sales in some of the Mediterranean countries. It may also be the basis of some industrial and business-to-business selling. Here the pricing decision is left to the sales professional; often with disastrous effects on profit.
- *Optional features.* The reverse of discounts may be that customers are offered a basic product to which they can add features, at extra cost (and often, unlike discounts, with much higher profit margins).
- *Product bundling.* Alternatively, they might be offered a 'bundle' of related products – such as a package of accessories with a camera – typically in this case at a reduced price, as compared with the prices of the separate items (although sometimes the separate items are not really sold apart from the special promotional 'bundle').
- *Psychological pricing.* Some suppliers deliberately set very high 'recommended' prices in order to be able to offer seemingly very high discounts ('massive savings') against them. However, this policy may rebound when consumers realize what is happening – and, in any case, such tactics are now often subject to regulation, and may even be illegal.

SELF-TEST QUESTION 7.9

List all the various types of discount that your organization operates.

What is the purpose of each? How effective is each in achieving that objective?

Pricing Strategy

Whatever the rationale behind the final pricing decisions, be it the most elegant of economic theory or the most pragmatic of competitive reactions, it is necessary to consolidate this as a pricing strategy.

This is needed, in the first instance, to ensure that what is being implemented matches what the participants in the decision actually thought they were agreeing to; too often there are major misunderstandings in management decision-making, which are only revealed when the damage has been done. Formalizing these decisions in writing should remove the possibility of such misunderstandings, although it may not always do so.

It is also needed to ensure that the individual prices are carefully managed, and that there is a balance across the whole portfolio.

Price Wars

Even though just over a third (38 per cent) of organizations say that they are committed to a strategy of competitive or cut prices,[26] price competition is most often seen to be the most savage and destructive form of commercial warfare. It is particularly destructive because at one end of the chain it destroys the profit of the suppliers (and with it the capacity to invest in the future of the market) and because at the other it often destroys the belief of the consumer in the quality of offering. Some of the reasons for indulging in the very risky pursuit of price competition may be:

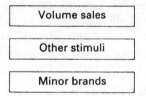

Volume sales

Not all price reductions are destructive. Some result in such increases in the volume of purchases that absolute profit is increased despite the relative reductions in price (and economies of scale may mean that even the relative profit per unit increases), and the whole market expands rapidly.

The key to making a success of price competition is in ensuring that it reflects a genuine cost advantage. Economies of scale, and hence the justification of lower prices to increase volumes, are one aspect. Another is that your own cost structure must offer advantages over those of the competitors. When these factors apply in your favour then price competition can be very advantageous, in exactly the same way that any other 'product' advantage would be.

Unfortunately, most price competition occurs between companies with very similar cost structures; and this frequently leads to a debilitating price war.

[26] D. Mercer, research to be published.

Other stimuli

Apart from a price reduction to reflect a genuine cost advantage, price reductions are often stimulated by:

> Market leadership
> targeting

> Excess capacity

> Falling brand share

- *Market leadership targeting.*   In an 'open' market, with a number of similar size brands (or a new market which has not yet stabilized), a brand owner may decide to make an investment to achieve market leadership (a 'penetration' policy in new markets); price is often the main weapon, particularly where there is a belief (often no more than an unjustified hope) that this may also lead to falling costs per unit.
- *Excess capacity.*   Perhaps the most dangerous move is where price is reduced to use up excess capacity, and hence to absorb more overheads. Unfortunately, this often takes place where there is spare capacity in the market as a whole; it is worth remembering that competitors are faced with similar problems – and will respond similarly.
- *Falling brand share.*   Defence of share often involves a more aggressive price position, and hence it may be wise to watch how rapidly share is being taken from competitors by non-price means (since too rapid erosion may stimulate a savage price war).

On the other hand, the dangers of initiating a price war include:

> Low-quality image

> Temporary advantage

> Investment potential

- *Low-quality image.*   A low price may be equated with low quality (and may actually represent just that, as the opponents shave quality in order to fund the cost cutting).
- *Temporary advantage.*   A price advantage is often only held in the short term, and consumers will be rapidly attracted to the even lower one (which you can be sure will eventually appear).
- *Investment potential.*   Above all, price reductions should be seen as an investment to generate greater sales (for, if they do not, they can only result in reduced profits). It is wise, under these circumstances, to work out which company has the deepest pockets and can invest in such a war of attrition the longest. History tends to show that it is often the initiator of the war who is the first casualty.

In the airline industry both Laker and People's Express fell into these traps, although – as always – other factors were also involved.

Minor brands

An exception to the strictures about price competition relates to minor brands in markets which are dominated by major brands. Thus, minor brands will typically make the largest offer (usually a price reduction) *per unit* (which represents the greatest impact they can make), whereas the response of the leaders is to promote (most economically) across the whole market, usually by advertising. This situation rarely leads to damaging price wars.

Reactions to Price Challenges

The first reaction to a price reduction should always be to consider the situation carefully (and metaphorically count to ten before indulging in self-righteous retaliation). Has the competitor decided upon a long-term price reduction, or is this just a short-term promotion? If it is the latter, then the reaction should be purely that relating to short-term promotional activity (and the optimum response is often simply to ignore the challenge). All too often, price wars have been started because simple promotional activities have been misunderstood as major strategic changes.

On the other hand, if it emerges that this *is* a long-term move then there are a number of possible reactions:

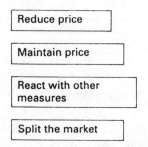

- *Reduce price.* The most obvious, and most popular, reaction is to match the competitor's move. This maintains the *status quo* (but reduces profits *pro rata*). If this route is to be chosen it is as well to make the move rapidly and obviously – not least to send signals to the competitor of your intention to fight.
- *Maintain price.* Another reaction is to hope that the competitor has made a mistake; although, if the competitor's action does make inroads into your share, this can rapidly lead to a loss of confidence as well as of volume.

- *React with other measures.* Reducing price is not the only weapon. Other tactics, such as improved quality or increased promotion (to improve the quality image, perhaps), may be used, often to great effect.
- *Split the market.* A particularly effective tactic (most notably used by Heublein, the owner of the Smirnoff brand of vodka) is to combine a move to increase the 'quality' of the main brand at the same time as launching a 'fighting brand' to undermine – by further price-cutting – the competitor's position.

Avoiding Price Wars

Avoidance is by far the best policy, but it is advice which may not always be taken if the benefits seem attractive (which, unfortunately, they may also be to the competitors). The dangers are summarized in a theory borrowed from the ethics branch of the social sciences.

The prisoner's dilemma

The basic, imaginary, dilemma (a 'philosophical problem' known for many years, and even described by Herodotus, but given this name and description by Alfred Turner) has two prisoners accused of a crime. If one confesses and the other does not, the one confessing will be released immediately and the other gaoled for 10 years. If neither confesses, each will only be held for a few months. On the other hand, if both confess they will each receive a sentence of five years. The problem, for the prisoners, is that they are not allowed to communicate with each other. The calculation is that self-interest will be best served for each by confessing, no matter what the other does. But, of course, this would be a less satisfactory solution for them than if they both held out. This 'game', together with its variants (as well as 'Chicken', which, in terms of who gives way first in a war of attrition, is also very relevant), is described in considerable detail by Eric Rasmusen.[27]

Fortunately the position in the case of price competition, while sharing some of the features of this dilemma – especially if the participants react without thinking – is somewhat more favourable. The 'prisoners' are not held incommunicado. They can exchange 'signals' which indicate their intentions. Under these circumstances, the best outcome can be achieved – and often is.

[27] E. Rasmusen, *Games and Information* (Basil Blackwell, 1989).

Price Increases

What is less often discussed, but is often more important, is the topic of price increases. The normal reason for these is inflation. The resulting increase in cost has to be passed on if profits are not to be adversely affected. Fortunately, the widespread expectation of inflation usually means that they can be imposed without too many problems.

Price increases are also often expected (at least by economic theorists) where there is 'excess demand'. While this is a situation which is very welcome to the suppliers, it is actually a fairly rare phenomenon and even more rarely lasts for any length of time.

On the other hand, where costs rise but price increases cannot be easily imposed, the solution may be to reduce the specification; to produce smaller packs, as the confectionery manufacturers often do. Adams et al.'s[28] research indicates that the best approach to 'downsizing' is:

1 'Downsize to the point where it is not noticeable'
2 'Focus consumers' attention away . . . by highlighting other benefits'
3 'Increase couponing temporarily'
4 'Implement . . . before it becomes a hot consumer issue'

The success in the UK of Jacobs 'Club Biscuits' against the brand leader, Kit Kat, after Rowntree had reduced the amount of chocolate in the covering of the latter, indicates the risks involved. Rowntree learned from that lesson, though, and subsequently launched 'Yorkie', a more substantial chocolate bar, against Cadbury's 'Dairy Milk' bar, with some success. Alternatively, it may be possible to remove some elements from the support package.

John Winkler[29] gives a six-part practical guide to making price increases:

- Put the prices up when everyone else does. (Don't hold back for the sake of competitive edge: you will have to increase eventually and the action will be more noticeable then.)
- Not too much at any one time. (Incremental increases – around the level of inflation – are less noticeable.)
- Not too often. (Buyers react against too frequent change.)
- Move something down when you move something up. (Try to lower a price even if it is only that of a minor product.)
- Look after your key accounts. (The 80:20 Rule says that it is the reactions of your key accounts which are most important.)
- Provide sound – and true – explanations. (Customers understand that prices sometimes have to go up when costs increase.)

[28] Anthony Adams, C. Anthony Di Benetto and Rajan Chandran, Can you reduce your package size without damaging sales, *Long Range Planning*, vol. 24, no. 4 (1991).
[29] J. Winkler, Pricing, *The Marketing Book*, ed. M. J. Baker (Heinemann, 1987).

SELF-TEST QUESTION 7.10

Produce a pricing strategy for your organization covering no more than two A4 pages. Your strategy document should:

- state what the overall policies should be for existing and new products or services
- identify individual prices for the major products or services, if these are different from the overall policy
- explain how the portfolio is balanced
- say how the policy will develop in future

FURTHER READING

Much of the theory of pricing can be found, as specific chapters, in the general undergraduate textbooks on economics; such as Begg, Fischer and Dornbusch, *Economics* (McGraw-Hill), or Lipsey, *An Introduction to Positive Economics* (Weidenfeld & Nicolson). However, these are substantial textbooks, the greater part of which may not be relevant to your needs – and they do document economic *theory*. Specific texts on pricing, on the other hand, tend to be very specialized – and hence even less readable.

SUMMARY

There is an argument which says that price is just one of the elements which go to make up the product package. However, it is generally considered important enough to warrant its own 'P'.

Much of the theory is, however, derived from economics; especially from supply and demand theory. This is encapsulated in the famous set of curves:

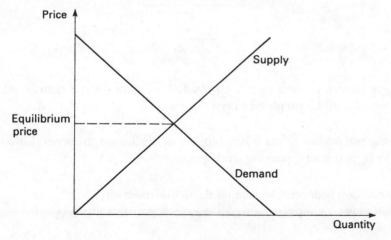

As this shows, the price is set by the point where the curves intersect. The degree to which demand is susceptible to price changes (*price elasticity of demand*) is another concept borrowed from economics.

Again in theory, but rarely in practice, these curves can be obtained from statistical analysis of historical data, survey research and experiment. Rather less theoretically, factors affecting the pricing policies of a specific organization may be:

Organization factors

- Life-cycle
- Portfolio
- Product line pricing
- Segmentation and positioning
- Branding

Factors derived from customers may be:

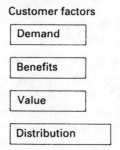

Customer factors

- Demand
- Benefits
- Value
- Distribution

Of these factors, *perceived value* is especially important since it defines what the customer should be prepared to pay.

Pricing new products offers a different set of challenges. In general, there are seen to be two main opposing strategies:

- skimming – high price, to skim off the short-term profit
- penetration – low price, to maximize long-term market share

Practical pricing policies for existing brands may include:

> Cost plus pricing

> Target pricing

> Historical pricing

> Range pricing

> Competitive pricing

> Market-based pricing

> Selective pricing

It should not be forgotten that price can also be a major factor in determining a product's or service's *image*, ranging from *quality-price* to *cut-price*.

A wide range of *discounts* may be offered: trade, quantity, cash, allowances, seasonal, promotional and individual.

Prices may also be set at levels which are judged to be 'psychologically' appropriate ($9.95, for instance). Other ways of achieving a price effect may lie with other parts of the offer, such as *product bundling*, at one extreme, and charging separately for 'options', at the other.

Alternatively, price may be *negotiated*, as it often is in capital goods markets.

Organizations may indulge in *price competition* for several reasons:

> Volume sales

> Other stimuli

> Minor brands

On the other hand, the dangers of initiating a price war include:

> Low-quality image

> Temporary advantage

> Investment potential

Practical reactions to *price challenges* could include:

| Reduce price |

| Maintain price |

| React with other measures |

| Split the market |

REVISION QUESTIONS

1 How does the equilibrium price come about? What is the price elasticity of demand?
2 How may supply and demand curves be established in practice?
3 What organizational factors, derived from related marketing theory, might influence price? How may positioning or branding be used to raise prices?
4 What customer-related factors might, in theory, affect price? Why may perceived value be important?
5 What opposing pricing policies may be applied to new products, and how do they work?
6 What is the impact of pricing roulette on price premiums.
7 List the pricing policies used in practice. What are the drawbacks of cost plus pricing?
8 How is competitive pricing different from market-based pricing? What selective pricing policies may be employed?
9 What discounts may be offered? What is psychological pricing? What are the differences between product bundling and charging for options?
10 Why might price competition be employed? When can it be justified in terms of volume sales? What are the dangers posed by price wars?
11 What responses to price competition may be available? How may they be successfully employed?

8 Distribution Decisions

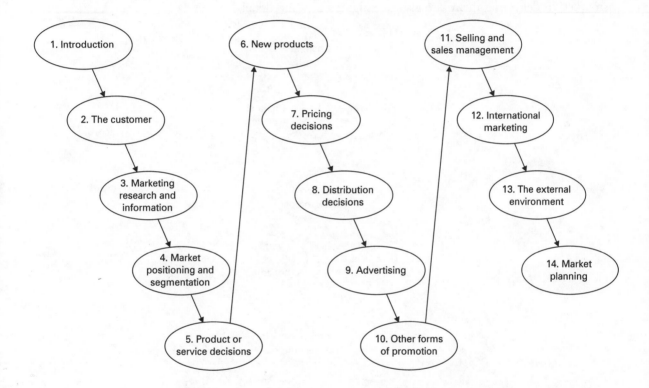

Introduction

'Place' is the least meaningful of the 4 Ps. Indeed, it has largely become the 'catch-all' of the 4 Ps. In addition to the major element of distribution, it covers what seem to be very diverse elements, including channel decisions, logistics, channel management, retailing and customer support. There may be some (albeit occasionally tenuous) shared logic between these various aspects of moving the goods or services between various levels of supplier and the end-user. Even so, *it is probably more productive to look at each of these in isolation from each other.*

The exact nature of the channels and distribution methods to be used is a fundamental, strategic, decision for the organization.

The logistics of distribution represent a specialized, but important function of management, ranging from data processing through inventory management to 'make or buy'. As this is a specialized subject, it is not explored in this edition – though it was in the previous one.

Retailing, as the ultimate link in many distribution chains, has special needs. Again, as this is a specialized subject, this is no longer covered in detail as part of this edition.

Customer service levels (resulting in customer satisfaction), and the special needs of the 'inner market' in delivering them, are also investigated in some detail.

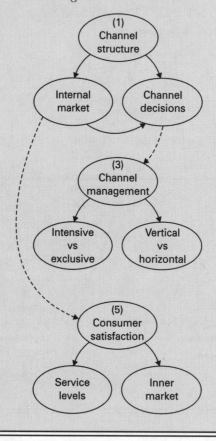

The ideal sales situation is that where the supplier and the customer meet face to face for a dialogue. In its most impressive form, where for example IBM sales personnel respond to the needs of major customers, this process could involve a team of experts meeting with a range of customer personnel over a number of months, so that the resulting individually tailored product exactly meets that customer's needs.

However, there are many products and services where the value of the individual sale does not justify such an approach, nor any other form of direct approach from the producer. The sale then has to be made through intermediaries, who can spread their costs across a range of products or services from different producers. The most obvious examples of these intermediaries are the retailers from whom we buy our consumer goods. But such intermediaries can be found in a wide variety of situations; after all, universities are merely the independent intermediaries that the government uses to deliver one form of higher education to the consuming students. In addition, the relationship between these intermediaries and the producers may be much more complex, and a whole spectrum of organizations may be involved.

The Distribution Channel

Frequently there may be a chain of such intermediaries, each passing the product down the chain to the next organization, before it finally reaches the consumer or end-user. This process is known as the *distribution chain* or, rather more exotically, as the *channel*. Each of the elements in these chains will have their own specific needs which the producer must take into account, along with those of the all-important end-user.

As Michael Baker[1] stresses, 'Consumption is a function of availability ... one can only consume products that are available.'

SELF-TEST QUESTION 8.1

What intermediaries does your organization use to service its end-users? (In this question, as well as in most of those in the later audits in this chapter, these intermediaries may be local authorities or voluntary agencies just as much as retailers or wholesalers.)

What function does each of these serve? How does your organization group these intermediaries?

---

[1] M. J. Baker, *Marketing Strategy and Management* (Macmillan, 1985).

Channel Members

Distribution channels can, thus, have a number of 'levels'. Kotler[2] defines the simplest level, that of direct contact, with no intermediaries involved, as the 'zero-level' channel.

The next level, the 'one-level' channel, features just one intermediary – in consumer goods a retailer, for industrial goods a distributor, say. In recent years this has been the level which, together with the zero-level, has accounted for the greatest percentage of the overall volumes distributed in, say, the UK; the very elaborate distribution systems in Japan are at the other end of the spectrum, with many levels being encountered even for the simplest of consumer goods.

In the UK, a second level, a wholesaler for example, is now mainly used to extend distribution to the large number of small, neighbourhood retailers.

The complexities which may actually ensue are best demonstrated by Benson Shapiro's[3] well-known illustration of Clairol's appliance division distribution system. The same picture can be applied, at least in principle, to 'service' channels. For instance, John Nevin[4] describes the alternative routes for the provision of the performing arts (figure 8.1).

SELF-TEST QUESTION 8.2

Draw the complete distribution chain for your organization, paying particular attention to the channels of distribution it uses to service its end-users.

Channel structure

To the various 'levels' of distribution, which they refer to as the 'channel length', Lancaster and Massingham[5] also add another structural element, the relationship between its members:

- *Conventional or free-flow.*   This is the usual, widely recognized, channel with a range of 'middle-men' passing the goods on to the end-user. This will be discussed later in some depth.

---

[2] P. Kotler, *Marketing Management* (Prentice-Hall, 7th edn, 1991).
[3] B. P. Shapiro, Improve distribution with your promotional mix, *Harvard Business Review* (March–April 1977).
[4] J. R. Nevin, An empirical analysis of marketing channels for the performing arts, *Marketing the Arts*, ed. M. P. Mokwa (Praeger, 1980).
[5] G. Lancaster and L. Massingham, *Essentials of Marketing* (McGraw-Hill, 1988).

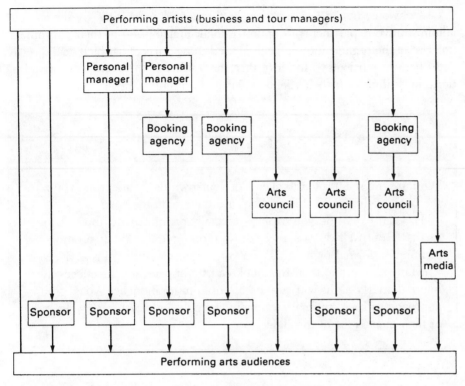

Figure 8.1   The marketing channels for the performing arts.

- *Single transaction.*   A temporary 'channel' may be set up for one transaction; for example, the sale of property or a specific civil engineering project. This does not share many characteristics with other channel transactions, each one being unique; therefore it is not discussed further.
- *Vertical marketing system (VMS).*   In this form, the elements of distribution are integrated; this is discussed further later in this chapter.

The internal market

Many of the marketing principles and techniques which are applied to the external customers of an organization can be just as effectively applied to each subsidiary's, or each department's, *internal* customers.

In some parts of certain organizations this may in fact be formalized, as goods are transferred between separate parts of the organization at a 'transfer price'. To all intents and purposes, with the possible exception of the pricing mechanism itself, this process can and should be viewed as a normal buyer–seller relationship. The fact that this is a captive market, resulting in a 'monopoly price', should not discourage the participants from employing marketing techniques.

Less obvious, but just as practical, is the use of 'marketing' by service and administrative departments to optimize their contribution to their 'customers' (the rest of the organization in general, and those parts of it which deal directly with them in particular). In all of this, the lessons of the non-profit organizations, in dealing with their clients, offer a very useful parallel.

SELF-TEST QUESTION 10.3

Who are the main internal clients of your own department or group (on the basis of the 80:20 Rule)? What are their requirements?

To what extent do you explore (formally or informally) those requirements? How well do you meet those requirements? What promotional techniques (formal or informal) do you use to enhance your service?

(Many of the audits in this book can be applied just as effectively to internal markets. If you are in a position to influence your group's approach to such internal customers, it might be worth reviewing some of the other audits in this light.)

Channel Decisions

Which channel to use is a major decision for most organizations. If the option is chosen of all sales being made directly to the consumer or end-user, there may be unacceptable cost penalties. On the other hand, introducing intermediaries can significantly reduce the amount of control that a producer has over the relationship with the end-user. The most likely factors to be taken into account in such a decision are:

- *Overall strategy.* The characteristics of the channel must be in line with the overall requirements of the marketing strategy.
- *Product (or service).* The characteristics of the product itself will play a part. For example, if it needs to be kept refrigerated, then a very specialized distribution chain will be required.

- *Consumer location.* Where the end-users themselves are located will also have an influence.
- *Cost.* Not least, of course, will be the comparative cost of the alternative channels.

Trade discounts

The organizations which form the various links in the distribution chains take over some of the producer's responsibilities. In general, their primary value to the producer is the wider distribution that they offer, which may increase the overall penetration of the brand. These intermediaries also hold stock, provide service support, and may also act as information gatherers and business consultants to the original producer. The exact relationship will depend in part upon the legal, contractual implications; a dealer will, for example, be totally independent of the producer, whereas an agent will act on behalf of that producer – typically operating the same terms and conditions.

In return for these services, these members of the distribution chains receive payments:

- *Trade discounts.* These are standard discounts, usually of a fixed percentage, offered to a channel member. However, the percentage may vary according to the 'category' in which the producer places the intermediary.
- *Quantity discount.* A quantity discount has the advantage that it offers an incentive for all intermediaries to try to sell the maximum volume, and hence trade-up to higher discount levels.

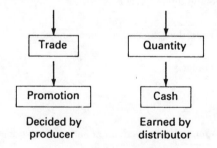

- *Promotional discount.* The producer may also attempt to 'push' the product or service by offering promotional discounts, in the belief that these will persuade the intermediary to substitute the brand in question for another, the end-user often accepting what is in stock. Alternatively, the intention may be to persuade the retailer to overstock; thus creating 'stock pressure', so that he is then forced to give the brand extra display space.
- *Cash discount.* Most producers normally offer trade intermediaries terms which require payment in 30 days. This is of considerable value to some retailers who have managed to reduce some of their stockholdings to less than five days. The extra 25 days' credit can in effect be used as a free loan. However, the producer may want to provide an incentive for retailers, or wholesalers, to pay earlier.

Hence, a cash discount, or a discount for immediate or prompt payment, is offered. This type of discount has, however, fallen into disfavour. The evidence suggests that the majority of customers will probably take the cash discount, and still pay late (often after 60 days rather than 30).

SELF-TEST QUESTION 8.4

For those in profit-making organizations: what trade discounts does your organization offer? Why does it offer these discounts? Are these goals achieved? Does it offer any cash discounts, and if so, to what effect?

For those in non-profit organizations: What fees or other incentives does your organization offer its intermediaries? What does it expect in return? How effective are these incentives in achieving the desired service to the end-users?

Channels

A number of alternative 'channels' of distribution may be available:

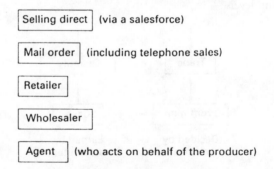

As suggested on a number of occasions, distribution channels may not be restricted to physical products. They may be just as important for moving a *service* from 'producer' to consumer in certain sectors; since both direct and indirect channels may be used. Hotels, for example, may sell their services (typically rooms) direct or through travel agents, tour operators, airlines, tourist boards, centralized reservation systems, and so on.

There have also been some innovations in the distribution of services. For example, there has been an increase in franchising and in rental services – the latter offering anything from televisions through to DIY tools. There has also been some evidence of service integration, with services linking together, particularly in the travel and tourism sector: for example, links now exist between airlines, hotels and car rental services. In addition, there has been a significant increase in retail outlets for the service sector; outlets such as estate agencies and building society offices, for example, are crowding out the traditional grocers and greengrocers from the high street.

Channel Management

The channel decision is very important. As we have seen, in theory at least, the cost of using intermediaries to achieve wider distribution is supposedly lower. Indeed, most consumer goods manufacturers could never justify the cost of selling direct to their consumers, except by mail order. In practice, if the producer is large enough, the use of intermediaries (particularly at the agent and wholesaler level) can sometimes cost more than going direct.

Many of the theoretical arguments about channels therefore revolve around cost. On the other hand, most of the practical decisions are concerned with control of the consumer. The small company has no alternative but to use intermediaries, often several layers of them, but large companies *do* have the choice.

However, many suppliers seem to assume that once their product has been sold into the channel, into the beginning of the distribution chain, their job is finished. Yet that distribution chain is merely assuming a part of the supplier's responsibility; and, if he has any aspirations to be market-oriented, his job should really be extended to managing, albeit very indirectly, all the processes involved in that chain, until the product or service arrives with the end-user. This may involve a number of decisions on the part of the supplier:

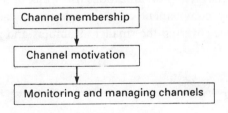

Channel membership.   To a degree, the supplier has some control over which organizations participate in the distribution chain, and what the structure of that channel might be. At one extreme, in mass consumer goods markets where members of the chain merely offer a logistical service, the supplier's main concern may be to *maximize distribution levels* so that the maximum number of outlets 'stock' the product or service. At the other extreme, where dealers, for example, take over some of the supplier's responsibility for supporting sophisticated technical products, the supplier may be primarily concerned about the *quality* of the individual dealer. Under these circumstances in particular, the choice of channel members becomes a very important activity, almost as though they were being hired as direct employees. These approaches can also be thought of as representing the intensity of the distribution:

- *Intensive distribution.*   Where the majority of resellers stock the 'product' (with convenience products, for example, and particularly the brand leaders in consumer goods markets) price competition may be evident.
- *Selective distribution.*   This is the normal pattern (in both consumer and industrial markets) where 'suitable' resellers stock the product.
- *Exclusive distribution.*   Only specially selected resellers (typically only one per geographical area) are allowed to sell the 'product'.

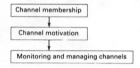

Channel motivation.   It is difficult enough to motivate direct employees to provide the necessary sales and service support. Motivating the owners and employees of the independent organizations in a distribution chain requires even greater effort. There are many devices for achieving such motivation. Perhaps the most usual is 'bribery': the supplier offers a better margin, to tempt the owners in the channel to push the product rather than its competitors; or a competition is offered to the distributors' sales personnel, so that they are tempted to push the product. At the other end of the spectrum is the almost symbiotic relationship that the all too rare supplier in the computer field develops with its agents – where the agent's personnel, support as well as sales, are trained to almost the same standard as the supplier's own staff.

Monitoring and managing channels.   In much the same way that the organization's own sales and distribution activities need to be monitored and managed, so will those of the distribution chain.

In practice, of course, many organizations use a mix of different channels; in particular, they may complement a direct salesforce, calling on the larger accounts, with agents, covering the smaller customers and prospects.

Vertical marketing

This relatively recent development integrates the channel with the original supplier – producer, wholesalers and retailers working in one unified system. This may arise because one member of the chain owns the other elements (often called 'corporate systems integration') – a supplier owning its own retail outlets is called *forward* integration. It is perhaps more likely that a retailer will own its own suppliers, this being *backward* integration. (For example, MFI, the furniture retailer, owns Hygena, which makes its kitchen and bedroom units.) The integration can also be by franchise (such as that offered by McDonald's hamburgers and Benetton clothes) or simple co-operation (in the way that Marks & Spencer co-operates with its suppliers).

Alternative approaches are 'contractual systems', often led by a wholesale or retail co-operative, and 'administered marketing systems' where one (dominant) member of the distribution chain uses its position to co-ordinate the other members' activities. This has traditionally been the form led by manufacturers.

The intention of vertical marketing is to give all those involved (and particularly the supplier at one end, and the retailer at the other) *control* over the distribution chain. This removes one set of variables from the marketing equations.

Research indicates that vertical integration is a strategy which is best pursued at the mature stage of the market (or product). At earlier stages it can actually reduce profits. It is arguable that it also diverts attention from the real business of the organization. Suppliers rarely excel in retail operations and, in theory, retailers should focus on their sales outlets rather than on manufacturing facilities (the most successful retail operator in the UK, Marks & Spencer, very deliberately provides considerable amounts of technical assistance to its suppliers, but does not own them).

Horizontal marketing

A rather less frequent example of new approaches to channels is where two or more non-competing organizations agree on a joint venture – a joint marketing operation – because it is beyond the capacity of each individual organization alone. In general, though, this is unlikely to be justified by marketing synergy alone.

SELF-TEST QUESTION 8.5

How does your organization formally manage the membership, motivation and monitoring of its channels of distribution?

Are there any significant differences in terms of the more informal, pragmatic procedures?

Has it employed either vertical or horizontal marketing? If so, how and why?

Customer Support

We now move on to look at another aspect of marketing; delivery of support for the customers.

Customer service levels

Perhaps the most important aspect of customer or client service, in terms of delivery of a product or service, is that it should be available when and where the customer wants it. If this is not the case, an immediate sale may well be lost. More importantly, long-term sales may also have been lost if the customer is forced to change to another brand, and then decides to stay with that brand.

The percentage availability is described as the *service level*. It might seem that the simple answer would be to achieve 100 per cent availability, but the cost of achieving this rises very steeply as the service level approaches 100 per cent, as the diagram by Thomas and Donaldson[6] (figure 8.2) shows. There is a very clear trade-off here between customer service (level) and cost. Fortunately the indications are that, in terms of demand generated, customers are not significantly affected by minor variations if there are generally high levels of availability. The usual 'S' shaped curve probably applies.

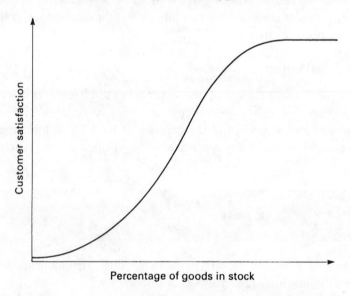

Lead time

However, there are other elements of customer service level, one of which relates to the time it takes to meet an order (where, unlike the situation described earlier, the product is not delivered 'ex-stock'). This is called the 'lead time' (or sometimes the 'order cycle time'). Clearly, the shorter the lead time, the better the service.

[6] M. J. Thomas and W. G. Donaldson, Customer service/customer care, *Marketing Handbook*, ed. M. J. Thomas (Gower, 1989).

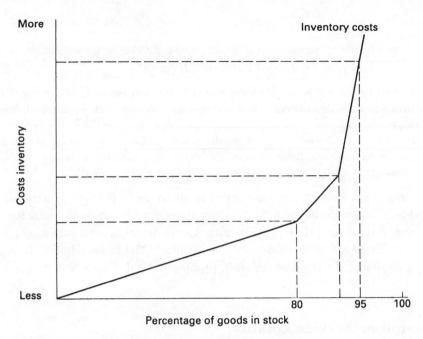

Figure 8.2 Cost of stockholding and service levels.

On the other hand, it is frequently the case that it is the *reliability* of the lead time that is more important. A customer who has to arrange a number of other activities to mesh in with the delivery of the product will often prefer that the delivery date is certain – even if it is later than it might have been – rather than face uncertainty. Another important element is the response time: how long it takes a customer to find out what is actually happening to the order.

In the specific context of queues associated with provision of a service, David Maister[7] lists a number of 'proportions':

1 Unoccupied time feels longer than occupied time ...
2 Preprocess waits feel longer than in-process waits ...
3 Anxiety makes waits seem longer ...
4 Uncertain waits are longer than known, finite waits ...
5 Unexplained waits are longer than explained waits ...
6 Unfair waits are longer than equitable waits ...
7 The more valuable the service the longer the customer will wait ...
8 Solo waits feel longer than group waits ...

These are all reasonably well known, indeed almost obvious, principles, yet how often have you recognized a management that has taken full note of them?

[7] D. H. Maister, The psychology of waiting lines, *Managing Services: Marketing, Operations and Human Resources* (Prentice-Hall, 1988).

Faults

The other measure, perhaps most immediately obvious to the customer, is the fault rate. This may be divided into two categories:

- *Errors.*   Errors involving the wrong 'product', quantity or price, or delivery to the wrong address, should not happen; but they do – and far more frequently than you might expect.
- *Faulty or damaged goods.*   This is usually what 'quality' is seen to be about; and customers, understandably, expect 100 per cent performance in this area (but rarely get it, except in the standardized mass consumer markets).

In many markets, this means that in order to avoid delivery of out-of-date products, or goods beyond their expiry date, the distribution chain has to operate a rigorous FIFO (First In First Out) control system; whereas LIFO (Last In First Out) is more normal and natural – the latest addition to stock being loaded at the front of the shelf, pushing the older stock to the back.

Customer Service Quality

The elements described so far largely relate to the narrow perspective of *service levels* in the consumer goods market. *In the other sectors, particularly that of industrial goods, 'customer service' may be even more important, and certainly more complex.* For example, it is often stated (not least by the company itself) that IBM's outstanding success – at its peak – as a marketing company was almost entirely due to its commitment to 'customer service'.

In the service sector (particularly in the area of personal services), customer service is often, by definition, the 'product' itself. The 'quality' of the customer service represents the quality of the 'product' the customer is buying. Indeed, in many service sectors the customer has to buy the service 'on trust', since it cannot be inspected before use. Monitoring such customer service, and maintaining standards, may be particularly difficult for some service providers, especially where there is a high content of personal service (for example, in hotels and catering in the private sector, and in hospitals in the public sector).

David Maister[8] formulates two 'Laws of Service'. The first of these is expressed by the formula:

> Satisfaction equals perception minus expectation. If you *expect* a certain level of service and *perceive* the service received to be higher, you will be a satisfied customer. If you perceive this same level where you had expected a higher one, you will be disappointed and therefore a dissatisfied customer. The point is that both what is perceived and what is expected are psychological phenomena

[8] Maister, The psychology of waiting lines.

– not reality [and it is the *relative* level of service, related to expectations, which is important, not the absolute one] ...

Second Law of Service: It is hard to play 'catch-up ball'. There is also a halo effect created by early stages of any service encounter ... the largest payoff may well occur in the earliest stages of the service encounter [a problem early in the provision of the service sours the whole process].

Bitner et al.[9] highlight one major problem when they say:

... exemplary firms understand that managing the service encounter involves more than training employees to say 'have a nice day' or to answer the phone on or before the third ring [although even these actions might represent a great step forward for many organizations] ... Effective management of the service encounter involves understanding the often complex behaviour of employees ...

... Employees must be empowered (given discretion and latitude) to take what action is proper in a specific situation. Many companies appear to believe that a management philosophy of endorsing action will empower employees. Broad endorsements and guide-lines such as 'the customer is always right' or 'we put service first' are not enough. As all customer employees soon find out, not all customers are right, and some are even abusive and out of control.

Customer Complaints

Godley[10] states that 'it is essential to record all complaints and the manner in which they are dealt with'. This may seem obvious, but even the UK's Open University Business School found to its surprise, and dismay, that its students had no formal means of complaint; this was only discovered when the students managed to find alternative, unofficial means. 'Customer complaints' is one of the most important aspects of business operations needing management control, yet it is often one of the most neglected.

Such complaints are often treated as a nuisance by many organizations, and yet they have considerable value for a number of reasons:

1 Although there will always be a small proportion of 'frivolous complaints', a complaint usually highlights something which has gone wrong with a part of the overall marketing operation; usually, a sufficiently high quality has not been achieved. Whatever the reason, the sensible marketer will want to know exactly what has gone wrong, so that remedial action may be taken.

2 The way in which a complaint is handled is often seen by customers, and their many contacts, as an acid-test of the true quality of support. What is more, it is

[9] M. J. Bitner, B. H. Booms and M. S. Tetreault, The service encounter: diagnosing favourable and unfavourable incidents, *Journal of Marketing*, vol. 54 (1990).
[10] C. G. A. Godley, Marketing control, *The Principles and Practice of Management*, ed. E. F. L. Brech (Longman, 1975).

also a powerful reminder to the organization's own staff of just how important quality is.

3 Not least, customers who complain are usually loyal customers (those who are not loyal simply tend to switch to another supplier), and will continue to be loyal and valuable customers – as long as their complaint is handled well.

The first rule is that *complaints should be positively encouraged*. Theodore Levitt[11] states:

> One of the surest signs of a bad or declining relationship [with a customer] is the absence of complaints from the customer. Nobody is ever that satisfied, especially over an extended period of time. The customer is not being candid or not being contacted.

That is not the same as saying that the *reasons* for complaints should be encouraged. But, assuming that despite your best efforts the problems have occurred, you should put nothing in the way of any customer who wants to complain; and, indeed, positively encourage such complaints – since the main problem lies with the many more customers who do not complain [and instead change to another supplier] rather than the few who abuse the complaints system.

Hart et al.[12] report:

> Many businesses have established '800' numbers so customers can report problems easily and at the company's expense. American Express has installed such lines and estimates it achieves responses more quickly and at 10 per cent to 20 per cent of the cost of handling the correspondence.

General Electric has gone further still, by providing a centralized, expert, round the clock, general support service: anyone who just has a query, not necessarily a complaint, about one of its products may call free of charge.

The second rule is that *all complaints should be carefully handled by painstakingly controlled, and monitored, procedures*. Complaints must be handled well, and must be seen to be handled well: by the complainant, and by the organization's own staff.

The third, and most important rule, is that *the complaint should then be fully investigated, and the cause remedied*. Complaints are only symptoms. The disease needs to be cured! There may be an understandable temptation to overlook complaints until they reach a 'significant level', but holding off until the complaints reach this 'pain threshold' usually means that they have already become damaging to the organization's image. It is far better to assume that 'one complaint is too many':

[11] T. Levitt, After the sale is over, *Harvard Business Review* (September–October 1983).
[12] C. W. L. Hart, J. L. Heskett and W. E. Sasser Jr, The profitable art of service recovery, *Harvard Business Review* (July–August, 1990).

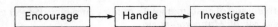

The reality in most organizations is very different. The number of complaints are minimized not by remedying the reasons for them but by evading the complainants. The erroneous assumption is usually made that complainants are troublemakers, and have to be handled in a confrontational manner.

Customer satisfaction

As mentioned above, most dissatisfied customers do not complain (up to 97 per cent, according to a US survey[13]), but they do tell their friends [the same survey showed that 13 per cent complained to more than 20 other people].

On the other hand, as Philip Kotler[14] points out, a satisfied customer:

1 Buys again.
2 Talks favourably to others about the company [although, as reported in the survey quoted above, only to three others – compared with an average of eleven others when complaining].
3 Pays less attention to competing brands and advertising.
4 Buys other products that the company adds to its line.

To emphasize these depressing statistics, Goodman and Malech[15] designed a chart which reports results from the US Office of Consumer Affairs (figure 8.3). Table 8.1 details the results that they themselves obtained on surveys for Coca-Cola and General Motors.

Clearly, any organization should be highly motivated to make certain that its customers are satisfied; however, in practice, remarkably few do so. It is essential, therefore, that an organization first monitors the satisfaction level of its customers. This may be done at the 'global' level, by market research. Preferably, though, satisfaction should be assessed at the level of individuals or groups. The results should be analysed to produce overall satisfaction indices, and also provided to field management so that they can rectify any individual problems.

It is possible that many retailers may not be able to use such information at the individual level, though the 'loyalty' (club) schemes being introduced may aid this, and some service providers may want to at least keep track of the satisfaction of their *regular* customers. However, more may track satisfaction

---

[13] K. Albrecht and R. Zemke, *Service America* (Dow-Jones Irwin, 1985).
[14] Kotler, *Marketing Management*.
[15] J. A. Goodman and A. R. Malech, The role of service in effective marketing, *Handbook of Modern Marketing*, ed. V. P. Buell (McGraw-Hill, 2nd edn, 1986).

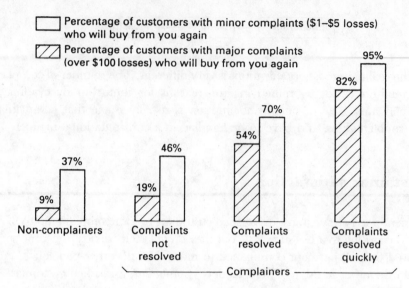

☐ Percentage of customers with minor complaints ($1–$5 losses) who will buy from you again

▨ Percentage of customers with major complaints (over $100 losses) who will buy from you again

Figure 8.3 How many of your unhappy customers will buy from you again?

Table 8.1 Word-of-mouth behaviour

	Satisfied	*Dissatisfied*
Median persons told of experience		
Small problems	4–5	9–10
Large problems	8	16

levels by branch, to detect unwelcome deteriorations before they do untold harm.

There are a number of advantages to conducting satisfaction surveys (particularly where any individual problems highlighted can subsequently be dealt with):

- like complaints, they indicate where problems lie
- if they cover all customers, they allow the 96 per cent of non-complainants to communicate their feelings, and vent their anger
- they positively show even the satisfied customers that their supplier is interested
- they help to persuade the supplier's staff to take customer service more seriously

The importance of very high standards of customer service can be demonstrated by two examples. The marketing philosophy of McDonald's, the world's largest food service organization, is encapsulated in its motto 'Q.S.C. & V.' ('Quality, Service, Cleanliness and Value'). The standards, introduced somewhat quixotically to its franchisees and managers at the 'Hamburger University' in Elk Grove Village, Illinois, require that the customer receive a 'good tasting' hamburger in no more than five minutes, from a friendly host or hostess, in a spotlessly clean restaurant. It is salutary to observe how few of their competitors manage even the simple task of keeping their premises clean. The second example, Disneyland, also insists on spotlessness, and on the customer being 'the Guest'; whereas the terms used in the fairground trade (with which Disney competes, albeit at a very different level) usually see the customer as some form of victim – 'pigeon', 'mark', 'punter' and so on – to be fleeced before the fair moves on.

The Inner Market

By definition, marketing is primarily concerned with the world *outside* the organization. On the other hand, if it is to optimize the use of resources, it also has to be concerned with what lies *inside* the organizational perimeter.

Increasingly, the most valuable resource of any organization (particularly in the service sector) is its people, and the skills that they possess. In tapping this internal resource, so that the organization can face up to its external environment, it turns out that many of the traditional tools of marketing can be used to great effect in the very important areas of internal communication and motivation. It would be foolish to pretend that marketing will supersede the human resource management needed to optimize the contribution from the workforce, but it can help to motivate and focus the efforts of the diverse parts of the organization.

Recent campaigns have tended to focus on Total Quality Management (TQM), on the basis that the overall quality that the customer perceives comes from every part of the organization. 'Inner marketing' is in many ways the ultimate extension of TQM in that it fixes 'quality' exclusively in terms of the marketing context (of what is important to the customer) *for every employee.*

What is increasingly being recognized is that the marketing function may effectively be distributed widely across the whole organization, rather than just concentrated in the marketing department. Christian Grönroos[16] makes the point that:

---

[16] C. Grönroos, Defining marketing: a market-oriented approach, *European Journal of Marketing*, vol. 23, no. 1 (1989).

This [marketing] function is not the same as the marketing department's. The latter's is an organizational solution only, whereas the size and diversity of the former depend on the nature of the customer relations. Hence, the marketing function is spread over a large part of the organization outside the marketing department, and all of the activities which have an impact on the current and future buyer behaviour of the customer cannot be taken care of by marketing specialists only.

Many organizations in the service sector, and not a few in the manufacturing sector, have 'customer service programmes'. These use many of the promotional devices of marketing – advertising, incentives, seminars, and so on – to persuade employees (particularly those in contact with customers) to adopt the correct attitude to those customers.

As Bitner et al.[17] report, however, this is insufficient where the organization's *systems* are ineffective. It is compounded by the fact that the employees experience considerable dissatisfaction themselves with customers whose behaviour is inappropriate or unreasonably demanding; and this requires a deeper appreciation of these relationships by management.

Piercy and Morgan[18] explain:

In working with a variety of organizations we have identified this problem as the *internal marketing strategy gap*. Our thinking is simply that in addition to the development of strategies aimed at the *external* marketplace, in order to achieve the organizational change needed to make these strategies work, it is necessary to carry out exactly the same process for the *internal* marketplace in companies – in short, we have both internal and external customers.

Customer service programmes have received a mixed response. The problem has often been that the management implementing them were themselves unconvinced of the message; and it was unrealistic, under these circumstances, to expect the employees to react more favourably than their betters. Probably the most frequent shortcoming is that such campaigns are run as very short-term programmes, which is bound to reduce their impact.

The *inner market* (not to be confused with the internal market) is a much more powerful concept. Quite simply, employees should be 'marketed' to in exactly the same way as customers. Implicit in this concept is that *all* the aspects of marketing as a whole should be incorporated; in particular, that a 'dialogue' should take place. 'Inner marketing' is as much about finding out what the employees want as persuading them to do what the organization wants.

The first requirement, and the one which distinguishes it from almost all other 'customer service programmes', is some form of marketing research;

---

[17]Mary Jo Bitner, Bernard H. Booms and Lois A. Mohr, Critical service encounters: the employee's viewpoint, *Journal of Marketing*, vol. 58 (October 1994).

[18] N. Piercy and N. Morgan, Making marketing strategies happen in the real world, *Marketing Business* (February 1990).

exactly as with any other marketing programme, but here conducted on the organization's own employees. This should be used to determine where they stand, for example, in relation to their perception of the customer, and of the customer service programmes which are likely to be the main focus of the research. Furthermore, as with any piece of sound research, it should also attempt to find out where employees might stand in the future, exploring their attitudes and motivations:

- Is the customer seen as friend or foe?
- Does anyone do anything more than pay lip-service to customer research programmes, and why?
- Do employees really want to offer a good service? If not, why not?
- How can they be persuaded to change their views?

Incidentally, this research may have additional benefits. One of IBM's most powerful tools, in developing its justly famed relationship with its staff, was the 'Opinion Survey'. Every two years, every IBM employee took part in an anonymous survey of how they felt about the company and its activities, as well as how they felt about their immediate management (since the results were published, this was a remarkably powerful device for ensuring that managers took note of the opinions of their subordinates). The results were very publicly acted upon to the benefit of the 'inner market', not least because the employees recognized that IBM was listening to them. Such 'opinion surveys' are remarkably effective devices for obtaining information on the 'inner market'. If applied regularly to all staff, they are also remarkably good motivators, and contributors to a positive culture. Unfortunately, remarkably few managers use them. Those that do (for example, David Ankerson[19] of the Chef & Brewer division of Grand Metropolitan, from whom the term 'inner market' came) report that they are essential to the development of their 'customer service' programmes.

SELF-TEST QUESTION 8.6

How important to the success of the *marketing programmes* are the various categories of staff – field support personnel, accounts and ledgers staff, administrative staff, warehouse personnel and shopfloor workers – in your organization?

What programmes are in place to educate these various groups in customer service? How effective are these programmes? How much genuine support do they receive from senior management?

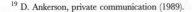

[19] D. Ankerson, private communication (1989).

> What programmes and research are in place to listen to employees?
> What impact might the implementation of inner marketing have?

'Cultural' Factors

In the ultimate extension of 'inner marketing', Peters and Waterman[20] stress that the 'culture' of an organization (generally speaking, the common values that its employees share) can be a very important contributor to its success. Such 'culture' can be even more important in determining what 'customer service' is provided. They conceptualize this cultural element as 'shared values', which are central to their framework of the 'Seven Ss'.

Even in the manufactured goods sector, the customer sees his customer service in terms of *all* his contacts with the company. He does not restrict his view to the narrow confines of product availability, or to just those members of the salesforce who are supposed to be the 'ambassadors' of the company. He is even less influenced by advertisements that tell him how good the service is, if his own experiences tell him otherwise.

The 'culture' of the company is often what conditions this 'customer service'. As already mentioned, IBM maintained a philosophy of 'customer service' throughout the whole company (applying to all employees) as its only marketing objective for more than half a century – with spectacular results. Both McDonald's and Disney have similarly strong cultures.

The problem of addressing the 'cultural dimension', even though it is an essential element which must be allowed for in any marketing operation, is that changes in the culture of an existing organization may literally take years to be completed. If existing cultures are strong, and the changes are major, the process may take decades. Both IBM and the Japanese corporations, who probably have the strongest cultures of all, needed as much as 15 years to develop fully all the detailed aspects of the new, and rich, cultures they were introducing.

Henry Mintzberg[21] explains:

> As the organization establishes itself, it makes decisions and takes actions which serve as commitments and establish precedents that reinforce themselves over time. Actions become infused with value. When the forces are strong enough ideology begins to emerge. Furthermore, stories – sometimes called 'myths' – develop around important events and the actions of great leaders in the organization's past. Gradually the organization develops a history of its own ... Over

---

[20] T. J. Peters and R. H. Waterman, *In Search of Excellence* (Harper & Row, 1982).
[21] H. Mintzberg, *Power In and Around Organizations* (Prentice-Hall, 1983).

time this tradition influences behaviour, and that behaviour in turn reinforces the tradition. Eventually, an ideology may become established.

Culture is not, therefore, a topic to be taken lightly; although minor changes – particularly those which 'complement' the existing culture – may be accepted more rapidly.

FURTHER READING

Most of the material detailed in this chapter seems to be covered, at one end of the spectrum, by chapters in the standard textbooks. At the other end of the scale are specialist books which are not usually of great value to the general manager. Of the latter, that by Peter Attwood, *Planning a Distribution System* (Gower, 1971), is rather out of date but still gives a good feel for what is involved in the logistics of distribution. *Marketing Channel Management* (by Kenneth G. Hardy and Alan J. Magrath, Scott Foresman & Co., 1988) gives a more up-to-date picture.

SUMMARY

It has to be admitted that 'Place' is little more than a name of convenience given to a miscellaneous rag-bag of functions; although they often do have some, albeit tenuous, links with distribution.

Thus, *distribution*, and in particular the *channels* used, are the key elements of this chapter. The channels can typically range from *zero-level* (with no interme-diaries) to *two-level* (using one or more wholesalers to supply retailers); and even then tend to ignore the important *internal markets*, which exist within organizations. *Channel strategy* tends to revolve around:

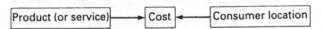

Channel management typically involves three types of decision/activity:

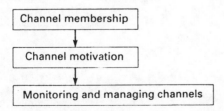

Customer service may depend upon the *service level*, or the lead time, or just an absence of faults. *Complaints handling* is, however, a very important function which should require that complaints are:

- encouraged (most customers do not complain, but simply take their business elsewhere)
- handled (customer satisfaction depends upon rapid resolution of the problem)
- investigated (complaints are symptomatic of underlying problems)

Customer satisfaction should, indeed, be tracked; for instance, by regular customer surveys.

In many organizations, especially those in the service sector, the '*inner market*' may be what determines the quality (sometimes referred to as TQM) of the offering. *Inner marketing* deploys all the techniques of conventional marketing, to find out what employees need and want – so that their support can be matched to the customer needs and wants. Not least, the *organizational culture* needs to be taken into account, or even modified – although this will normally take a very long time.

REVISION QUESTIONS

1 What are the roles of the different levels of distribution channels? How do internal markets fit in?
2 What make up the three main areas of channel management? Why might intensive distribution be more difficult to control, and channel members harder to motivate?
3 What is the inner market? Why is it important? How can it be addressed?

9 Advertising

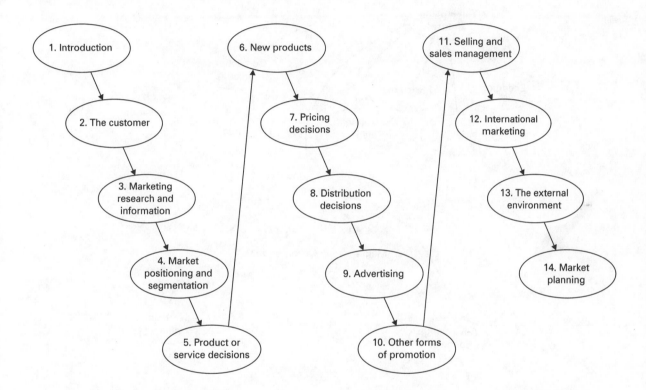

Introduction

Advertising is perhaps the most visible manifestation of marketing even if it is, at least on the large scale, the province of a minority of organizations. There is a well developed range of theory which addresses how advertising communicates, and the various elements of this are explored in this chapter. They include how messages reach consumers, with models which include encoding as well as those based on diffusion.

These traditional theories are, however, challenged by the use of 'conviction marketing', which is based as much on personal vision as on marketing research – and follows rather different rules. Indeed, the most prevalent practice is 'coarse marketing', which follows few, if any, of the guidelines.

Advertising practice is examined in terms of both the overall promotional mix and – in some depth – media, with a review of the main media types. However, it is mainly described through the workings of advertising agencies, in terms of both creative and media departments.

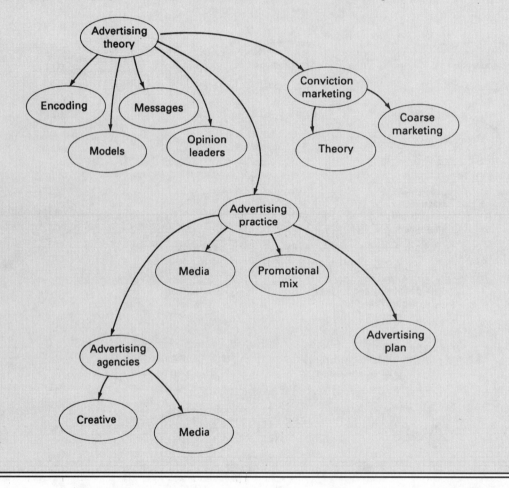

In earlier chapters we developed the model of marketing as a 'dialogue'. Specifically, we saw how market research was used to *listen* to consumers:

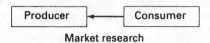

Market research

We now come to the other half of the dialogue, that of *talking* to the consumer:

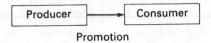

Promotion

The ideal form of promotion is the conversation which takes place between the expert sales professional and his or her customer. It is ideal, when properly handled, because, as well as being interactive, the communication in each direction is specific to the needs of both; and, if successful, should end in the best possible solution. Other forms of promotion, which deal in the 'average' needs of groups of people, can only hope to approximate to this ideal.

Dialogue

One key factor which must, therefore, always be remembered about promotion is that it is only one half of a dialogue. If the advertising does not respond to the customer needs, which should have been discovered by listening to the result of the marketing research, for example, it will probably fail – no matter how creative the treatment by the advertising agency.

Effective promotion is thus inextricably linked with sound market research, in one form or another. This is also an on-going dialogue, since the promotion itself will change what the customer thinks and needs.

Encoding

The most generally quoted model of the communication process stresses the element of 'encoding':

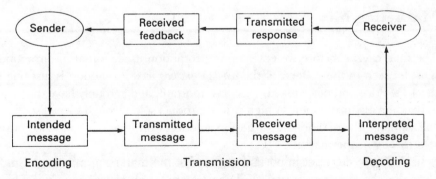

This is an elaborate way of saying that human-to-human communication is a *very* complex process, and that there is considerable latitude for misinterpretation. More fundamentally, it illustrates the need for considerable skill in creating the messages which the receiver (the consumer) finds persuasive: hence the justification for highly-paid advertising agency copywriters. But it also demonstrates the fact that the medium of transmission (press or television) can also change the message, again justifying the need for the copywriters and media buyers.

This 'electronic' metaphor does, however, illustrate the point that 'noise' is a major problem for any promotional message. The message itself may be distorted in transmission, in the few seconds which the reader spends on it before the page is turned or before the viewer is distracted from the message of the commercial. The recipient may, accordingly, obtain a very fragmentary message (hence the emphasis on simplicity in advertising messages). Worst of all, though, will be the torrent of other 'noise', the potentially more interesting editorial matter surrounding the advertisement, or just the distractions of everyday life, through which the advertisers' messages have to be heard: hence the reliance on multiple 'opportunities to see' – to 'turn up the volume' or to break through the noise barrier. There is also a need to invest in creative talent to optimize the impact of the individual message.

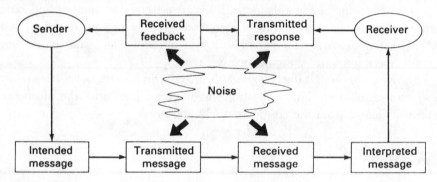

Marketing Mix

The final caveat, before we enter upon promotion itself, is that all promotion must be seen in the context of the *whole marketing mix*. Promotion is just one of the 4 Ps. Price and place may be just as important, and certainly have their own impacts on any promotion. A high-priced product sold through specialist outlets will demand a very different form of promotion from that of a cut-price brand sold through supermarkets.

In addition, the most important element of the marketing mix must almost always be the *product or service* itself. Despite popular misconceptions, it is a hard fact of advertising life that consumers will not buy – at least not more than once – a product or service which does not meet their needs, no matter how persuasive the promotion. At the same time, the form of the promotion itself, the message and even the medium, may be largely determined by the specification of that product or service. Thus, by defining the product, you largely define the whole marketing mix, which explains the heavy emphasis on the 'product' in the earlier chapters.

In this way, then, all the elements of the marketing mix (all Four Ps) contribute to the overall promotion of a product or service or company; and the 'input' into promotion may come from areas even further afield.

Promotion of services

Despite the fact that services follow much the same pattern of promotion as products, there may be some differences:

| Personal Selling and employees |
| Word of mouth |
| Tangibility |
| Consistency |

- *Personal selling and employees.* We have already seen that services are usually produced and consumed at the same time, and frequently this is also the time of the sale itself. This means that the sale is often made personally by the staff who are providing the service. In this way, perhaps the majority of the staff in effect become sales personnel; and, to persuade them to provide the requisite quality of service, 'advertising' may have to target them as much as the external customers.
- *Word of mouth.* Because of the problems of demonstrating quality and value, and the customer's need to build up trust, word of mouth recommendation by loyal customers may be correspondingly more important – particularly for those services, such as personal services, which are based upon local branches with relatively small catchment areas.
- *Tangibility.* The promotional campaign needs to make tangible the intangible, possibly by the use of symbols such as Marlboro's cowboy or Legal and General's coloured umbrella.
- *Consistency.* As 'trust' can easily be destroyed by a single bad experience, it is important that the service, and its promotion, maintains consistency. It must continue to offer, and deliver, what was promised to the customer.

Promotion in non-profit organizations

It should be easy to see that service providers in general have the same promotional needs as manufacturers of physical products, although the detailed messages may be very different. However, those managers working in non-profit organizations may fail to see any requirement to 'sell' or promote their 'products' or organizations. A national health service, for example, does not need to advertise for customers, although its private-sector competitors do.

One thing *is* clear: such organizations still have to communicate with their 'customers'. They need to let their consumers know that the organization exists, what it offers and how they can use it; hence the plethora of 'promotional' booklets that social services departments offer to the unemployed. The requirements imposed by these 'communications' are often indistinguishable from conventional service industry promotions. Indeed, government 'information' campaigns – such as those to combat cigarette smoking and drug addiction – often dominate the mass media.

Corporate Promotion versus Brand Promotion

Most advertising, along with other forms of promotion, relates to specific brands. It is very direct in attempting to increase sales of that product or service. However, a growing element is that of corporate advertising, which promotes the overall organization rather than its individual brands. Indeed, in order to reduce advertising costs – in relative terms – many organizations have now started to promote this *corporate brand* as their main investment, with individual products running – on reduced budgets – under this umbrella. Thus, the rationale may be that it is the support to be obtained from the organizational umbrella which ultimately sells the brands; and such a case can certainly be made for Marks & Spencer (whose corporate name is better known than its 'St Michael' brand name) or IBM. On the other hand, it may well be also because of a degree of nervousness induced by the increasing possibility of even very large corporations falling to hostile takeovers.

The principles of corporate advertising follow those of brand advertising very closely: in this context, the corporation is the brand writ large. The example of corporate advertising does, however, illustrate a more general point: that an organization may conduct a number of different types of promotional campaign, often aimed at different audiences. That targeted on consumers is usually self-evident, but there may also be a significant amount of promotion – often in the form of direct mail – directed at shareholders and other members of the financial community, with a view to protect the share price and reduce the risk of takeover activity.

All of these different forms of promotion follow broadly similar rules, but each must be designed to meet the needs of its specific target audience. One word of caution is necessary: if these separate campaigns obviously come from the same supplier, they must also be *consistent* with each other – even if, as often happens, they are developed by different agencies. When British inventor Clive Sinclair launched the disastrous C5 electric car he was using the financial 'vehicle' of a separate company, but this did not stop the eventual bad publicity from rebounding on his main money-spinner, the personal computer company; to the extent, perhaps, that this led to his eventual decision to sell that company, and his name, to Amstrad.

Push versus Pull

Where a supplier uses any form of distribution chain, as most of those in the mass consumer markets in fact do, he or she is faced with two extremes in terms of promotion;

In the case of *push* the supplier directs the bulk of the promotional effort at selling the 'product' into the channel (into the various organizations which make up the chain of distribution) in order to persuade the members of that channel to 'push' the product forward until it reaches the final consumer. It tends, thus, to revolve around sales promotion and push is sometimes referred to as 'below the line' (derived from the days when advertising agencies managed all promotional activity – and the items on the accounts which did not relate to advertising were put below the line which divided off the agency's main activity on the expenditure reports). This is a technique particularly favoured by organizations without strong brands which are involved in price competition.

In the case of *pull* the supplier focuses the promotional effort (typically advertising) on the consumer, in the belief that he or she will be motivated to 'pull' the product through the channel (by demanding it, for example, from retailers). It is (due to its association with advertising) sometimes referred to as 'above the line'. This is the technique usually favoured by the owners of strong, differentiated brands.

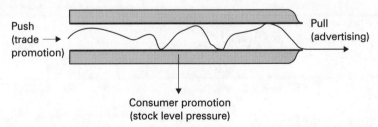

In practice, most suppliers choose a route somewhere between these two extremes; blending both elements to obtain the optimum (balanced) effect. In any case, brand share is often dependent upon the percentage distribution; and, in turn, distribution just as often reflects brand share.

Choosing a Promotional Method

A major decision to be taken before 'talking' to the customer is what promotional mix to use. Just as there are separate elements to the overall marketing mix, so there are different 'media' which may be used to reach the customer. Choosing which of these to use is a key decision, because – depending upon the individual product and the customer set – different 'media' may have varying degrees of effectiveness.

Typically, the major decision is on what medium to concentrate the main message(s). The campaign may often revolve around just one medium, be it a television commercial or personal selling. Even so, other media will probably be used, and the balance between them must be considered carefully.

There is a wide variety of specific techniques which may be used to communicate with customers. Broadly speaking, they can be grouped into three main categories, in terms of decreasing impact on the customer:

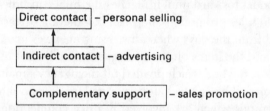

SELF-TEST QUESTION 9.1

Which of the following forms of promotion does your organization use?

- direct contact – personal selling?
- indirect contact – advertising?
- complementary support – sales promotion?

The Promotional Lozenge

To put these in a more memorable context than just the rather amorphous 'marketing mix' (even though that does convey exactly what is involved) I like to look at the 'promotion lozenge'. Once again it is shaped like a diamond, but I prefer to call it a lozenge because (unlike the earlier research diamond) it does not have any clear cutting edges. It is generally much less well defined, softer at its extremes. And there is definitely a quality of trial and error involved – suck the lozenge and see!

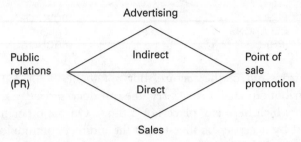

This lozenge is not as arbitrary as it may seem. It actually is organized along two dimensions. Hopefully, the vertical one is obvious. *It is the move from direct (sales) to indirect (advertising) contact with the customer.*

Perhaps less obvious, but in many respects more important, is the horizontal dimension. This shows the flow over time, from the start with the establishment of a general interest via public relations (PR), through investment in image building with advertising and much of the selling process, to the very immediate impact of sales promotional devices at the point of sale. It also demonstrates the gradation from the long-term investment in PR and advertising/sales to the very short-term effect of promotion.

The demands posed by your product/service package determine the actual shape of the lozenge – another reason for choosing a soft, malleable lozenge rather than a hard diamond. If you need the face-to-face (sales) contact to explain a complex package, and the price of this is sufficiently high to cover the high costs this implies, then the lozenge becomes almost an inverted triangle:

The advertising element is almost missing, though even in the almost pure sales environment there will remain some element of indirect contact – often in the form of direct mail – to generate prospects for the face-to-face contact. The 'point of sale' here is a time (not a place), and the promotional element is usually only seen in the form of discounting the price. Despite my earlier comments though, sales professionals would argue that this does need to have a very sharp cutting edge.

Almost the exact reverse occurs for fast moving consumer goods where the low unit price means that face-to-face selling is simply not an economic proposition:

Here 'sales' drops out of the picture, but not totally – for someone has to persuade distribution chains to carry the product/service package to the 'point of sale' (which here is a place not a time). On the other hand, most of the effort must by necessity be invested in the indirect communications. Once again, though, the promotion (here used at the point of sale) is very short term – again usually in the form of some price reduction (either directly or indirectly). You can play many different games with the lozenge, but I will finish with one which distorts it to show – quite realistically – advertising (for, say, a consumer durable or a car) preceding face-to-face sales activity in the retail outlet.

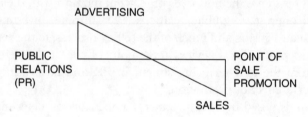

Personal Selling

As already stated, this is potentially the *ideal* form of promotion, assuming that the salesforce lives up to its promise, which, unfortunately, is not always the case. Face-to-face contact offers promotion which is:

- *interactive*
- *responsive*
- *flexible*

but, as it requires a salesperson to talk to every customer, it is inherently:

- *expensive*

If the value of the individual sale is high enough, and the customers may be contacted economically, personal selling will usually be the chosen approach. Selling, and sales management, is covered in more detail in chapter 11.

Selling services

In practice, face-to-face selling tends to be more prevalent in the service industries. This is, in large part, because many such services are also 'delivered' in a personal form; with some service providers using 'professionals of the specialism' rather than salespersons. It is also because personal contact may be seen as necessary to establish the 'credentials' – the integrity – of the service provider, where the service itself is an intangible quantity. In these situations the sales professionals, and the way they personally handle the sale, may be seen by the customers as the best measure of the service being offered; the method of promotion may become, by default, the 'product'.

Because of the involvement of so many personnel in face-to-face contact during the delivery of such a service, the 'sales' role may become diffused. *All* personnel providing the service are, in one way or another, 'salespersons'. This means that 'sales training' (often described, in this context, as 'customer service training') has to be provided on a much wider front, throughout the organization; hence the emphasis on 'customer care' programmes in the retailing and financial services sectors. This is equally true of non-profit organizations; the doctor's 'bedside' manner represents an important 'sales' activity (and, by improving the consumer's perception of the 'service', may actually improve the 'medicine').

Advertising Theory

On the other hand, most contacts with consumers or end-users, which are individually relatively low in value, must inevitably be handled by indirect means. Of these, the main process used to 'talk' to consumers is advertising. Indeed, the 1979 research by Farris and Buzzell[1] concluded (largely without any great surprises) that advertising/promotion ratios are higher where:

- the product is standardized, rather than produced to order
- there are many end-users (e.g. almost all households)
- the typical purchase amount is small
- sales are made through channel intermediaries rather than direct to users

This list represents almost the classic definition of where advertising should apply. More tellingly, however, they found that the ratios are also higher where:

- auxiliary services are of some importance
- the product is premium priced (and, probably, premium quality)
- the manufacturer has a high contribution margin per dollar of sales

---

[1] P. W. Farris and R. D. Buzzell, Why advertising and promotional costs vary: some cross-sectional analyses, *Journal of Marketing* (Fall 1979).

Again, this emphasis on higher-quality/higher-margin products is not totally unexpected. Rather more unexpectedly, but perhaps reflecting the tactical use of advertising as a weapon for buying share and volume (especially at the time of new product launches), they also concluded that the ratios are higher where:

- The manufacturer has a relatively small share of market, and/or has surplus production capacity
- A high proportion of the manufacturer's sales come from new products

The question which has long been asked is 'Just how effective is advertising?' Lord Leverhulme (the founder of the Unilever empire) was supposed to have made the famous comment that he was sure that half his advertising didn't work – but the problem was that he did not know which half. This view is reinforced by Abraham and Lodish,[2] whose research apparently showed that only 46 per cent of advertising campaigns for established brands showed a positive impact on sales (although the ratio was slightly higher, at 59 per cent, for new products). Clearly, it is important that organizations understand what they are doing in this field.

As with any 'conversation' there may be many topics which could be addressed, and many different styles of delivery – as shown by the many different creative devices used by advertising agencies. In general, though, there are three main groups of activities:

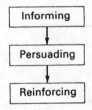

- *Building awareness (informing).*   The first task of any advertising is to make the audience appreciate that the product or service exists, and to explain exactly what it is.
- *Creating favourable attitudes (persuasion).*   The next stage, and the one that preoccupies most advertisers, is to create the favourable attitudes to the brand which will eventually lead the consumers to switch their purchasing patterns.
- *Maintenance of loyalty (reinforcement).*   One of the tasks which is often forgotten is that of maintaining the loyalty of existing customers, who will almost always represent the main source of future sales.

There are a range of separate functions involved in producing successful advertising, and these are reviewed in the rest of the chapter.

---

[2] M. M. Abraham and L. M. Lodish, Getting the most out of advertising and promotion, *Harvard Business Review* (May–June 1990).

Advertising Investment

Traditionally, advertising and promotion has been treated as current *cost*, with an immediate, but short-term, effect. Although this view probably is justified in terms of most forms of sales promotion it seriously underestimates some important longer-term impacts of advertising and PR. A more useful view in this context is that *advertising investment should in effect be treated as a fixed asset.*

Adopting such a long-term perspective has a number of important implications. The first of these revolves around the patterns of performance which might be expected. Thus, the basic pattern is not that of the short-run supply and demand curves, but that of the '*longer term competitive saw*'[3] which we looked at in the earlier chapter. Indeed, it is a level saw; its overall trend is relatively flat but it has the teeth representing the impact of the individual campaigns (or even that of individual insertion, or even of words within the single advertisement).

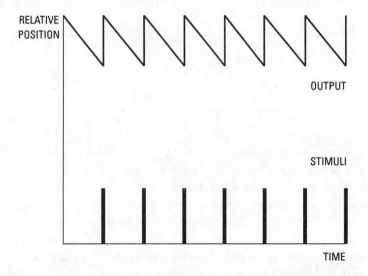

Following the implied principle of the fixed asset, this sawtooth maintenance pattern can be overlaid on a gradually declining trend in performance, notionally equivalent to *depreciation* in financial accounting (which we examined in an earlier chapter). Thus, over time there may be a slow drift away from the ideal position – as the customers' needs and wants change and/or competitive positioning improves. Your own response to this may take two forms. The first, and perhaps the most effective, is that of: '*dynamic repositioning*' – change in relative positions should be regularly tracked and the brand's position readjusted to take account of this in much the same way that an autopilot's feedback mechanisms ensure that an airliner follows the correct flightpath. The emphasis here is on

[3] David Mercer, Death of the product life cycle, *ADMAP*, September 1993.

the dynamic approach to (current) change – where most of traditional marketing theory revolves around decisions based upon static (historic) positions.

If such dynamic repositioning is not possible, perhaps because the necessary product changes come in discrete steps, then periodic readjustments may be needed. This is where the concept of '*advertising depreciation*' allows the build-up of reserves to cover the significant costs of major repositioning exercises.

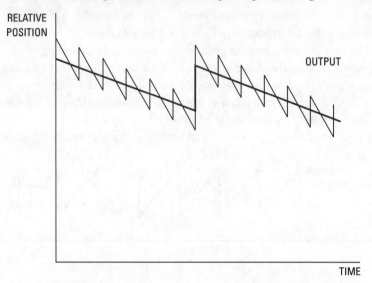

This long-term asset investment aspect of brand performance is largely ignored by traditional marketing theory; though Kent and Allen[4] have recently shown that 'the effect of familiarity suggests that well-known brands have important advantages . . . consumers appear to better remember new product information for familiar brands . . . less affected by exposure to competitive advertising'.

The above pattern of responses assumes, however, a complementary repositioning process – which builds upon existing strengths. This process cannot, though, be held to be true of two situations. The first of these is well recognized. It is the new product launch, where the logistic curve may be most effectively used to represent the relatively slow build-up of brand position which results from even quite high levels of investment; for the key aspect is the level of investment needed. It is seen in two main dimensions. One is the amount of (financial) investment needed. To buy your way into a market is a very expensive process indeed. The main practical feature, though, is the level of risk. Most managements believe, quite incorrectly, that risk is reduced if the levels of investment are minimized; the reverse is true. Once you accept the basic

[4] Robert J. Kent and Chris T. Allen, Competitive interference effects in consumer memory for advertising: the role of brand familiarity, *Journal of Marketing*, vol. 50 (July 1994).

level of risk the more money you invest in a major change, the lower you reduce the risk.[5]

If you want to make a major impact on a market (one that will, for instance, put you into the most profitable Rule of 123 slots) you must recognize that the level of investment needed will be correspondingly high; in practice it will probably be beyond the reach of all but the largest Japanese corporations where major markets are concerned (and hence the earlier emphasis on segmentation).

The second dimension is time. Any new penetration of a market takes far longer than is expected. Rather than the one to two years that optimists expect and the three to four years that pessimists allow for, *the reality of new launches, even for successful introductions, is a mean of eight years to break-even.*[6]

Industrial Advertising

Whereas consumer goods advertising has to handle almost all of the 'contact' with the end-user audience, that of industrial advertising (often called 'business-to-business' advertising) typically only forms part of the overall communication. It is often designed just to create the initial awareness, and to generate 'leads' (frequently based on reply-paid 'coupons' included with the advertising) before the face-to-face sales process (conducted by the producer's own salesforce or, perhaps more likely, by its agent's and dealer's salesforces) takes over.

Much of industrial advertising is, therefore, designed to elicit responses leading to a sales visit. It also often needs to convey more information than equivalent consumer advertising: capital goods, for example, are significantly more complex than repeat-purchase consumer goods. The advertising campaigns may also have to work over much longer periods, since purchases may be more infrequent; and the purchase process itself may be extended.

The other major point is that the average advertising budget, reflecting the secondary importance of advertising compared with face-to-face selling, is usually much lower; normally it is less than seven figures and often less than six figures, even for relatively large organizations. The average target audience is also much more specifically selected; and this has led to the emergence of a specialist group of media – pre-eminent among whom are the trade press. In this context, media buying has become a correspondingly specialist activity, frequently focusing on identification of the few publications which *can* reach the specialist target audience, rather than producing a balanced schedule for reaching them most economically (as is the task with consumer goods

[5] Ralph Biggadike, The risky business of diversification, *Harvard Business Review* (May–June 1979).
[6] Ibid.

campaigns). Yolanda Brugaletta[7] provides a useful list of the main differences from consumer advertising:

Business-to-business advertisers	*Consumer advertisers*
1 Have complex and multitiered buying influence.	1 Simple, one-person or family influence.
2 Advertising is generally 'support' to the sales influence.	2 Advertising is the major sales influence.
3 Purchase decisions are long-range and considered; immediate, measurable sales results rarely occur.	3 Purchase decisions are more spontaneous, i.e. if you need it, buy it; immediate, measurable sales results often occur.
4 Product usage cycle is long.	4 Product usage cycle is short for most items.
5 If purchase is not satisfactory buyer is challenged – his job is on the line.	5 If purchase is not satisfactory, repercussions are minimal.
6 More *advertising* planning – less '*marketing*' planning – so less result oriented.	6 Product management (marketing) systems are based on results.
7 *Little* 'test' marketing.	7 'Test' marketing is the *norm*.
8 Advertising budgets are based on 'last year's sales – and historical spending levels.	8 Advertising budgets are based on '*task*' or '*need*' from test results.
9 Reliance on 'readership scores' and 'did you buy?' to evaluate success of advertising.	9 Communications, recall, and image measurements.
10 Advertising is technical/factual in copy content. Often very potent – very informative – persuasive.	10 Advertising emphasis is on 'brand image'. Sometimes even *dumb* sell vs *smart* sell – *often persuasive*.
11 Editorial environment is naturally business oriented.	11 Editorial environment tends to be personal fulfilment/entertainment oriented.
12 Attitude of '*catching up*' to *marketing world*.	12 Great confidence. 'Knows everything' attitude.

Creating the Correct Messages

Clearly, the prime objective of most promotion is to make the 'sale' (where the 'sale' in the case of a non-profit organization might, for example, be to persuade the target audience to adopt a different behaviour pattern; say, give up smoking). To achieve this result, though, it will almost certainly need to communicate one or more messages (whether the promotion consists of face-

---

[7] Y. Brugaletta, What business-to-business advertisers can learn from consumer advertisers, *RC*, no. 131 (June 1985).

to-face selling or advertising on television). The tasks that these messages must undertake closely shadow the model described in chapter 2, where they were explored in more detail:

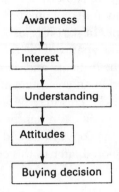

Awareness

The first task must be to achieve awareness, to gain the attention of the target audience. All of the different models are, predictably, in agreement on this first step. According to David Ogilvy,[8] one of the great gurus of advertising:

> On average, five times as many people read the headlines as read the body copy. It follows that unless your headline sells your product, you have wasted 90 per cent of your money.

Achieving awareness means, therefore, that the messages must first of all be seen and 'read'. They must *grab* the audience's attention. Advertising agencies have spent decades honing down the techniques involved: from challenging headlines (like the famous Avis 'We try harder') in the press to memorable images on television (such as the Coca-Cola 'We'd like to teach the world to sing'). One of the most influential campaigns of recent years has been that for Perrier, created by Leo Burnett.

On the other hand, you should be aware that there is often a tendency by advertising agencies to concentrate almost exclusively on this element of awareness, which suitably impresses the copywriter's peers in other agencies, but does not necessarily achieve the end result of 'making the sale'.

Again, David Ogilvy[9] makes the point in a forthright fashion:

> There have always been noisy lunatics on the fringes of the advertising business. Their stock-in-trade includes ethnic humor, eccentric art direction, contempt for

---

[8] D. Ogilvy, *Ogilvy on Advertising* (Pan Books, 1983).
[9] Ogilvy, *Ogilvy on Advertising*.

research, and their self-proclaimed genius. They are seldom found out, because they gravitate to the kind of clients who, bamboozled by their rhetoric, do not hold them responsible for sales results.

'Attention getting' is in part a function of 'size'. A full-page advertisement is more likely to command attention than a quarter-page, a two-minute commercial more than a 15-second one. In part it is, as suggested above, having some feature which breaks through the apathy of the reader or viewer; using a 'visual' or a headline which is out of the ordinary and demands attention – remembering that this has to be achieved in an environment in which every other advertiser is attempting the same trick. This may be so successful, indeed, that the advertising becomes almost 'generic', as it has for Benson & Hedges cigarettes.

Arguably, then, *creativity* (of the copywriters and visualizers in the advertising agency, whose role will be explored later in this chapter) is the key to this first stage.

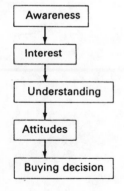

Interest

It is not sufficient to grab the reader's attention for a second or so, until it wanders again. In that brief time the message must *interest* that reader, and persuade him or her to 'read' on. The content of the message(s) must be meaningful, and clearly relevant to the target audience's needs.

This is where *marketing research* can come into its own as the basis for effective advertising. In the first instance, the 'advertiser' needs to know exactly *who* the audience is. Then the advertiser has to understand the audience's interests and needs, which must be addressed, and what are the exact benefits (in the consumer's own terms) the product or service will provide. In short, the message must be in the language of the consumer, and must make an offer that is of real interest to the specific audience.

This may mean that the message is boring to all other audiences (including those who are commissioning and creating the advertisement), but that is not the point; it has only to be of interest to the specific target audience. The messages which are of interest to teenage pop record buyers may well be very different from those aimed at middle-aged buyers of Volvo cars; and if the latter are commissioning advertising campaigns for the former, they had better appreciate the difference.

The second stage, therefore, largely depends upon an excellent appreciation of the results of *marketing research*.

Understanding

Once interest is established, the message has to explain the product or service, and its benefits, in such a way that readers can understand it; and can appreciate how well it may meet their needs – again as revealed by the marketing research. This may be no mean achievement when the copywriter has just 50 words, or ten seconds, to convey the entire message. This is one reason why complex capital goods sales are the province of the sales professional (who may take many hours, in total, to explain the product fully) and, on the other hand, why there is such a demand for good copywriters who can actually describe consumer goods – in meaningful terms – in such few words on an advertisement. On the other hand, David Ogilvy[10] advises: 'long copy – more than 300 words – actually attracts *more* readers than short copy'.

This stage is, thus, a mix of sound *marketing research mediated by professional copywriting skills*.

Attitudes

The message must go even further, to *persuade* the reader to adopt such a positive attitude towards the product or service that he or she will purchase it, albeit as a trial. There is no adequate way of describing how this may be achieved. It is down to the creative *magic of the copywriter's art*, based on the strength of the product or service itself.

Buying decision

All of the above stages might happen in a few minutes, while the reader is considering the advertisement in the comfort of his or her favourite armchair. On the other hand, the final decision to buy may take place some time later, perhaps weeks later, when the prospective buyer actually tries to find a shop which stocks the product. This means that the basic message will probably need to be reinforced, by repeats, until the potential buyer is finally in the position to buy. Above all, it also means that the product or service must be distributed widely enough for the prospective buyer to be *able* to find it.

These stages are most evident in the AIDA[11] ('Attention', 'Interest', 'Desire', 'Action') model, which is frequently advocated as the structure for the selling process. Similar stages are also described in the 'Hierarchy of Effects'[12] model (where 'Interest' and 'Understanding' are paralleled by 'Knowledge', 'Liking' and 'Preference').

After AIDA, the most often-quoted model within the advertising industry is DAGMAR (Defining Advertising Goals for Measuring Advertising Results), which splits the process down to the four steps of 'Awareness',

---

[10] Ogilvy, *Ogilvy on Advertising*.
[11] E. K. Strong, *The Psychology of Selling* (McGraw-Hill, 1925).
[12] R. J. Lavidge and G. A. Steiner, A model for predictive measurements of advertising, *Journal of Marketing* (October 1961).

'Comprehension', 'Conviction' and 'Action'. There are a number of other models in the literature, but they all tend to describe the same processes from differing viewpoints.

'Stepwise' models are limited, however. In particular, although they may work in a cold sales call, in other complex real-life marketing situations they do not take into account *time and experience*. As Mark Lovell[13] suggests, the attitude changes are likely to be more gradual, and much of advertising succeeds 'by virtue of marginally increasing the frequency of purchase of the brand among consumers who already have experience of it'.

Thus, one of the major weaknesses of much of advertising theory is that it fails to take into account the history of the brand. Buying decisions are rarely taken in isolation. They are an accumulation of months, even years, of experience on the part of the buyer. Abraham and Lodish[14] observe:

> On average, 76% of the difference observed in the test year persisted one year after the advertising increase was rolled back. Over a three-year period, the cumulative sales increase was at least twice the sales increase observed in the test year.

On the other hand, they also say:

> If advertising changes do not show an effect in six months, then they will not have any impact, even if continued for a year.

SELF-TEST QUESTION 9.2

Take a representative sample of your organization's promotional material (advertising, mailings, brochures and so on). What do you think it achieves in each of the areas of awareness, interest, understanding, attitudes and the buying decision?

(Keep the promotional material you have collected, for use in later audits.)

The Message

The main message will usually be based on the specific *benefit* which the advertiser has identified as the main advantage which the product offers over its

[13] M. Lovell, Advertising research, *Consumer Market Research Handbook*, ed. R. Worcester and J. Downham (McGraw-Hill, 1986).
[14] Abraham and Lodish, Getting the most out of advertising and promotion.

competitors. This may not be the main benefit which the buyer will receive from the product, for that may also be offered by all the competitors; although it is the foolish advertiser who does not check that the consumer really is *aware* that all products are identical in offering the main benefit.

The advertiser will aim to find a *USP (Unique Selling Proposition)*, an important benefit which is unique to the product or service. This USP may be based on 'physical' (or intangible) *features* associated with the product, ranging from what it actually does, through to the quality of the support services. Most advertising follows this route; and it is particularly easy to target, communicate and monitor messages of this type. David Ogilvy[15] recommends:

> Wherever you can, make the product itself the hero of your advertising. If you think the product is too dull, I have news for you: there are no dull products, only dull writers. I never assign a product to a writer unless I know he is personally interested in it.

On the other hand, the USP may occasionally be based upon a *psychological* appeal. It may even be based on fear, which is often a hidden feature of much of financial services advertising, as well as that for condoms. It may be based on guilt (educational toys, perhaps?). It may be based on positive emotions such as love; and this is the emotion which usually features, in one guise or another, in those advertisements that are sometimes expanded into 'mini-soaps', either in the family context (Oxo) or the more direct personal drama (Nescafé Gold Blend). It may frequently be based upon humour. If this is successful (as it has been for Heineken lager) the viewer or reader shares the joke, and develops positive attitudes to the product. Unfortunately, if the joke is not shared – and humour is a notoriously difficult art-form – it may be just as likely to alienate.

Finally the message may be communicated by *association*; either directly by association with a specific well-known personality (such as Pepsi Cola's use of Michael Jackson) or sometimes just in terms of the voice-over (Victor Borge's distinctive voice was used for the earlier Heineken commercials). But it may also be by association with a particular situation; as, for example, with the family in the Oxo soap operas.

David Ogilvy,[16] once more, adds the important footnote:

> When faced with selling 'parity' products [that is, products that are the same as their competitors, as many are], all you can hope to do is explain their virtues more persuasively than your competitors, and to differentiate them by the style of your advertising. This is the 'added value' which advertising contributes . . .

---

[15] Ogilvy, *Ogilvy on Advertising.*
[16] Ogilvy, *Ogilvy on Advertising.*

However, as *The Economist*[17] reported:

> Creative advertising is as difficult to produce as it is to describe. Aldous Huxley,
> who worked in advertising, reckoned it was easier to write ten passable sonnets
> than one effective advertisement.

Message consistency

One factor which is often ignored by marketers, and in particular by agencies, is
the need for successive campaigns to be consistent with their predecessors. Too
often, campaigns are seen in isolation, with just the current 'task' to carry out.
In reality, in most cases, they will be building upon what has gone before; and
to achieve the maximum effect they must be consistent with these previous
messages (or, at least, allow for the inherent 'investment' in consumer image
built up by these messages). All too frequently, the new campaign ignores past
history and has to fight to overcome this unnoticed legacy of the past, as well as
its current opposition.

The first recourse in creating new advertising should be to the 'guard book',
the historical record of all past advertising, kept by every wise marketer and
agency, to see exactly what has gone before.

Advertising investment

Thus, what you need to achieve with the message determines not just its content
but the medium which conveys it. Most important, though, will be the message
itself – how well it relates to the existing positioning and how well it achieves the
planned repositioning (or maintains the existing one). This is not a simple task.
The most obvious feature is that of the general decline which the investment in
brand position experiences over time – as evidenced by the Long-Term
Competitive Saw, for instance. In the chart opposite this arises from two
main components. One, referred to as '*depreciation*', simply represents the attrition which the brand suffers as customers' attention is distracted by all the other
stimuli which continuously inundate them. It also reflects the drift away from
optimal positioning, over time, as tastes change. The second, '*external obsolescence*', reflects the attrition caused by the activities of competitors. Their promotion will reshape the market, so that your own brand's positioning again drifts
away from the optimum.

The chart shows one further element, '*internal obsolescence*'. This is a polite
description for the self-inflicted wounds, often caused by overly-anxious creative
departments, where the brand positioning is actively moved *away* from the
optimum position by new advertising! The chart reflects the work which, as
we saw earlier, needs to be carried out before a combative advertising campaign can even start to work.

[17] J. Micklethwaite, The advertising industry, *The Economist* (9 June 1990).

ADVERTISING INVESTMENT

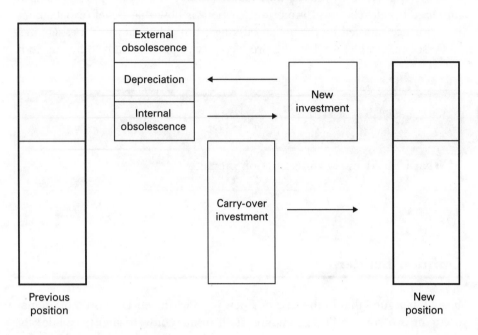

Advertising believability

Indeed, there is in general one dimension of advertising which is usually forgotten – that of believability:

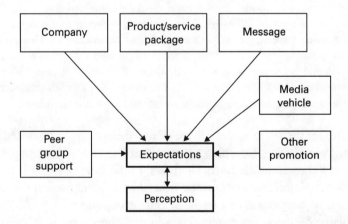

The inputs to the believability equation are many, and – as can be seen from the diagram – often lie outside of the advertising itself, so that the whole process is complex and difficult to manage. These outside factors often place quite constricting limitations on what may reasonably be said within the advertisement itself.

Most important of all is that the equation does not just cover pre-purchase belief. The most important element is how that belief (expectations) is in practice satisfied by the actual offering – a highly believable message may cause serious problems when the product/service package fails to live up to it.

Opinion Leaders

It is often argued that in the case of a new product the effect of promotion may occur in two stages. The promotion itself (usually advertising) persuades the more adventurous *opinion leaders* in the population to try the product or service. These opinion leaders then carry the message to those who are less exposed to it; and in the mass markets this often means to those who may be less exposed to the mass media. As Gatignon and Robertson[18] describe it:

> The extant two-step model depicts mass media reading opinion leaders who, in turn, influence a set of followers. This information-giving flow may, in fact, be valid for some percentage of personal influence transactions. However, other flows are possible, including information seeking and information sharing . . . Most personal influence is transmitted within a network of peers who possess similar demographic characteristics . . . The probability of such influence is high simply because people are most likely to interact with similar others.

Thus, this is *not* the same as the 'trickle-down' theory, much favoured in certain parts of the social sciences, which assumes that patterns of consumption are led by the upper classes and then 'trickle down' to the lower classes. It is important to note that 'opinion leaders', on the other hand, influence *members of their own class* and do so horizontally in terms of class groupings.

Whichever of these approaches is adopted, however, it is clear that the impact of media advertising may be much more complex than many of its practitioners allow for.

[18] H. Gatignon and T. S. Robertson, A propositional inventory for new diffusion research, *Journal of Consumer Research*, vol. 11 (1985).

Word of mouth

A more generalized aspect of communications within the community as a whole is 'word of mouth'. Much of advertising theory concentrates upon the 'direct' receipt of these 'indirect' communications; it assumes that the consumer receives the message directly from the media, and only from the media. In practice, as we have seen in the preceding section, the message may well be received by word of mouth from a contact (who may have seen the advertising – or may, in turn, have received it from someone else). Equally, even if the consumer has previously seen the advertising, word of mouth comments may reinforce (or undermine) what this has achieved directly.

Cognitive dissonance

One, perhaps unexpected, feature of 'audience behaviour' was reported by Leon Festinger.[19] This is that interest in all forms of promotion, particularly advertising, reaches a maximum *after* the consumer has made his or her purchase. The usual explanation for this apparently illogical behaviour is that the consumer is then searching for proof to *justify* his recent decision. In looking at the competitive advertising, say, the consumer is trying to seek out its flaws, in comparison with the chosen product or service, in order to obtain reassurance that his or her decision was correct.

The importance of this, from the advertiser's point of view, is that advertising still has a job to do even after the sale has been made. In addition, the messages needed to address cognitive dissonance may be subtly different: they need to provide reassurance, and allow for the fact that these purchasers will also represent the main source of future sales.

Message Selection

The advertising messages to be used, which will usually have been created by the advertising agency's creative department, need to be evaluated carefully. *Experts recommend that an effective advertisement should concentrate on just* one *central selling proposition.* Complicating advertisements by adding further messages will generally dilute the main message, as well as the overall impact.

The most effective method of selection is that of 'pre-testing' the advertisement on a sample of the target audience. This is a specialized form of marketing research, which is usually the province of specialized research agencies. An audience is typically shown a new commercial (sometimes in 'storyboard'

---

[19] L. A. Festinger, *A Theory of Cognitive Dissonance* (Row, Peterson & Co., 1957).

form, although this is a very difficult approach to use), and questioned to determine its impact (before seeing it, as well as after, to detect shifts in opinion).

SELF-TEST QUESTION 9.4

Return to the promotional material you collected for the last audit. How effective are the messages contained in the various items? Do they communicate with you?

More importantly, do you think they communicate with their target audiences? Indeed, is it obvious who their target audiences are?

Are the messages simple, and described in the language of the audience, without jargon? How much impact do they have?

Conviction Marketing

At this point I shall divert into an important – but little recognized – aspect of marketing, which is rather more general in its impact but which is most closely linked with 'message selection' (hence, the reason for its presence here).

'Conviction marketing' – sometimes called '*commitment marketing*' – is, in many respects, alien to most of the concepts of traditional marketing. Yet it is probably more prevalent than the genuine use of pure marketing, and arguably it is not infrequently more successful. It has a long and chequered history. The propaganda machines developed by the Nazis offered some of the most potent, and widely deplored, demonstrations of its power (and this represents one possible reason why discussion of this style of marketing is even now generally avoided). The religious 'marketing machines' had been even more effective in earlier generations (and can even now be very powerful, as is evidenced by the case of Islamic fundamentalism). In the commercial sector, though, its use has sometimes been just as powerful – and very productive! Indeed, the majority of the few truly global brands have embodied it to some degree: IBM, with its philosophy of 'Customer Service', McDonald's with Q.S.C. & V., Coca-Cola with its embodiment of the American teenage dream, Marlboro and the wide open spaces of the frontier!

It is different from 'selling', which is conventionally seen as the main alternative to marketing, in that its focus is very firmly on the consumer – as all marketing is supposed to be, where the focus of 'selling' is internal (the customer is to be persuaded to take what the organization has to offer). On the other hand, conviction marketing's focus is still *one-sided*. There is little or no attempt to use market research to find out what the consumers need or want, though research is sometimes used to justify the organization's existing prejudices – and is frequently used, to great effect, to optimize the presentation of its chosen message.

The power-house of such 'conviction marketing' is the powerful *idea* (the 'conviction' to which the organization has made its 'commitment'), which the organization *believes* the consumers are also committed to (despite any evidence to the contrary!) or need (for their own good!). Despite the focus on the consumer, and frequent reference to the importance of that consumer, the real organizational commitment is to the overarching idea (or set of ideas, often a 'life-style'). The essence of, and the strength of, such 'conviction marketing' is the power it gives to the marketing organization, to 'evangelize', where – in many respects – religious as well as political parallels are often more relevant than those of conventional marketing theory.

In turn this power derives from a number of factors. The concept being marketed must be *distinctive*. Successful conviction marketing is not the province of the marketer who is dedicated to pallid incrementalism. It has to be readily identifiable, as Coca-Cola is in terms of the very powerful image of the bottle (if not necessarily of the product contained). Beyond that, however, it has to be based on an *identity, a brand personality*. The beneficiaries of conviction marketing are typically not products where the technical features are predominant. Coca-Cola and Marlboro are a matter of personal taste, but it is the images associated with them, their brand persona, which add the necessary *richness* to the relatively mundane. Even in the case of IBM it was the marketing and support (rather than the very complex technology) which was its outstanding feature. The richness, the depth, to the identity seems to be necessary (at least in the most successful examples), to give it almost human characteristics.

Despite the richness of the concept it has to be instantly communicable, which demands that it be *clear*, and preferably *simple*. It has to be conveyed by simple messages, such as the shape of the bottle (or now the graphics on the can) of Coca-Cola, or the cowboy and Marlboro. Where the product is complex, and none could be more complex than that of IBM, it has to be enshrined in an associated philosophy, 'Customer Service' (personified by the field personnel in the now rather outdated, but very necessary, dark suits and white shirts). It is frequently associated with a distinctive form of quality: McDonald's 'Hamburger University', for example.

Conviction marketing is, above all, dependent upon the consumers' belief in what its communicators say. Being somewhat unrelated to the basic needs, the '*vision*' of the 'product' (of its identity) has to be conveyed to the target audience. They, in turn, have to enter into a '*belief*' in the 'product' before they can fully appreciate it. This means that the message being communicated has to be believed; and that, in turn, means that the communicators themselves need to believe.

In some cases the 'communicators' can be those of conventional marketing: the Marlboro cowboy in the advertising, or the bright clean image of McDonald's outlets. But behind them there is often a human face. In IBM it was the salesforce, immensely capable and imbued with (many would argue indoctrinated in) the IBM culture – and which of their customers could resist such evangelists. But, above all, it usually requires a strong (and almost obsessively dedicated) human personality at the centre, to make the vision work; the Watsons at IBM and Ray Kroc at McDonald's developed very rich cultures which were aimed more at their own employees (the 'communicators' the public see) rather than at their markets.

Although *customer* needs are at the heart of conventional marketing, they are only an 'enabling' factor in the case of conviction marketing. If the 'vision' is too far removed from the consumer's view of reality, it will not be accepted. Even so, Clive Sinclair's C5 electric/pedal-power car (eventually, derisively, called the 'electric clog') was initially accepted with praise by the media, based on his own charismatic image and obvious commitment to it; it took nearly three months for commentators to admit that the idea was in reality laughable. The resultant shock to believability, on the other hand, probably brought down the remainder of his business empire (which was unconnected to the C5, and more soundly based)! There have been other spectacular mismatches to reality: IBM's PC Junior, Ford's Edsel, for example. These are, however, the *recorded* exceptions; most mismatches fail at the 'new product' stage – and quietly disappear with the 90 per cent of such new products which do not achieve acceptance.

Conviction marketed products can be broadly divided into two groups;

The former are products, or services – frequently in the high technology field, whose creator has a blind faith in what product or service features are needed. Steve Jobs, at Apple, believed in the special technology of his products (even after IBM set new standards – and John Sculley had to be recruited from Pepsi, to inject more conventional marketing expertise), Alan Sugar believed in his personal ability to put together low-priced electronics packages. The problem with conviction marketed products in this category is that they can be very rapidly overtaken by changes in the market; typically, new technology supersedes them (as the Commodore Pet, one of the original PCs, was displaced from the business market by Apple, which in turn was superseded – as brand leader – by IBM), or tastes change (as Woolworth found out as its traditional place on the high street was undermined). As already indicated, the strongest 'conviction marketed' brands are those in very general markets where the distinctiveness comes from the image – from the intangible *values* associated with the brand.

These brands are usually much more capable of change, since their identity is not usually locked into 'physical' features. The customers (and the organization's own employees) can easily accommodate developments in technology and taste. IBM's 'Customer Service' carried it through decades of revolutionary change and Disneyland is constantly absorbing new rides – but still keeping them immaculately clean! Even McDonald's, which should perhaps be one of the most product-based of retailers, is in reality based on conviction marketing of values: Q.S.C. & V. (Quality, Service, Cleanliness & Value). It has managed to change what it serves (adding a breakfast menu – and lines based on chicken and fish, as well as pizza) and how it serves (increasing the size of its 'sit down' sections – so that it has become a restaurant rather than just a take-away outlet).

The challenge for less charismatic marketers, committed to the wisdom of the 'outside-in' viewpoint, is to understand to what extent the success of 'conviction marketing' undermines traditional marketing theory. This is a question mark which implicitly hung over much of marketing theory through the 1980s; it drove practitioners and academics alike to look for alternative approaches – such as competitive advantage. The reality is that *most* products and services (at least in terms of numbers of lines, if not of value of sales) are managed without reference to the principles of marketing, and have been throughout history. The difference is that 'conviction marketers' have very successfully extended this common 'inside-out' approach by adopting some of the tools of marketing. Indeed, the conviction marketers probably make greater use of marketing tools (albeit to somewhat perverted ends) than do many of those who would pay lip-service to traditional marketing. Philip Morris, which owns the Marlboro cigarette brand, also owns the Miller Brewing Company of Milwaukee. In applying the same sort of charismatic (and 'macho') image to 'Miller High Life' they used extensive market research to fine tune the positioning. More important, the company continued to be aware of the demands of its marketplace, and subsequently launched the highly successful 'Miller-Lite' (low calorie beer) as a 'less filling' beer which fitted this image.

At the end of the day, the basic justification for *conventional marketing*, in the absence of the blinding (and hopefully viable) vision of the conviction marketer, is simply that it is generally the most successful approach to product or service management. Giving the customer what he or she wants rarely fails!

As already stated, what often makes the task easier for conviction marketers is that their competitors seem even more mesmerized than their customers. Many organizations are *'dedicated followers'*; they *always* look to their competitors to take the lead. Their adherence to this creed goes beyond that required of 'followers', the subsidiary brands in a market which are simply not in any position to set the pace, as described in the later chapter on the 'Environment'. It goes beyond the IBM approach of *'constructive following'*, where that organization (in its days of market dominance) deliberately let other, smaller, organizations explore (and take the risks inherent in) new developments; only to recapture the initiative (by deploying the vast resources at its command) when the markets proved viable – a strategy which usually proves successful (if potentially risking loss of the leadership, as IBM eventually found out).

'Dedicated followers', though, assume that the market leader *always* knows best. So that even IBM's mistakes were ascribed to covert machinations, which must have some ultimate value, and these too were copied! 'Dedicated followers' represent a terminal case of myopia. They are organizations which, in effect, sub-contract their policy-making to their competitors. As such, they deserve to, and usually do, pay the ultimate price for this! The main problem facing conviction marketers is that the necessary strength of their commitment may blind them to the realities facing them and their customers. It is difficult enough for any marketer to adopt the unbiased perspective essential to understanding the customer's needs and wants. It may be impossible for a conviction marketer, whose 'vision' may be so powerful that it precludes any doubts about the 'product'. The Concorde airliner development team were convinced of the market for their 'baby', and their market research supported that view – it was only the market which disagreed. Even IBM can fall foul of this problem, as it did with its personal computers when its immensely strong corporate 'vision' got in the way of any meaningful recognition of the scale of the problem posed by its wayward dealers.

Creative marketing

Kotler[20] approaches the question from a slightly different direction. He describes conventional 'base-line' marketing as 'responsive marketing', and the highest level of this – where marketers recognize emerging trends and produce products and services ahead of this – as 'anticipatory marketing'. He reserves the highest level of all for 'creative marketing' – somewhat along the lines of conviction marketing – where 'the company creates something that no one explicitly asked for . . .'

Gut reaction

For most of the time the marketing manager is likely to be using his or her considerable intelligence to analyse and handle the complex, and unique, situations being faced, without easy reference to theory. This will often be 'flying by the seat of the pants', or 'gut-reaction'; the overall strategy, coupled with the knowledge of the customer which has been absorbed almost by a process of

[20] Philip Kotler, Reconceptualizing marketing: an interview with Philip Kotler, *European Management Journal*, vol. 12, no. 4 (December 1994).

osmosis, will determine the quality of the marketing employed! *Thus, the most successful marketer is often the one who trains his or her 'gut-reaction' to simulate that of the average customer!*

This, almost instinctive management, is what I would call '*coarse marketing*', to distinguish it from the refined, aesthetically pleasing, form favoured by the theorists. It is often relatively crude and would, if given in answer to a business school examination, be judged a failure of marketing. On the other hand, *it is the real-life world of most marketing!*

SELF-TEST QUESTION 9.5

To what extent does your organization communicate by conviction marketing? Do any of your competitors adopt such an approach? How successful is it?

If there were to be such conviction at the heart of your marketing, what would it be? What would the message be?

Returning to the promotional material you collected earlier, can you detect any signs of 'coarse marketing'?

Let us now return to the more traditional requirements of advertising theory.

Media Selection

In theory, media selection should be the process of choosing the most cost-effective media to achieve the necessary coverage, and number of exposures, among the target audience. Performance is typically measured on two dimensions:

Coverage (or 'reach'). To maximize overall awareness, the maximum number of the target audience should be reached by the advertising. There is a limit, however, for the last few per cent of the general population are always difficult (and accordingly very expensive) to reach; since they do not see the main media used by advertisers. Indeed the cost of *cumulative* coverage typically follows an exponential pattern. Reaching 90 per cent can cost double what it costs to reach 70 per cent, and reaching 95 per cent can double the cost yet again. The coverage decision is, in practice, a balance between the desired coverage and the cost of achieving it. A large budget will achieve high coverage, whereas a smaller budget will limit the ambitions of the advertiser.

Frequency. Even with high coverage, however, it is not sufficient for a member of the target audience to have just one 'Opportunity To See' (OTS) the advertisement. It is generally reckoned that around five OTS are needed before any reasonable degree of impact is achieved; and significantly more may be needed to build attitudes which lead to brand switching. To achieve five OTS, even across a coverage of only 70 per cent of the overall audience, may require 20 or 30 peak-time transmissions of a commercial, or a significant number of insertions of press advertisements in the national media. A related point is that, as the above figures suggest, most consumers simply do not see the commercials all that frequently (whereas the brand manager, say, looks out for every one; and has already seen them many times before their first transmission – and so becomes justifiably bored). The message is that the life of advertising campaigns can often be extended far beyond the relatively short life which is usually expected of them. Indeed, as indicated above, the research shows that advertisements *need* to obtain a significant number of exposures to consumers before they even register. As David Ogilvy[21] recommends, 'If you are lucky enough to write a good advertisement, repeat it until it stops selling. Scores of good advertisements have been discarded before they lost their potency.'

The more sophisticated media planners will also look at the *spread* of frequencies. Ideally *all* of the audience should receive the average number of OTS (since those who receive less are insufficiently motivated, and the extra advertising is wasted on those who receive more). Needless to say, it is impossible to achieve this ideal. As with coverage, the pattern will be weighted towards a smaller number, of heavy viewers for example, who will receive significantly more OTS, and away from the difficult last few per cent. However, the good media buyer will manage the resulting spread of frequencies so that it is weighted close to the average, with as few as possible of the audience away from the average.

Frequency is also complicated by the fact that this is a function of time. A pattern of 12 OTS across a year may be scarcely noticed, whereas 12 OTS in a week will be very evident to most viewers. This is often the rationale for advertising in 'bursts' or 'waves' (sometimes described as 'pulsing'); with expenditure concentrated into a number of intense periods of advertising – which are noticed – but with these bursts spread throughout the year, so that brands do not remain uncovered for long periods.

As a final footnote, it should be noted that longer commercials may often be more cost-effective than shorter ones. Based on results of direct response advertising, which might be somewhat different from other forms, a BARB study[22]

---

[21] Ogilvy, *Ogilvy on Advertising*.
[22] Meg Carter, Direct response ads gain respect, *Marketing Week* (5 July 1994).

found that 60-second commercials were twice as efficient as 10, 20 and 30-second ones; which in turn were six times as effective as shorter ones.

In the end, it is the media buyers who deliver the goods; by negotiating special deals with the media owners, and buying the best parcels of 'slots' to achieve the best cost (normally measured in terms of the cost per thousand viewers, or per thousand household 'impressions', or per thousand impressions on the target audience). The growth of the very large, international, agencies has been partly justified by their increased buying power over the media owners.

SELF-TEST QUESTION 9.6

In very broad terms, what coverage and OTS do you think your organization achieves? Is coverage wide enough and OTS high enough to achieve its objectives?

Types of Media and their Characteristics

In terms of overall advertising expenditures, media advertising is dominated by press and television, which are of comparable size (by value of 'sales'). Posters and radio follow some way behind, with cinema now representing a very specialist medium.

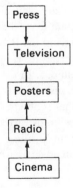

Press

In this medium, spending is dominated by the national and regional newspapers, the latter taking almost all the classified advertising revenue.

The magazines and trade or technical journal markets are about the same size as each other, but are less than half that of the newspaper sectors.

National newspapers.   These are traditionally categorized, from the media buyer's viewpoint, on the basis of class; even though this is of declining importance to many advertisers. 'Quality' newspapers, for example, tend to have a readership profile of in excess of 80 per cent of ABC1 readers, though it is more difficult to segment readerships by age categories. They are obviously best matched to national advertisers who are happy with black and white advertisements, although limited colour is now available – and high-quality colour is available in some supplements. National newspapers in general, and the quality press in particular, are supposed to carry more 'weight' with their readers (since they are deliberately read, not treated just as 'background'); therefore an advertisement placed in one is taken more seriously than a comparable one in a regional newspaper, although it may be more transitory (since it is not kept for reference as some local weeklies may be).

Regional newspapers.   These may be dailies, which look and perform much like the nationals, or weeklies, but are rather more specialized, although they dominate the market for classified advertising. Indeed, there is usually much more advertising competing for the reader's attention, and the weekly newspaper is fast becoming the province of the 'free-sheets' – which are typically delivered free to all homes in a given area – obtaining all their revenue from the very high proportion of advertising which they carry, and accordingly having the least 'weight' of all.

Advertisements in newspapers, referred to as 'insertions', are usually specified as so many centimetres across so many columns. In these days of metrication, a multiple of 3 cm is used as the standard measure, instead of the previously traditional inch. Thus, a '30 cm double' is an advertisement that is 30 cm long, down the page, and across two columns of type, where the width of columns varies from paper to paper – an important consideration when you are having the printing 'blocks' made. The position is also often specified so that, for example, an advertiser of a unit trust will probably pay extra to make certain that the insertion is next to the financial pages.

Magazines.   These offer a more selective audience (which is more 'involved', with the editorial content at least). Magazines are traditionally categorized into general interest, special interest and trade or technical. The advertiser will, therefore, be able to select those which match the specific profile demanded by the advertising strategy. The weight, or 'authority', of magazines is correspondingly high, and they may be kept for a considerable time for use as reference – and passed to other readers (so that 'readership' figures may be much higher than 'circulation' figures). They can offer excellent colour printing; but, again, the clutter of many competing advertisements may reduce the impact of the advertiser's message.

Trade and technical.   In the trade and professional fields there are now a significant number of 'controlled circulation' magazines. These are like the 'free press', in that they are delivered free to the recipients; but, at least in theory, those recipients should have been carefully screened to ensure that they are of value to the advertisers – and the circulation can, if properly controlled, represent a wide cross-section of the buyers, and influencers, in the advertiser's target audience. The rates for positioning are usually more varied than for newspapers, with premiums being paid for facing editorial matter and, of course, for colour.

Television

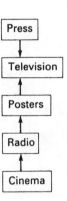

This is normally the most expensive medium, and as such is generally only open to the major advertisers, although some regional contractors offer more affordable packages to their local advertisers. It offers by far the widest coverage, particularly at peak hours (roughly 7.00–10.30 p.m.), and especially of family audiences. Offering sight, sound, movement and colour, it has the greatest impact, especially for those products or services where a 'demonstration' is essential; it combines the virtues of both the 'story-teller' and the 'demonstrator'. However, to be effective these messages must be kept simple – and have the impact to overcome the surrounding distractions of family life.

The medium is relatively unselective in its audiences, and offers relatively poor coverage of the upper class and younger age groups, but as it is regionally based it can be used for regional trials or promotions (including test markets).

The price structures can be horrendously complicated, with the 'rate card' (the price list) offering different prices for different times throughout the day; and this is further complicated by a wide range of special promotional packages, and individual negotiations. It is truly the province of the specialist media buyer.

Satellite television is now supposed to be the medium of the future, and has already become a significant competitor, for advertising budgets at least, in a number of countries. Cable television was similarly supposed to represent the future a decade ago. This promise has been largely fulfilled in the USA, where the average household can now tune into 31 channels. It has yet to achieve comparable levels of penetration in other countries; though it is extending its coverage, often in combination with satellite television, in many countries.

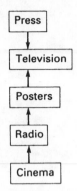

Posters

This is something of a specialist medium, which is generally used in support of campaigns using other media. On the other hand, some advertisers, particularly those in brewing and tobacco, have successfully made significant use of the medium; to achieve this, they have developed the requisite expertise to make efficient use of its peculiarities.

The main roadside posters are described in terms of how the poster is physically posted on to them (pasted on, one sheet at a time, by a bill-poster); as 16 sheet (the main, 10' x 6'8" size in vertical format) and 48 sheet (10' x 20', in horizontal/landscape format). Those smaller ones, seen in pedestrian areas, are typically four sheet (5' x 3'4"). The best sites are typically reserved for the long-term clients, mainly the brewers and tobacco companies (hence one reason for their success in use of the medium), so that new users may find this medium relatively unattractive.

Radio

The use of radio has increased greatly in recent years, with the granting of many more licences. It typically generates specific audiences at different times of the day; for example, adults at breakfast, housewives thereafter, and motorists during rush hours. It can be a very cost-effective way of reaching these audiences (especially as production costs can also be relatively cheap), although the types of message conveyed will be limited by the lack of any visual elements, and may have a 'lightweight' image.

Cinema

Although the numbers in the national audience are now small, this may be the most effective medium for extending coverage to the younger age groups, since the core audience is aged 15–24.

The Henley Centre for Forecasting[23] neatly summarizes the positions of the various media (figure 9.1).

SELF-TEST QUESTION 11.7

Which of these media does your organization use, and why?

Do you think the media characteristics listed above represent a suitable media schedule for your organization? What changes would you recommend?

---

[23] Henley Centre for Forecasting, *Planning for Change* (1989).

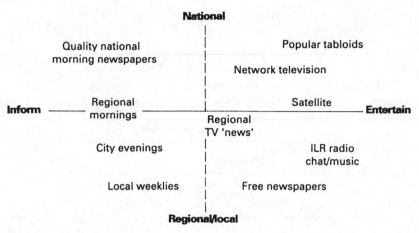

Figure 9.1 Media positions.

Audience Research

Finding out exactly who is the audience for a particular newspaper, or who watches television at a given time, is a specialized form of market research, which is usually conducted on behalf of the media owners. In the UK the Joint Industry Committee for National Readership Surveys (JICNARS), a twice-yearly survey of 30 000 individuals, establishes the readership of more than 100 national newspapers and magazines; while the Broadcasters Audience Research Board (BARB) provides a weekly report on a panel of 3000 homes equipped with metered television sets.

The Press figures are slightly complicated by the fact that there are two measures: those of *readership*, which represents the total number of readers of a publication, no matter where they read it, and *circulation*, the number of copies actually sold, which is mostly independently validated by the Audit Bureau of Circulation (ABC).

The Promotional Mix

The ideal promotional mix will be specific to an individual product or service, and to the marketing objectives which have been set for it. In deciding that optimal mix, however, a number of general factors may need to be taken into account:

- *Available budget.* The prime practical determinant of the promotion mix, and one that is often ignored by theory, is usually the amount of money available. For

Available budget

Promotional message

Complexity of product or service

Market size and location

Distribution

Life-cycle

Competition

example, if you do not have a budget running well into six or seven figures then you need not consider television. In particular, if your budget is below six figures you will need to look at the specialist press.

- *Promotional message.* The message which has been chosen will also largely determine the medium to be used. A demonstration of the product will demand either face-to-face selling, of some form, or television (or cinema). A coupon response will only work in the press or by direct mail (or door-to-door).
- *Complexity of product or service.* Sometimes the product or service will determine the medium. If, as often happens in industrial and capital goods markets, the product is complex or requires significant amounts of service support, then face-to-face selling may be the only route open.
- *Market size and location.* Where the target audience is located will be a determinant of the media chosen. If the audience covers a large part of the population, and the budget can afford it, television will usually be the best choice. If it is very specialist, but spread throughout the whole population, then the relevant specialist press or even direct mail may be most suitable.
- *Distribution.* Obtaining distribution, in particular through retailers, may often be the key to success. The promotional mix chosen may, therefore, be designed as much to sway the buyers in the distribution chain as the end-users.
- *Life-cycle.* The life-cycle stage may be critical. If the product or service is in the introductory stage, building awareness is the main aim; whereas if it is in the growth stage, the requirement is to persuade potential consumers to switch their buying patterns.
- *Competition.* Finally, any marketer needs to take account of what his competitors are doing. If the main competitor launches a high-spending television campaign, and you have a low-spending press campaign, then you will have to take some serious decisions. Do you also move into television, and probably increase costs to the extent that your profits will be hit? Or do you stay where you are, and possibly have to accept a reduced market share?

The Major Elements of an Advertising Agency

If you are ever likely to use, or even come into contact with, an advertising agency – and our research[24] shows that more than two-fifths of all organizations employ one – you will find that it is rather different from most other commercial organizations. There are many variations on the general theme, of course, but the traditional agency is structured around three main functions:

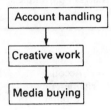

The support functions behind these might be:

- production
- control
- administration

In addition, the agency might offer specialist support functions (closely paralleling those of the advertiser) such as:

- market research
- marketing
- public relations
- direct mail
- promotions

Apart from market research and marketing, which are as important for the agency as for its clients, these other functions typically operate as autonomous groups within the agency. Brian MacCabe[25] shows the typical organization of an agency (figure 9.2).

Account handling

For an agency, which usually has relatively few clients – each of whom is important to its success – the interface with the client is of paramount importance. For this reason, the 'account executive', the person who is in charge of the account, is often the most important individual in the agency. He or she will handle all contact with the client, in this respect acting much like any high-level

---

[24] D. Mercer, research to be published.
[25] B. F. MacCabe, The advertising agency, *The Practice of Advertising*, ed. N. A. Hart and J. O'Connor (Heinemann, 1978).

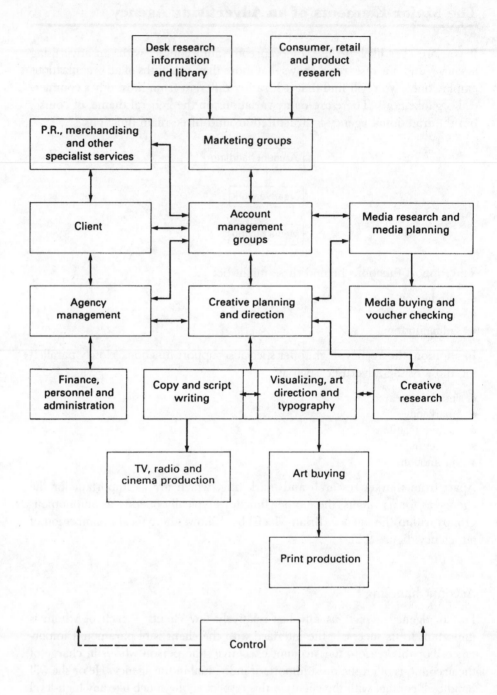

Figure 9.2   Workflow in an advertising agency.

sales professional. But this individual will also manage all activities on the account within the agency; in this context acting very much like a brand manager – and, indeed, the two functions closely parallel each other.

From the client's point of view, the key element of the account executive's job is that he or she understands what the client wants to achieve. This may mean that the account executive needs to understand almost as much about the organization's activities as the brand manager, so that the internal briefings within the agency (which are usually the prerogative of the account executive) will be comprehensive and accurate, and that the subsequent supervision of the work of the various creative and media departments will also be directed towards meeting the strategies of the client. The effective account executive has, therefore, to be the agency's representative to the clients, but also the *client's representative to the agency*. Account executives are frequently organized in teams, each headed by an account supervisor or account director.

Creative work

The *raison d'être* for most agencies is their creative skill. They, and often they alone, have the expert talent to take the mundane marketing objectives of the client and turn them into eye-catching, memorable advertisements. This is reflected in the importance ascribed to creativity by agency clients. A *Marketing Week* survey[26] of the clients of the top UK advertising agencies showed that their average ratings of importance (on a scale where 10 was 'most important') in terms of their 'overall assessment of agency performance' were as follows:

Creativity	8.7	Media buying	7.7
Value for money	8.3	Marketing strategy	7.1
Attentiveness and adaptability	8.0	International coverage	3.3
Quality of account managers	8.0		

To achieve this, the large agency may well have a number of creative specialists:

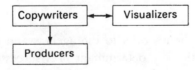

[26] D. Torin, Saatchi suffers fall from grace, *Marketing Week* (16 November 1990).

- *Copywriters.* The creative powerhouse of an agency is often its copywriters. They write the words or the scripts, but they are often also expected to be the source of the original creative ideas, which turn the dull market objectives into sparkling advertising.
- *Visualizers.* The visual elements of press advertisements are provided by artists, usually called 'visualizers' (or, more grandly, 'art directors'). They work hand-in-hand with the copywriters, to the extent that it is frequently difficult to determine which member of this creative team has produced a specific creative idea. Specifically, the visualizer provides the various 'roughs' (draft sketches) of the visuals, including 'storyboards' (rough cartoons illustrating what visuals will be included in the final commercial) which accompany the scripts. These visualizers do not usually produce the finished artwork: their input is purely creative, and there are specialist photographers and illustrators, subcontractors to advertising agencies, who undertake the high-quality finished work.
- *Producers.* For a television, radio or cinema commercial, an outside production company and director will be chosen (to meet the specific needs). The agency producer, in the mirror image of the account executive's role, will supervise relations with this outside team, to ensure that the finished commercial meets everyone's requirements.

Creating the Advertisement

As seen by the client, the typical process in the creation of an advertisement will follow a number of stages:

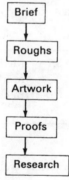

Brief

As we have seen, the client's brief to the agency, and how that is translated within the agency, is the key determinant of a successful advertisement. No matter how brilliant the creative treatment, it will not succeed if it fails to meet the marketing objectives. From the brief the agency creative team will, by a variety of techniques ranging from brainstorming to simply staring out of the window, slowly develop some creative ideas.

Roughs

After being developed by the creative team as thumb-nail sketches, these ideas will be brought together as 'roughs', relatively crude impressions (albeit usually laid out as advertisements) of the concepts being considered. Eventually, a number of these will be presented to the client, for discussion. From these alternatives one (or perhaps several) will be chosen for further development.

As we have already seen, in the case of a commercial this 'rough' will typically be in the form of a script accompanied by a 'storyboard'.

Further stages of 'roughs', with both visuals and copy developing (usually in consultation with the client, and certainly with the account executive), will gradually approach what is finally agreed as the ultimate concept.

The client should then formally approve these final roughs (sometimes referred to as 'finished layouts'); and, indeed, should make certain that they are *completely* happy with what is being proposed – for changes beyond this stage can be very expensive, with new artwork often costing thousands of pounds (and new commercials usually being, literally, prohibitively expensive).

Artwork

The concept, by that time in the form of a 'working layout' in which all the elements are accurately positioned, will then usually be turned into finished artwork by specialist, external, suppliers.

The agency's skill is in knowing which of these will produce the best results in terms of the desired advertisement; and, to a certain extent, in knowing even at the 'roughs' stage just what might be achievable.

The finished artwork will, once more, be presented for the client's approval. It is unusual, and expensive, for the basic material to be altered; but it is quite normal for the details to be changed, usually in the 'body copy' (the descriptive paragraphs in the advertisement, as opposed to the headlines) or the detailed arrangement of the visual elements (which will just require 'cut and paste').

Proofs

The final stages of approval will be those when the blocks for the press advertisement, or the final cut of the commercial, with its matched sound-track, have been produced; the client can now see *exactly* what has been paid for. It is very rare and inordinately expensive – but not unheard of – for changes to be made at this stage.

It is worth noting that while the 'closing date', the date by which the blocks must be provided to the publisher, may be only a few days before publication in the case of a newspaper, it may be as much as two or three months ahead in the case of magazines, which can extend the lead times for the whole creative process quite significantly.

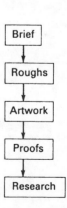

Research

As we have seen elsewhere in this chapter, the impact of advertising should always be checked. If substantial sums are to be committed to media, this research may be run at each and any stage from the concept (the 'rough') through to the final proofs (when testing is most usual, to ensure that the required attitude shifts are achieved; and, perhaps more importantly, that unwanted side-effects are not observed).

If affordable, research should always take place when the final advertisement is run in the media: the resulting 'awareness' ratings will give a first indication of the 'creative' impact of the campaign. The best measure, of course, is sales.

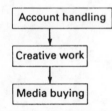

Media Buying

The third aspect of the traditional agency is the department which buys the space, or time, in the media to meet the client's marketing objectives. This also follows a number of stages:

Brief

Yet again, the first and most important step is the client's brief. In this case the need is for the media buyers to understand exactly who the advertising is supposed to reach. This will primarily be specified, in the media buyer's terms, as a profile of who is to be included in the target audience. The relatively crude measures of age and class have now been expanded by a range of more sophisticated tools, which allow a more sophisticated audience profile to be met. In addition to specifying the coverage, however, the client may also wish to indicate the spread of OTS (Opportunities To See) desired. Good coverage may still be ineffective if most of the audience only see the commercial, say, once; whereas a minority wastefully see it many times unnecessarily (as can happen with a schedule built from very cheap off-peak slots). Again, the onus is on the client to say exactly what is expected to be achieved.

Media schedule

On the basis of this profile, and taking into account any restrictions imposed by the likely creative treatment, the media buyer will construct the optimum media schedule to provide the best match; and which will deliver the profile most economically. In the case of mass consumer goods, this task is sometimes handled by computer, but it should be noted that the use of computers has actually declined since the 1970s, as it has been found that human creativity is just as applicable. A careful selection of media can reduce the *per capita* costs quite significantly. In the case of more specialist campaigns, such as those in the trade press, specialist media buyers will have the advantage. Here the profiles (both from the client and from the media) are likely to be inexact, and scheduling becomes much more of an art than a science.

Once more, the final schedule is approved by the client since it can – and often does – represent the major element of the marketing budget.

Tactical media buying

This stage is the province of the expert media buyer alone, to negotiate the best deals and achieve the lowest possible costs. Although the core of any schedule will probably be based upon a number of peak-time spots, the overall costs are typically reduced by shopping around for suitable bargains in off-peak time; seeing which slots are going cheap, taking advantage of last minute bargains, and pressuring the media owners into offering more favourable packages. Few agreed media schedules are ever implemented exactly. They are normally modified 'in flight' to allow for these bargains and, hopefully, to achieve better than forecast costs. This, in particular, is an area in which the client must have confidence in the abilities of the chosen agency.

Research

When the campaign has ended, the client should establish, through the agency, exactly what has been achieved. The research in this case is relatively routine, for all the various forms of media have their own research organizations; and the output from these, especially those relating to television, should be an accurate measure of who was exposed to the advertisement. This research report is the acid test of an agency media buying department and, as such, is essential reading for any client.

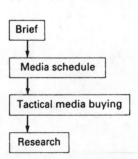

ACTIVITY 9.1

Prepare an advertising agency brief (of no more than 500 words, but covering both creative and media briefs) on your organization's main product or service. Use your colleagues, or family, to criticize the content and style.

SELF-TEST QUESTION 9.8 (for advertisers only)

In the context of the preceding material, how does your organization use its agency (if at all)? How does the agency respond?

What improvements could be made in your organization's management of the relationship? What improvements could be made in the agency's work?

How successful do you believe the resultant advertising is (in terms of both creative platform and media schedules), and why?

How do you think it might be improved?

(You will find it a considerable help if you can arrange a visit to your advertising agency, to see how it is organized and to meet some of the personalities involved. If this is a one-off request the agency should welcome your visit, since it will also help them gauge what other members of management are like, and how they see the agency – and their own organization.)

The Advertising Plan

As with all marketing activities, objectives must be set for advertising, and should include the following:

- *Who and where.* It is critical to define the target audience as exactly as possible, since this allows the 'media buyers' in the advertising agency to plan to achieve an economical coverage of this audience; to build up the media schedule to give a cumulative coverage of the desired audience. It is also important to agree what percentage coverage of this desired audience will be acceptable.
- *When.* Timing needs to be balanced with the requirement for each separate campaign to have sufficient impact.

- *What and how.* The message that the creative team from the agency will encapsulate, in interesting advertising, has to be the right message for the product and the audience; and the impact required may also determine the medium used.

The most important aspect of an advertising plan is that, as far as possible, it should be *quantified* so that the subsequent performance of the advertising itself can be measured. The typical quantities which, if affordable, should always be measured after each campaign are:

- awareness – unless it was already very high, the advertising should have achieved a measurable increase in awareness
- attitude – it should also have created the planned attitude shifts

Advertising Budgets

Ideally, advertising should be set on the basis of profit maximization models. Thus, in theory, the demand curve for a product or service against advertising expenditure is plotted, in much the same way as is that of the more traditional demand against price. Needless to say, however, there are very few products or services for which this ideal can be achieved. Where it is an option, where there are lengthy series of historical data and competitors are consistent in their actions, it is sometimes attained by sophisticated (computerized) 'regression analyses'. Sometimes, more pragmatically, the shape of the curve is guessed, judgementally, by the experts involved. Then 'marginal analysis' (the same principle as marginal costing) can be applied; and advertising can be increased just up to the point at which the additional income just offsets the additional costs. Unfortunately, due to the inherent complexities of promotion (and its long-term 'investment' impact), such calculations are rarely possible. Where they are possible (such as by Gallahers in the 1960s) they are remarkably effective, largely because they can justify significantly higher budgets than discretion would otherwise dictate.

More generally, the advertising budget is determined by even more basic means. Thus, for example, some of the more popular ways that the advertising 'spend' is decided may be as follows:

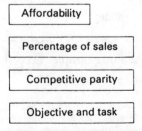

Affordability

Percentage of sales

Competitive parity

Objective and task

- *Affordability*. The management may decide on what they think is a 'reasonable' figure, often just based on last year's spend, or on whatever is left over when the expected revenue is offset against the projected costs and the required profits.
- *Percentage of sales*. This is virtually the classic method, where a fixed percentage of sales revenue is allocated. It is fast and easy to calculate, but it does not take into account any changes in conditions in the market – and perhaps implies that sales create advertising, rather than the other way round.
- *Competitive parity*. In competitive markets, the share of the advertising spend is often equated with the share of the market. There is evidence (from the UK car industry, for example) that advertising shares do broadly follow the same pattern as market shares (although the work shows that it is the advertising which positively *creates* the market share, rather than the other way round). Even so, the approach still suggests that the competitors know better what they are doing than you do.
- *Objective and task*. This simply asks what needs to be done (although with carefully calculated and quantified objectives), and then costs it. Unfortunately, it is rarely applied.

As suggested earlier, it would be ideal if a general model could be found which allowed the advertiser to forecast the sales outcomes of his spending, but in most markets the complexity of the other factors involved precludes this. So there is, perhaps, some excuse for the 'rules of thumb' described above; and, in practice, many marketers use all of these techniques, weighting the budget by which one seems most applicable to the task in hand.

Keith Crosier[27] comments that only three approaches are in common use. Aggregating the results of six surveys covering the period 1970 to 1985, he reports the usage as:

Advertising/sales ratio	44 per cent	Objective and task	18 per cent
Executive judgement	21 per cent	All others	17 per cent

More subversively, perhaps, Thomas Bonoma[28] reports, on the basis of his research:

> . . . the egalitarianism in resource allocation creates 'global mediocrity'; marketing that is excellent at nothing. Because the company spreads its resources thinly over many programs, the most vital marketing projects don't get the funding and attention they need. The creative marketing manager subverts this parody of equality by allocating resources on the basis of merit, often through budget switching of loose 'shoe-box' money.

Perhaps less obviously, the pattern of spending could be most efficiently linked to the brand position. For example, according to a survey[29] based on

[27] K. Crosier, Promotion, *The Marketing Book*, ed. M. J. Baker (Heinemann, 1987).

[28] T. V. Bonoma, Marketing subversives, *Harvard Business Review* (November–December 1986).

[29] Hashi Syedain, In pursuit of the perfect mix, *Marketing* (31 October 1991).

PIMS data, brand leaders should spend 70 per cent or more of their budget above the line (to achieve a ROCE, Return On Capital Employed, of better than 40 per cent) where a fourth brand should only spend 30–50 per cent (for 10 per cent ROCE).

The wise marketer also monitors what is happening throughout the year, as the various campaigns progress, to see if the budgets need reviewing; and, in any case, formal reviews would be conducted on a quarterly basis.

SELF-TEST QUESTION 9.9

How does your organization set its advertising budgets? How would you set them?

Advertising Research

This marketing research process, which follows the same rules as usual, is frequently used to test individual pieces of advertising, press advertisements and (in particular) commercials, before they are used, to ensure that they actually meet the objectives which have been set for them.

As already indicated, the coverage achieved by the advertising will almost certainly be tracked directly if television commercials are used (the BARB research monitors the performance of all television advertising, by each individual time slot). In the case of press advertising it is sometimes considered worthwhile to conduct separate research to measure the proportion of the target audience that has actually seen the advertisement; and, more importantly, can remember seeing it. The same techniques can also be used for commercials (whereas the BARB results have been limited to which television sets are switched on and who is in the room at the time, which may not always give the result that the advertiser is seeking). It is normal to monitor any advertising campaign's performance against the objectives set for it, typically in the areas of:

- *Awareness.* 'Spontaneous awareness' is measured as the proportion of those who can remember the brand without any prompting. 'Prompted awareness', which is usually much higher, measures the proportion who can recognize the brand when a prompt card (listing its name, amongst other competitive brands) is shown to the respondents. On the other hand, 'recall' tests explore what consumers can remember about the elements within the advertising (in the case of 'aided recall', with the benefit of being shown the advertisement).
- *Attitudes.* Most advertisements are normally designed to have an impact upon specific attitudes. Ideally, in the most sophisticated approaches, the research should check that the brand has achieved the new (multidimensional) 'position' which was set as the objective.
- *Sales offtake.* The acid test of advertising, though, should be the additional sales generated. Due to the multitude of other factors usually involved, this is normally a difficult, if not impossible, measurement to make. However, it is an exercise which should be undertaken – no matter how approximate the results – for a campaign which results in *reduced* sales, no matter how inaccurately measured, is unlikely to be judged a success.

'Test markets' can also be used to compare different campaigns in different regions, but in view of difficulties of comparison between regions and the urgency of most advertising campaigns they are rarely employed in practice.

Coupon response

One particularly effective measure of the effectiveness of press advertising, along with that of direct mail, can be implemented where the purpose of the advertising is to elicit a direct response, typically in terms of motivating the reader to ask for further information through a 'coupon' included in the advertisement or mailed material.

Each such advertisement or mailing can then be given a code; the usual means being to include a dummy 'department number' (which equates to the publication used, say) as part of the mailing address. The response obtained from each of the publications (or each of the mail packages) can then be measured accurately, at least in terms of the percentage coupon response rate. Although, of course, that may not be an appropriate measure if what is primarily being attempted is a shift in attitudes.

This technique can also be used to test, and directly compare, two or more advertisements where the media owner offers 'split runs', in which the overall print run is split (usually geographically) or the television is run by regions. Comparison of the results, for each part of the test, may give a good indication of performance; although geographical variations will need to be allowed for (and may even be partly compensated for by 'flip flop testing', where the test is repeated with the regions reversed). You should be aware that coupon response may not be the best measure of the performance that you want to gauge; for example, long-term image building will not be demonstrated.

SELF-TEST QUESTION 9.10

Does your organization measure the effectiveness of its advertising and, if so, how? What do the results (if any) show? What action is taken on the basis of them?

FURTHER READING

This subject is, once more, covered by most of the general textbooks (including, of course, that by Philip Kotler). Probably the most readable advertising book, which still offers just about the best insight into what advertising is really about, is that by David Ogilvy (*Ogilvy on Advertising*, Pan, 1983). *Advertising* (2nd edition, by Kenneth E. Runyon, Charles E. Merrill, 1984) gives a very comprehensive coverage, which is also quite readable – and is suitable for the general audience, although the book is lengthy.

SUMMARY

Put very simplistically, advertising represents the *talking* part of the dialogue referred to at the beginning of the book. In practice, it is a much more complex process, as is hinted at by the *encoding* model:

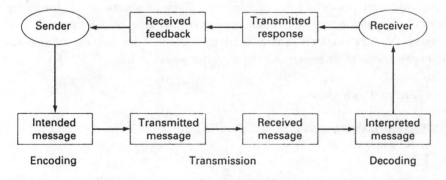

However, it is just one element of the promotional mix which includes personal selling and word of mouth, particularly in the case of services. It may be just as applicable to many non-profit organizations. It is also, increasingly, a vehicle for *corporate promotion*. In all these cases it is a *pull* technique (persuading consumers to pull the product through retailers), rather than *push* (selling, by sales promotions for instance, into the channels).

Advertising is generally, but perhaps simplistically, recognized to carry out three progressive tasks:

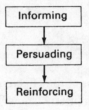

It does this with a *message* which may create:

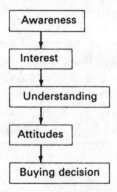

The message should ideally contain a *USP*, although it should also be consistent with past campaigns. It may be advisable to recognize that this message is also passed by *word of mouth*, with *opinion leaders* playing an important role.

A particularly powerful form of marketing is *conviction marketing*. This concentrates on the talking part of the dialogue, to convey an especially strongly held message. Market research is only used to fine tune the delivery of this all-important message. It is particularly powerful where it has:

- a distinctive, rich identity
- a clear, simple idea
- believable communicators
- weak opponents

It may be *product-based* or, with even more power, *value-based*. It can be used by market leaders to ensure that their competitors are followers rather than challengers. On the other hand, much of marketing – described as *coarse marketing* – is based on pragmatic reaction rather than theory.

Media selection and buying require specialist knowledge and skills, but essentially aim to achieve satisfactory (cumulative) *coverage* with the requisite *OTS* (Opportunities To See) at an economic cost.

The main *media* are:

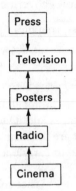

An *advertising agency* will include a number of specialist departments:

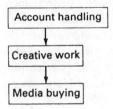

The *advertisement* will typically go through a number of stages:

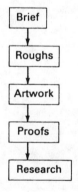

Like other budgets, *advertising budgets* are fixed by a number of means:

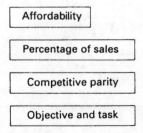

Research also has an important role, covering:

- performance (awareness, attitudes, coupon response, sales levels and so on)
- copy testing (pre and post)

REVISION QUESTIONS

1 What are the main elements of the promotional mix? Which may be 'push' and which 'pull'? What are the advantages and disadvantages of personal selling?
2 What is meant by encoding? What are the main functions of advertising? What does the advertising message need to do to carry out these functions?
3 How may advertising depreciate?
4 Is a USP compatible with consistency? What role do opinion leaders play?
5 What is conviction marketing? How does it differ from traditional marketing theory? What are the factors which favour its use?
6 What are the main measures of media performance? Why are they important? What are the differences between the two most popular forms of media?
7 What are the main departments within an advertising agency? What do they do?
8 What are the main stages in the production of an advertisement? What happens at each of these stages? What is the client's responsibility at each?
9 How may advertising budgets be set? How may performance be measured?

10 Other Forms of Promotion

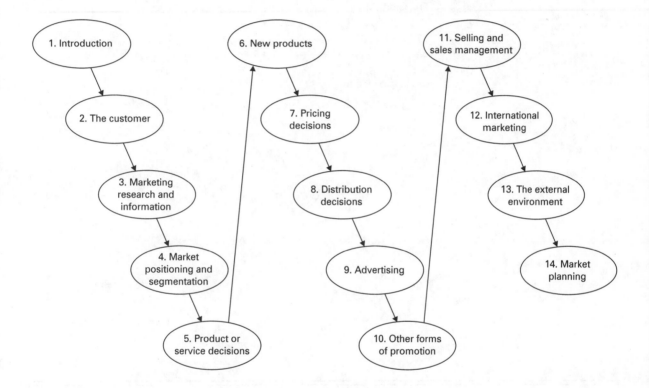

1. Introduction

2. The customer

3. Marketing research and information

4. Market positioning and segmentation

5. Product or service decisions

6. New products

7. Pricing decisions

8. Distribution decisions

9. Advertising

10. Other forms of promotion

11. Selling and sales management

12. International marketing

13. The external environment

14. Market planning

Introduction

There are other possible methods of promotion. 'Precision Marketing', for instance, is set to expand significantly over the present decade, with the advent of the computing power and data collection techniques needed to drive it. Currently, though, this is best evidenced by direct mail activity, but branch marketing also shares some of the characteristics, as does telesales.

On the other hand, sales promotion should be used almost exclusively in support of other promotional activities since it offers essentially short-term gains, whether or not it takes the form of price-based promotions. Despite its limited effectiveness, however, this form of promotion reportedly accounts for a greater proportion of the overall spending than advertising.

Public relations is a neglected resource in most organizations. In terms of press relations it offers a very cost-effective vehicle for promotion. In terms of corporate relations, it is the vehicle for dealing with many of the contacts with the external environment, at least those in the very important area of political activity. In both functions, professionalism is essential.

Exhibitions are specialized activities which may, however, have much to offer some organizations.

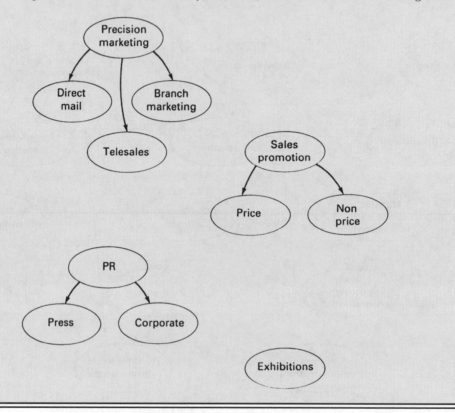

Precision Marketing

The explosion of data over the past decades has only recently been harnessed in the most direct way; that of marketing directly to the individual customers or small groups of customers. We believe that this is, in general, best described as precision marketing, but popular usage has recently focused on the more specific term of 'database marketing'. Martin Baier[1] describes some key aspects of this:

[1] M. Baier, *The Elements of Direct Marketing* (McGraw-Hill, 1983).

Direct marketing, with its historical roots in direct mail (an advertising medium) and mail order (a selling method), has evolved as an aspect of the total marketing concept. It is characterized by *measurability* and *accountability* as well as reliance on *lists* and *data*.

He goes on to offer a definition:

Direct marketing is an interactive system of marketing which uses one or more advertising media to effect a measurable response and/or transaction at any location.

Petrison et al.[2] summarize the trend towards direct (database) marketing as 'Marketers began by addressing their customers as a mass; today, they use database marketing to view them as individuals. This trend . . . is likely to continue . . .'. This is a view which is now gaining much wider acceptance amongst marketers in general, not just those at the leading edge, as direct marketing (albeit renamed, and newly respectable) comes out of the closet!

Another – more traditional – form of 'direct marketing', which will be described in detail in chapter 11, has been the normal selling approach employed, for example, in the industrial (complex sale) markets; the salesperson often spends a considerable time, face to face with the customer, tailoring the sale to that individual's specific needs.

The key to success in *both* of the fields described above is *detailed information about individual customers*.

Availability of Data

Until recently, however, those suppliers in the mass markets were not allowed the luxury of employing a face-to-face salesforce; the cost was, and still is, prohibitive. The new factor, which can go some way towards achieving the same impact, is the increasing availability of much more detailed information on large numbers of individual customers (or groups of these), together with the processing power to handle this data. The main drivers for change are:

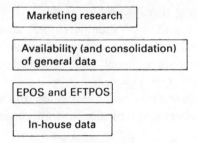

| Marketing research |
| Availability (and consolidation) of general data |
| EPOS and EFTPOS |
| In-house data |

---

[2] Lisa A. Petrison, Robert C. Blattberg and Paul Wang, Database marketing: past, present and future, *Journal of Direct Marketing*, vol. 7, no. 3 (Summer 1993).

Marketing research

Over recent years there has been a growing awareness that the broad averages hide considerable variations in terms of specific groups. At one level, this has been explored by very large surveys (such as TGI, the Target Group Index), which are statistically significant in terms of the smaller groups and, for example, allow the complementary relationships between different brands (as well as their relation to quite specific life-style groups) to be investigated.

At another level, the geographical dimension has been developed by organizations (such as ACORN and PIMS in the UK) which have categorized local neighbourhoods, so that suppliers can target specific groups with greater accuracy.

As John Whitehead[3] says:

> Neighbourhood classifications have spawned a whole portfolio of techniques that are able to dissect markets in great detail. Geodemographics is used primarily to analyse customer addresses and market research data; to target door-to-door advertising; and in the use of census and other demographic data to describe and model markets locally.

He goes on, though, to describe the most recent developments which link this data with life-style data, for instance:

> CON Marketing, linking up with National Shoppers Survey, has launched Persona, a 'behaviourgraphic' classification, defining electoral roll households by categories such as 'Bon Viveurs' and 'Wildlife Trustees', which relate to consumers' priorities and lifestyles.

Availability (and consolidation) of general data

More data is becoming available from existing sources. The ACORN work, for example, is based upon census data, which is now generally available in computer-readable form. In addition to this, many organizations are recognizing the value of what they hold on their own databases (membership lists, for example) and are making them available for sale.

A more fundamental, and as yet little developed, approach is to consolidate these various databases and thereby to provide a greater amount of information about, and a more 'three-dimensional' picture of, the individuals involved. To date, at least in the UK, this approach has been most effectively explored in terms of consolidating 'warranty card' information (the 'market research' information provided by consumers returning warranty cards) from different suppliers.

---

[3] J. Whitehead, Paying attention to detail, *Marketing* (22 February 1990).

In the longer term, the consolidation of the very large databases (including those of the credit card companies, always assuming that this will be allowed under the terms of the relevant legislation) will provide quite detailed information on at least one of the activities of most individuals in the population.

EPOS and EFTPOS

The most immediate stimulus, albeit probably more in theory than in practice, is the introduction of EPOS (Electronic Point Of Sale), together with EFTPOS (which adds the electronic transfer of funds), by the major retailers. Using EPOS, details of an individual transaction (but not the identity of the individual purchaser) can be tracked. Using EFTPOS it should also be possible to relate these transactions to any individual. In this way, retailers in particular will be able to build up a very detailed picture of the buying habits of individual customers.

In this way, for instance, at the beginning of 1995 the supermarket chain Tesco used a new 'Club Card' to recruit more than 5 million members, whilst raising its turnover by 7 per cent, in less than three months!

Following this theme, in the specific context of supermarket retailing, Cathy Bond[4] comments:

> Database marketing is on the way, ushered in by the growth of EPOS and direct debit scanning tills. It is worlds away from the kind of mass coupon drops and mailers which typically herald a new store opening, or which try to drum up seasonal extra business. Database experts dream of a world where mailshots will look as if they were tailor-made for every recipient. Where grocery retailers will value individual customers and not think of them as just so many feet through the door each week. The attitude will be caring, but not patronising – and definitely not tainted with the intrusive commercialism that is conventional direct marketing's big drawback.

In-house data

A number of organizations, ranging from direct mail houses to domestic appliance retailers, already have detailed information available on their existing records. Even organizations in the FMCG field, such as Nestlé, Pedigree Petfoods and Kraft General Foods, are also reported to be consolidating data that they accumulate about their consumers. It is claimed[5] that Heinz has already built a database of nearly six million homes in the UK that are

---

[4] C. Bond, Customer conscious, *Marketing* (8 March 1990).

[5] Philip Kotler, Reconceptualizing marketing: an interview with Philip Kotler, *European Management Journal*, vol. 12, no. 4 (December 1994).

heavy users of its products. According to Kotler,[6] 'The question is only whether companies will find it worth doing.'

In the USA, for example, Sears-Roebuck uses the computerized database information on its 40 million customers to promote special offers to specific target segments.

Manipulation of Data

The theory of precision marketing is simple: it is merely a matter of matching the requisite marketing approach to the individual. Thus, for example, Sears-Roebuck targets those of its customers who have purchased a number of domestic appliances without any associated maintenance cover, in a drive to sell them general maintenance contracts. A salesperson, in face-to-face contact, follows much the same process.

The problem comes in manipulating the vast quantities of data involved. Until recently even starting on this task was near impossible, just because of the amount of data involved, but now computers (which almost all organizations already have) have developed to the stage where they can easily handle the amount of this 'paperwork'.

Unfortunately, computers cannot – as yet – take decisions, without being fed very elaborate sets of rules to govern every possible situation.

There are two main solutions to this dilemma:

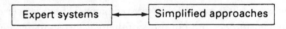

Expert systems. The longer-term solution may well be to teach the computers how to make the necessary decisions, including some 'learning from experience', using artificial intelligence or 'expert systems'-based approaches. This is a subject which is beyond the scope of this book.

Simplified approaches. In the shorter term, the answer may be to develop simpler ways of dealing with the data which, while not releasing the true potential of precision marketing, will still allow some of the benefits to be gained. There are two main routes:

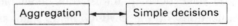

• *Aggregation.* The individuals (or separate stores) can be aggregated with others which share broadly similar performance or behaviour patterns; this is the broad principle on which ACORN already works. The precision is limited, but at least 'individual' approaches are possible at the group level.

[6] Ibid.

- *Simple decisions.* Instead of exactly matching the total purchasing profile of consumers, the decisions can be made to relate to relatively simple factors, as in the example of the Sears maintenance contracts. This approach can be developed incrementally, adding new decisions based upon simple combinations of factors as justified by experience.

Promotional Delivery Systems

The final requirement of a precision marketing system is that it should be capable of delivering the promotional effort where it is needed. Many forms of media will claim to deliver to tightly defined audiences (and some of the specialist and trade magazines do exactly that), but in general the minimum size of group which can be targeted (often no smaller than an individual town) excludes them from precision marketing. The traditional approach, and probably still the cheapest and most effective in this context, is direct mail.

Direct Mail Advertising

Direct mail advertising is just one – albeit very large – part of the overall direct marketing effort; but it can make an important contribution to closely targeted, precision marketing, campaigns – especially those in the industrial sector.

Thus, one effective way of generating numbers of prospects for the face-to-face, industrial salesforce, is to undertake mass mailings. The normal response rate for such mailings is often claimed to be as much as 1 or 2 per cent;[7] but in practice rates can be much lower. On the other hand, when mailing to specialized markets with a particularly powerful message, the response can reach almost 10 per cent. Whatever part of this very wide range a mailing falls into, you will still have to distribute large numbers to obtain even reasonable numbers of prospects – it is a 'numbers game' with a vengeance.

Pierre Passavant[8] says:

> The psychology of direct marketing is somewhat special. It tends to blend aspects of selling with elements of advertising.

He goes on to make the further point, which is not widely appreciated, that:

> The direct marketer allocates a far larger proportion of the sales dollar to promotion than manufacturers or most sellers of packaged goods . . .

[7] *The Dartnell Sales Promotion Handbook*, ed. O. Riso (Dartnell Corporation, 1979).
[8] P. A. Passavant, Direct marketing strategy, *The Direct Marketing Handbook*, ed. E. L. Nash (McGraw-Hill, 1984).

As with all forms of promotion, however, before conducting any mailing you have to be clear what are your specific objectives. Most mailings are designed to produce immediate sales enquiries. Even then you may decide that you want to make this route more clearly defined; and may decide to set your specific objective as attracting people to a free seminar, or to 'buy' enquiries by offering a free sample. There are many ways of achieving results; but it is important, before you go further, that you know *exactly* what you wish to achieve.

The advantages and disadvantages of direct mail

Advantages include the following:

- *Specific targeting.* Clearly, the most important aspect of direct mail is that it can be directed *exactly* at the specific, individual, customer. In 1990 Porsche were able to target the 300 000 Americans most likely to spend $75 000 on a German car.
- *Personalization.* Direct mail can address the customer personally. If the full benefits of precision marketing are exploited, it can be directly tailored to his or her needs (interactively based upon prior experience, as recorded on the database). Needless to say, the Porsche mailing was elaborately personalized.
- *Optimization.* Because of its direct response nature, the marketing campaign can be tested and varied to obtain the optimal results.
- *Accumulation.* Responses can be added to the database, allowing future mailings to be even better targeted.
- *Flexibility.* A direct mail campaign can be mounted quickly on a wide variety of topics within an overall promotional campaign.

Disadvantages include the following:

- *Cost.* The cost per thousand will be higher than almost any other form of mass promotion (although the wastage rate may be much lower).
- *Poor-quality lists.* The mailing lists may initially be of poor quality (with duplicate names, for example): they may be expensive to 'clean' and may even contribute to offending customers.
- *Relative lack of development.* The techniques of direct mail are, as yet, relatively unsophisticated, and this may mean that the medium is less effectively used.

Perhaps the greatest disadvantage, certainly in terms of consumer marketing, is the poor image that direct mail still holds. Its popular description, as 'junk mail', is well deserved, and historically accurate. Many mailings have been poorly planned, poorly targeted and poorly presented.

The mailing list

The first question to ask is to whom you wish to mail. The answer will probably come most frequently, and most successfully, from your own database of customers and prospects. On the other hand, even though you may have a great many names on your files, it may still be worthwhile being selective, choosing just those who will be susceptible to the mailing. This saves on cost, but it also protects the investment in the database by not exposing recipients to mounds of irrelevant 'junk mail'.

If you do not have a suitable list of prospects on your database, you may be able to use the services of a specialist mailing house which does maintain such a list (often compiled from customer and prospect lists bought from other suppliers such as yourself). Mailing houses will usually sell a list for one-time use, providing labels (or sometimes computer readable material for your own use) or even a complete mailing service.

In the UK, the best list of such mailing houses is probably that contained in the *Direct Mail Databook*.[9] The most important question to ask in buying such a list is how accurate it is. The source of many lists may be suspect (they are frequently derived from subscribers to magazines, for example, or respondents to free offers, who may not be the ideal prospects), but then this may be the only way in which you can reach your target audience. Lists may also be out of date (12 per cent of the UK population changes address every year)[10] and may need 'cleaning' (for example, to remove duplicate entries or to update contacts within organizations). Usually the only satisfactory way of finding out how useful they are is to run a test mailing, even though that represents an investment of time and money.

Investing in your own database

As the above section implies, the most productive mailing list is usually the one that you have built for yourself. As Edward Nash[11] comments, in the context of mail order operators:

> The single most valuable list used by the majority of advertisers is their own house list. Tragically, it is often the most neglected. For most direct marketing companies, it is the single most precious asset – the one whose loss could put them out of business. It is usually the most responsive list to a company's additional offers.

Even in organizations with more general fields of operation, the data obtained as a result of those operations (enquiries, face-to-face selling, exhibitions, direct mail, and so on) should all be regarded as precious. Data should be consolidated and protected so that they are usable, and useful, as a direct input to all marketing activities – especially for precision marketing.

[9] *Direct Mail Databook*, ed. J. Durlacher (Gower, 4th edn, 1983).
[10] R. Fairlie, Starting your own direct mail operation, *Direct Mail Databook*, ed. J. Durlacher (Gower, 4th edn, 1983).
[11] E. L. Nash, *Direct Marketing: Strategy, Planning, Execution* (McGraw-Hill, 2nd edn, 1986).

The direct mail offer

The basis for a mailing has to be a clear-cut 'offer'. This may be simply a statement about the products or services, or it can be a specific promotion. As with all forms of promotion, you need to be very clear what your real offer is and, despite the apparent opportunity to convey large amounts of material, you will usually need it to be kept as simple as possible. The material will almost inevitably arrive through the prospect's letterbox among half a dozen other similar mailings. Thus, as with all advertising, your direct mail message will have just a few seconds to grab the recipient's attention. The much quoted sales acronym, KISS (Keep It Simple, Stupid), is nowhere more applicable than in mailings.

Finally, as direct mail is almost always only a part of a wider campaign, there must be a clear action associated with the message. This may be just the suggestion (but a strong one) that the recipient should return the reply-paid card; or it may be stronger, telling the recipient to be prepared for a telephone call from a salesperson.

The letter

It is, of course, quite possible to send out a mailing without any letter; and perhaps most mailings in consumer markets simply comprise such unaccompanied 'flyers'. But most mailings sent out as part of overall campaigns in the industrial sales environment, even mass mailings, usually include a letter. In any case, the evidence suggests that enclosing a letter improves the response rate; and enclosing a *personalized* letter improves it significantly. Market research among personal computer buyers showed that between 60 per cent and 80 per cent of them read a letter addressed to them by name, whereas less than 40 per cent read one addressed to them by title, and in just over 20 per cent of cases where it was addressed to the company. *According to this evidence, personalization can improve the performance by a factor of four.* There is some controversy as to what is the best form of letter. Clearly, a simple price promotion (still one of the most powerful ways of gaining attention) will benefit from a short, punchy, style; whereas the more 'serious' nature of a technical brief on a sophisticated new product might be better suited to a longer format. Whatever its format it should be written (preferably by a trained copywriter) in a style that is easy for the reader to understand – with the minimum of jargon, for example.

Howard Dana Shaw (one of the most respected US authorities on writing mail order letters) has produced 'six checking points for writing that gets people to do things':

1 Be natural instead of literary
2 Simplify your sentences

3   Write in pictures
4   Make things move
5   Use personal pronouns
6   Don't inflate

The one point that most commentators seem to agree on is that the areas at the top and foot of the letter receive the most attention from the recipient. At the top, try to encapsulate the overall message in a punchy headline; and then make the hottest offer immediately, in the first paragraph. The best way to use the area at the foot is to include an important postscript.

Inserts

The most frequently used item in a mailing is a brochure. Once more, the rule is to keep it simple, and in line with the message of the letter: conflicting messages will just confuse the reader. If two mailings are needed to avoid confusion, take consolation from the fact that the most effective mailing campaigns are those with a *number* of separate mailings – like most advertising, the effect is cumulative.

Over the years, the large number of devices, such as gifts, 'Yes/No' stamps, samples and so on, have (on the basis of testing) been found to be effective. These are usually the province of the specialist mailing house. On the other hand, as with all marketing, the 'product' offer itself must be attractive to the recipient.

Reply-paid cards

A reply-paid (or FREEPOST) card improves the chances of generating a response. According to *The Dartnell Sales Promotion Handbook*:[12]

> The cheapest way to get inquiries for a product or service is the post-paid reply card. An offer to send some helpful booklet, or to send some article of use, to a list of prospects has been known to produce as high as 37 percent replies at a cost of less than 54 cents each. Returns of five percent to ten percent on reply paid cards of this kind are common.

Better results (by a factor of three or four) can be obtained if the reply-paid card is personalized.

The best results of all are generated by sending a personalized reply form, together with a ready *stamped* envelope (rather than a reply-paid cover), even though this approach increases costs dramatically.

---

[12] *The Dartnell Sales Promotion Handbook.*

Timing

The timing of mailings can influence their impact. Clearly, they have to be integrated with the overall campaign. On the other hand, there are some times of year, particularly July, August (holidays) and December (Christmas), when it is traditionally believed to be unproductive to mail. Even the day of the week can have an impact. *The Dartnell Sales Promotion Handbook,*[13] for example, reports that:

> Care should be taken, they say, to avoid reaching a businessman's desk on Monday, or any day following a holiday, when there is likely to be a large accumulation of letters needing attention . . . the best day is Tuesday, and Wednesday is next best.

Response rates

The great advantage of direct mail advertising is that every aspect of promotion can be tested, simply by measuring the resulting response rates. All that is required is that the reply-paid card (or the response coupon in an advertisement) can be identified with the specific element of the campaign under test. The most useful, and most frequently used, technique is to include 'Department xxxx' (where xxxx is the number of the test) in the address; this is sometimes called the 'key number'.

In this way, every element of direct mail promotion may be optimized. The mailing list can be categorized, and the letter (and other promotional material) designed to have the greatest impact (as measured by response).

This technique has been honed to a fine edge by large-scale users, such as Reader's Digest. Every part of the mailing will have been tested, and selected precisely because it is the most effective in terms of generating measured responses. This testing is often carried out using 'split runs', in which some of the (randomly selected) customers receive one version of the mailing and other customers receive the one with which it is to be compared. In this way, the effectiveness of two may be directly compared.

The trap into which such organizations may fall is that this incremental approach may gradually concentrate on an ever smaller group of the population, who are particularly susceptible to these direct mail techniques – in the process, neglecting the much larger part of the population which is less susceptible.

Other Forms of Direct Mail

Some organizations have recently started to use telex and fax in the same way as direct mail. This is more expensive, but may be more likely to be read by the

---

[13] *The Dartnell Sales Promotion Handbook,* edited by Ovid Riso (Dartnell Corporation, 1979).

recipient because of its novelty value. The use of such electronic communications is less of an innovation than it might seem; according to Ed Burnett, over 90 per cent of Sears-Roebuck's catalogue sales are *telephoned* in. It is likely that this approach will also be extended to computer electronic mail when this becomes more widely used.

Door-to-door

An alternative, and cheaper, approach is to employ a door-to-door distribution company to deliver unaddressed mailings to all addresses in a specific area. This loses many of the advantages of direct mail, but where the area is tightly defined it can still offer a high degree of precision. In particular, it now offers a very good vehicle for 'sampling' new users on a tightly targeted basis (which, once again, can be optimized by testing).

The maximum coverage by delivery organizations (such as Circular Distributors and Donnelly Marketplace) is 16.5 million homes in the UK (85 per cent of the total).

Publications

It is also now possible for those publications reaching the bulk of their readers by mail to produce tailored versions to suit even relatively small groups of consumers. Rapp and Collins,[14] for instance, describe how *Farm Journal* uses computer-collated binding to send out a minimum of 2000 different versions (and, at that time, a maximum of 8896 versions) to its 825 000 readers. Advertisers are similarly matched to readers, on the basis of computerized subscriber profiles.

Computer-mediated Communications (CMC)

One new vehicle for precision marketing, which is likely to emerge as the century draws to a close, is that of computer communication. During the 1980s this was largely limited to communication within organizations, and then within relatively few pioneering organizations; although those that did develop it on a large scale – such as IBM and DEC – found that it had dramatic implications for their internal communications (and even forced structural changes). With the rapid development of various forms of the super-highway, especially the Internet, this type of communication is expanding dramatically. There have already been – as yet relatively ineffective – attempts to use these media for direct selling.

[14] S. Rapp and T. Collins, *The Great Marketing Turnaround* (Simon & Schuster, 1990).

Even so, by 1990 Murray Turoff[15] estimated that there were well over 10 000 active bulletin board systems in the USA, and remarked: 'It is amazing that they exist almost ignored by either the communicators or the computer industry.' The essential features of the more advanced CMC systems are described by Kaye et al.[16]

Most CMC systems provide an integrated range of facilities. These generally include:

- electronic mail for one-to-one communications
- one or more asynchronous group communications (conferences)
- a 'chat' mode for real-time exchange of short messages with other users
- a directory of all users, with their résumés and information on when they last accessed the system
- a directory of all listed conferences, and brief details of each one . . .

CMC can be used to 'talk' individually to thousands of contacts (simultaneously if necessary) – with all the power of the accumulated database information immediately at hand. More importantly, perhaps, it has the potential of becoming a *new* medium of communications, positioned mid-way between individual communications and the mass media.

Branch Marketing

One alternative, as a device for precision marketing, is that based upon branches. This is typically only open to those in the service sector (especially those in retailing), but for these fortunate few it represents a particularly powerful form of marketing; and is likely to grow considerably in use over the next few years as the service sector learns to make use of marketing in general, and of precision marketing in particular.

The 'precision' enters this form of marketing in a number of ways:

- *Location.* In the first instance, the actual site of the branch can be chosen to optimize its catchment area, so that the maximum number of potential customers can be attracted. This is normally carried out using a geographic database, such as ACORN or PIMS in the UK, to locate the clusters of potential customers; and then to optimize (by Monte Carlo or other statistical method) the number covered.
- *Range.* The exact range of products or services to be offered can be matched to the profile of the exact catchment area, and subsequently modified by practice in the light of actual sales.

---

[15] M. Turoff, The anatomy of computer application innovation: computer mediated communications (CMC), *Technological Forecasting and Social Change*, vol. 36 (1989).

[16] T. Kaye, R. Mason and L. Harasim, *Computer Conferencing in the Academic Environment*, Center for Information Technology Paper no. 91 (Open University, 1989).

| Location |
| Range |
| Direct mail |
| Personal contact |
| Experimentation |

- *Direct mail.*   Once again, direct mail can be very effectively used to attract new prospects, and to rejuvenate lapsed customers, by targeting precisely those promotions which might be most attractive.
- *Personal contact.*   Once in the branch, and in a face-to-face sale, feedback from an EPOS system could allow personalization; even if only to allow the assistant to say 'Thank you, Mrs Patel', but possibly also to say, 'We have just received a shipment of the perfume you particularly like, which was out of stock the last time you called.'
- *Experimentation.*   As with direct mail, branches have the luxury of being able to try out new ideas, and measure how effective they are. This is the most powerful form of research; it tests exactly the factors which the question demands, rather than extrapolating from indirect indicators.

ACTIVITY 10.1

Design a mailing (to an intermediary, a retailer or agent) for your organization's latest product or service. First of all, you should decide upon the objective of the mailing, and how this may be achieved in terms of the messages contained. Then write the letter, and decide what inserts will be needed. Finally, decide when and how it should be mailed.

You can obtain a criticism of the final result from a colleague, or even from a member of your family (spouses make excellent critics in this respect, since they will have received more than their fair share of junk mail).

SELF-TEST QUESTION 10.1

What direct mailing does your organization undertake? What are its objectives, and how well does it succeed? What changes would you suggest? What further mailing programmes would you suggest?

> What branch-level precision marketing does it undertake, and how well does it succeed? What changes would you suggest?
>
> What other precision marketing does it undertake? What other, as yet neglected, opportunities for precision marketing can you see?

Other Direct Contacts

A direct salesforce is usually an optimal approach, but can be very expensive. This problem has been nicely side-stepped by some organizations which have recruited part-time agents (typically housewives, at low rates of 'pay'). Avon Cosmetics have developed this to near perfection, with reportedly around a million 'representatives' world-wide. The friendly relationship between seller and buyer (who often know each other socially) reinforces the sale – and also motivates both seller and buyer. Tupperware – and 'erotic' lingerie – parties extend this approach further.

These techniques can be considered as precision marketing in that they involve a very direct – and often a very knowledgeable – approach to the customer. On the other hand, since the organization employing the seller has not as yet obtained access to this knowledge, but depends upon the informal relationship being handled by its 'agents', it encounters some problems in terms of applying the other techniques of precision marketing.

Sales Promotion

Sales promotion should normally be an adjunct to personal selling or advertising. Some techniques can be applied to services as well as to products. Kenneth Runyon[17] succinctly defines its key characteristics as:

1 A relatively short-term activity.
2 Directed towards sales force, distribution channels, or consumers, or some combination of these groups.
3 Used in order to stimulate some specific action.

In recent years, however, spending on sales promotions, in both the USA and Europe, reportedly has overtaken that on advertising. WPP Group reported as early as 1988 that sales promotions had equalled advertising in terms of revenue (at around $200 billion globally). This might seem to challenge the consensus drawn from theory. It may, though, be seen more pragmatically as evidence of

[17] K. E. Runyon, *Advertising* (C. E. Merrill Publishing, 2nd edn, 1984).

the short-termism afflicting corporate strategies rather than as evidence of well-founded marketing campaigns.

Sales promotion covers a wide range of possibilities; as demonstrated by the list in table 10.1, developed by Malcolm McDonald,[18] to which *sponsorship* (typically of events, such as sports meetings) should be added.

Advantages and Disadvantages of Sales Promotion

Despite its recent widespread use as a key element of marketing campaigns, at least in terms of money spent, the essence of sales promotion is that it is intended as a very short-term influence on 'sales': it typically has an insignificant long-term effect, but may be used as a powerful additional factor, included in the competitive balance, in the short term, to sway sales in the supplier's favour, and to bring sales forward.

Advantages

- sales increase – the main short-term benefit
- defined target audience – it can be targeted on specific groups (especially selected retailers and their customers), especially now that it can be linked, by computer-generated POS coupons, to actual purchases going through the checkout
- defined role – it can also be targeted to achieve specific objectives, such as increasing repeat purchase – again POS dispensers can target these more accurately
- indirect roles – it can also be used to achieve other objectives, such as widening distribution or 'shelf facings'

Disadvantages

- short term – almost all of the effect is immediate. There is rarely any lasting increase in sales. Research by Andrew Ehrenberg[19] has shown that 'shoppers simply exploit [them] . . . and then return to the brand they used before . . . Nothing happened in terms of repeat purchase and . . . brand switching.'
- hidden costs – many costs, not least the management/salesforce time and effort, do not appear in the direct costs
- confusion – promotions can conflict with the main brand messages, and confuse the customer as to what the image really is. It is believed, for instance, that Burger King's promotional activities, in its war with McDonald's at the end of the 1970s, may have actually had an unfavourable influence on consumers' brand perceptions![20]

[18] M. H. B. McDonald, *Marketing Plans* (Heinemann, 1984).
[19] Andrew Ehrenberg, LBS report debunks the effectiveness of promos, *Marketing* (29 August 1994).
[20] J. P. Jones, The double jeopardy of sales promotions, *Harvard Business Review* (September–October 1990).

Table 10.1 Types of sales promotions

Target market	Money		Goods		Services	
	Direct	Indirect	Direct	Indirect	Direct	Indirect
Consumer	Price reduction	Coupons Vouchers Money equivalent Competitions	Free goods Premium offers (e.g. 13 for 12) Free gifts Trade-in offers	Stamps Coupons Money equivalent Competitions	Guarantees Group participation events Special exhibitions and displays	Co-operative advertising Stamps, coupons Vouchers for services Event admission Competitions
Trade	Dealer loaders Loyalty schemes Incentives Full-range buying	Extended credit Delayed invoicing Sale or return Coupons Vouchers Money equivalent	Free gifts Trial offers Trade-in offers	Coupons Vouchers Money equivalent Competitions	Guarantees Group participation events Free services Risk reduction schemes Training Special exhibitions, displays Demonstrations Reciprocal trading schemes	Stamps, coupons Vouchers for services Competitions
Salesforce	Bonus Commission	Coupons Vouchers Points systems Money equivalent Competitions	Free gifts	Coupons Vouchers Points systems Money equivalent	Free services Group participation events	Coupons Vouchers Points systems for services Event admission Competitions

- price-cutting – which can persuade users to expect a lower price in future, and potentially damage 'quality'

Perhaps its greatest disadvantage, though, may be the lack of effectiveness. Abraham and Lodish[21] report that:

> . . . only 16% of the trade promotion events we studied were profitable, based on incremental sales of brands distributed through retailer warehouses. For many promotions the cost of selling an incremental dollar of sales was *greater* than one dollar.

They go on to record that, despite this:

> . . . promotions have become so popular that they now account for more than 65% of typical marketing budgets.

In line with its essentially short-term objectives, a promotion may realistically be expected to achieve a number of limited objectives:

| Trial purchase |
| Extra volume |
| Repeat business |
| Point of sale impact |

- *Trial purchase.* Some promotions are expressly planned to induce consumers to try the product or service. The classic example is that of 'money-off' coupons, or samples of the product, at the time of the launch (possibly 'banded' as a free gift on a related product).
- *Extra volume.* Other promotions are designed to stimulate the user's decision at point of sale; on-pack price cuts are the obvious example. It may often be found that a cheaper alternative is to offer more of the product ('free 20% extra') for the same price.
- *Repeat business.* Yet others are meant to build repeat business. A good example is that of 'money off next purchase' coupons.
- *Point of sale impact.* Free gifts, for example, may provide additional interest for an advertising campaign, or a competition may lead to a better display at the point of sale; but it is the extra shelf space that sells the product, rather than the promotion itself.

It should be added that sales promotion and advertising (or, indeed, any of the other forms of promotion) are complementary; and the most effective, well-balanced, campaign will often include a mix of several types of promotion.

---

[21] M. M. Abraham and L. M. Lodish, Getting the most out of advertising and promotion, *Harvard Business Review* (May–June 1990).

Promotional Pricing

One of the most frequently used sales promotional techniques is that of offering promotional discounts; that is 'buying' extra sales – albeit only in the short term. These can be grouped into a number of main categories:

> Price reductions
>
> Free goods
>
> Banded offers
>
> Vouchers or coupons
>
> Cash refunds
>
> Money off next purchase
>
> Loyalty schemes
>
> Loss leader pricing
>
> Cheap credit
>
> Special events

Price reductions.   The simple 'money-off' promotion is the most direct and hence may have the most immediate impact on sales levels. As it is shown on the 'pack', it is also difficult for any retailer to avoid passing it on to the consumer. It is the most expensive technique, because to be effective it usually needs to represent 15 to 20 per cent off the regular retail price. It may also prove difficult to restore the price to its original level at the end of the promotion, as consumers, and in particular retailers, may decide to stock-pile in order to hold off their purchases until the next promotion (indeed, Schultz and Robinson[22] report that 'more than 25 per cent of all retail customers are considered regular "price-off" buyers'). It may also do considerable damage to the image of quality products or services, especially where the price-off 'burst' or 'flag' may visually dominate the label.

Free goods.   The offer of more product for the same price has a number of advantages. It often costs the supplier significantly less than a price cut, and it forces the customer to buy more than usual, possibly setting a new pattern of usage. Also, it possibly has less impact on the established price, although it can set an awkward precedent.

Banded offers.   Two or more products, often banded together using adhesive tape, almost invariably at a lower price (although one product may be offered as a

---

[22]D. E. Schultz and W. A. Robinson, *Sales Promotion Essentials* (Crain Books, 1982).

'premium') are typically meant to offer greater 'value'; but this normally poses problems in terms of requiring changes to the production lines – often with considerable reductions in productivity. With, however, the increasing sophistication of EPOS, the products can now be linked electronically rather than physically – which means that similar benefits can be gained without these costs.

Vouchers or coupons.   Where the aim is to extend the penetration (or trial) of the product or service to new customers (particularly in the case of a new product launch), coupons are often used. They are most effectively delivered door-to-door, where they achieve high redemption rates; though, computer controlled POS dispensers, linked to purchases, are now proving very effective. Schultz and Robinson[23] report that 'About 60 per cent of homes that receive direct mail coupons actually use them', although they also report that the redemption levels for individual coupons are around 10 per cent. In the USA it is claimed that 80 per cent of these are now delivered via FSIs (Free Standing Inserts, books full of coupons). They may also be incorporated in press advertisements – which are cheaper to run but have a considerably lower redemption rate (Schultz and Robinson,[24] again, report between 2 per cent and 3 per cent). Depending upon the generosity of the offer, this is supposed to tempt consumers away from their existing brands to try the new one. This can be a very effective type of promotion if coupon redemption levels are high enough, and may be more cost-effective than sampling; and it clearly has only limited impact on the prices paid by existing customers. 'Stamps', the popularity of which has fluctuated over recent years, are a special form of this type of promotion; they are intended, in particular, to buy very long-term loyalty, or for use on a staple item of purchase. However, they can be expensive and very complex to administer, particularly where they lose their 'competitive edge' and are taken for granted.

As already mentioned a number of times, a recent development has been the issuing of coupons at supermarket checkouts – the coupons being related, by computer, directly to the specific customer's purchases. The ASDA supermarket chain, in the UK, for instance, uses this approach, which is based on the Catalina Electronic Marketing System.[25]

Cash refund.   A cash refund (from the retailer or by mail), usually on the basis of a 'voucher' which is attached to, or is part of, the pack, is a way of offering a controlled price reduction. On the other hand, the redemption procedures may be complex (and unwelcome to the trade). It can also be expensive; sometimes (when 'trial' is being sought) the refund may even be as much as the whole purchase price, although the redemption rates reported[26] (of only a few per cent) indicate that many purchasers never redeem the offers – and so actual costs may be significantly reduced.

Money off next purchase.   A somewhat similar coupon offer, this time on the label of the product itself, may be used to extend buying patterns and build customer loyalty. For instance, the UK jewellery chain Ratners offered a £50 voucher for every £150 spent;

| Price reductions |
| Free goods |
| Banded offers |
| Vouchers or coupons |
| Cash refunds |
| Money off next purchase |
| Loyalty schemes |
| Loss leader pricing |
| Cheap credit |
| Special events |

---

[23]Schultz and Robinson, *Sales Promotion Essentials.*
[24] Schultz and Robinson, *Sales Promotion Essentials.*
[25] Anne Massey, Hi-tech promotions, *Marketing Business* (May 1994).
[26] Schultz and Robinson, *Sales Promotion Essentials.*

although (typically for a promotion) the indications are that this was possibly used to boost short-term sales and reduce stock levels rather than to build loyalty; indeed, Hawkes[27] emphasizes that 'customers who are bribed for their orders are significantly more prone to competitive action . . .'.

Loss leader pricing. In the case of the service and distribution industries, a product or service may actually be priced below cost in order to attract customers into the branch, in the hope that they will buy other products or services which *are* profitable.

Cheap credit. Where credit is offered, lower-priced or even free credit may be used instead of a simple price reduction. This may be cheaper to the vendor who has access to cheaper lines of credit (although the cost of bad debts must also be covered). It may be particularly attractive to the more naïve consumer who sees it as a way of getting something now, and paying later. It may also be a means of introducing the consumer to the use of the supplier's credit facilities.

Special events. Certain sectors of the retail trade offer 'special', usually seasonal, events to encourage buying during periods of traditionally low turnover.

Loyalty schemes

The Tesco supermarket chain, in the UK, has focused on 'loyalty' (and massive amounts of customer information) generated by a 'club' scheme. The customers are identified (for the computer database) by a magnetic striped card, very similar to that described[28] in use by A & P in the US. The Tesco venture proved a great success, achieving 5 million cards issued in just three months;[29] whilst at the same time recording a 7 per cent increase in revenue (for an effective discount on the card of less than one per cent!). American Express have claimed almost as many members for its world-wide 'Membership rewards' scheme.

Other suppliers' loyalty schemes – which have depended upon customers writing in to join their clubs – have, though, recorded more questionable degrees of success – typically only recruiting a small proportion of customers.

'Non-price' Promotions

There are a number of other forms of promotion which aim to offer 'added value', but which are not so directly price-related:

---

[27] Paul Hawkes, Building brand loyalty and commitment, *Journal of Brand Management*, vol. 1, no. 6 (1994).

[28] Jim Bessen, Riding the marketing information wave, *Harvard Business Review* (September–October 1993).

[29] Martin Croft, It's all in the cards, *Marketing Week* (24 March 1995).

Competitions

Personality
promotions

Free gifts and
mail-ins

'Self-liquidating'
offers

Multibrand
promotions

Competitions.   In this case the purchaser receives the right to one or more entries in a competition. Exceptionally, if the main prize is very large (and it is the size of the top prize which reportedly determines the interest of the consumer), this can be a very attention-getting form of promotion. It can be very easy and cheap to mount, and has a guaranteed fixed maximum cost. In its normal form, though, it has a lower level of interest for the consumer, with a low 'redemption' rate; and is now often just used as a means of gaining extra in-store impact.

Personality promotions.   In former times, in particular, teams of 'sales promoters' toured the country (sometimes dressed in the most outlandish of costumes), offering incentives such as 'instant prizes' to potential users. More recently, this has been largely super-seded by 'in-store promotions', staffed by personnel who are usually part-timers employed by specialist agencies. The process can be expensive, and difficult to control, although it may occasionally generate some of the benefits of face-to-face selling.

Free gifts and mail-ins.   These give the customer an additional offer (a 'giveaway' either 'on-pack', or at point of sale, or by mailing in). They can be expensive to run (depending on the value of the 'free offer'). The technique can be used to establish repeat purchase if a *number* of coupons (and hence packs) have to be collected. However, the administration can be complex, and additional sales may just come from heavy users buying forward. A special form of the 'giveaway' is one where the container itself is 'reusable' (for instance, a shelf-storage jar containing instant coffee). Such free gifts are not restricted to FMCG products. Some banks, for example, have offered free legal help and surveys to those taking out a mortgage.

Competitions

Personality
promotions

Free gifts and
mail-ins

'Self-liquidating'
offers

Multibrand
promotions

'Self-liquidating' offers.   In this case the offer is not free, as a result of which some writers call it a 'premium' offer. Like a competition it can add interest and the impression is usually given that the supplier is subsidizing the offer, so that the customer will obtain a good deal on the item. In practice, the intention is usually to cover the cost within the amount paid by the customer; in effect it offers the customer only the benefit of the supplier's buying power (or the special deal which has been negotiated). It is now seen as having low consumer interest (according to Schultz and Robinson:[30] 'It's estimated

---

[30] Schultz and Robinson, *Sales Promotion Essentials.*

that less than 10% of the population have ever sent away for a self-liquidating premium . . . redemption of self-liquidating premiums is usually less than 1% of the media circulation where it is offered'), and is only used in the few situations in which such marginal impact is worthwhile; though there would appear to be few of these. It can also have significant hidden costs, since it is difficult to administer; and forecasting stock levels is a very problematic experience.

Multibrand promotions. A number of brands, typically from one supplier, share a single promotion, in order to maximize impact for given costs. This technique can be used to recruit new users to these other brands, but it will only work well if all these brands are in widespread distribution, and there is some logic to the link.

Sampling

This is generally the most powerful form of promotion for 'new products', the immediate aim being to obtain 'trial' by users. It is normally used as one of the very early elements in a launch. Interestingly, though, Schultz and Robinson[31] say that:

> Sampling seems to work best for new products when it is preceded by four to six weeks of advertising. That generates interest which the sample then converts into trial.

For example, to follow the launch of 'Radion' detergent, Target Group (on behalf of its client, Lever Brothers) delivered 200 gram trial packs of this product to 10 million households in the UK.

It is a very expensive promotional device, often less cost-effective than any of the other forms of promotion. But it is the most effective, direct and immediate way of obtaining consumer trial. Retailers also recognize its power to pull in customers, and it may accordingly also help to achieve distribution. Indeed, it is often combined with a money-off voucher, to ensure that a successful trial is rapidly followed by a purchase. Thus, the Radion sample mentioned above also carried a '20p off' coupon.

Charles Frederick Jr of Ogilvy & Mather Inc. (reported in Schultz and Robinson)[32] tabulates the value of the technique (table 10.2). This shows that while sampling is better than coupons at obtaining trial, some of this advantage is clawed back because coupons have a higher conversion rate from trial to full users.

---

[31] Schultz and Robinson, *Sales Promotion Essentials.*
[32] Schultz and Robinson, *Sales Promotion Essentials.*

Table 10.2 Effectiveness of sampling

	Sample	*Mail coupon*
Total homes	100	100
Trial	80	20
Usage	20	7
Rate of conversion	25%	35%

Measurement of Promotional Performance

Unlike most other forms of promotion, which can be considered – at least in part – to have a cumulative effect over the longer term (and hence can be considered as partly an investment), sales promotions are almost always developed to have a direct, and immediate, effect. As a result the extra sales should be directly linked to the sales promotion.

Each such sales promotion can, and should, be set specific performance objectives. The performance should be monitored to ensure that these objectives are attained, and as a basis for judging the usefulness of such promotions in similar future situations.

The exception to this rule of measurement of results may be the many promotions which are run solely as an 'incentive' for the retailer to give additional temporary support to the brand.

SELF-TEST QUESTION 10.2

What 'sales promotions' does your organization undertake? What are they intended to achieve? Do they succeed? What improvements would you suggest?

Telesales

Somewhere between direct mail and the face-to-face sales call lies 'telesales'. To a degree this is a personal technique, and it can certainly be interactive whereas a mailshot cannot. It is a 'medium' most often used in the industrial goods sector (where the relatively high cost per call can be more easily justified), but some consumer 'capital goods' suppliers, such as those offering double glazing, and Ford, in the USA (which once made 20 million calls to produce leads for its sales personnel), also use it. On a more typical scale, one 'Midland Bank' campaign in the UK at the end of the 1980s required close to 40 000 outbound calls, together with the handling of 7000 inbound calls.

The great advantage of telesales over face-to-face selling is the rate at which calls can be made. It is quite realistic for even untrained sales personnel to make more than 50 such telephone calls in a day (compared, say, with as few as 300 face-to-face calls in a *year*). When specialist telesales personnel are used, the call rate can rise into hundreds per day.

The great advantage over direct mail is the success rate, which is estimated to be as much as ten times as high. It is not unusual to achieve a 10 per cent 'response rate' when, for instance, the intention is to invite contacts to a suitable 'seminar' as a preliminary to face-to-face selling. Edward Nash[33] declares that it can be as high as 25 or 30 per cent of all calls made.

The clear disadvantages are that teleselling is limited in comparison with face-to-face calls; there are no visual stimuli (for either side), and the calls have to be much shorter. It is considerably more difficult to be persuasive as a disembodied voice, which is why the technique is often only used as a first step towards a face-to-face call. This technique is several times more expensive than direct mail, but much less expensive than a face-to-face call. Moriarty and Moran,[34] for instance, quote a rate of $17 per hour (compared with $300 per hour for direct face-to-face representatives).

Telesales agencies

It is expensive to maintain a telesales team: accordingly, many organizations use specialist telesales agencies, set up to handle the difficult task of controlling and motivating their personnel – for most sales personnel nothing could be more soul-destroying than spending all day making 'cold' telephone calls.

The basis for such calls is usually a 'script', which will be produced in co-operation with, and agreed with, the client. This calls for a high degree of skill, since it takes the telesales staff through the various levels of 'conversation' with their contact, and the wide range of possible responses. Equally, though, this means that the call can only deal with very simple, superficial matters – as an introductory device.

Inbound telemarketing

A telesales (or 'enquiry handling') team also receives calls from customers and prospects. These calls may be part of 'business as usual', in which case they may

[33] Nash, *Direct Marketing: Strategy, Planning, Execution*.
[34] R. T. Moriarty and U. Moran, Managing hybrid marketing systems, *Harvard Business Review* (November–December 1990).

be handled by in-house teams. On the other hand, they may be part of a one-off promotional campaign, an advertised offer being directed, for example, to a standard 'freephone' number (0800 in the UK, or 800 in the USA). Again, these are typically handled by specialist agencies which have the computer systems and, especially, the extensive telephone lines necessary for these peak loads.

'Enquiry-handling' in general is a weak link in the marketing operations of most organizations. Very few organizations indeed have formally planned and carefully monitored enquiry-handling systems. It is very difficult to demonstrate 'quality' when the customer cannot find anyone to handle an enquiry, and complaints are definitely exacerbated when nobody seems willing to listen. A very simple, but often very enlightening, test is to ring your own organization with such an enquiry, and see just how well – or how disastrously – it is handled.

Press and Public Relations

Face-to-face selling, advertising and sales promotion can all be described as the primary sources of communication. They are under your direct control, and you pay for them. But there are also *secondary* sources of communication, which are not under your direct control and for which you do not pay – including word of mouth, editorial comment, personal recommendation and so on. These secondary sources may still be influenced by your promotional activities. In turn, because of their supposed 'impartial' nature, they may carry considerable weight with your consumers (possibly even more so than direct primary sources).

The most important element of secondary sources of communication is that of the press. It can be a very effective (and very inexpensive) part of the marketing mix, but it is one that many companies neglect. Although there is a limit to the amount that can be productively spent on PR, up to that point it is often the case that (pound for pound) the investment can be many times more productive than that spent on other types of promotion (including advertising). This is just as true of a small company (which may find such PR the most effective vehicle for promoting its products, whereas it simply cannot afford large advertising budgets). Again, though, the specialist expertise of a PR agency is really called for.

PR is often a particularly valuable promotional device for services since the 'authority' offered by independent recommendations in editorial matter can add vital credibility to an intangible service. PR is a particularly easy promotional device for non-profit organizations to use; the UK-based Open University, for example, has little need to advertise – where it is considered by editors a very legitimate topic for considerable comment. It is claimed that Anita Roddick built her 'Body Shop' empire without a single advertisement.

There are a wide range of vehicles available to PR: a good PR practitioner will use any opportunity to further the cause of the client. Some of the main ones are as follows:

Media contact

News stories

Media events

Press office

Media contact

One of the most important tasks of the PR professional is to maintain contact with the key journalists in the relevant media (usually the national press, journals, radio and television). This is a two-way process: the PR professional learns about, and can contribute to, features which will appear in the media; while, in the other direction, journalists become more receptive to news stories from the PR professional.

It is, indeed, an 'investment' process. The relationship with the media (and especially with individual journalists) has to be cultivated until a mutual trust has been earned. When working properly this is not a process of exploitation by either side, but of mutual respect.

It is significant that a US survey (carried out by Sheila Tate, Press Secretary to Mrs Nancy Reagan – as reported by Roger Haywood)[35] revealed that more than 90 per cent of journalists rated 'candour' as the key quality that they required in an executive responsible for public relations; and the same percentage said they were more likely to deal with PR people whom they knew personally.

News stories

The backbone of PR is the interesting and entertaining news item, either genuine or 'manufactured', which shows the client product or service in a good light. Such stories are best placed by personal, professional contact. For more general distribution (to the local press, for example) carefully written press packs (with suitable black and white photographs) also demand expert attention.

Public relations handbooks tend to stress that you must have good writing skills to deliver such stories, but that is only the starting point. PR is like any

[35] R. Haywood, *All About PR: What to Say and When to Say it* (McGraw-Hill, 1984).

other form of marketing. You must know the customers (here the journalists) and provide – and sell – the right 'product', the story they want.

The personal touch helps. Surprisingly, perhaps, the US survey quoted above showed that most press releases were read by journalists (who were even happy to be reminded, by telephone, of press events). This finding is tempered by a UK survey[36] which showed that press releases achieved only a 22 per cent rating as a 'source of information most useful to your work as an editor', compared with 86 per cent for articles in other newspapers.

Media events

One device often used is a media event, the launch of a new product for example, which is an excuse for inviting journalists to a free lunch and exposure to the accompanying PR messages. Unfortunately, this device rarely works, unless the groundwork has already been done and the personal contacts with the media well and truly established.

The US survey showed that two-thirds of journalists believed that news conferences were abused as a communications technique. On the other hand, discreet contact with bona fide executives from the organization may pay better dividends. The UK survey mentioned above rated interviews with 'company officials' at 58 per cent compared with 19 per cent for 'company public and/or press relations officers', and a mere 14 per cent for 'public relations agencies'.

Press office

It is just as important that you are able to react to press enquiries. A continuously manned press office, which can handle any level of questioning from journalists, and is almost effusively enthusiastic to help, is essential if PR is to be taken seriously. Again, professionalism is essential.

It is well worthwhile ensuring that all senior executives who come into contact with the media are trained in handling such interviews (not least in avoiding giving 'hostages to fortune'). It is also a sound investment to have suitable executives who are professionally trained in the techniques of handling radio and television interviews, as this requires some skill.

Plans and budgets

As mentioned above, PR is very cost-effective. In addition, it is usually the case that the amount which can be spent on it is relatively low, in comparison with

---

[36] B. MacArthur, Editors prefer to ransack the rivals, *The Guardian* (7 January 1991).

the other promotional spends, and is self-limiting (there are only so many events that you can arrange, and only so many journalists that you can entertain). Thus, there is a good argument for saying that PR budgets should come at the head of the queue. Only when you have obtained the maximum you can achieve from PR should you allocate the remaining funds to other promotional activities. Since you get what you pay for, it is thus also better to pay more for high-calibre personnel than waste the rest of the PR budget.

You can use any of the methods normally deployed in calculating promotional budgets, but Roger Haywood[37] states that:

> Experience shows anything less than 15 per cent of the total promotional budget being spent on PR will not achieve anything substantial; with smaller budgets or more specialized markets the minimum proportion will rise. For example, an industrial marketing company will probably need to spend upwards of 30 per cent on the PR area.

It may be difficult to overspend on PR, but even so it is very easy to lose control of PR costs (PR agencies do like to indulge in *very* expensive entertaining), so they must be agreed in advance, and controlled as closely as any other part of the overall promotional budgets.

To be most effective, PR needs to be a continuous activity; with carefully planned events and activities scattered throughout the year − to maintain press interest − or alternatively concentrated at the times of the year when they can be most effective.

SELF-TEST QUESTION 10.3

To what extent does your organization use PR? Who undertakes this? (Is it an internal department, or has a specialist agency been appointed to handle it?) How effective is it?

What would be your suggestions for greater use of PR in its widest sense? What would be your suggestions for its more effective use?

Corporate PR

PR is often used as a global term to cover a wider range of activities. Of these, perhaps the most important may be that of acting as the corporate interface

---

[37] Haywood, *All About PR: What to Say and When to Say it.*

with the outside world. This aspect of PR is much more likely to be the province of corporate PR personnel. Some of the routine tasks include:

- communications to 'stakeholders' – annual reports and newsletters (including, perhaps, company magazines, sponsored journals, and so on) to the various stakeholders, from shareholders through to (most importantly) the workforce
- speeches – 'ghostwriting' the various speeches and presentations (both external and internal) in which senior management become involved
- community contact – acting as the channel for the 'corporate citizen' activities which organizations feel, usually with some justification, will help their image in the community

ACTIVITY 10.2

Prepare a 200-word press release, aimed at your customers, about a recent major development in your organization. Prepare similar releases, on the same subject, aimed at financial stakeholders and the workforce. How do they differ? What happens if the wrong version of the release reaches one of these groups?

Again, you can obtain useful criticism of the style and content from a colleague or a member of your family.

However, there may be a 'strategic' element to corporate PR. This may operate from both ends of the spectrum:

Defensive PR

The organization will often be exposed to the activities of external pressure groups. The corporate PR department, if one exists, will typically be the one that 'defends' the organization against these onslaughts, and handles the external interface with such groups.

Indeed, the corporate PR group may be the source of the organization's knowledge of such groups. Roger Haywood[38] states:

> It is the responsibility of the PR adviser to understand the position of all important external groups – particularly those trying to exert pressure for change, such as a campaigning consumer body, a group of dissident share-holders . . . What is their case? Is it factually based? Who are they trying to influence? How are they attempting this?

He goes on to suggest an important first line of defence, one which is often ignored in the heat of the moment, actually remedying what these groups are attempting to rectify themselves:

> Of course, if the PR adviser feels there is validity in their claims then, especially, it becomes his or her responsibility to advise management and try to institute appropriate policy changes within the organization.

How the organization then responds to such pressure, usually in terms of its own submissions to the bodies which wield power, is most clearly the responsibility of the corporate PR function. As Roger Haywood,[39] again, comments:

> Certainly the organization should think very carefully before refusing to communicate in sensitive areas. Any communications should be through the same media used by the pressure groups and every critical comment or negative news story should be dealt with promptly with a properly counterbalanced company statement . . . lobbies have been more successful because of the inability of the opposition to handle their case properly.

Proactive PR

Rather fewer organizations use PR to influence 'external' activities, such as those in the political arena, to their advantage. However, those that do may gain considerable advantage. On the other hand, in view of the investment required this may be the province of the larger organizations. It also requires special personnel, with expert skills and knowledge, and will usually (even in the case of larger companies) demand the employment of an outside agency; for example, one that specializes in 'lobbying' politicians. The scale of resource required can be substantial. One of the oil multinationals, for instance, maintains a 'lobby' office of ten people in Washington and one of eight people in London (also handling the European Commission).

There are, in fact, a wide range of audiences to be contacted in this proactive role, including:

General public	Press	Financial community	Government

---

[38] Haywood, *All About PR: What to Say and When to Say it.*
[39] Haywood, *All About PR: What to Say and When to Say it.*

Other influential bodies (such as trade unions, religious groups and international bodies) should not be ignored.

In many of these fields, top management will have, and will build upon, the most important contacts; but the corporate PR function should provide co-ordination and support. It should be assumed, incidentally, that lobbying is best handled in house (or by agencies employed directly). Roger Haywood[40] reports that:

> . . . much of the lobbying undertaken by some trade associations . . . is extremely rudimentary; it may make them *feel* good, but will have very little influence on the shape of legislation. Too often, the case is being presented far too late and without enough authority or substantial evidence.

Some trade associations (particularly those of the professions and farming) *are* powerful lobbyists, but rather more are not. In any case, the lobbying (and power struggles) *within* trade associations, to capture their 'votes' for 'interested groups', often means that individual members may find their interests not represented – and sometimes even opposed.

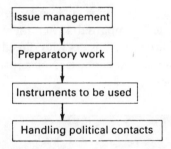

Issue management   The first task of corporate PR is to determine what 'issues', relevant to the future of the organization, are likely to emerge over the next few years. As in 'scanning' the environment, this is not an easy task. It can, in this case, be more directly based upon opinion research – although this may be expensive. Alternatively, it can be obtained by buying syndicated reports from the specialist consultancies, such as the Henley Centre for Forecasting or Stanford Research Institute (SRI). It is recommended, however, that no more than 10–20 issues are 'managed' at any one time.

Once the issues have 'emerged', it is important to try and understand them; and, in particular, to obtain political input on their perceived importance. It is also important to start 'lobbying' (possibly on an international scale) as soon as possible. At the highest level, the multinational will lobby at a very senior level indeed. BP, for instance, lobbied the 1989–90 GATT round *directly*, since it had doubts that individual governments would lobby as effectively on its behalf.

---

[40] Haywood, *All About PR: What to Say and When to Say it.*

Preparatory work Another aspect of proactive corporate PR may be working, perhaps over a number of years, to prepare the ground for future developments. At least one multinational puts a PR/lobby team into a country anything up to two years in advance of a major move so that, when that move takes place, the politicians have been primed and ideally legislation has been put in place to support the move. The PR team then works alongside the corporate negotiators, as the move is implemented, to smooth the way.

Instruments to be used Having decided what issues or preparatory work are to be addressed, the next move is to decide what PR instruments (press contacts, events, publications, and so on) are to be used – and how. Again, a detailed plan is essential, not least to co-ordinate the 'contacts' undertaken by the various managers involved, and this needs to be tracked and reported upon regularly, perhaps every quarter. An annual operating plan is also required, especially where the budget can run into millions of dollars per annum for the larger multinationals.

Handling political contacts Various levels of political contact may be cultivated. At the lowest level there are the senior civil servants, who are very influential (but who want to be seen to be impartial). Then there are the many interested politicians. Highest of all are the ministers who directly decide policy; needless to say, they are the most important contacts. Not surprisingly, they are available to only a few organizations.

SELF-TEST QUESTION 10.4

What proactive corporate relations does your organization undertake? How does it handle the contacts involved? How effective are they?

   (This information may be difficult to find. Probably this will be because there is no such activity. Alternatively, the organization may not wish to make it public.)

Sponsorship

This very specialized form of promotion can be very expensive indeed (whether it is in the field of arts or sport or whatever). It requires careful justification, and too often it is based solely upon the private interests of the members of the board. However, it can be very productive for those organizations (such as tobacco companies) that have limited access to the media, or have more complex objectives (such as arranging events in order to meet customers).

Such sponsorship can be quite discreet or highly public. In 1990, for instance, the Rover (Car) Group in the UK committed £600 000 over three years to raise the standard of British Junior Tennis. At the same time Barclays Bank paid £7 million to extend its very visible sponsorship of the English Football League for a further three years – its previous period of such sponsorship having, presumably, proved to be good value for money.

SELF-TEST QUESTION 10.5

To consolidate the work you have done on promotion, you should now undertake your next major exercise, and produce a promotional plan on no more than two A4 pages. You should cover all promotion from advertising through to sales promotion.

As suggested in the earlier sections of this chapter, this plan should include references to:

- target audience
- targets (coverage, awareness and so on)
- timing
- media
- creative message
- budgets
- measurement of results

Exhibitions

This area of promotional activity is generally related to 'selling' because many prospects expect to find their suppliers at such venues. For example, market research showed that just under 30 per cent of personal computer buyers expected to find their suppliers at exhibitions.

Martyn Davies[41] summarizes the main benefits when he says:

> Exhibitions afford you the double benefit of demonstration with personal contact . . . Prospective buyers can see and handle your product, try for themselves and ask questions.

---

[41] M. Davies, *The Effective Use of Advertising Media* (Business Books, 1981).

These are powerful benefits but, like any other promotional activity, exhibitions demand careful planning – and not a little expertise – in order to reap these rewards.

The main aspects involved are:

- objectives
- selection
- location and design

- *Objectives.* As Thomas Bonoma[42] suggests, one of the most important and frequently neglected activities relating to exhibitions is deciding the objectives. Just why are you there?
- *Selection.* Every exhibition organizer thinks that his offering is essential, but very few of them really are; and most organizations will need to select very carefully those which they *must* attend. Clearly, the organizers should be able to provide statistics of attendances at previous events, and the exhibitor list for the forthcoming one should convey the best flavour of that show. If the main vendors in the industry are not attending, then ask yourself why.
- *Stand location and design.* The main requirement, whatever the chosen size and shape of your exhibit, is to obtain the best location. As John Fenton[43] stresses, the three main priorities are 'Position, position and position', echoing the well-known dictum about the location of retail outlets. The best positions are typically along the central aisles, as close as possible to the larger, more spectacular, stands.

ACTIVITY 10.3

If your organization attends any exhibitions, ask to help on a stand. You should find no difficulty in obtaining permission, as it can be one of the most boring jobs (which is why stand organizers are always looking for helpers).

SELF-TEST QUESTION 10.6

What exhibitions does your organization attend? What stand locations and designs does it choose, and why? How does it organize its activities on the stands?

How effective is this activity?

---

[42] T. V. Bonoma, Get more out of your trade shows, *The Marketing Renaissance*, ed. D. E. Gumpert (John Wiley, 1985).
[43] J. Fenton, *How to Sell Against Competition* (Heinemann, 1984).

FURTHER READING

There is a wide variety of handbooks about direct mail, but almost all of them are intensely 'practical'. Martin Baier (*Elements of Direct Marketing*, McGraw-Hill, 1985) does, however, approach the subject of 'direct marketing' from the more traditional marketing viewpoint. Another recent text, which also covers at least part of the field of precision marketing, at a rather more sophisticated level than many of the other books, is *Direct Marketing: Strategy, Planning, Execution* (by Edward Nash, McGraw-Hill, 1986).

Sales promotion is also a specialized area. *The Dartnell Sales Promotion Handbook*, edited by Ovid Riso (Dartnell Corporation, 1979), may be somewhat out of date, but gives the most comprehensive coverage. The most useful (and readable) coverage may well be that provided by Don E. Schultz and William A. Robinson (*Sales Promotion Essentials*, Crain Books, 1982); although John Williams (in *The Manual of Sales Promotion*, Innovation Ltd, 1983) also gives a very concise and pragmatic coverage.

A comprehensive, and well written, text on the subject of public relations is *All About PR: What to Say and When to Say it*, by Roger Haywood (McGraw-Hill, 1984). For a comprehensive introduction to 'lobbying', in the UK environment, Charles Miller's book (*Lobbying: Understanding and Influencing the Corridors of Power*, second edition, Basil Blackwell, 1990) is particularly valuable.

SUMMARY

Precision marketing is growing in importance, as increasingly sophisticated computerized databases allow the possibility of tailoring promotional messages to ever smaller groups. It utilizes data provided by:

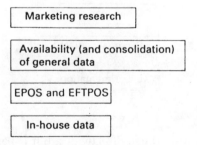

As yet there are problems in handling the complexities posed by the large quantities of data involved. These may eventually be addressed by the use of expert systems, but currently are most practically dealt with by simplified techniques (simple decisions and aggregation).

The main vehicle currently employed is *direct mail* advertising. Its advantages are:
- specific targeting
- personalization

- optimization
- it is cumulative
- it is flexible

Disadvantages are:

- cost
- poor-quality lists
- it is relatively undeveloped

The main elements of a *mailing* typically are:

- mailing list
- offer
- letter
- inserts
- reply-paid card

Other forms of precision marketing are:

- door-to-door – an alternative delivery system for large drops
- computer-mediated communications – CMC, as yet undeveloped
- personal (agent) selling – including party sales

Branch marketing already has the ability to make use of precision marketing, in terms of:

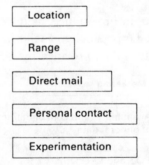

Location

Range

Direct mail

Personal contact

Experimentation

Sales promotion covers a wide range of activities, but it has a very specific set of advantages:

- sales increase – immediate
- defined target audience and role – to meet specific short-term objectives

But, even though it may account for almost two-thirds of the overall promotional budget, it may be less effective, and has a number of major disadvantages:

- short term – it has no lasting effect
- hidden costs – the total costs may be uncontrollable
- confusion – in the minds of consumers
- price-cutting – it may damage the brand image

It is best used to meet specific short-term objectives, usually in the areas of:

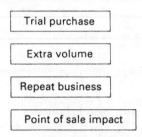

Trial purchase

Extra volume

Repeat business

Point of sale impact

Promotional pricing may include a number of devices, ranging from price cuts in various forms (reductions, cash refunds, money off next purchase, loss leaders and cheap credit) to free goods (banded offers, vouchers or coupons). *Non-price promotions* include competitions, mail-ins, self-liquidating offers and multibrand promotions.

Probably the most powerful, but also the most expensive, form of sales promotion is *sampling*, which is, as a result, primarily used for new product launches.

Public relations is arguably the most cost-effective, but often most neglected, form of promotion. The activities involved include:

Media contact

News stories

Media events

Press office

The evidence is that contact by senior executives (rather than by PR personnel) may represent the most effective approach; though it needs to be professionally co-ordinated.

Corporate PR has two faces. The first is routine:

Communications to 'stakeholders'

Speeches

Community contact

The second, *proactive PR*, is less frequently employed but may be very powerful in persuading specific groups on issues key to the future of the organization:

| General public | Press | Financial community | Government |

The stages involved are:

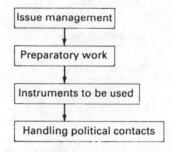

Issue management
↓
Preparatory work
↓
Instruments to be used
↓
Handling political contacts

They require expert, professional management.

REVISION QUESTIONS

1 Why is precision marketing growing in importance? How may the complexity of data be handled?
2 What are the main advantages and disadvantages of direct mail? How may it be used?
3 What are the key elements of a direct mailing? How may they be optimized?
4 What other forms of precision marketing are available? How may the principles be used in branch marketing?
5 What are the advantages and disadvantages of sales promotions? How may they be best used?
6 What price promotions and what non-price promotions are available? How may sampling be used?
7 What are the main elements of public (press) relations? How may its effect be optimized?
8 What are the routine aspects of corporate PR? What may be the proactive elements? Who may be the target audiences? What are the activities involved?

11 Selling and Sales Management

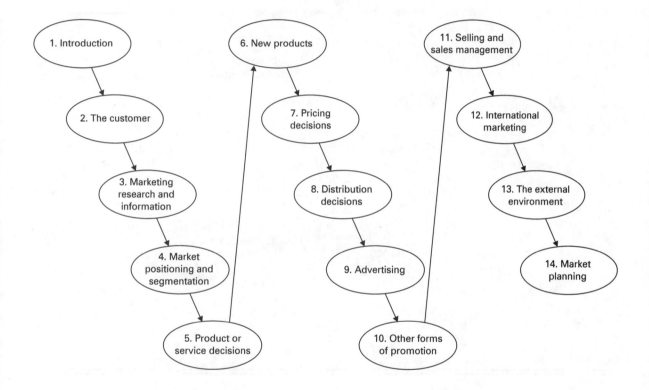

1. Introduction

2. The customer

3. Marketing research and information

4. Market positioning and segmentation

5. Product or service decisions

6. New products

7. Pricing decisions

8. Distribution decisions

9. Advertising

10. Other forms of promotion

11. Selling and sales management

12. International marketing

13. The external environment

14. Market planning

Introduction

Although it is given relatively little prominence in most textbooks, selling and sales management are generally the most important elements of marketing for the majority of organizations. An understanding of sales, in its widest sense, and of sales management is, therefore, an essential requirement for most managers.

The sales role itself revolves around a variety of management processes. The basic building block is territory management, the territory being in many respects a small business in its own right.

This involves a considerable degree of resource management; but the most important element is that of managing customers and prospects.

The heart of the sales process is the sales 'call'. However, this often has more to do with myth than reality; particularly in the 'complex sale', where 'relationship management' (and 'account management') comes to the fore.

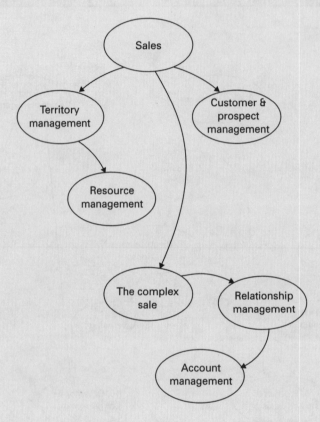

In most organizations more money is spent on personal selling than on advertising and sales promotions combined – in acknowledgement of its effectiveness. Accordingly, many organizations are prepared to spend a high proportion of their communications budget on personal selling (which also indicates just how expensive it is).

On the other hand, use of the salesforce is qualitatively different from almost all other aspects of marketing, being much more dependent upon relationships between individuals, between sales personnel and customers, and between sales management and their sales personnel. It is generally the management of these human relationships, rather than the logistics, which is most important.

As with most other management tasks, the management of this selling process (at the sales management level) starts with a definition of how the sales activities are to be organized.

Territory Management and Planning

The first decision is how responsibilities are to be allocated within the sales team; the now traditional basis for this is the individual territory. In fact, the concept of sales professionals being entitled to their own territory is a relatively recent one. It was only just before the First World War that John Patterson instituted the concept of territories as a fundamental aspect of the NCR sales operation; and shortly afterwards Thomas J. Watson, then at NCR, took it to IBM – and there used it as a basis for building that company's legendary salesforce. Prior to that time, there had been no 'territories': all prospects were fair game for all salesmen; and their main competitors could just as easily be from the same company as themselves.

Although such territories are normally thought of as geographical areas, there can be a number of bases for the way they are structured:

| By geography |

| By industry |

| By product |

Geographical territories

Most territories are based on a geographical area, ranging from a whole country downwards to a single postal district. One advantage of such an approach is that the areas are relatively easy to define, and hence should avoid unnecessary contention. On the other hand, very few sales professionals rigorously check what their territory is; and this situation may be complicated by the fact that such territories often split along main roads, with one sales professional calling on the businesses on one side and another on the opposite side.

By industry. A territory split which is used much less frequently than geography is that by industry, but this can be a very powerful choice. For many years, IBM split its main business by industry and this had the great benefit that the sales professionals dedicated to each industry were steeped in the knowledge and folklore of that industry – although their geographical range was wider.

| By geography |

| By industry |

| By product |

By product.   This approach is often necessary because it may be time-consuming to get to know the products in sufficient depth, and sales personnel may not have the personal resources to apply equal expertise to all products in the range.

The Sales Professional

The basic building block of all sales operations is the individual sales professional. His or her actions will build up to produce the overall sales impact. The next part of this chapter will, therefore, look at individual sales activities. These are conventionally not treated as management activities, but they are as much 'tools' of marketing as any of the other techniques I have described. Accordingly, you should appreciate what they imply, and thus what lies behind one of the most important operations of almost all commercial organizations (and, probably under a different name – such as 'client services' – of many non-profit organizations as well).

Individual management of sales

As I have said above, the traditional view of selling has been that it is a 'professional' role rather than a management one (very few sales professionals manage teams of subordinates). In practice, much of the sales professional's role is actually concerned with management. The typical, competent, sales professional should manage a number of resources and processes:

Territory.   The sales professional is typically solely responsible for his or her territory. He or she is responsible for everything that happens in this territory; for all activities, with the range of responsibilities comparable with those normally assumed by a brand manager, or even by the chief executive of a subsidiary.

Sales plan.   In particular, within that territory he or she has to create a sales plan – a 'cut down' and probably simplified version of the marketing plan. Performance against that plan will have to be monitored, and tactics changed to allow for deviations against target – just as in the overall organizational plan.

Organizational resources.   Every sales professional will have some organizational resources at his or her command; including service support, marketing support and, possibly, even budgeted amounts of territory-based promotional funding. All of these resources will have to be managed in exactly the same way as the rest of the organization's resources.

Support personnel.   It is conventionally assumed that sales professionals do not manage people: indeed, as mentioned earlier, very few do actually have formal responsibility for subordinates. Yet many indirectly control the activities of support personnel. What is more, they have to achieve this management control, often under difficult circumstances on customer premises, without any formal authority.

Customer interface. Above all, the sales professional manages the 'customer interface', that most important asset of any organization, the 'goodwill'. This demands a great deal of skill and is a role which contains many of the key elements of management.

The Territory Sales Plan

The sales plan for an individual sales territory should include, either formally or informally, most of the following elements:

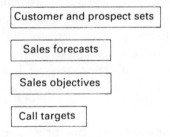

Defining the customer and prospect sets

At this stage the customer and prospect database will usually be built, since each of these will, to some extent, require individual attention:

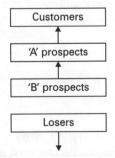

Customers   Without any doubt, the most important split on almost all territories is that between customers and prospects. Customers are almost universally more productive than prospects; and indeed more productive than many sales professionals (or their management) allow for. What is more, assuming that the organization has previously offered good service, customers are already tied to it; and competitors will have to justify breaking these links before they can even begin their selling process. In such customers the organization already has an existing base on which it is natural to build.

However, many sales professionals devote little time to customers. The 'macho' image often promoted by sales trainers persuades them to spend their time unproductively – touting for new business, when common sense should tell them to spend at least adequate time defending, and developing, their customer base.

This problem was particularly evident in the earlier days of the personal computer market. All of the research showed that the one group who were almost guaranteed to buy a new system were the existing customers, who had already bought a previous system – typically within the past year. On the other hand, cold prospects were unlikely to show a better than 10 per cent chance of buying a system. Yet most sales professionals still sadly neglected their customers; the industry had an appalling reputation of poor service to customers.

Therefore the first priority of any sales professional must be to allocate resources to the *customer* set, but also to differentiate between customers according to what they are worth. Some will be 'bankers' and will bring in a large part of the easy 80 per cent of business – and these investments must be cosseted. On the other hand, some will be totally unproductive, demanding resource for little return, and in these cases the plan must be to contain the 'bleeding'.

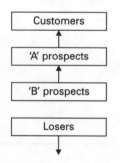

'A' prospects   The sales team should know their customers well enough to be able to predict the sales performance of each. But the real skill comes in being able to separate out the sheep from the goats among the prospects. The question of which are the 10 per cent or so who will bring in 50+ per cent of the new business is partly a function of their size (in terms of potential business) and partly of their probability of closing. These are the prospects who should have first claim on the resources left after the planned support of customers.

'B' prospects   Similarly, the sales team will have to determine the remaining prospects who will bring in the remaining 50 per cent of new business. This needs careful planning, and a ruthless determination to control resource exposures, in order to ration out the small amount of resource remaining after customers and 'A' prospects have been catered for.

Losers

All others have to be treated as outcasts. No matter how much they plead, the productive salesforce will have to be ruthless and refuse to fritter away resource on unproductive areas. The main danger is that they will allocate some of their precious resources to 'tyre-kickers' (in the jargon of the sales discipline – which does not always hide its questionable origins in the used car trade), happy for the sales professional to spend considerable time talking to them – indeed demanding this – but never really likely to buy. The true professional must be ruthless and insist that they *prove* their good intentions. This sounds like the reverse of good salesmanship, but at times good salesmanship is as much about managing scarce resources as it is about winning friends and influencing people.

As indicated earlier, husbanding resources, for the 20 per cent of accounts that will bring in 80 per cent of business, is a critical aspect of all territory and account planning. It is one of the 'management' aspects of professional sales-manship that many sales professionals find most difficult to implement; they more naturally 'shoot from the hip', rushing to the account that immediately demands attention, without considering the long-term implications. Planning is essential to the sales professional, and is often the activity that distinguishes him or her from less professional juniors.

Forecasts of Business

The most productive phase of any planning usually starts with the forecasts of where the business, usually in the relatively near future, will come from:

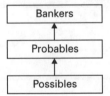

Bankers

The easiest part of any forecast should be to deal with the 'bankers', those accounts that the sales personnel know will soon complete the formality of signing the order.

Even then, forecasting exactly *when* they will sign is not necessarily that easy. Paradoxically, it is somewhat more difficult to control if they have already stated that they *will* be placing the order. As far as they are concerned, they have already given their sales contact the order; they see their formal signature as a petty administrative detail. However, bankers are still the easiest to predict, and should form the core of any forecast.

Probables versus possibles

Looking at the forecasts of sales professionals it has been my own experience that probables and possibles fall into three main groups. Those accounts labelled '80 per cent chance of closing' can usually be regarded as genuine 'probables'; sales professionals tend to be unduly optimistic, but an 80+ per cent confidence level is usually indicative of a good chance of success.

Below 50 per cent, however, the 'possibles' that most sales professionals would hope for are more normally 'likely losers'. The main question to be asked of this category is whether it is worth putting any more resource into them. The experienced sales professional (and, in particular, his or her manager) will usually include in the overall forecast only the business rated to have a better than 50 per cent chance.

In any event, the wise sales manager will then still divide the aggregated forecasts of the sales team by a factor of two when making his or her own submission to senior management.

SELF-TEST QUESTION 11.1

In the context of the above topics, what are your observations of your own organization's salesforce?

Sales Objectives

The specific sales objectives should be derived in part from these investigations, but they will also emerge from the overall marketing plan, which will be discussed later. They should include at least three major elements:

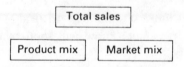

- *Total sales to be achieved.* This is quoted in terms of volume or value, or possibly both; for example, 400 cases (volume) or £2 000 000 (value).

- *Product mix.* This is the relative contribution of each product to total sales: for example, 80 per cent of sales to be product A, 15 per cent to be product B, and 5 per cent to be product C.
- *Market mix.* This is the proportion of total sales in each market: for example, 10 per cent in France, 20 per cent in the UK and 70 per cent in Benelux; or 80 per cent to the financial services sector, 15 per cent to retailers, and 5 per cent to the rest of industry.

Call targets – the numbers mountain

The basic building block of any sales campaign has to be its calls. Generally speaking a number of calls are needed to get the business; and it is certainly true that the more contacts which are made the greater will be the business booked.

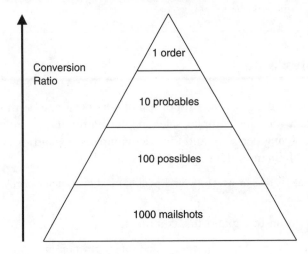

This is often described in sales circles as the '*numbers game*'. I prefer to call it the '*numbers mountain*', for each level must rest firmly on the one below if you are to be able to climb to the peak.

Thus, for every 1000 mailshots sent out there will be a certain percentage of returns which justify a sales professional calling personally; and telesales and cold calling will also generate proportional results. From these subsequent calls a proportion will turn into serious prospects (some of whom will progress to demonstrations and proposals). And out of these serious prospects a proportion will place orders, and a proportion (hopefully a good proportion) will place those orders with the organization undertaking these activities rather than with its competitors.

At each stage, therefore, there is a *conversion ratio*. It is clearly the sales professional's personal skills (backed by sound account management) which ensure that this conversion ratio is as high as it can be. Converting a good prospect into a customer requires all the skills a sales professional possesses, but it is a basic fact of the sales game that providing the raw material, the *numbers* of prospects to feed into the 'machine' which eventually converts them into business, is just sheer hard work. The more mailshots sent out, the more teleselling done and the more cold calls made, the greater the raw material for the conversion process. *The eventual outcome is almost directly proportional to the numbers that are fed in.*

SELF-TEST QUESTION 11.2

What performance targets are set for the sales personnel of your organization?

How is actual performance against these targets measured? What targets do you think should be set?

The Complex Sale

The sales professional, a growing proportion of sales personnel, is more likely to come into contact with the 'complex sale', in which a number of individuals are involved in the buying decision, and the sales campaign extends over a number of calls. Miller, Heiman and Tuleja[1] define it as follows:

> A Complex Sale is one in which several people must give their approval before the sale can take place.

However, they go on to expand this comment:

> In a complex sale, you have short-term and long-term objectives. In the short term, you must close as many individual deals as you possibly can, and as quickly as possible. In the long term, you want to maintain healthy relations with the customers signing the deals, so they'll be willing to make further purchases in the months and years to come. It would be great if these two objectives always coincided, but you know that they don't.

Thus, in many ways this environment is very different from that of the single call sale, which has been the staple diet of many (if not most) sales trainers; though it is a rapidly declining aspect of selling.

As Miller, Heiman and Tuleja[2] put it:

> Because most sales-training programs emphasize tactical rather than strategic skills, even very good salespeople sometimes find themselves cut out of a sale at the last minute because they failed to locate or cover all the real decision-makers for their specific sale.

---

[1] R. B. Miller, S. E. Heiman and T. Tuleja, *Strategic Selling* (William Morrow, 1985).
[2] Miller, Heiman and Tuleja, *Strategic Selling*.

Decision-makers and influencers

Perhaps the most obvious difference is the complexity introduced by the multiplicity of 'buyers' involved. It is no longer sufficient to persuade just one buyer: instead, sales professionals have to convince a whole range of individuals, all with different (and often contradictory) requirements.

Identifying the buyers

The first problem that this poses is quite simply that of identifying who the various buyers are. In a complex sale it is no longer an easy task: the 'buyers' involved can range from the Chief Executive to members of the typing pool.

The convention is to split these 'buyers' into 'decision-makers' and 'influencers', with the clear implication that the small group of 'decision-makers' should be the prime target – although 'influencers' should not be neglected. This is a useful distinction in that it correctly focuses the sales professional's attention on the key decision-makers, and forces him or her to contact them; too many sales personnel remain bogged down among the 'influencers'. It was certainly true, in the early days of the personal computer market, that dealer salesmen rarely contacted more than one person in their prospect (even in the larger corporations). He or she was usually a buyer in the purchasing department, and was usually only an 'influencer'. The real decisions were taken elsewhere, untroubled by the attentions of salesmen; though, because in the absence of any sound marketing effort the only sales message was price, the lack of face-to-face contact with the 'decision-maker' was not really a critical factor.

The problem with this two-way split is that both 'decision-makers' and 'influencers' are very general categories – probably too general (and too confined within the sales perspective) to best help the sales professional to home in on the exact decision-making structure. In their book, Miller, Heiman and Tuleja[3] seem to offer a better (if at times much more complex) structure. They identify four 'buying influences', the first three of which relate to the more conventional structure:

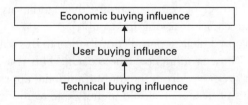

---

[3] Miller, Heiman and Tuleja, *Strategic Selling*.

Economic buyer   The 'economic buyer' is the ultimate decision-maker. He is a single entity, usually a single person (but possibly a group, such as a board). He holds the purse strings, and *must* approve the decision. Clearly this buyer is the most important in the whole structure:

> Almost by definition you don't find people who give final approval far down on the corporate ladder.

User buyers   These are the people who are going to use whatever is being offered. In the more conventional model they would lie uncomfortably between 'decision-makers' and 'influencers'; a virtue of the more complex model is that it allows sales professionals to handle this important group most effectively.

The role of the User Buyer is filled by someone who will actually use (or supervise the use of) your product or service. The role of the User Buyer is to make judgements about the impact of that product or service on the job to be done.

Technical buyers   These are the true 'influencers' of the simpler model; but they have a powerful power of veto, which could still be fatal for the sale. They vet the specification for technical conformance. Paradoxically, in many complex sales situations (certainly in the case of computers of any sort) the purchasing department falls into this category.

> The Technical Buyer's role is to screen out unsuitable offering. They're gate-keepers.[4]

Miller, Heiman and Tuleja make the important point that these categories are not a function of the titles on the doors; they are a result of specific relationships to the 'purchase'. Even more importantly, the authors emphasize the fact that the structure is not fixed. The relationships change for different purchases, and people move from one category to another.

In practice, the decision-making process is normally deeply embedded in the 'user' process. Users have a great deal of delegated power. In many cases, although the final decision may have to be approved by higher authority, it is in reality only a power of veto (any board that saddles its user departments with an unwelcome choice is asking for trouble).

Miller, Heiman and Tuleja's special contribution to this search is to identify a fourth category of 'buying influence', the 'coach'. This is a powerful concept, but it is quite a way removed from the more traditional approaches. In essence, it says that the sales professional should identify one or more contacts who can (and are willing to) guide them through the complexities of the sale:

[4] Miller, Heiman and Tuleja, *Strategic Selling*.

The role of a coach is to guide you in the sale by giving you the information you need to manage it to a close that guarantees you not only the order, but satisfied customers and repeat business as well.[5]

SELF-TEST QUESTION 11.3

Take one or two of your organization's leading customers or clients. For each of them, can you identify the three categories – economic buying influence, user buying influence and technical buying influence – of buyers?

Organizational Buying Situations

Some writers, such as Robinson, Faris and Wind,[6] also identify different buying situations:

```
Straight rebuy
```

```
Modified rebuy
```

```
New task buying
```

- *Straight rebuy.* This is the repeat purchase of an existing product or service which has given satisfactory performance: no new information is needed for the buying decision. The 'sitting tenant', the existing supplier, is usually difficult to displace in such situations. Webster and Wind[7] postulated a 'source-loyalty' model, which maintained that buyers favour existing (known risk) suppliers, since much of their buying is routine.
- *Modified rebuy.* The buyer may be dissatisfied with the existing product or service, and in this case the buying decision has to be re-evaluated. This is the occasion when new suppliers are most likely to make changes to existing purchasing patterns. However, it does imply that in many markets it is the existing supplier who loses the business, by incompetence or inattention, and not the new one who wins it.
- *New task buying.* In this situation there is no previous history, so the buyer has to start from scratch, and all suppliers begin with the same chance.

---

[5] Miller, Heiman and Tuleja, *Strategic Selling*.
[6] P. J. Robinson, C. W. Faris and Y. Wind, *Industrial Buying and Creative Marketing* (Allyn & Bacon, 1967).
[7] F. E. Webster and Y. Wind, *Organizational Buying Behaviour* (Prentice-Hall, 1972).

Inter-organizational Relations

Selling has traditionally been seen as a *confrontational* activity, with the salesperson 'hierarchically' subservient to the buyer – the former trying to persuade the latter to buy something not wanted or needed. It is seen as a 'zero-sum game', in which each of the participants can gain only at the expense of the other.

In recent years, however, it has been argued that the most productive relationship in such sales deals is based on a 'win–win' approach, in which it is expected that both sides will gain from the deal (albeit in different ways), so that they start out with the intention of producing a mutually beneficial arrangement. An increasing number of organizations have, indeed, come to see the relationship as one of *interdependence* – where the two sides adopt a 'peer-to-peer' relationship. The sales role here is sometimes described as *relationship management*.

As this type of relationship requires a higher level of personal support, from a more skilled sales professional (a 'relationship manager'), it will typically be limited to the five or ten most important customers.

Win–Win

Miller, Heiman and Tuleja[8] have encapsulated this philosophy in terms of the 'win–win matrix'. In practice, this is something of a gimmick, since their comments show that all of the remaining quadrants tend to be unstable; and degenerate into the lose–lose situation. Even the lose–win situation degenerates, since it sets up unrealistic expectations for the future. On the other hand, the win–win concept is very powerful; and the only real alternative, of lose–lose, serves to highlight this. Partnership, or win–win, must always be looked for.

	Seller (I)	
	I win you win	I lose you win
Buyer (you)	I win you lose	I lose you lose

Dave Ulrich[9] puts the same point in a rather different way, in a longer-term perspective:

---

[8] Miller, Heiman and Tuleja, *Strategic Selling*.

[9] D. Ulrich, Tie the corporate knot: gaining complete customer commitment, *Sloan Management Review* (1989).

In the turbulent and increasingly competitive 1990s, firms need to go beyond customer satisfaction. Firms earn customer satisfaction in the short term by assessing and meeting needs; they earn customer commitment in the long term through hundreds of small, heroic acts that create loyalty and devotion . . . committed customers look beyond short-term pleasures and develop an allegiance to the firm . . . committed customers become interdependent with the firm through shared resources and values.

Relationship Management

Indeed, as Theordore Levitt[10] says:

The relationship between a seller and a buyer seldom ends when the sale is made. In a great and increasing proportion of transactions, the relationship actually intensifies subsequent to the sale. This becomes the critical factor in the buyer's choice of the seller the next time around . . . The sale merely consummates the courtship. Then the marriage begins. How good the marriage is depends on how well the relationship is managed by the seller.

He illustrates the point by comparing the typical reactions of the seller versus those of the buyer (table 11.1). Regular contact is essential in order to maintain rapport, to maintain the partnership. It is also very productive in terms of developing the account. Buck Rodgers[11] says:

Successful salespeople understand the importance of long term customer corrections. The size of their paycheck is determined to a large extent by their ability to develop sound, lasting relationships with enough customers. For the best of them, it's easy enough. They are respectful and thoughtful and go out of their way to be helpful.

Table 11.1   When the sale is first made

Seller	Buyer
Objective achieved	Judgement postponed; applies test of time
Selling stops	Shopping continues
Focus goes elsewhere	Focus on purchase; wants affirmation that expectations have been met
Tension released	Tension increased
Relationship reduced or ended	Commitment made; relationship intensified

---

[10] T. Levitt, After the sale is over, *Harvard Business Review* (September–October 1983).
[11] B. Rodgers with R. L. Shock, *The IBM Way* (Harper & Row, 1986).

In general terms, Christopher et al.[12] compare relationship marketing with traditional marketing, which they describe as 'transaction marketing', as follows:

TRANSACTION MARKETING	RELATIONSHIP MARKETING
Focus on single sale	Focus on customer retention
Oriented to product features	Oriented to product benefits
Short timescale	Long timescale
Little customer service	High customer service
Limited customer commitment	High customer commitment
Moderate customer contact	High customer contact
Quality set by production	Quality set by all

Pine et al.,[13] however, make an important point when they describe the process as a 'learning relationship' '. . . an ongoing connection that becomes smarter as the two interact with each other . . .'. Reinforcing the importance of this process of learning Kalwandi and Narayandas[14] demonstrated that 'maintaining close relationships with customers in the long run can lead to higher profitability through a better understanding and servicing of customer needs'.

The emphasis that IBM places on this aspect is demonstrated by the example of account planning, also described by Buck Rodgers:

> What IBM calls account-planning sessions are conducted annually. Here, both line and customer-support people spend from three days to a week reviewing the entire status of an account. With a major customer like Citibank or General Motors, as many as fifty IBM people could be involved. In the case of a small account, the session might include a handful of IBMers . . . The customer has a well documented action plan that covers the upcoming year as well as years to come.

The investment in a satisfied customer may not show on the balance sheet, but it contributes handsomely to the bottom-line profit.

SELF-TEST QUESTION 11.4

What philosophy does your organization adopt in terms of its dealings with its customers? Could it be described as 'win–win'? If not, what changes would a 'win–win' approach require, and what would the outcome be?

[12] Martin Christopher, Adrian Payne and David Ballantyne, *Relationship Marketing* (Butterworth Heinemann, 1993).

[13] B. Joseph Pine II, Don Peppers and Martha Rogers, Do you want to keep your customers forever, *Harvard Business Review* (March–April, 1995).

[14] Manohar U. Kalwandi and Narakesari Narayandas, Long-term manufacturer-supplier relationships: do they pay off for supplier firms, *Journal of Marketing*, vol. 59 (January 1995).

Account Planning

As usual in marketing, the most important activity in developing these key relationship accounts is the development of a sound plan – the *account plan*. However, unlike the overall sales plan, which deals with groups of customers, each account plan (or 'key account plan') deals quite specifically with a *single* customer.

For each of these key accounts, a unique plan should be developed which matches (at least in its scope of content) the overall marketing plan. It should detail the specific objectives, which will be individually related to the customer's needs and wants, and the activities that are planned to meet these objectives, and to build the 'relationship'.

If such a plan is produced internally within the selling organization it will be a productive exercise. If it is produced in co-operation with the customer, so that the resulting plan becomes a shared plan, it may make a major contribution to the development of that business relationship; it then becomes a genuine peer-to-peer relationship. Such an account plan was the basis of much of IBM's success in selling to its large accounts.

As I have already stressed, I also believe that account management (in its most general sense, covering prospects as well as customers) is the essence of professional salesmanship. Customer account management, in particular, is the epitome of this. It is probably the most important single skill (apart from selling itself) required of a sales professional; and yet, perhaps typically, it is almost entirely neglected by sales trainers.

FURTHER READING

There is a vast range of books written about selling; and, be warned, most of them are not worth the paper they are printed on. They tend to concentrate on the minutiae of the dubious techniques of 'persuasion', such as 'objection hand-ling' and 'closing', which have (rightly, in my opinion) brought the sales profes-sion into disrepute.

Surprisingly, the best book is just about the oldest, *How to Win Friends and Influence People*, by Dale Carnegie (Simon & Schuster, 1936). If you can cope with the fact that the President Roosevelt he refers to, as a contemporary, is Theodore (not even Franklin Delano) then the ideas that it contains are excel-lent. A rather more up-to-date approach, and one which encapsulates much of the reality of complex sales, is *Strategic Selling*, by Robert B. Miller and Stephen E. Heiman (William Morrow, 1985). This is a much better guide to effective selling than all those offering glib formulae for 'success'.

SUMMARY

In most organizations the main marketing resource is the salesforce. Use of this resource is qualitatively different from almost all other marketing activities because of its dependence upon relationships between individuals. The role of the salesforce mainly covers:

- prospecting
- selling
- supporting

The building block of a sales organization is the *territory*, which may be defined:

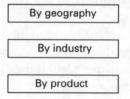

The whole of the selling operation revolves around the individual *sales professional*, whose role holds many similarities with management in general:

- territory management
- resource management
- management of support personnel
- management of the customer interface

The last aspect, the *customer interface*, may represent the major investment of the organization; although this may be unrecognized.

The territory sales plan will include:

- identification of customer and prospect sets – 'A', 'B' and losers
- sales objectives – including product and/or market mix
- sales forecasts – totals, with bankers, probables and possibles
- call and activity targets – mailings, and so on

Prospecting (generating new customers) is a *numbers game*: the more mailings, say, are sent out the more prospects, and ultimately customers, will be generated. On the other hand, much of the work of sales professionals revolves around the *complex sale*. This employs long-term sales campaigns to multiple personnel in an organization:

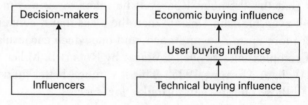

The individual sale may fall into a number of categories:

Straight rebuy

Modified rebuy

New task buying

The *inter-organizational relationships* are particularly important, and a *'win–win' philosophy* is most successful:

Seller (I)

	I win you win	I lose you win
Buyer (you)	I win you lose	I lose you lose

Accordingly, *relationship management* and *account planning* are important activities; and with them *project management skills.*

REVISION QUESTIONS

1 What are the main roles of the salesforce? What are the main differences between prospecting and selling/supporting?
2 What are the main management aspects of the sales professional's role? What is the investment in the customer interface?
3 Who may be the parties involved in the complex sale? What categories of individual sale may be involved? What are the differences from consumer goods purchases?
4 How does account planning support relationship management? What skills does this require? How does the salesman stereotype have an impact on the process?

International Marketing

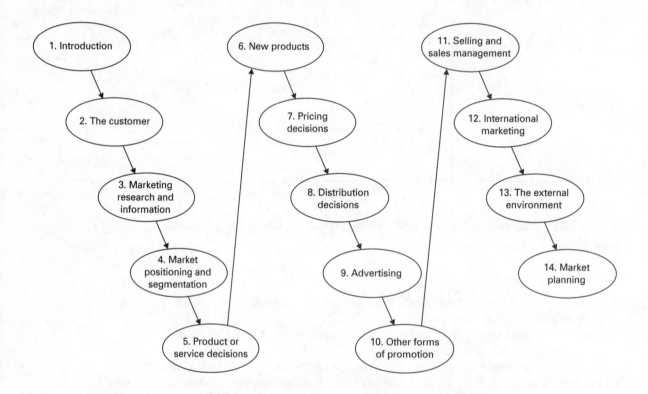

1. Introduction → 2. The customer → 3. Marketing research and information → 4. Market positioning and segmentation → 5. Product or service decisions → 6. New products → 7. Pricing decisions → 8. Distribution decisions → 9. Advertising → 10. Other forms of promotion → 11. Selling and sales management → 12. International marketing → 13. The external environment → 14. Market planning

Introduction

In this chapter, we look at the two extremes of this specialized area, in order to illustrate what is involved. Globalization is much discussed by experts, but apparently less often implemented in practice. However, the theories are explored in this chapter, in some detail, as are those relating to multinational operations.

The basic market entry decision is, however, the focus of the central part of the chapter.

The decision having been taken, the detailed product and price decisions are then investigated, before the main tactical approaches are developed in some depth.

The latter part of the chapter moves to the other end of the spectrum, dominated by agents who support small and medium-sized exporting organizations.

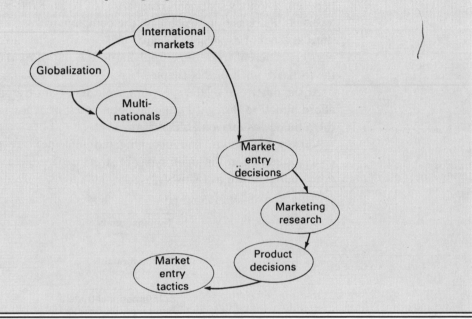

So far I have talked about marketing as if the geographical dimension was one of the least important. But even within one country there may be significant regional differences. Within countries as large as the USA regional differences may be dramatic: from New England to the West Coast, and from Alaska to Texas, the range of natural environments (as well as the range of population groups) varies enormously, as do the market needs, hence the greater emphasis on regional marketing in that country.

However, the biggest difference is that between countries. The thin red lines drawn upon maps may appear to be less significant than the geographical features they so often parallel; but they are no less important in terms of the influences at work in the marketing environment that they encircle – despite the much reported emergence of globalization, and country groupings such as the EU.

This chapter is, accordingly, an introduction to the various ways in which these differences affect marketing, and to the special techniques which may be deployed to deal with these differences. It is a general overview, though, and those who become involved in international marketing would be well advised to study one of the books dedicated to this topic, for it is a very specialized form of marketing.

Structure

The most important factor in any organization's relationship with the various national markets is its own structure. The stereotypical relationship is that between a purely national company, such as Rolls-Royce Cars, and its 'overseas' markets – in which case the company will see almost all its relationships as those of exporting. Because these relationships are, in many important respects, different from those applying to the rest of marketing, they will form the focus of much of this chapter.

At the other end of the spectrum are a few giant transnationals, which can afford almost to disregard national boundaries; or at least are able to consider them merely as unavoidable nuisances.

Various definitions, and matching terminologies, are offered by different commentators; but the main types of structure, in terms of handling international business, are as follows:

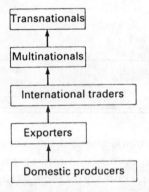

- *Transnationals.* These are the truly global organizations, such as IBM or Shell, which operate in most countries; they have marketing organizations in all the countries, and production units (and even development laboratories) in a fair number. These organizations can afford to view national markets as purely regional affairs, with each region having its own marketing characteristics, but otherwise with no special marketing problems.
- *Multinationals.* These organizations, such as Unilever and General Mills, also operate in many countries. On the other hand, they tend to have individual operating companies in each country, which market to (and 'manufacture' for) that market. Country organizations are, therefore, subsidiaries which control their own operations largely independently of the other country organizations. The marketing process is, thus, almost a purely national operation; with the parent only controlling the operations at the group level (and then typically in terms of the flow of funds).
- *International traders.* These are organizations, such as Renault and Cinzano, which are typically based in one country, and produce most of their output there. In other

countries they have sales subsidiaries (and sometimes limited production – often assembly – operations). They are largely in the business of export, facing the problems which are described later in this chapter. On the other hand, they already have an international structure which can address these problems and compart-mentalizes them, so that they may largely be dealt with as normal marketing activities.

- *Exporters.* These represent the majority of the organizations that trade interna-tionally. Their main base, often overwhelmingly so, is their 'domestic' (home) market. Exporting, as a minority activity, is subject to the problems described later in this chapter.
- *Domestic producers.* These form the largest number of organizations in any national market. They do not involve themselves in overseas markets; perhaps wisely so, as many small export operations are loss-makers, although the formation of 'international' groupings such as the EU may force them to face the issue.

SELF-TEST QUESTION 12.1

Into which of these categories does your organization fall? Into which categories do your main competitors fall?

Globalization

There has been much talk of globalization. Indeed, the impact of the transna-tionals and multinationals cannot be ignored: they often account for a major part of any nation's business activity. Warren Keegan[1] identifies a number of forces which have led to the expansion of international business:

- the international monetary framework – the rapid development of the international financial markets
- the world trading system – in particular the influence of GATT
- global peace – now reinforced by the demise of communism
- domestic economic growth – making these markets more receptive to imports
- communications and transportation technology – so that business can be carried out on a global basis
- the global competition – one of the responses to the above factors

Michael Marien[2] offers a slightly different analysis, but with much the same message:

---

[1] W. J. Keegan, *Global Marketing Management* (Prentice-Hall, 4th edn, 1989).
[2] M. Marien, Driving forces and barriers to a sustainable global economy, *Futures* (December 1989).

An impressive array of current and potential driving forces propels this development. Among technologies, communications and computers are in the forefront in linking the world (and are themselves being linked), and air transport has facilitated physical movement of people. Leading idea-drivers include transnational corporations, 'Europe 1992', the new capitalism of deregulation and global competition, and the thawing Cold War.

This theme has been reinforced by Theodore Levitt:[3]

> The result [of technology] is a new commercial reality – the explosive emergence of global markets for globally standardised products, gigantic worldscale markets of previously unimagined magnitudes.

At its most basic level, when one now walks into a supermarket, be it in Europe or the USA, one is immediately at home. The layout is much the same, and the products are much the same – and are promoted in much the same way.

As might be expected, in the light of his general work on competitive strategy, Michael Porter[4] has identified a range of factors which revolve around two main areas of activity: comparative advantage and economies of scale.

Comparative advantage

Production can be located in those countries which have the most favourable cost or quality factors; which is why the computer component industries have established plants in Taiwan.

It should be noted that conventional economic theory explains the whole of international trade on this basis. One country has an 'absolute advantage' over another in terms of producing a specific product, because the factors of production are more favourable (lower wage costs, material costs, capital costs, and so on). In bilateral trade, therefore, the country with the comparative advantage will export the product, in return for products with regard to which the other country has a comparative advantage.

As with most economic theories, the theory is then overlaid with additional levels of complexity, to try to explain why real life diverges from the basic theory. In practice, the patterns which emerge in the developed world are very much more complex; particularly because the almost random fluctuations in the international money markets (often led by government intervention) make the scale of such 'absolute advantage' difficult to gauge. In any case, global organizations seem to carry this 'absolute advantage' with them; they base their country by country allocations of production and other functions on factors other than simple price advantage.

[3] T. Levitt, The globalization of markets, *Harvard Business Review* (May–June 1983).
[4] M. Porter, *Competitive Strategy* (Free Press, 1980).

On the other hand, there is little doubt that management accounting in a multinational context has failed to reach the levels of provision of useful information which are now deemed essential on the national level. As Kenneth Simmonds[5] comments:

> Rather than relying on transfer prices to signal cost information indirectly and inefficiently, a direct indication of short and long-term cost-volume-profit relationships would enable market units to propose actions that would fit an overall strategy. Management accounting has traditionally advocated the use of cost-volume-profit data within the single market firm. But management accounting within multinationals has not moved to provide system-wide cost-volume-profit relationships. There is no body of literature about how to transmit and use international cost-volume-profit data. In fact, there is nothing about how management accountants might construct cost-volume-profit calculations on a system basis for multi-plant multinationals with all the differences in costs and currencies this implies.

Thus, a comparative disadvantage may simply appear to occur because all the developmental (and/or head office) overheads are being charged against the home country. In any case, providing low-cost countries with experience in new technology can also very quickly lead to the creation of new international competitors.

In addition, as Yoram Wind[6] points out:

> . . . there is no evidence that consumers are becoming universally more price conscious. In fact some of the products often viewed as global are fairly expensive – Cartier watches, Louis-Vuitton handbags or Canon cameras. Furthermore, the desirability of focusing on price positioning is very questionable.

Economies of scale

Concentrating the total demands of a number of countries on a limited number of plants, and sharing the accumulated experience (as well as engaging in joint purchasing across these plants), should lead to economies of scale. Procter & Gamble, for example, successfully concentrated detergent production on fewer plants than Unilever, potentially gaining a cost advantage in the process (although this was possibly undermined by the shift to liquid detergents, which may have been less susceptible to economies of scale). Similarly, there might be some economies to be achieved by global marketing; for example, expensive commercials could be used in several countries. McCann-Erickson, as reported by Quelch and Hoff,[7] said that they saved $90 million in production costs, over 20 years, on Coca-Cola commercials in this way.

---

[5] K. Simmonds, Global strategy, achieving the geocentric ideal, *International Marketing Review* (Spring 1985).
[6] Y. Wind, The myth of globalization, *Journal of Marketing*, vol. 3, no. 2 (1986).
[7] J. A. Quelch and E. J. Hoff, Customizing global marketing, *Harvard Business Review* (May–June 1986).

Hamel and Prahalad,[8] however, make the important point that the impacts of global organization may be complex:

> It is more difficult to respond to the new global competition than we often assume. A company must be sensitive to the potential of global competitive interaction even when its manufacturing is not on a global scale. Executives need to understand the way in which competitors use cross-subsidization to undermine seemingly strong domestic share positions.

In other words, a company's business may be destroyed by 'dumping' when a foreign competitor is determined to buy entry into the market.

What is less clear is the degree to which the many multinationals (as opposed to the relatively few transnationals, or 'global corporations' as Levitt calls them) themselves actually see, and exploit, a global marketplace. Some of the suppliers of expensive industrial capital equipment, IBM in computer mainframes and Boeing in airliners for example, may be able to bestride the world. To a lesser – usually continental – extent, suppliers of 'consumer durables', such as Ford in cars and Electrolux in washing machines, can also tap wider markets. On the other hand, Yao-Su Hu[9] claims – with some justification – that in general there are no corporations which are genuinely multinational. The exceptions, he says, fall into just two categories: the few bi-national companies, which are owned in two countries (such as Shell and Unilever), and firms from small nations which do not have a large home market. All others still depend upon a disproportionate amount of business coming from their home market; they are, according to him, national companies with international subsidiaries.

What is interesting, in marketing terms, is how few truly global consumer brands there are. Coca-Cola, Heinz, Kellogg's, Marlboro and McDonald's spring immediately to mind, representing, at least to some, symbols of US economic domination. But, beyond these and a few other similar examples, there are fewer global brands than might be expected. Unilever has developed Lux soap as an international brand for decades, and has more recently promoted Timotei shampoo across a wide range of countries. But, like many other companies (including its main competitor, Procter & Gamble), most of its brands are purely national – even when the national companies produce virtually identical products (but under different brand names).

Many of the 'international brands' are national brands translated (often literally as exports) to the world stage. Thus Johnny Walker scotch whisky, Volkswagen German cars, and Dole Hawaiian pineapples are firmly based on national identities. There is no doubt that many would argue for a different categorization, and that the difference between transnational and international

[8] G. Hamel and C. K. Prahalad, Do you really have a global strategy?, *Harvard Business Review* (July–August 1985).
[9] Yao-Su Hu, Global or stateless corporations are national firms with international operations, *Californian Management Review* (Winter 1992).

brands is not that significant. Even so, it should not be so surprising that there are so few genuinely global brands. Marketing theory assumes, correctly in most cases, that the product or service (and the whole marketing mix) has to be matched to customer needs and wants. The theory of global brands, on the other hand, assumes that 'global customers', with almost exactly the same 'global tastes', can be found. But even Luciano Benetton, quoted in a Harvard Business School Case,[10] said:

> When speaking of 'second-generation' Benetton, I am thinking of a new business reality which is extra-European in scope. But we have to take into account the diverse requirements of the markets we are planning to enter.

The complication is that 'global marketing', in its purest sense, requires the differences between countries to be negligible, or at least so small that they can be ignored in practice (but compare, for instance, Japan with the USA, or Nigeria with Italy). In most instances this is just not realistic; each national market has to be approached separately, and often in a very specific way.

Returning to that supermarket mentioned earlier, the products may look the same in Europe and the USA, but the brands will typically be very different. This will partly be due to genuine differences in the formulation, to match local tastes, but it will also reflect the comparative strengths of the corporations (and their history of acquisitions) in those markets.

Perhaps the most dramatic example of the failure of 'global marketing' was that of the Parker Pen Company. In the mid-1980s it set out to bring its marketing, across 154 countries, under a 'global marketing' umbrella, with all major decisions and standards centralized. Unfortunately, as it soon found, the markets *were* different. As a result the single, world-wide, campaign ('Make Your Mark With Parker') was a failure, and Parker Pen has apparently lost much of that world-wide business.

True globalization has only been achieved in a few markets, which seem to require one or more of the following characteristics to be present:

> Technological development

> Innovation

> Concept-based

> Conviction marketing

[10] J. L. Heskett and S. Signorelli Benetton, *Multinational Marketing: Cases and Readings*, ed. R. D. Buzzell and J. A. Quelch (Addison-Wesley, 1988).

- *Technological development.*   A number of these markets are driven by highly developed, and rapidly changing technology; and it is this technology itself which gives the cross-country and cross-cultural uniformity. At the same time the expense of developing the technology also offers economies of scale to justify the globalization process.

- *Innovation.*   Some markets have been conquered by the global organizations which first marketed an innovatory product or service, which they have then rolled out to the national markets before significant competitors have begun to emerge.

- *Concept-based.*   Some brands have developed such powerful concepts or images (verging on 'mini-cultures' in their own right) that they have been able to overwhelm local cultures – at least in the field in which they hold sway.

- *Conviction marketing.*   Similarly, the owners of most of these brands have been so convincing that they have been able to overpower, and often obliterate, local differences. Thus, Hunt et al.[11] make the point, about the dramatic success of Honda in the motorcycle market, that 'Honda turned market preference around to the characteristics of its own products and away from those of American and European competitors.' It is also interesting that some of the most successful global brands seem to be able to embody a considerable element of what is best in their original national cultures.

Standardization versus Adaptation

In the literature, this whole debate has now been condensed down to a dichotomy between 'standardization' (that is, global marketing, the standardization of products across all markets) versus 'adaptation' (the classic marketing approach to the individual needs of markets and consumers). Segmentation theory would suggest that the adaptation approach might be most powerful, but the work of Szymanski et al.[12] suggests that 'the standardized approach evokes similar performance responses in Western markets'. Henzler and Rall[13] usefully summarize the debate in the form of a matrix (figure 12.1). They then come to three critical questions. First:

1. *Is our business suited to globalization?* . . .

What might peak demand for the product in the major markets amount to, and what factors will affect it? Realistically, how uniform are customer needs from one country or region to another? . . . What further performance potential in the value-added chain could be realized by a shift to a global orientation . . .

[11] T. Hunt, M. E. Porter and E. Rudden, How global companies win out, *Harvard Business Review* (September–October 1982).
[12] David M. Szymanski, Sundar G. Bharawaj and P. Rajan Varadarajan, Standardisation versus adaptation of international marketing strategy: an empirical investigation, *Journal of Marketing*, vol. 57 (October 1993).
[13] H. Henzler and W. Rall, Facing up to the globalization challenge, *McKinsey Quarterly* (Winter 1986).

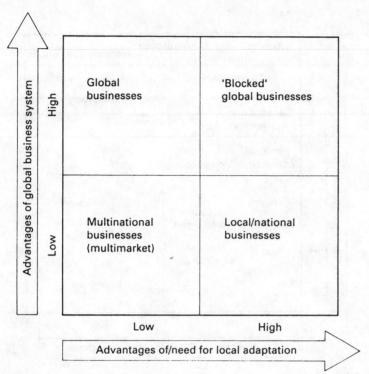

Figure 12.1   The global/local trade-off.

They illustrate this aspect using an analysis of various industries across their matrix (figure 12.2). The two further questions, assuming that the first test is passed, are:

2. *What is our best strategy?* . . .

3. *Can we implement this strategy?* . . .

If the company has no significant competitive advantage and the market is already occupied by global competitors, a globalization strategy may make little or no sense. In such a situation, the wise course may well be to retreat into a specialized niche or a customer segment with extremely high service requirements.

More obvious still has been the decision actually to rename brands in various countries, in order to have truly global brands. Thus, the UK 'Marathon' brand (chocolate bar) was very expensively renamed by Mars as 'Snickers', to bring it into line with other countries.

Triad power

'Global' markets are made up of 'national' markets which have very different weightings, and the major economies of the developed world account for a

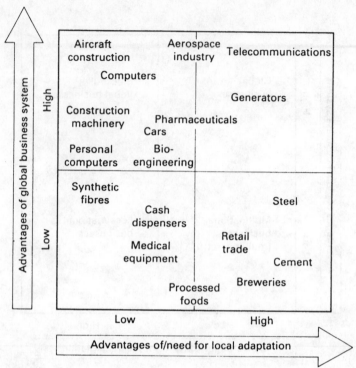

Figure 12.2   Examples of global/local trade-off.

dramatically disproportionate share of these markets. While not denying the importance of other markets, Kenichi Ohmae[14] stresses the key role of the three major markets (which he terms the 'Triad'):

> By now, the strategic significance of Japan, the United States and Europe should be obvious: This Triad is where the major markets are; it is where the competitive threat comes from; it is where the new technologies will originate. As competition becomes keener, it is where preventative action against protectionism will be needed most. To take advantage of the Triad's markets and forthcoming technologies and to prepare for new competitors, the prime objective of every corporation must be to become a true insider in all these regions.

Transnationals/Multinationals and Exporters

Subject to their decisions as to how they will treat their brands around the world (as global, international or merely, but most frequently, national) the

[14] K. Ohmae, *Triad Power: the Coming Shape of Global Competition* (Free Press, 1985).

marketing departments of multinationals and transnationals can largely ignore the complexities of international marketing. All they need do is apply the practices taught in the rest of this book. Paradoxically, therefore, the theory of international marketing is least relevant to its most significant practitioners.

Indeed, the major requirement for international success would appear to be established success in a (strong) domestic market, and usually dominance of that domestic market. Only then do the organizations have the financial and structural strengths to penetrate overseas markets on the scale that is necessary to dominate them too. In particular, the flows of funds cross-subsidize the emerging overseas operations (which often have to invest very heavily to overcome locally entrenched competitors), until these become self-funding and then, in turn, cash generators on the large scale. Therefore, the truly global corporations have their roots in very strong national marketing, and eventually manage to treat the whole world as one national market.

It is true, as Hamel and Prahalad[15] suggested, that:

> Global competitors must have the capacity to think and act in complex ways. In other words, they may slice the company in one way for distribution, in another for investments, in another for technology, and in still another for manufacturing.

Thus, for example, IBM has a truly global strategy for its development laboratories, a continental strategy for its manufacturing plants, but a largely nationally-based strategy for marketing (although based on globally enforced standards and prices). The main thrust of the rest of this chapter is, accordingly, concerned with those organizations which are essentially national, based primarily in one country, but which have extended, or wish to extend, their operations 'overseas'. The main question for them is how best to handle this genuinely alien marketing environment.

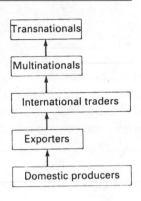

SELF-TEST QUESTION 12.2 (for those whose organizations are transnational or multinational)

To what extent is your organization globally structured? Does it make use of comparative advantage or economies of scale, in this context?

To what extent is its marketing organized globally? Does it pursue policies of standardization or of adaptation?

To what extent does it have global 'brands'?

To what extent do the 'Triad' markets dominate global sales for your organization's products or services?

---

[15] Hamel and Prahalad, *Do you really have a global strategy?*

Export or Not

In general, there are three main initial decisions in international marketing:

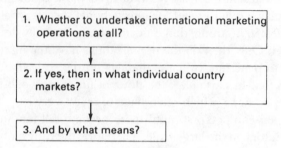

1. Whether to undertake international marketing operations at all?

2. If yes, then in what individual country markets?

3. And by what means?

The first question to be asked therefore, of organizations which are currently limited to their national market, is quite simply whether they should export at all. There is often a considerable amount of 'emotional' pressure on medium-sized firms, not least from governments which want to improve their sagging balances of trade, to 'export'. The reality is that, apart from the ubiquitous multinationals, probably very few organizations benefit significantly, at least in financial terms, from their 'international operations'.

There are, of course, the notable exceptions. On the other hand, the many achieve, at best, only mediocre results. *Any organization needs to ask, very carefully indeed, why it should export.* What will it gain from its planned overseas operations, and can it handle them efficiently?

SELF-TEST QUESTION 12.3

Does your organization operate overseas (or has it done so in the past), and if so, where and how? What proportion of its annual turnover and what part of profit is generated abroad?

If it operates overseas, why does it do so; and if not, why not?

There is, of course, one major constraint on any organization's global ambitions: will its products or services translate to other markets? It is not clear, for example, that there is as yet a large-scale market for haggis in England, let alone in the rest of Europe.

SELF-TEST QUESTION 12.4

How suitable for foreign markets is your organization's product or service? Can it be changed to make it suitable?

In relation to these questions, and those in the rest of the chapter, base your answers upon an overseas operation that your organization has recently been involved in, or on one in which it is thinking of becoming involved. If your organization has no overseas ambitions this chapter may only be of academic interest to you. If you wish to continue to play this market audit 'game' (in this case only as an activity, since it will not be part of the picture that you are building up of your organization) then you should focus on a foreign country which you know reasonably well where your organization might choose to operate.

In the context of this foreign operation, what do you believe are the key variables (factors) that are important in your existing, national, marketing operation? They might include 'good distribution', or 'a product matched to consumer tastes', or 'the correct advertising platform', and so on. List, say, the five most important factors in the form of the related objectives that you will be trying to achieve; for example, to obtain sound distribution, to research consumer needs and then match them, to produce measurably effective advertising, and so on.

How workable are these objectives? How precise are they? How can they be predicted and monitored? How comprehensive are they?

If you are considering an actual marketing operation, how well do these objectives match what your organization has actually achieved? What are the differences, and why do you believe that these have occurred?

The purpose of clarifying these objectives is that, when the information about the target market has been collected, any significant divergences will become immediately obvious. If the strategic objectives cannot be met, no amount of brilliant tactical manoeuvring will rectify the situation.

Eliminating Unsuitable Markets

One approach to targeting export markets is to select, for consideration, just those countries where 'experience' (or hearsay) has suggested there may be worthwhile business. This approach (sometimes called an 'expansive' one) starts with a 'cluster' of countries (often those located, in geographical terms, close to the original domestic market) which have characteristics similar to those that the organization is familiar with. Styles and Ambler[16] would, for instance, recommend – on the basis of research into 67 winners of the 1992 Queen's Award for Export Achievements – that this approach (which they describe as 'psychic distance') be adopted.

Another approach (sometimes described as 'contractible'), and one which might be worth pursuing, even if in parallel with the first one, is to start with *all* countries and then eliminate those which are proved to be unsuitable. The effect may ultimately be the same, but this approach has the virtue of not unnecessarily eliminating the potential markets which are less than obvious.

There are a number of methods which can be used to filter out unsuitable markets. However, I will simply examine a number of the factors which may be used to initially screen out the most obvious non-runners:

| Common sense |

| Size of population |

| 'Regulatory considerations' |

| Economic considerations |

| Social and business structures |

| Living standards |

| Accessibility |

In the elimination of export markets, the first filter is obvious, while the remaining sets of filters will require more information. One part of this information, the key 'product' and market parameters, should already have been derived from the work you have done in the rest of the book. The remaining information, about the various markets, will be derived from the sources to be described later in this chapter:

| Common sense |

| Size of population |

| 'Regulatory considerations' |

| Economic considerations |

| Social and business structures |

| Living standards |

| Accessibility |

Common sense.   For some products or services, there may be groups of countries which are clearly unlikely to buy significant quantities. For example, some strict Islamic countries are poor markets for alcoholic drinks, and the poorest of the Third World countries are unlikely to be large-scale purchasers of mainframe computers.

Size of population.   Some countries (for example, Belize or Bhutan) are so small as to be smaller than some English or American counties; and their markets for imported goods

[16] Chris Styles and Tim Ambler, Successful export practice: the UK experience, *International Marketing Review*, vol.11, no. 6 (1994).

may be smaller than some towns in the developed world. The 'infrastructure' which is needed to export to these countries may only be justified, therefore, by products with very large sales world-wide.

State of development. Even the larger Third World countries (such as Ethiopia or Bangladesh)[17] may be so underdeveloped that a population the size of a European country will, once more, generate a market that is scarcely larger than a French or American town.

Regulatory considerations. There are a number of countries which have regulations or laws that can constrain the marketing of certain products, or the activities of certain organizations (particularly foreign companies). The main areas of concern will probably be:

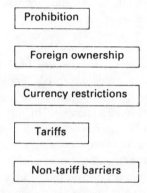

- *Prohibition.* Certain categories of product may be legally barred; for example, alcoholic drinks in Saudi Arabia. Less obvious are bans such as that which the US government imposes on high-technology equipment being shipped to some third countries, and which can apply even to products which only contain small elements of US technology (and even then perhaps made under licence).
- *Foreign ownership.* In order to protect emerging local industries, a number of countries impose restrictions on the 'ownership' of local companies. This may mean that it becomes impossible to establish a local branch, or that the conditions which would be imposed are unacceptable.
- *Currency restrictions.* Because of their fragile economies, some countries have controls on the 'export' of currency, sometimes to the total exclusion of commercial money transactions. This may make it impossible to extract any profit from the country – or even to receive payment for a product shipped into the country – unless a complex web of barters is set up.
- *Tariffs.* By far the most common (official) trade barriers are those enforced by tariffs. For a variety of reasons, some countries, including some of the strongest trading nations, will require extra duties, payable on certain categories of imported goods, so that these will be at a cost disadvantage (and hence a price disadvantage,

---

[17] M. Kidron and R. Segal, *The State of the World Atlas* (Pan Books, 1981).

typically of between 5 per cent and 30 per cent, but sometimes more than 100 per cent) against local goods.

- *Non-tariff barriers.* At least tariff barriers are highly visible. 'Non-tariff' barriers can be much less obvious. For example, before the EC harmonization of standards, France and Germany required imported products to have expensive changes made to them to meet local standards. 'Structural' barriers, such as very complicated distribution systems, are even more difficult to detect.

Common sense

Size of population

'Regulatory considerations'

Economic considerations

Social and business structures

Living standards

Accessibility

Economic considerations. GDP (Gross Domestic Product) in total, and its growth rate – and, in particular, GDP *per capita* – can say a lot about the potential spending power and patterns of a country's population. These figures are available in reference books, such as the OECD economic surveys or the United Nations Yearbooks, which may often be found at the larger reference libraries. However, care should be exercised in using any such data on a comparative basis, since the bases for the different sets of data may not be strictly comparable.

Social and business structures. The regulatory implications of social structures have already been mentioned. However, the culture itself can play a decisive role in deciding whether a product is to be accepted. The special problems of Islamic countries have already been cited, but there are many other cultural barriers. Business cultures also have their idiosyncrasies. In certain countries, for example, it is a way of life for 'access' to be 'purchased'; in US and European eyes this may be seen as bribery, but locally it is often seen simply as part of the normal costs of trading. Equally, in certain countries the structure of business may be very informal, so that it takes a deal of accumulated expertise to understand exactly what the deal that you have just struck actually means. In other countries still the negotiation procedures are alien, ranging from the haggling of the bazaar (which is meant to be an entertainment in itself for both participants) to the sophisticated nuances of Japanese business (most of which are lost on Western businessmen). The state of development of the society can be gauged by the degree of literacy, and the employment levels – as well as employment by sector (service versus manufacturing versus primary agriculture, for example). The level of education may become a deciding factor in the use of any product which requires a degree of skill, or the following of written instructions.

Living standards. Individual living standards may often be estimated by reference to a few simple measures, such as ownership of television sets or telephones or cars. Indications of the 'infrastructure' may be obtained from measurements such as the percentage of houses with mains drainage. Certain infrastructure elements may be very important to specific products or services: General Foods failed to make a success of selling packaged cake mixes in Japan, despite heavy promotion, because very few Japanese households own ovens in which to bake cakes. The 'skew' of living standards can be estimated from the distribution of income in general, or by the extent of the 'luxury' industries.

Accessibility. The final set of questions to be asked relates to the ease of access to a given market. The potential that it offers may be placed on one side of the scale, but the costs of tapping that potential (of providing the necessary exporting infrastructure) must be put on the other side before any sensible decision can be made. Key factors may be:

```
┌─────────────────────┐
│     Distance        │
└─────────────────────┘

┌─────────────────────┐
│   Language and      │
│     culture         │
└─────────────────────┘

┌─────────────────────┐
│ Business infrastructure │
└─────────────────────┘
```

Distance.   With the advent of the 747 airliner and container ships, the world can now sometimes be thought of as a 'global village'. Trade between many countries is now an easy matter in physical terms, and electronic communication is even easier in terms of remote contacts. However, there are still many places – and indeed whole countries – which are not tied into the trade routes; and where the transport of goods, and even of visiting businessmen, may impose significant problems.

Language and culture.   It may be quite possible to obtain a local agent who speaks your language well (or to find an interpreter), but an ignorance of the local language can bar an exporter from many of the 'signals' which he or she could expect to use in interpreting a market. 'Aesthetic' considerations also must not be ignored. In Japan, for instance, the McDonald's 'clown' advertising failed, because a white face signifies death. Of course, taste varies considerably. Heinz Ketchup is a global brand, but its formulation is different in different countries, to account for local tastes.

Business infrastructure.   The support available to assist import business in a given market can vary widely, and needs to be taken into account. In the first place, are there suitable agents to handle the product or service? Does your own government have a sound trade department in its local embassy, to provide accurate information and advice? What is the 'bureaucracy' like, in terms of importing? What is the business etiquette? Punctuality, for instance, may vary considerably across national boundaries, and may wreak havoc with carefully crafted schedules for visits.

Nachum's research[18] indicates that – in general terms – for industrial goods the key factors favouring import demand are trade figures, consumption in general, energy production and the monetary situation; whereas those for consumer goods are income and stability of the currency.

Country Portfolio

Having made the various decisions, having entered the market and having achieved an adequate level of sales, the transnational/global corporation will

---

[18] L. Nachum, The choice of variables for segmentation of the international market, *International Marketing Review*, vol. 11, no. 2 (1994).

then need to consider how its 'portfolio' of country operations is balanced, and how their different strengths (and weaknesses) complement the overall operation. Carol Kennedy[19] looks at this in terms of a matrix which measures position in terms of competitive strength against development (or 'life-cycle'). She illustrates this with reference to 3M's position (figure 12.3).

SELF-TEST QUESTION 12.5

Using the above categories of filters (and any others which are relevant), remove those countries which do not pass the various levels of screen:

- common sense
- size of population
- regulatory considerations (prohibition, foreign ownership, currency restrictions, tariffs and non-tariff barriers)
- economic considerations
- social and business structures
- living standards
- accessibility (distance, language and culture and business infrastructure)

	Maturity stage			
Competitive position	Embryonic	Growth	Mature	Ageing
Leading		Brazil Canada Italy		
Strong	Scandinavia Japan		France	
Favourable	Afr. M–East UK	USA Germany		
Tenable				
Weak				

Figure 12.3 Strategic condition of 3M business by geographical market.

[19] C. Kennedy, Planning global strategies for 3M, *Long Range Planning*, vol. 21, no. 1 (1988).

Marketing Research

As with any new venture, the next stage in the approach to an overseas market should be to conduct market research. In many respects this will follow the same paths as those of domestic market research, as described in chapter 3; any research overseas must follow as rigorous an approach.

There are, though, other aspects, in particular those relating to sources of data and in the handling of remote research agencies, which are also peculiar to export marketing.

As usual, you can undertake the desk research yourself, or you can 'subcontract' it to a specialist department in your own organization or use an outside consultant. Whichever the route, the first step, as always, is to search through the existing 'literature'. The sources of data are very different and perhaps more limited than those for the larger home markets of many exporters:

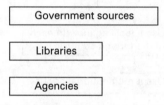

Government sources

Libraries

Agencies

Government sources. Most governments are anxious to promote exports, and invest considerable sums in research around the world, for the benefit of their exporters. They will, typically, maintain trade departments in each of the main embassies; collecting commercial intelligence. In many countries this information is usually provided to exporters via an overseas trade agency, but local chambers of commerce and the main banks may also be able to help.

In addition, there are a number of commercial publishers, such as:

- Euromonitor – *Market Research Europe, International/European Marketing, Data and Statistics* and *Consumer Europe*
- EIU (Economist Intelligence Unit) – *Marketing in Europe*

SELF-TEST QUESTION 12.6

What desk research does your organization normally undertake in the context of overseas markets?

If you wish to carry out a more detailed task, use the resources of your local library to collect the information that is available on the chosen overseas markets.

> This may be an extensive exercise, which will be productive only if you are actually involved in export management. For most managers a visit to the library (to establish what material is held) should prove sufficient to determine how valuable this data is – and possibly to give a superficial indication of the potential and problems of these overseas markets.

Ad hoc Research

This largely follows the rules described in chapter 3; the most obvious difference is that the work will be conducted in another country. To handle this problem there are a number of possible solutions, including:

Do-it-yourself. The conditions for conducting market research (the sampling framework, the regulatory requirements, the social environment, who is available to use as interviewers, and so on) vary considerably from country to country. In Muslim countries, for instance, the housewife may not be permitted to be interviewed unless her husband is present. Vern Terpstra[20] reports that almost 30 per cent of domestic mail in Brazil is never delivered, somewhat limiting the validity of mail surveys there. The research of Parameswaran and Yaprak[21] resulted in the conclusion that:

> . . . the same scales may have different reliabilities in different cultures, and the same scales may exhibit different reliabilities when used by the same individual in evaluating products from different cultures . . . This argues against simple comparisons of research results in cross-national marketing.

DIY is, thus, even less advisable than in domestic market research.

Use a local agency (in each of the foreign countries). This follows the usual national practice, of appointing a research agency to carry out the fieldwork, as described in chapter 3;

---

[20] V. Terpstra, *International Marketing* (Dryden Press, 1987).
[21] R. Parameswaran and A. Yaprak, A cross-national comparison of consumer research measures, *Journal of International Business Studies* (Spring 1987).

but in this case the agency is in the foreign country. However, this approach does require a significant amount of (expensive) time, visiting the market to brief the agency and supervise activities.

Use a multinational agency. This is the easiest approach, as easy as using an agency in your own market (which is where the office you deal with will be located). The 'global' agency is, on the other hand, only as strong as its local links (which will probably be subcontractors in the smaller countries). This may cause problems for specialist investigations, for example those in industrial markets, where the local subcontractor might not have the skills needed to handle such work.

Use a domestic agency (to co-ordinate foreign agencies). This allows for a free choice of local agencies in the foreign markets; but it assumes that the domestic agency has a good grasp of the foreign local scene, comparable with that of the multinational agencies.

It is generally recommended that one of the last two alternatives is adopted; to organize research locally (in the foreign market) is beyond the capacity of most organizations.

SELF-TEST QUESTION 12.7

What market research does your organization carry out in overseas markets? How reliable is it? How does it compare with the domestic research? What improvements might you suggest?

Market Entry Decision

Once the screening process has reduced the number of potential countries down to a relatively small number, these can be categorized (and prioritized) by the techniques that you would use in judging any move into a new market. You should recognize, however, that such a move should be considered as a diversification, even though the products or services involved may be the main-line ones from the home market. Diversification, you will remember, should be the subject of that much more serious consideration.

At the end of this process of prioritization you should have divided your potential overseas markets into a number of categories, each requiring different courses of action. Three of these categories may, for example, be:

- markets not to be exploited
- markets to be covered by agents or distributors
- markets for major development

Depending upon the strategies adopted (based on the portfolio planning, say) some of the major markets will be scheduled for development at some time in the future, whereas others will require immediate attention.

Country risk

One of the factors which needs to be taken into account, particularly by the multinationals, is the risk that their investments in a particular country will be nullified; either by 'investment recovery risk', resulting from government action (such as expropriation or war), or by 'cash flow risk', due to radically reduced economic returns (from strikes, debt and currency problems, and so on). John Stopford[22] categorizes such risks diagrammatically:

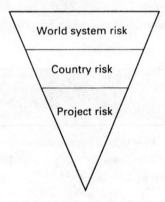

- *World system risk.* This is the risk to the whole system of international trade, posed by problems such as the 'North/South Divide' and Third World debt.
- *Country risk.* This is the general risk of doing business in the particular country (which is often the only 'country risk' discussed, even though it may only be of direct interest to international banks).
- *Project risk.* Most importantly, John Stopford identifies the fact that the specific risk of each project may vary considerably (an exploiter of raw material supplies may be in danger of nationalization, whereas at the same time a supplier of essential 'high-tech' equipment may be received with open arms). However, this element is often not taken into account.

There are a number of suppliers of 'country risk analyses', based on tracking political and other indicators in these countries (with an overall risk factor calculated from these), including Frost & Sullivan and Business International. Their reports are of greatest use to the major banks, whose country-level lending may be at risk. They may be of less direct use to corporations involved in specific market sectors, which are not addressed by such reports.

[22] J. Stopford, Personal communication (1989).

The best advice is to include an assessment of such risks in the overall research, and then to monitor developments (including political developments) closely.

Product Decision

A further level of decision to be taken, even if the 'entry decision' is made, is 'With what product?' Many global marketers appear to use the same product world-wide, a simple 'extension' of what is offered in the home market; and it is true that McDonald's and Coca-Cola, for example, offer identical products world-wide.

On the other hand, many multinationals market very different products in diverse countries. These are often marketed as different brands: however, some-times the brand name is the same, but the formulation is different, to meet local needs. General Foods (the manufacturer of Maxwell House), for instance, blends different coffees for the UK (where it is mainly taken with milk), for France (where it is often taken black) and for Latin America (whose consumers like a taste of chicory). This may be a matter not just of taste or culture but of physical needs; the Japanese, being physically small, demand smaller versions of almost everything – including some consumer durables.

Even if the product, or service, is the same in all markets, the promotional vehicles – and the promotional messages – may be very different. The cultural constraints may mean that exactly the same basic message has to be told in different ways to be meaningful to different national audiences.

Price decision

Some global organizations, such as IBM, might choose to maintain much the same prices world-wide (although, typically, these will be higher than those in the domestic market of the parent company), always subject to the limitations imposed by varying currency exchange rates. Others, such as those in the pharmaceutical industry, may set prices by what each market will bear, leading to very different prices in each country.

The problem with significant variations in price between countries, particu-larly where the countries are close to each other, is that customers may indulge in 'cross-border shopping' to take advantage of the lower prices; or, even worse, wholesalers may do so – and create a 'grey market' in the higher price country (thus destabilizing marketing operations in that country).

The price that the parent company charges for the product it ships into the country is called the 'transfer price'. This can be based upon actual, or notional, costs; IBM, for instance, is very careful to ensure that it reflects true costs.

However, it can occasionally be manipulated to avoid or minimize local taxes. In any case, as we saw earlier in this chapter, Kenneth Simmonds[23] believes that international management accounting practices are not sound enough to provide for accurate transfer prices.

On the other hand, some exporters have been known to set very low prices in some overseas markets; they 'dump' the product, with the intention of undermining local suppliers, so that there will ultimately be less competition, and the prices can then be raised to a profitable level.

Counter-trading

This category of international trading, which includes barter deals, counter-purchasing, buy-backs, switch trades, offset deals and compensation trading, accounts for a significant proportion of international trade. According to Shipley and Neale[24] it 'now forms 20–30 per cent of world trade, with total yearly value possibly exceeding $100 billion'. The main forms are:

- barter – payment for goods by goods, with no direct involvement of money, usually as a one-time exchange which leaves the supplier having to find a market for the goods that have been received in exchange
- buy-backs (sometimes called 'compensation agreements') – the supplier (usually of technology or capital equipment) agrees to buy back some of the resulting product, to cover the cost of the deal
- switch-trades – deals involving various partners (usually specialist institutions) which aim to achieve a balance of trade
- clearing arrangements – bilateral trade agreements between countries rather than individual organizations

Needless to say, most organizations would prefer cash, but if this is not available then a counter-trade may be better than nothing. But it has to be recognized that it is difficult and time-consuming, and often leaves the vendor with products which are difficult to sell.

SELF-TEST QUESTION 12.8

What is the product philosophy behind your organization's product or service offerings in the various national markets?

[23] Simmonds, Global strategy: achieving the geocentric ideal.

[24] D. D. Shipley and C. W. Neale, Successful countertrading, *Management Decision*, vol. 26, no. 1 (1988).

Market Entry Tactics

Having decided to enter a specific market, that entry may be made via a number of routes. Simon Majaro[25] illustrates the alternatives diagrammatically (figure 12.4).

I will settle for a rather simpler categorization:

Domestic-based (direct) export sales

In this case, all activity will be handled by an office located in the organization's home headquarters, although the documentation and shipping are often sub-contracted to a third party. This will necessarily be a limited operation; handling unsolicited orders from overseas, and selling to foreign government buying offices (often by bidding against tenders) or those of other foreign buying groups (retail chains, for example). This approach can very occasionally (where the exporter has special expertise or can offer a very low price) generate high volumes with low overheads (as the Taiwanese personal computer component suppliers have shown). This approach is unlikely to work for a service.

Indirect export sales

In this case, the whole overseas operation is subcontracted to an export–import house, which takes over all responsibility for export and distribution of the product (or, much less likely, the service) overseas. An alternative might be to let another organization, which is well established in overseas markets but which wishes to spread its overheads, handle export sales; this is sometimes

[25] S. Majaro, *International Marketing: A Strategic Approach to World Markets* (George Allen & Unwin, 1982).

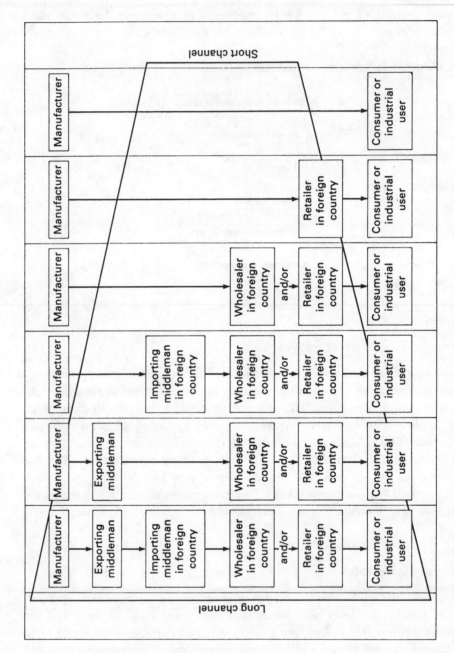

Figure 12.4 Major types of distribution channels in international marketing.

called 'piggy-back marketing' or 'mother-henning'. For many years the largest Japanese organizations were the giant trading houses ('Sogo Shosha', including C. Itoh – the largest – Mitsui and Mitsubishi) which handled the export sales of many Japanese corporations. Again, this is a route unlikely to be used for services.

Licensing

This may be a means of rapidly, and cost-effectively, entering a large number of markets, including services markets. It does not require the investment of resources which direct entry would demand. Coca-Cola, for example, used to license local bottlers in some markets, although it has since switched to direct operations in the main markets. Pilkington licensed its float glass technology in some of the smaller, more difficult markets. Even Philip Morris licenses its global brands in markets where governments hold a monopoly of cigarette production.

A wide range of different forms of licensing agreements and contracts (including those relating to franchising) is available; so this is an area where specialist legal expertise is essential. The clear advantage is that it requires no knowledge of the local market, only of the areas of expertise that the organization already possesses.

The disadvantage is that this approach may limit future development of the organization's position in the market. Indeed, it may not only limit future access to that market, but may also create competition in third markets, as the licensee gains experience and know-how.

Joint ventures

These have much in common with licensing. Both usually involve a local organization handling the marketing (and typically also production) in the foreign market. The difference is that the international partner has an equity holding in the local operation.

The skills for setting up a local joint venture, and sharing the running with the local partner, are not those of conventional marketing (and are, perhaps, more related to those of diplomacy). They are beyond the scope of this book.

Co-operative distribution

Suppliers, for example those in commodity (typically agricultural) markets, sometimes join together to export as a group. Occasionally, an export consortium (an essentially short-term grouping) may be formed to tender for a specific bid (usually for a large-scale, turn-key contract).

One device that the Japanese, and their later imitators, have very successfully used to break into markets has been to supply 'own' ('private') brands to distributors. Thus, for example, Fujitsu has supplied mainframe computers to Amdahl and Siemens, just as Taiwanese suppliers of consumer electronics and personal computers have provided supplies for a wide range of retailers; all for 'badging' by the local distributors. They have thus been able to gain 'technical' experience of the market, by riding on the known brands of existing companies.

If the position in the market is to be consolidated (and not to be left at the whim of the distributor who owns the local brand) there remains the transfer to full-scale marketing, with the organization's own brands. This is a transfer that some of the Japanese corporations, at least, have managed with great success, but it is definitely not guaranteed.

| Domestic-based export sales |
| Indirect export sales |
| Licensing |
| Joint ventures |
| Co-operative distribution |
| Local sales organization |
| Middlemen/agents |

Local sales organization

The largest, and most attractive, markets may well justify the establishment of a local sales operation (although this often occurs after the market has been tested by using an agent for a period). A number of possibilities are open for such a sales organization:

- *Subsidiary/branch office.* This is the vehicle chosen by most truly international or multinational organizations; the classic example, once more, was IBM, which used to have sales organizations in 130 countries.
- *Joint selling company.* A joint venture may be set up with a local partner or another supplier. Even IBM had to accept such arrangements in certain countries (such as Saudi Arabia), where local trading practices make direct control impossible.
- *Purchase of an existing organization.* If sufficient resources are available, then the quickest route to widespread distribution may be to buy into an existing company, which is already in the market (either with a 100 per cent takeover, or with a controlling interest; or even with a minority interest that guarantees co-operation). This approach was adopted, for example, by Nestlé (on the very large scale) in its takeover of Rowntree.

SELF-TEST QUESTION 12.9

Which of these approaches has your organization used? Which were the most effective, and why? Why have the others not been used?

Middlemen/Agents

By far the most widely-used approach (in terms of the number of exporters using it, if not in terms of the volumes shipped) is to use agents or distributors. This offers a relatively low initial cost and risk; and bypasses many of the barriers which countries erect against the direct entry of foreign companies.

On the other hand, open-ended agency agreements may also exclude the exporter when later direct operations might be more productive. Letraset, for example, had at one stage to 'buy back' many of its earlier agency agreements.

The Agent's Balance

Most agency agreements are not open-ended. The result is, therefore, an 'incentive balance' for the local agent, which the exporter should be aware of:

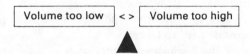

- *Volume too low.* If the agent does not put in sufficient effort and sales are low, then the exporter will become dissatisfied and switch to another agent.
- *Volume too high.* On the other hand, if sales become too high the exporter will be tempted into entering the market direct. This is an aspect which is at the forefront of many agents' minds, but is rarely considered by exporters.

Agents or distributors

In many respects these two different forms of legal entity operate, from the exporter's point of view, in much the same way. They will both handle all the exporter's local operations, from import through to the customer. The legal distinctions between them (which can become important in certain litigation, so that – once more – expert legal advice is necessary) are:

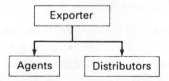

- *Agents* are independent intermediaries, between buyer and seller, who may act in the name of, and for, their client organization; receiving, in return, commission on business transacted. Their contracts usually define exactly how, and where (in terms of territory), they may act for the organization.

- *Distributors* sell in their own name, and on their own behalf ('taking title' to the goods they purchase from the exporting organization for the purpose of resale). Their territory may also be defined, but their compensation comes from the profit margins they can get on the sales made.

Strategic (International) Alliances

A much more positive approach to using 'third parties', used in particular by the larger corporations (who are often already multinationals in their own right) is very deliberately to build strong marketing links with other organizations – 'strategic alliances'.

As Kenichi Ohmae[26] says:

> Companies are just beginning to learn what nations have always known: in a complex, uncertain world filled with dangerous opponents it is best not to go it alone . . . But managers have been slow to experiment with genuine strategic alliances. A joint venture here and there, yes, of course. A long-term contractual relationship, certainly. But forging the entente, rarely . . . Alliances mean sharing control . . . Globalization mandates alliances, makes them absolutely essential to strategy. Uncomfortable – but that's the way it is.

He goes on to explain:

> Alliances are not tools of convenience. They are important, even critical, instruments of serving customers in a global environment . . . Few companies operating in the Triad of Japan, the United States, and Europe can offer such topflight levels of value to all their customers all the time all by themselves.

He also highlights the problems of finding the resources needed:

> To compete in the global arena, you have to incur – and sometimes find a way to defray – immense fixed costs. You can't play a variable cost game any more. You need partners who can help you amortize your fixed costs . . .

Such strategic alliances are, therefore, created to engender monumental economies of scale – truly global undertakings.

David Lei[27] makes the same point:

> The higher costs and risks of R&D, production, financing and market penetration brighten the prospects for expanded strategic alliances between global companies as top management believes that no company can manage all of the high risks associated with world-scale ventures.

But he goes on to add the caution:

[26] K. Ohmae, The global logic of strategic alliances, *Harvard Business Review* (March–April 1989).
[27] D. Lei, Strategies for global competition, *Long Range Planning*, vol. 22, no. 1 (1989).

Yet joint ventures raise several questions of great corporate strategic importance since this vehicle for cooperation can also seriously undermine the company's long-term competitiveness if management is not careful in defining and implementing its 'foreign policy'.

Michael Geringer,[28] however, points out the amount of effort and investment involved in such a process:

> Because of the presumed long-term nature of most joint ventures and the costs associated with premature dissolution, there tend to be relatively high financial and human costs associated with the selection of partners for successful ventures. Firms must be willing to incur substantial search costs, including those associated with developing selection criteria and evaluating partners, as well as the extensive resource expenditures typically involved in the negotiation stage. In addition, the process needs to be approached with considerable patience and realistic expectations.

Pitfalls

At the end of the day, when all the various selection procedures have been completed and truly international marketing has been put in place, what can go wrong? Kamran Kashani's research[29] highlighted five pitfalls:

INSUFFICIENT RESEARCH . . . nearly half the programmes included no formal research before startup and most of the companies paid for this omission afterwards . . .

OVERSTANDARDIZATION – when a local program is burdened with too many standards, local inventiveness and experimentation close to the market dry up . . .

POOR FOLLOW-UP –

NARROW VISION –

RIGID IMPLEMENTATION . . . standardized marketing is a means to reaching an end, never an end in itself.

SELF-TEST QUESTION 12.10

Has your organization used agents or distributors? If so, what has been its experience? What lessons have been learned?

---

[28] M. J. Geringer, Selection of partners for international joint ventures, *Business Quarterly* (Autumn 1988).

[29] K. Kashani, Beware the pitfalls of global marketing, *Harvard Business Review* (September–October 1989).

FURTHER READING

My own preference among the books dedicated to international business or marketing is *International Marketing* by Vern Terpstra (4th edn, The Dryden Press, 1987), which is both comprehensive and readable. It gives a very sound grounding, illustrated by many examples, in the specialized form of marketing which is needed to handle such operations. On the other hand, there are a number of other books, such as *International Marketing and Export Management* by Gerald Albaum et al. (Addison-Wesley, 1989) and *Global Marketing* by Warren J. Keegan (4th edn, Prentice-Hall, 1989) which also provide good coverage.

Kenichi Ohmae's book, *Triad Power: the Coming Shape of Global Competition* (The Free Press, 1985), concentrates on the importance of the main markets, and on examples of multinationals working within them; it offers some very challenging insights for those who are faced with competition at this level.

SUMMARY

A number of organizational structures may be employed to undertake international business in general and *international marketing* in particular:

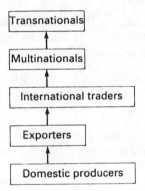

The requirements of the *transnationals and multinationals* are very different from those of exporters. The former's interest may be in *globalization* (based possibly, at least in theory, on economies of scale or comparative advantage). Even so, there are relatively few genuine global brands, and these tend to revolve around:

The main debate, however, is between *standardization* (globally controlled marketing policies) and *adaptation* (national policies), although Kenichi Ohmae concentrates on the *Triad* of the three main markets.

At the other end of the spectrum, the first of the key *exporting decisions* revolves around *market entry*, and eliminating unsuitable markets on the basis of:

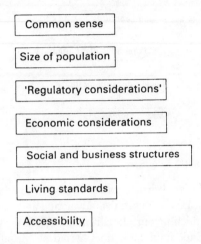

Sources of *marketing research data* may be *desk research* (via government services, libraries and agencies) or *ad hoc research*:

The *market entry decision* should take into account risk, but will also incorporate decisions on *product or service* and *price* (which may involve counter-trading). A spectrum of *market entry tactics* are then available to the exporter:

Domestic-based export sales

Indirect export sales

Licensing

Joint ventures

Co-operative distribution

Local sales organization

Middlemen/agents

REVISION QUESTIONS

1 What different organizational structures are employed to address international marketing? How important may comparative advantage and economies of scale be?

2 What are the factors which favour globalization? What are the differences between standardization and adaptation? How does 'Triad power' affect this?

3 What are the factors which may be taken into account when selecting markets for possible entry? What regulatory considerations may be most important?

4 What sources of material for desk research are available? How would you choose between alternative sources of *ad hoc* research?

5 What needs to be taken into account in the market entry decision? What risks are involved? What 'product' and price decisions need to be made?

6 What market entry tactics are available? How do joint ventures compare with licensing? What are the advantages and disadvantages of a local sales organization versus use of agents?

13 The External Environment

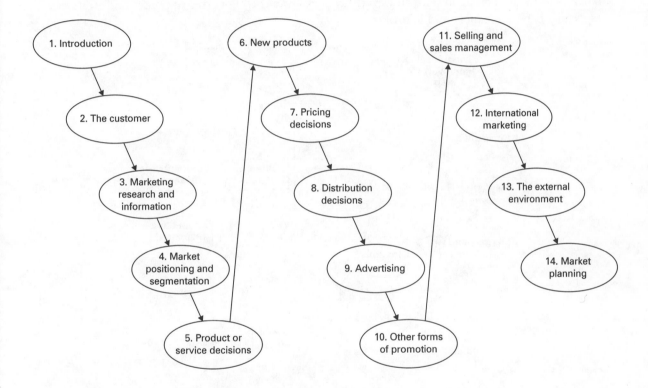

1. Introduction

2. The customer

3. Marketing research and information

4. Market positioning and segmentation

5. Product or service decisions

6. New products

7. Pricing decisions

8. Distribution decisions

9. Advertising

10. Other forms of promotion

11. Selling and sales management

12. International marketing

13. The external environment

14. Market planning

Introduction

In recent years the horizons of 'marketing' have been expanded to encompass the wider environment. It has been recognized that, at least in the longer term, the survival of organizations is very dependent upon that environment. A number of theoretical frameworks have been put forward, but the simplest and most widely used is STEP (Sociocultural, Technological, Economic, Political); this is the framework adopted in this chapter. Thus, the sociocultural domain of the environment is explored; with particular reference to the main 'drivers for change'. The technological, economic and political domains are similarly investigated; with particular reference to mergers and acquisitions, and the 'multiple publics' which an organization faces. The latter part of the first half of this chapter, though, is devoted to environmental analysis in general, and to 'scanning' in particular (especially for 'weak signals').

The second half of the chapter is devoted to the element of the environment that has the most immediate impact, and one which dominated management activities in the 1980s – competitive strategy. Following the widely-accepted frameworks developed by Michael Porter, this initially concentrates on the competitive features of different industry types, and in particular the entry barriers to them. The main part, however, revolves around competitive responses and strategies, especially between leaders and followers.

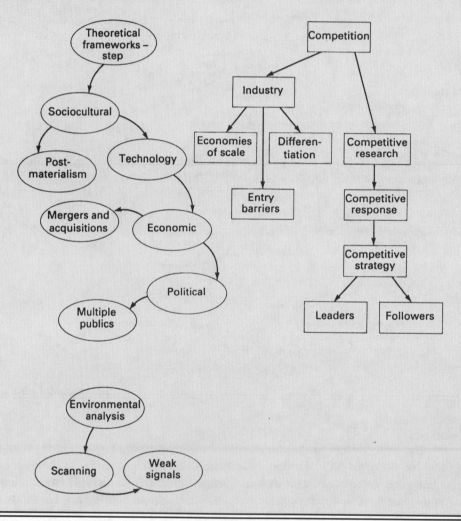

Pfeffer and Salancik[1] make the following comment:

> The key to organizational survival is the ability to acquire and maintain resources. This problem would be simplified if organizations were in complete control of all the components necessary for their operation. However, no organization is completely self-contained. Organizations are embedded in an environment composed of other organizations. They depend on those organizations for the many resources they themselves require. Organizations are linked to environments by federations, associations, customer–supplier relationships, competitive relationships and a socio-legal apparatus defining and controlling the nature and limits of those relationships.

They add:

> Despite the importance of the environment for organizations, relatively little attention has been focused there.

They also quote the results of a survey by Lieberson and O'Connor[2] of 167 companies in which 'the administrative impact (the effect of the company management) was dwarfed by the impact of the organization's industry and the stable characteristics of the given organization . . .'.

In essence, this research showed that *most organizations were more susceptible to the impact of their external environment than to the actions of their own management.* Their bottom-line profits were more dependent upon the vagaries of external events than upon how well their internal operations were managed. In recent years, indeed, this impact has become more unpredictable.

Most organizations, however, seem (at least formally) to ignore this dimension of their business. If they are well managed, they devote immense efforts to optimizing the internal factors which are within their control; but they barely notice what is happening outside, and make little attempt to formally manage that side of their activities, except for some marketing responses. Yet a survey by Greenfeld et al.,[3] of 200 CEOs in Baltimore, showed that the average CEO spent 27 per cent of his or her time dealing with external matters. A major element of that outside environment is indeed made up from the factors which are now grouped under the global heading of 'marketing'. Beyond this, however, there is a whole range of social and political factors which may have even greater impact. Not least is the impact of government regulation, which may make or break whole sectors of industry.

Douglas Brownlie[4] summarizes the position when he states three 'premises':

- 'the determinants of success are dictated by the business environment'

---

[1] J. Pfeffer and G. R. Salancik, *The External Control of Organizations: A Resource Dependence Perspective* (Harper & Row, 1978).

[2] S. Lieberson and J. F. O'Connor, Leadership and organizational performance: a study of large corporations, *American Sociological Review*, vol. 37 (1972), pp. 117–30.

[3] S. Greenfeld, R. C. Winder and G. Williams, The CEO and the external environment, *Business Horizons* (November–December 1988).

[4] D. Brownlie, Environmental analysis, *The Marketing Book*, ed. M. J. Baker (Heinemann, 1987).

- 'the firm's response to environmental change represents a fundamental choice'
- 'a knowledge of the business environment must precede the acquisition of any degree of control over it'

Philip Kotler[5] approaches the subject from a different direction, adding a further two Ps, 'power' and 'public relations', to create '*Megamarketing*':

> 1. Power. The megamarketer must often win the support of influential industry officials, legislators, and government bureaucrats to enter and operate in the target market . . . Thus the megamarketer needs political skills and a political strategy. The company must identify the people with the power to open the gate. It must determine the right mix of incentives to offer . . .
>
> 2. *Public Relations.* Whereas power is a push strategy, public relations is a pull strategy. Public opinion takes longer to cultivate, but when energized it can help pull a company into the market . . . Before entering a market, companies must understand the community's beliefs, attitudes and values. After entry they need to play the role of good citizen by contributing to public causes, sponsoring civic and cultural events, and working effectively with the media . . .

SELF-TEST QUESTION 13.1

What external factors, other than marketing, have a significant impact on your organization? What social pressures are applied to it, and what legislation constrains it? What industry factors determine its profitability?

Theoretical Frameworks

As is frequently the case in marketing, a number of alternative frameworks for studying this wider environment are offered, the most conventional of which describes it in terms of an '*onion*':

[5] P. Kotler, Megamarketing, *Harvard Business Review* (March–April 1986).

This is a useful approach, since it distinguishes between three different degrees of interaction:

- *Organization (or internal environment).* This includes those activities, contained totally *within* the organization itself, which make up the daily life of most organizations.
- *Marketing environment.* This is the area of the external environment which has the most immediate impact on organizations, and is generally recognized by them (and is the subject of much of this book).
- *External environment.* This is often not recognized as a force impinging on organizations; and yet, as we have seen, it may well contain the *major* factors which determine the performance of those organization.

There is, however, no agreed terminology for the various components of the environment; possibly the simplest approach is to group them into market and non-market components.[6]

These external factors are most often grouped as the *STEP* factors (Sociocultural, Technological, Economic and Political). They can have dramatic effects on organizations. The (political) results of legislation, for example, determine the boundaries of the actions of most organizations, and yet they are often 'taken as read', and are a relatively unnoticed element of organizational

```
┌─────────────────┐
│  Sociocultural  │
└─────────────────┘
┌─────────────────┐
│  Technological  │
└─────────────────┘
┌─────────────────┐
│    Economic     │
└─────────────────┘
┌─────────────────┐
│    Political    │
└─────────────────┘
```

performance.

For most of the rest of this section, covering the main 'domains' of the external environment, we shall follow this simple STEP approach. This offers the easiest way to break a very complex subject down into manageable pieces. It is, however, an arbitrary approach, which does not necessarily do justice to the complexity of the factors involved, and may even hide some of the more important interactions.

We shall, accordingly, look at each of these four factors separately, even though they normally act in combination. In each case we will not just look at the techniques involved, but will also explore the key 'facts' that distinguish that 'domain'. In particular, we shall look at the main 'drivers' for change.

[6] David P. Baron, Integrated strategy: market and non-market components, *California Management Review*, vol. 37, no.2 (Winter 1995).

Sociocultural

Cultural traditions are not easily overturned, but over the years they can change quite significantly – without the organizations involved noticing. Over the 1970s and 1980s, for example, the role of woman in society – and, in particular, woman's role at work – changed dramatically; and this was of considerable significance to those supplying services to women. No longer could they assume that the average woman was the stereotypical housewife. The women's magazine industry, as one example, was changed out of all recognition.

Over the past two decades there have been major changes in a number of areas of the overall sociocultural environment. The 'Information Revolution' has begun to have a measurable impact on the patterns of employment, with economists pointing to a degree of 'structural unemployment' caused by its progress. It is arguable, indeed, that the social effects of this particular 'revolution' have barely been felt as yet, and that it will dominate many of the changes in society over the coming two decades.

Related to this particular 'technological' driver, there have been a number of predictions made about how society will change. One of the earlier ones, and also one of the most influential, was that by Daniel Bell,[7] concerning the development of the *post-industrial society*:

> The concept of the post-industrial society is a large generalization. Its meaning can be more easily understood if one specifies five dimensions, or components, of the term:
>
> 1. Economic sector: the change from a goods-producing to a service economy;
>
> 2. Occupational distribution: the pre-eminence of the professional and technical class;
>
> 3. Axial principle: the centrality of theoretical knowledge as the source of innovation and of policy formulation for the society;
>
> 4. Future orientation: the control of technology and technological assessment;
>
> 5. Decision making: the creation of a new 'intellectual technology'.

As with many such 'forecasts', the pace of change has been slower than Daniel Bell expected. However, Bell recognized that his 'forecast' was based as much on hope and desire as on rational projection. In the context of his fifth element, for instance, he added:

> The goal of the new intellectual technology is neither more or less to realize a social alchemist's dream: the dream of 'ordering' the mass of society . . . That this dream – as utopian, in its way, as the dreams of a perfect 'commonwealth' –

---

[7] D. Bell, *The Coming of Post Industrial Society: a Venture in Social Forecasting* (Heinemann, 1974).

has faltered is laid, on the part of its believers, to the known human resistance to rationality.

Post-materialism

From the point of view of the marketer, perhaps the most important predicted change is that from a materialist society to a post-materialist one. Inglehart and Appel[8] explain the driving force behind this:

> Some of the most basic values that motivate the publics of Western societies have been changing gradually but steadily during recent decades. Through a process of intergenerational and population replacement, 'Materialist' values, emphasizing economic and physical security, have been giving way to 'Post-Materialist' values, that place greater emphasis on such goals as self-expression and belonging . . .

Elizabeth Nelson,[9] following a similar post-materialist theme, plots the results from a number of European countries on a multidimensional map (figure 13.1). As she explains:

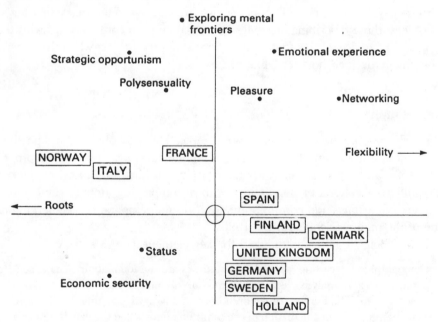

Figure 13.1 Sociocultural positioning of countries.

[8] R. Inglehart and D. Appel, The rise of postmaterialist values and changing religious orientations, gender rules and sexual norms, *International Journal of Public Opinion Research*, vol. 1, no. 1 (1989).

[9] E. Nelson, Marketing in 1992 and beyond, *RSA Journal* (April 1989).

The trends at the top are the dynamic trends which are going to operate increasingly in the 1990s. The ones at the bottom are the older, 1940s and 1950s trends and those in the middle are two of the protest trends of the 1960s and 1970s.

It is only fair to report that 'post-materialism' is taking longer to arrive than its most ardent supporters would wish.

Post-Modernism

This is a development, originating in sociology, which has been embraced by some marketing academics. For many other marketers, though, it may represent a confusing topic – not least because there are so many different definitions; it confuses me, and I am supposed to be an expert in the field! To give a flavour of what is involved, not least of the complexity, Firat et al.[10] say that it 'posits that social experience is an interplay of myths that produce regimes of truth . . .'. They do, however, also stress the important role of marketing in the whole process, concluding that 'Marketing can no longer pretend to be an instrumental discipline that *affects* consumers and society but has to become reflexive and has to be studied as the sociocultural process that *defines* postmodern society.' Indeed, not a few sociologists are starting to use marketing terms – not least those describing life-styles – in an attempt to come to grips with the subject. My advice, at this stage, is to worry about the subject when the experts have finally decided how to define it!

Demography

Some changes are, however, totally predictable. The most obvious, and possibly the most important, are those resulting from demography. The 'baby boom' of the 1960s, and the subsequent dramatic decline in birth rates, have produced very different cohorts of population, with accompanying (totally predictable) changes in earnings and consumption. As a result, demography is emerging as one of the major 'sciences' of the 1990s.

Daniel Bell,[11] again, summarized the key elements:

Demographic forecasting – population statistics are the foundation of most economic and social analysis – is a curious mixture of indeterminacy and a modified closed system. The number of children born in any particular time is subject to changes in values, the fluctuation of economic conditions, and the like. But once a given number are born we can predict from actuarial tables, with a high degree of probability, the numbers that will survive, and the rate of the cohort's diminu-

---

[10] A. Fuat Firat, Nikhilesh Dholakia and Alladi Venkatesh, Marketing in a postmodern world, *European Journal of Marketing*, vol. 29, no. 1 (1995).
[11] Bell, *The Coming of Post Industrial Society: a Venture in Social Forecasting*.

tion over time. From this one can estimate such social needs as education, health and so on . . .

You would be well advised to develop, or acquire, up-to-date demographic analyses relating to your own organization's specific needs. But, as an indication of some of the global trends which should be watched, a particularly interesting table developed by Geoffrey Hobbs[12] is shown (table 13.1). This shows rapidly increasing domination, in population terms, by the less-developed world. The same demographic driver, however, results in ageing populations across almost all Western countries. For example, the US figures are as shown on figure 13.2. The impact of these demographic changes is translated by Hugues de Jouvenel[13] into the related social expenditure needs (figure 13.3).

Table 13.1 Average annual population increases in selected decades (actual and UN medium variant projections)

	1950–59		1980–89		2010–19	
	million	*%*	*million*	*%*	*million*	*%*
More-developed world	11.3	22.5	7.3	9.2	4.5	5.5
Less-developed world	39.0	77.5	72.4	90.8	78.8	94.5
Total	50.3	100.0	79.7	100.0	83.3	100.0

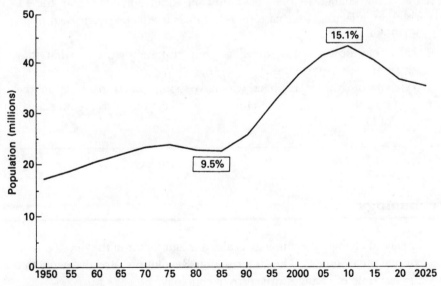

Figure 13.2 US population aged 45–54 years.

[12] G. D. Hobbs, The commercial, social and political implications of future demographic change, Paper presented at 'Exploring the Future: Trends and Discontinuities', Chatham House, London, October 1989.
[13] H. de Jouvenel, *Europe's Aging Population: Trends and Challenges to 2025* (Butterworth, 1989).

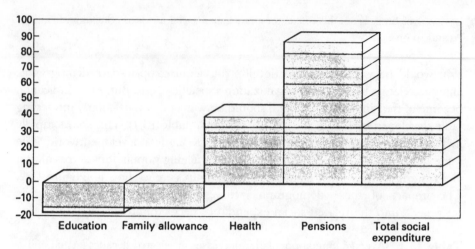

Figure 13.3 Evolution of social expenditure due to demographic factors, 1980–2040 (average of seven OECD countries).

Technology

The impact of changing technology is also a major factor in the development of the external environment. The 'Information Revolution' already mentioned is just one example of changes driven by technology.

The direct impact of new technology on organizations may be obvious. Even then, 'marketing myopia'[14] – where they are so involved in short-term problems

---

[14] T. Levitt, Marketing myopia, *Harvard Business Review* (July–August 1960).

that they cannot see wider perspectives which will determine the future – may blind them to the obvious. Less apparent, though, are the social or 'structural' changes generated by such new technology. The 'Information Revolution' is having its wider impact, for one example, by allowing much smaller organizations to achieve 'economies of scale'. In the larger organizations it is having a different effect by encouraging horizontal communications (via electronic mail) to take over from the traditional vertical (hierarchical) organization; and in the process creating new structures which are close to those of Japanese companies.

Peter Senker identifies four main 'drivers' in the field of technology:

- information technology
- new materials
- environmental issues
- biotechnology

SELF-TEST QUESTION 13.3

What are the main technological changes and 'drivers' facing your customers? What are those which will affect your own organization's products/services and processes?

Economic

Some of the 'theory' of marketing is also shared with other academic disciplines – or at least appears to be! Thus, although the 'market' is clearly at the heart of marketing, it has also become central to economic theory; and, indeed, to the basic philosophies of 'capitalism'. The way in which each of these two disciplines approaches the concept of the market could not, however, be more different.

The population in general, and the business community in particular, have uncritically accepted the basic tenets of economics as the given fundamentals of business life. Put simply, it is widely believed that economic theory accurately describes what happens in the wider business world. As we shall see, the reality (at least as described by marketing theory – and, even more clearly, by marketing practice) is often very different.

In the earliest days there was very little practical difference between economics and any theory of business management – or of 'marketing' as then practised – in a society which had few surpluses to exchange. Adam Smith[15] wrote his

---

[15] A. Smith, *An Inquiry into the Wealth of Nations* (1776).

justifiably renowned *Wealth of Nations* as a treatise to be studied as much by businessmen as by government.

Even in the Victorian period, 'neoclassical' economics, as developed by Alfred Marshall[16] for example, was still spending much of its time trying to describe practical business processes, albeit in more scientific terms. The 'laws of supply and demand', which now lie at the heart of modern micro-economics, represented a practical attempt to describe how prices were set at a time when almost all major markets were commodity markets, and the one variable which the seller could control was price.

At that time the political debate, led by Karl Marx,[17] revolved around the ownership of the capital involved (and hence, most importantly, ownership of the profit), together with the associated division of wealth and income. 'Capitalism' was about just that – about who owned the capital. It too, in its own perverse way, was firmly based on conventional economic theory. Even so, business economics, or the related 'micro-economics', remained closely linked to actual business activities through the first half of the twentieth century.

Economists, however, increasingly focused on the need to create a body of theory which would justify their claim that economics was a legitimate academic discipline. At this time 'macro-economics', that element which described the factors pertaining to the economy as a whole (and was clearly the responsibility of government rather than business), was split off as a separate subject – particularly after the pioneering work of Lord Keynes[18] became generally accepted – to become the part of economics which received the most publicity.

The debate about whether the government should control demand or supply was won, in the 1970s, by the latter view (now espoused by many governments).

Over the same period, the political basis of capitalism has also shifted. As described above, the key factor had been seen to be the ownership of capital; the prime need was for 'profit' to stimulate the 'entrepreneur' to innovate, and improve business efficiency. Indeed, it had previously been widely believed that the strength of the capitalist West derived from that profit motive, which by itself led to enterprises almost automatically being better managed – for the good of all involved.

Unfortunately, by the 1970s, after the development of the global money markets, and after Kenneth Galbraith's very influential teachings,[19] it had become clear that, at least in terms of routine operations, ownership of capital had largely become divorced from the management of most large organizations.

The political theme then became that of the 'market'. The great benefit of 'capitalism', it thus emerged, was that the 'market' was the best (and only

[16] A. Marshall, *Principles of Economics* (1890).

[17] K. Marx, *Das Kapital* (1867).

[18] J. M. Keynes, *The General Theory of Employment, Interest and Money* (1936).

[19] J. K. Galbraith, *The Affluent Society* (Hamish Hamilton, 1958).

'natural') mechanism for allocating resources; for deciding how demand could be met. 'The discipline of the market' or the 'virtue of market-led economies', then became the central theme of 'capitalist' governments; and is now espoused almost as enthusiastically by the governments of the former communist bloc, though their lack of success in gaining all the benefits claimed for it, and the pain involved in its implementation, has now caused some disillusionment. Social democracy, often as yet unspecified, has replaced pure market economies in many of these countries.

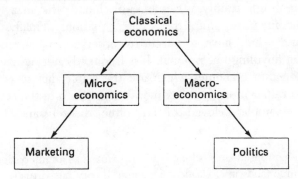

Micro-economics and marketing

Modern micro-economics experiences no theoretical problem in describing the activities of the *'perfect firm'*. This 'ideal' organization is involved in perfect competition, where price is the one dominant factor (and this, above all, is the element manipulated in the many economic equations which are used to describe that firm). All decisions are taken rationally, based upon maximization of monetary outcomes (profit), where all the relationships are exactly known and can be plotted upon definitive graphs.

Even here, R. H. Coase[20] points out in connection with commodity exchanges and stock markets:

> It is not without significance that these exchanges, often used by economists as examples of a perfect market and perfect competition, are markets which are highly regulated (and this quite apart from any government regulation that there may be). It suggests, I think correctly, that for anything approaching perfect competition to exist, an intricate system of rules and regulations would normally be needed . . .

This *transaction cost* approach explores the relationships between economic theory and business management, by looking at the difference in 'transaction costs' between the alternatives considered, as the reason for the logical choice made.

[20] R. H. Coase, *The Firm, the Market and the Law* (University of Chicago Press, 1988).

This field of theory has, in particular, concentrated upon business structure – including the 'make' or 'buy in' decision. Here it argues, with some success, that the firm's decision as to whether to 'make' a component itself or buy it from a supplier is (or at least should be) taken on 'cost' grounds (though the definition of 'cost' here is more complex than normal).

Whatever the approach, micro-economics finds considerable difficulty in dealing with '*imperfect competition*', since no generally agreed model for representing this state of affairs has yet emerged. Worst of all, particularly in the current climate of uncertainty, it cannot easily handle the 'fuzzy' relationships which do not fit neatly into the exact equations. Finally, as Kenneth Galbraith[21] and others have so succinctly observed, management decision-making is often anything but rational. It is frequently not designed to achieve the simple monetary outcomes which are the staple diet of economics, but instead reflects rather more complex motivations. Even in the context of small business, the example beloved of economic theoreticians, Colin Gray[22] observes:

> Although the entrepreneur has long been recognized as an interesting character in the economic landscape, classical economic theory has virtually ignored the importance of the owner-manager's personality on the firm's economic behaviour. Indeed . . . economic 'agents' or 'actors' are treated in classical economics as abstractions rather than individuals.

Marketing, which has grown as a business function over this period (while economics has waned, in terms of its comparable use as a business management tool), thrives on precisely these elements, which are the stuff of real business life. Thus, the aim of every brand manager is to make competition ever *more* imperfect (aiming for the 'ideal' brand which holds a monopoly over its customers, who will stridently demand Carlsberg beer and reject any alternatives). In this environment the 'intangible' (and often seemingly irrational) needs and wants of the customer predominate. The tools of marketing are frequently the 'creative' tools which address the 'fuzzy' areas of formulating the most attractive product or service, and of developing the most effective promotions. Having to compete on price, as the micro-economists would ideally wish for, is usually seen as defeat by such marketers.

Thus, there are many disadvantages to adopting the pure economic viewpoint. On the other hand, there still remain some clear advantages to investigating such an economic perspective. In particular, economics has benefited from almost a century of concentrated academic activity; developing a rigorous, logical, framework. It is the rigidity of thinking imposed by this framework which has often now detached it from real life. But the very strength of this

[21] J. K. Galbraith, *The New Industrial State* (1967).
[22] C. Gray, The entrepreneur's self concept and economic theory (Open Business School Working Paper, March 1990).

body of academic theory means that economics can offer a useful reference framework with which to compare many marketing decisions.

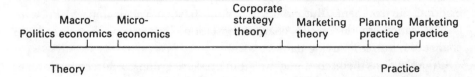

ACTIVITY 13.1

This 'activity' is a repeat of that included in the first chapter. Again, I will test your appreciation of the relationship between marketing and economics. The question to be answered (once more, I should add, without a great deal of research) is: how would *you* define 'the discipline of the market'?

Is it something remote and impersonal, which does not directly affect your life; one of those grand phrases which you read in the newspapers, but which seem to have no bearing on everyday life? Or do you automatically think of a political explanation, in terms perhaps of the traditional confrontation between right and left? Or do you think of economics – and, possibly, rather esoteric theory? Or is it something which impacts *directly* upon your business life?

SELF-TEST QUESTION 13.4

What are the main economic forces facing your customers? What are those which will affect your organization's products/services and ways of doing business?

Political

The boundaries within which organizations can operate are frequently set by legislation – from the ingredients they can legally put into their products to the buildings that their employees are allowed to work in. Indeed, our research[23]

---

[23] D. Mercer, research to be published.

Sociocultural

Technological

Economic

Political

shows that 'regulation' is generally seen to be the most important element deciding the long-term future of organizations – to the extent that more than half of them report this as the single most important such element affecting their external environment. But political actions have a wider impact. Pressure groups campaign directly to change legislation, but also work indirectly to change the public's buying habits.

Organizations themselves may well join pressure groups, to force government to protect their entrenched positions. Such groups are often very successful, to the extent that, for example, the UK's Ministry of Agriculture, which is, as part of its role, supposed to look after consumers' interests, has been accused of being simply the mouthpiece of the farming industry.

It might be thought that only the larger organizations are the direct targets of pressure groups or have the resources to be involved in pressure groups themselves; but it is just as important that the smaller organizations understand the political machinations which are taking place around them, and which have a major, albeit relatively unseen, impact.

On the other hand, there may be stronger forces at work. The Strategic Planning Society,[24] for instance, reported that:

> People are increasingly questioning the relevance of many established institutions. Some examples:
>
>> antipathy towards political parties
>> decline in organized religion
>> decline in trade union membership
>> an overriding concern by the business community that education lacks employment and social dimensions . . .

In the context of the US political scene, Fahey and Narayman[25] identified a number of significant political changes:

> Rise in the number of interest groups . . . there is a group for every cause . . .

> Rise in the activism of interest groups . . . many groups are expert at getting access to the media . . .

> Escalation of single interest groups . . . many of the interest groups that have appeared on the political horizon in the last two decades are dedicated to a single issue or cause . . . These groups are not easily distracted from their goals . . .

> Rise in the diversity of issues in the political arena . . . an increasingly broader array of issues now find their way into the political process . . .

> More intensive and protracted political conflict . . . many more conflicts among more groups now dot the landscape . . .

---

[24] D. Skyrme, The social environment, *Business Futures*, ed. R. Whaley (Strategic Planning Society, 1988).
[25] Fahey and Narayman, *Macroenvironmental Analysis for Strategic Management*.

Greater potential for interest groups to affect the political process . . . It is increasingly easy for interest groups to impact the political system . . .

Defending an organization against pressure groups requires skill and tact. Most important of all, it requires a sound understanding of their viewpoint; and, to be most effective, as sympathetic an approach to them as possible. It is rarely possible to defeat such groups head-on without incurring heavy costs, but it may be much more realistic to divert them – to solutions which are attractive to them, and are also preferable to your own organization.

At the other end of the spectrum, in using membership of a pressure group (an industry association, say) to gain advantage, skill is once again needed; to steer them in the direction which is advantageous to the organization. A discussion of techniques which might be used to handle some of these activities is included in the section on 'Public relations' in chapter 10.

Law

Most aspects of marketing transactions will be covered by one or other form of legislation, not least that of contract law. The marketing manager or sales manager, then, must be well aware of those aspects that most directly affect them; and this will vary from industry to industry, and from country to country. The chemicals industry, for instance, is driven by legislation on safety, whereas financial services providers in the UK look to the Financial Services Act. Most managers, however, should at least understand exactly what their own contract means; and, even more importantly, what the implications are when others insist that their own contractual terms are followed instead.

The laws which affect your business need to be handled expertly, by specialists, for two main reasons:

- specificity – there is a vast array of laws, only some of which affect individual industries or organizations in specific countries
- currency – more importantly, laws change, often quite rapidly

The recent world-wide move to 'deregulation', for example, has had major implications for organizations in areas as diverse as financial services and airline operation – both of which have seen, as a result, a significant number of their members go to the wall. Make sure that you invest in the best possible legal advice.

Consumerism

The pressure group which has had the most direct impact on organizations in recent years has been that of the consumer movement, to which can now be added the environmental lobby and the green movement. The motivation of these movements has been sincere, no matter how annoying they may have been to the producers that they have targeted. They have aimed to benefit the consumer – high ideals, which are in stark contrast with those of some of the rather more self-interested industrial pressure groups.

The views held by these consumerist groups are often closer to those of the average consumer than those of the supplier. What they urge often makes very good marketing sense; and their views are often a sound guide to what future legislation may bring. In this vein, Wills et al.[26] suggest that recognition of consumer rights (as shown in figure 13.4) would ensure that a more satisfactory relationship would be built up between organization and customer.

Multiple Publics

A concept which has recently emerged is that there are a number of different groups which can claim an interest or 'stake'. Gareth Morgan[27] actually refers to them as 'multiple stakeholders' in the organization. Using a now more usual terminology, Lusch and Lusch[28] define the 'public' of an organization as 'any group which has an actual or potential interest or impact on an organization's ability to achieve its objectives'. They also identify a number of major 'publics':

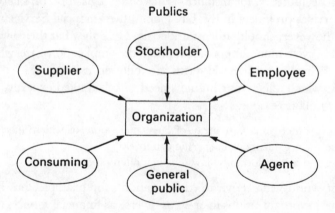

To this list Kotler[29] adds some 'important pressure groups' – citizen action publics, local publics and government publics – together with the related media publics.

Traditionally, especially in the view of economists, only the owners (the 'stockholders' in the above list) have been legitimately entitled to an interest

[26] G. Wills, S. H. Kennedy, J. Cheese and A. Rushton, *Maximising Marketing Effectiveness* (MCB University Press, 1989).
[27] G. Morgan, *Riding the Waves of Change* (Jossey-Bass, 1988).
[28] R. F. Lusch and V. N. Lusch, *Principles of Marketing* (Kent Publishing, 1987).
[29] P. Kotler, *Marketing Management* (Prentice-Hall, 7th edn, 1991).

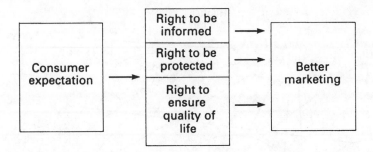

Figure 13.4 Consumerism's way to better marketing.

in what the organization does. More recently it has been recognized that employees' interests should also be taken into account.

Mergers and Acquisitions

The power of the financial stakeholders should not, however, be underestimated. It is often seen in its most active form (at least by the defenders) when acquisitions or mergers take place (not infrequently on an 'unfriendly' basis). The rationale for mergers and acquisitions is not always financial. It is, indeed, often for reasons related to marketing; in the diplomatic terms which accompany such manoeuvres, 'to obtain some synergy from complementary marketing assets', or in more forthright terms, 'to try and increase monopolistic control over customers'.

Pfeffer and Salancik[30] describe this in terms of 'controlling interdependence':

> We argue that merger is a mechanism used by organizations to restructure their environmental interdependence in order to stabilize critical exchanges . . . There are alternative theories of merger, including those that hypothesize that mergers are undertaken to increase profits or to achieve economies of scale . . . the available data do not support these other two interpretations . . .

Perhaps this effect is even more apparent in the strategic 'alliances' between various organizations, which do not result in any form of shared ownership, but which all the same result in formal links between them (usually in the guise of licensing, joint ventures or co-marketing). Devlin and Bleackley,[31] for instance, illustrate the complex web of alliances in the telecommunications industry (figure 13.5).

---

[30] Pfeffer and Salancik, *The External Control of Organizations: A Resource Dependence Perspective.*
[31] G. Devlin and M. Bleackley, Strategic alliances: guidelines for success, *Long Range Planning*, vol. 21, no. 5 (1988).

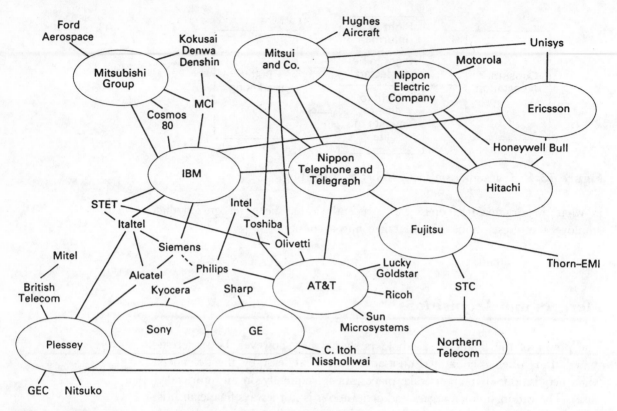

Figure 13.5 Alliances in the telecommunications industry.

It is argued by some[32] that 'networks' of such alliances will become even more important in the future; co-operation rather than competition may bring the greatest rewards!

Perhaps the best advice is to know your competitors (in the broadest sense), since this is frequently the direction from which such moves emerge.

SELF-TEST QUESTION 13.5

What pressure groups are attempting to influence the future of your organization? How? What problems and what opportunities do they pose?

On the other hand, to what pressure groups does your organization belong in order to further its various causes? How effective are they?

[32] Nigel F. Piercy and David W. Cravens, The network paradigm and the marketing organisation, *European Journal of Marketing*, vol. 29, no. 3 (1995).

> What regulation, and legislation, critically controls your organization's activities? How is it likely to change? How does consumerism affect this?
>
> To what publics and stakeholders is your organization generally answerable? What are their needs? Are these in conflict? How may any conflict be resolved?
>
> How exposed is your organization to merger and acquisition activity? How does it, or will it, defend itself against this?

Environmental Analysis ('Scanning')

The first step in addressing the wider, 'external' environment is that of discovering what threats and opportunities it holds for the organization. This is environmental analysis. The steps in this process are illustrated by Johnson and Scholes[33] (figure 13.6). The heart of this process has been called *scanning*. This is

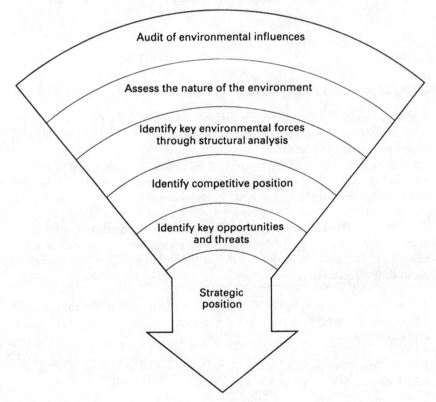

Figure 13.6   Steps in environmental analysis.

[33] G. Johnson and K. Scholes, *Exploring Corporate Strategy* (Prentice-Hall, 2nd edn, 1988).

a term which is much used by marketing experts, but which has been rarely defined – and even less frequently employed in practice.

'Scanning' is a very wide-ranging activity. In its broadest sense it encompasses all those activities which the organization uses, formally and informally, to keep abreast of those changes in the external environment which will affect its future. At its widest it can include all the factual (news and documentary) material to be seen on television or read in the newspapers and periodicals! Here the simplest advice must be to maintain the maximum exposure to the widest range of these media; certainly not relying on just one newspaper (even the *Wall Street Journal* or the *Financial Times*), which will almost inevitably be biased in one way or another, but taking a balanced range of these.

Some of the activities which need to be considered include the following.

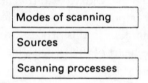

Modes of scanning

Sources

Scanning processes

Modes of Scanning

Francis Joseph Aguilar[34] distinguishes four modes of scanning:

Undirected Viewing.   This scanning is defined as general exposure to information where the viewer has no specific purpose in mind with the possible exception of exploration. This mode is characterized by the viewer's general unawareness as to what issues might be raised. The sources of information are many and varied, the amounts are relatively great, and the screening is generally coarse . . . alerting the businessman to the fact that *something* has changed . . .

Conditioned Viewing. This scanning is defined as directed exposure, not involving active search scanning, to a more or less clearly identified area or type of information . . . the viewer is sensitive to the particular kinds of data and is ready to assess their significance . . .

Informal Search. This scanning is defined as a relatively limited and unstructured effort to obtain specific information for a specific purpose . . . the information is actively sought.

Formal Search. This scanning refers to a deliberate effort . . . to seek specific information . . .

[34] F. J. Aguilar, *Scanning the Business Environment* (Macmillan, 1967).

He goes on to add the warning that:

> Scanning is costly; information is boundless. In practice an organization can attend to only a small fraction of the information that keeps pouring in upon it from its environment. The rules of scanning must be framed with reference to the economics of this activity, and costs must be weighed against benefits.

Of these processes it is the first, 'undirected viewing', which potentially represents the major expenditure of resource, but also the most important benefits in terms of long-term survival (although it is also the most neglected by many organizations).

Sources

Unfortunately, undirected viewing is the most difficult to control. Fahey and Narayman[35] describe its complexity and inherent difficulties:

> Scanning is the *most ill-structured* and ambiguous environmental analysis activity. The potentially relevant data are essentially unlimited. The data are inherently scattered, vague, and imprecise, and data sources are many and varied. Moreover, a common feature of scanning is that *early signals* show up in unexpected places. Thus, *the purview of the search must be broad*, but no guidelines exist as to where the search should be focused. In short, the noise level in scanning is likely to be high.

Even on a limited scale, however, these resource demands imply the necessity of a team approach. One of the most interesting suggestions for handling this came from an organization which asked *all* its employees to clip *any* news item they felt might be relevant to the future of the organization. All of these clippings were then 'scanned' by the environmental analysis group. When a pattern emerged, of a phenomenon being reported across a number of such sources, it was reasoned that these particular 'weak signals' possibly indicated an important underlying trend, and it was thereafter tracked in more detail.

John Naisbitt[36] extends the scope of the analysis, with his statement, 'The most reliable way to anticipate the future is by understanding.' He also puts the process of scanning the media into a more 'academic', historical context:

> We learn about this society through a method called 'content analysis', which has its roots in World War II. During that war intelligence experts sought to find a method for obtaining the kinds of information on enemy nations that public opinion polls would have normally provided. Under the leadership of Paul Lazarfel and Harold Lasswell . . . it was decided we would do an analysis of the content of the German newspapers . . . Although this method of monitoring

---

[35] Fahey and Narayman, *Macroenvironmental Analysis for Strategic Management.*
[36] Naisbitt, *Megatrends: Ten New Directions Transforming our Lives.*

public behaviour and events continues to be the choice of the intelligence community – the United States annually spends millions of dollars doing newspaper content analysis in various parts of the world – it has rarely been employed commercially.

He adds that the greatest strength of such analysis comes about because:

> For economic reasons the amount of space devoted to news in a newspaper does not change significantly over time. So, when something new is introduced something else or a combination of things must be omitted. The news-reporting process is a forced choice in a closed system. In this forced-choice situation, societies add new preoccupations and forget old ones. In keeping track of the ones that are added and the ones that are given up, we are in a sense measuring the changing *share of the market* that competing societal concerns demand.

He is probably correct in assuming that this degree of sophistication is employed nowhere outside of the intelligence services, but scanning might include the use of regular opinion surveys (most probably shared 'omnibus' surveys). Another approach is to take regular reports from consultancies which specialize in this field, such as the Henley Centre for Forecasting. An active industry association might also provide good support.

| Modes of scanning |
| Sources |
| Scanning processes |

Scanning processes

Continuous scanning, probably mainly of the mass media, is thus one of the most important, externally oriented, activities undertaken by any organization. However, John Diffenbach[37] found (from a 1977 survey of 66 firms, from the Fortune 500, replying to his questionnaire) that, at least in these larger corporations, the users of environmental analysis saw their activities in terms of more formal processes (table 13.2).

Perhaps the most important ingredient, however, is an *attitude*, particularly on the part of the management most directly involved. Douglas Brownlie,[38] again, suggests:

> Management attitudes have a vital role to play in creating an organizational climate that enables the firm, not only to operate what should in effect be an *open window of perception* on the past, present and prospective business scene, but also to act upon the insight it provides.

Possibly the simplest, and best, advice is to cultivate a deep, on-going, curiosity about that external world; coupled with an ability to recognize which

[37] J. Diffenbach, Corporate environmental analysis in large US corporations, *Long Range Planning*, vol. 16, no. 3 (1983).
[38] Brownlie, Environmental analysis.

Table 13.2 Use of environmental analysis techniques by large industrial corporations

Technique	Percentage of companies reporting use of techniques
Expert opinion	86
Trend extrapolation	83
Alternate scenarios	68
Single scenarios	55
Simulation models	55
Brainstorming	45
Causal models	32
Delphi projections	29
Cross-impact analysis	27
Input–output analysis	26
Exponential forecasting	21
Signal monitoring	12
Relevance trees	6
Morphological analysis	5

Percentages are based on the responses of the 66 firms that reported having environmental analysis activities.

signals, from amongst the mass of data which every new day brings, are relevant – and important – to the future of the organization. This philosophy should ideally be shared by others in your organization because, as a survey by Francis Joseph Aguilar[39] showed, 23 per cent of the information about the external environment was gained from subordinates (whereas superiors and meetings only provided 9 per cent).

An especially useful device for stimulating debate about the external environment, as well as bringing together existing knowledge, is the use of scenario planning; in which the group of participants, from across the organization, identify the forces for change; and group them into two alternative scenarios of the future.[40]

The ultimate incentive for investing the necessary time and resources in these processes is a realization of just how important these activities may be to preserving the long-term future of the organization.

[39] Aguilar, *Scanning the Business Environment*.
[40] David Mercer, Simpler scenarios, *Management Decision* (June 1995).

Weak Signals

There has been a considerable amount of largely academic discussion about 'weak signals', small pieces of information that signal important changes which are as yet unrecognized. The comment has concentrated upon retrospective analysis. Thus, for example, the 'signals' that Japanese manufacturers were coming to dominate certain industries (the motorcycle industry, for instance) are, once you look for them, quite obvious; and yet they were totally overlooked by the existing suppliers in these markets.

The problem, which most of these academics tend not to address, is that while it is easy to see these patterns with the benefit of hindsight, it proves very difficult indeed to detect them in advance.

Joseph Martino[41] suggests that the key is to look for 'patterns' (a *sequence* of signals). Two errors can be made. The first, and most likely, is to miss the signals altogether. The second, at the opposite extreme, is to find a pattern which is not really there: 'The human mind has an amazing facility for finding patterns in what is really nothing but random noise.' In the field of business, he suggests that the movements of key experts or management (or changes in management structure) may offer a useful, early, insight into competitive developments at least.

Joseph Martino also suggests that one way of trapping weak signals is to set 'thresholds' (for instance, that a senior politician has to become involved with an issue or that a journal considers it worth an editorial comment), above which signals are then tracked. It has to be recognized, however, that setting any such 'thresholds' requires considerable expertise.

Perhaps the most important advice, all too often neglected in practice, is that the suspected weak signals *must* then be tracked.

SELF-TEST QUESTION 13.6

What 'scanning' does your organization systematically undertake? If (as is likely) the answer is 'none', why not?

What 'scanning' does it undertake informally? What is it missing? What has it missed in the past?

What 'weak signals' can you detect in your current environment, in terms of factors which will significantly affect your organization? What should be done about these?

---

[41] J. Martino, *Technological Forecasting for Decisionmaking* (American Elsevier Publishing Company, 1972).

SELF-TEST QUESTION 13.7

?

In overall terms, which of the four main external factors (sociocultural, technological, economic and political) have the most impact on your organization? How does your organization react?

Competition

Competition is a major factor in most markets, and hence in most marketing activities. As was pointed out in chapter 1, 'competition' is at the centre of the Japanese definition of marketing. Even in the West it is a major determinant of product (and service) sales performance. The marketer must know, therefore, what his offering's relative performance is – on all fronts.

Led by Michael Porter,[42] the marketing developments of the 1980s (and indeed those of overall corporate strategy) were dominated by competitive policy. This focus remedied the previous neglect of the subject; but there has been a degree of over-reaction, to the extent that for some companies competitive policy is now seen as more important than all other aspects of marketing – including the customer.

The Industry

The first level of understanding of the competitive environment is that of the 'industry' (in its broadest sense, be it frozen foods or health service provision) within which the organization operates. The industry is defined as a group of firms (or organizations) which offer products (or services) which are near substitutes for each other: in economic terms, these 'products' have a 'high cross-elasticity of demand'.

The 'character' of that industry will often largely determine the competitive activities taking place within it, and the profits of most of the participants. Some of the factors which may contribute to this overall 'character' are shown on the next page. This appears to be a formidable list, but not all of the factors apply equally to all industries. In any case, you will see that many of these factors behave in exactly the way that you might expect, and so it may be a distillation of common sense. It is important to consider the alternatives, for it is too easy to overlook one when you think you have discovered why your profits are low.

[42] M. E. Porter, *Competitive Strategy* (Free Press, 1980).

Size of market
Number or organizations
Concentration or fragmentation

Product differentiation
Economies of scale
Investment and legislative barriers
Overcapacity

Age of market
Rate of change
Susceptibility to external factors

Size of market.   The larger the market the more attractive it will generally be to new entrants, and the more important it may become. On the other hand, the larger the market the more likely it will be that it will be segmented. This will allow 'niche' marketing, thus reducing competition.

Number of organizations competing and concentration of business.   It might seem that the greater the number of organizations in a market the more competitive it might be, and this is generally true – if the brands are of roughly the same size. But the level of competition may also be related to the pattern of concentration of the overall business into the hands of the major players; clearly, a monopoly or oligopoly will significantly reduce competitive forces. The most stable, and profitable, market (apart from a pure monopoly) is usually that with one or two dominant brands and a few smaller brands:[43] that is, imperfect, or monopolistic, competition. If, on the other hand, the comparable number of brands, say four or five, are all of the same size, then the market may be the most viciously competitive that there is.

Product differentiation
Economies of scale
Investment and legislative barriers
Overcapacity

Product differentiation.   The most sophisticated marketers will aim to differentiate their product or service from the others in the market. This may be achieved by unique features, or it may simply be achieved by strong branding such as Heinz has used to hold its position in the baked beans market. In general, the more that products or services are differentiated, the less direct the competition will be.

Economies of scale and investment barriers.   It is often considered that economies of scale are the main features of any market. The theory is that the greater the economies of scale,

[43] David Mercer, A two decade test of product life cycle theory, *British Journal of Management*, vol. 4 (1993).

the greater will be the benefits accruing to those with large shares of the market; and hence the greater the competition to achieve such larger shares. Economies of scale can come about because larger plants are more efficient to run, and cost relatively less per unit of output to build. They may come about because there are overhead costs which cannot be avoided, even by the smaller organizations, but which can be spread over larger volumes by the bigger players. They may also come about because of 'learning effects', in this case related to accumulated volume; the more that is produced the more the manufacturer learns – finding ever more efficient methods of production. All of these effects tend to increase competition, by offering incentives to 'buy' market share in order to become the lowest-cost producer. On the other hand, they also produce significant barriers against new entrants to the market. The higher the initial investment, the more difficult it is to justify an investment in a new entry. But such economies of scale do not always last for ever, particularly in view of the new computer-based manufacturing technologies; and the increasing move in many markets to offer wider choice to consumers. On the other hand, the evidence[44] – encapsulated in the Rule of 123 – seems to show that a clear brand leader (in most consumer goods markets at least) holds a significant advantage over the other brands; typically holding twice the share of the second brand, and three times that of the third – and able to employ marketing activities that enjoy substantial economies of scale.

Legislative barriers.   It has long been the case that sitting tenants in large markets have managed to persuade government, paradoxically often as a response to complaints about cartels, to enact legislation to govern the competitive behaviour of the main players – even if that was against the intention of the original government intervention. Pressure groups or lobbies that are used to redirect this process can often offer the most profitable form of investment, and can erect near impenetrable entry barriers. This is perhaps most obvious in the professions, but it also applies, for example, to the suppliers to the defence industry and to the airline market in Europe.

Control of distribution channels.   If the distribution channels can be denied to competitors, then competition can be limited. It is rare for single products to achieve this, although the brewers and the oil companies, with their 'tied' outlets, have achieved something along these lines. Supermarket chains, however, will often only stock the two leading brands – thus effectively limiting competition. This is a particularly important, but often overlooked, barrier to the development of minor (and especially, new) brands.

Overcapacity.   Perhaps the most sensitive indicator of price competition is the degree of overcapacity. Beware those markets, particularly those with economies of scale, where there is a significant amount of spare capacity. You can be sure that everyone will be focusing on sales (and hence production) levels, almost regardless of price; and that almost inevitably leads to low, commodity-based, prices.

Age of market
Rate of change
Susceptibility to external factors

---

[44] David Mercer, Death of the life cycle, *ADMAP* (September 1993).

Age of market and rate of change. Clearly, the dynamics of a market will have an impact on the players within it. According to life-cycle theory the older markets should be more competitive, as growth slows down and the competitors look for growth at the expense of each other. But the evidence[45] suggests that this has not happened in FMCG markets; even though, according to most theories, these should have been most susceptible.

Competitive history. As this last factor suggests, in most stable markets the best indicator is what has happened before. The previous reactions of competitors will to a large extent determine what the new competitive moves will be, particularly in terms of reactions to new entrants. If existing brands have shown that they will react strongly, by defending their position with aggressive promotion and pricing, then new entrants may be deterred. Instability may be created, however, if the organizations in the market differ in their structures, goals and cultures, and hence cannot easily 'read' what the intentions of their competitors are. This 'inscrutability' may have helped Japanese entrants to destabilize some markets, to their eventual benefit. Michael Porter[46] suggests that there are good and bad competitors. 'Good' competitors play by the rules that the industry has tacitly recognized; they typically limit price competition, help to expand the industry and do not aim to destroy other competitors. 'Bad' competitors, on the other hand, usually do the opposite; they break the 'rules', 'buy share' (often by starting a price war) and upset the equilibrium. To optimize their results, 'good' competitors should, within the very strict legal guidelines, aim to (co-operatively) constrain the 'bad'.

Susceptibility to external factors. All of the above factors may pale into insignificance if there are key factors outside of the market which determine its future: for example, the oil market was very stable until the 1973 Arab-Israeli war.

Michael Porter[47] more succinctly identifies five key factors engaged in 'extended rivalry' (figure 13.7).

- *Industry competitors* – rivalry amongst existing firms, which is generally considered to be what 'competition' is about.
- *Potential entrants* – the threat from new entrants, which may change the rules of competition, but against which 'entry barriers' can be erected.
- *Suppliers* – the bargaining power of common suppliers, which can change the structure of industries (as OPEC did in the 1970s).
- *Buyers* – the bargaining power of the customers (for example, the retailers control the destiny of many suppliers of consumer goods).
- *Substitutes* – the threat of substitute products or services, which may destroy the whole industry, not just the existing competitive structure (as the transistor did to the old-fashioned valve).

'Substitutes' are a particularly important element of competition, since they normally appear from directions where a challenge is not expected (and from

---

[45] David Mercer, A two decade test of product life cycle theory.

[46] Porter, *Competitive Strategy*.

[47] Porter, *Competitive Strategy*.

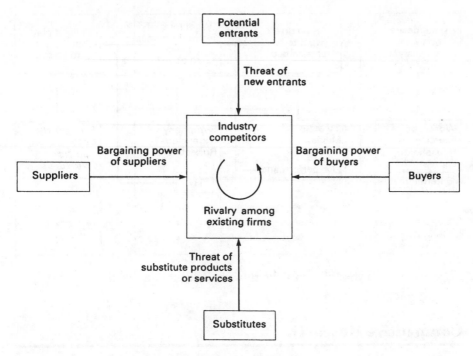

Figure 13.7 Forces driving industry competition.

which the organization is, accordingly, most vulnerable). Perhaps the most famous example is that of the British motorcycle industry, which was destroyed not by internal competition but by the Japanese, to whose growing experience the UK manufacturers had steadfastly remained blind.

In the case of service organizations, the choices offered by substitutes may sometimes represent the main competition. Kotler and Andreasen[48] illustrate the chain of 'competitive' decisions facing the audience which eventually arrives in a theatre (figure 13.8).

SELF-TEST QUESTION 13.8

How would you characterize the 'industry' within which your organization operates?

Which of the factors described – economies of scale, positioning, structural, switching costs and political – have a significant impact? What impact do they have? How does your organization allow for this?

---

[48] Kotler and Andreasen, *Strategic Marketing for Nonprofit Organizations.*

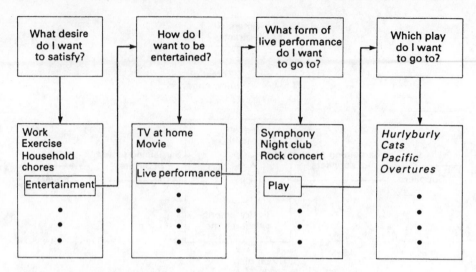

Figure 13.8 Types of competitors facing a legitmate theatre.

Competitive Research

Marketing managers need to be fully aware of all aspects of the competition. They need to know what their competitors' offerings are, what their plans are, and what results they are achieving.

Competitive performance

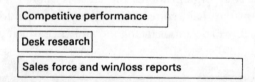

Information may be derived from market research (for example in terms of market shares and customer attitudes) or from articles in the trade or national press. The competitor may be looking for PR, but in the process it may provide you with invaluable information; even if you have to be wary of inflated claims.

It may also come from a source which is often overlooked, the competitor's annual report, which may reveal:

- turnover – how much muscle it really has in the marketplace, and whether its sales are growing
- cost structure – its variable costs and overheads, and where it lies in terms of economies of scale

- investment – what investments have been made, which may indicate new products or lower cost production
- financial stability – borrowings and their gearing, and its overall liquidity
- profit – in terms of percentage of revenue, margin and percentage return on investment (ROI), and whether this allows the company to invest in new developments.

Desk research

The prime source of competitive intelligence is, once more, desk research. But how reliable is it?

Apart from an analysis of the logistical strengths and weaknesses of each competitor, possibly the most important aspect of such research is to find out how each competitor thinks. In this context there are many analogies with warfare: the best generals spend a great deal of their time trying to understand their opponents; so that they may be able to predict how they will respond to each new situation. Some of the information may be gleaned from published material:

- objectives – the goals which the competitor's management, or its owners, have set
- culture and structure – how it is organized, both in terms of its management and logistical structures, and its overall philosophy
- industry view – how it assesses what is happening around it, and what assumptions it makes, about your activities for example

This information may be supplemented in the short term by what Michael Porter[49] calls 'signals' from competitors, statements of intent. These may include advance notice of new products or the actual launch of 'fighting products', designed specifically to undercut competitors.

Perhaps the best approach is to try as far as possible to compile something approximating to a marketing audit for each main competitor (perhaps with the aid of SWOT analysis, which will be described in the final chapter).

Salesforce and win/loss reports

In general, one of the best sources of competitive information is the salesforce. They will have regular contact with customers who, in turn, will of course have regular contact with the competitor's sales personnel.

In this context there are two requirements for sound marketing practice. The first is that you must persuade the salesforce to pass this information to you immediately; not a trivial task, because sales personnel are notoriously loath to

---

[49] Porter, *Competitive Strategy*.

prepare reports. The second is to recognize that your own indiscretions, made to impress your own salesforce, will inevitably be passed to your competitors.

Where the value of each sale is high, typically in the capital goods sector, one specific piece of information which can be demanded from sales personnel is a report on each win or loss. The sales professional should have a very good idea of why the sale was won or lost, and that information – much of it related to competitive strengths and weaknesses – can be invaluable.

Competitors' Response

Probably the most important, but often neglected, aspect of any such research is to determine how each of the competitors may respond to future changes. There are four main categories of possible response:

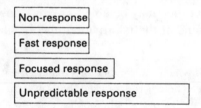

- *Non-response* (or slow response).   This competitor will not respond directly to any changes in the environment, or at least will not do so in the short term. It may be a dominant brand leader, which can afford deliberately to ignore most of the (minor) competitive threats. On the other hand, it may be a competitor in a particularly weak position.
- *Fast response.*   A few organizations, such as Procter & Gamble, have a policy of immediate and substantial response. If this strategy can be resourced it is usually the most effective and the most cost-effective, since the sooner the threat is removed the sooner high profits can be generated again.
- *Focused response.*   Some competitors will only respond to certain types of challenge (typically on price), either refusing to accept or simply not recognizing other forms of challenge (particularly those in the form of 'product' developments).
- *Unpredictable response.*   This is by far the most difficult to deal with.

SELF-TEST QUESTION 13.9

Which are your organization's main competitors? For each of these competitors, summarize (on a separate sheet of your exercise book) its main characteristics in the marketplace:

What is its position in the market (segment and percentage share)?

- What is its performance (turnover and profit)?
- What is its product line?
- What are its strengths?
- What are its weaknesses?
- What is its cost structure? (Does it have high overheads and need to make volume sales?)

Then consider its motivations and the resulting strategies:

- Who are the owners, and what do they want of it (profit or diversification, for example)?
- Is its strategy directed at volume, or profit, or long-term growth?

What key characteristics distinguish each of these organizations from your own, and from each other?

Competitive Strategies

Michael Porter,[50] who is the leading exponent of competitive strategy, states that there are just three 'potentially successful generic strategic approaches to outperforming other firms in an industry'. In figure 13.10, he lists overall cost leadership, differentiation and focus.

The first alternative has come to prominence in recent years. Organizations have invested vast sums to achieve economies of scale. Markets have been expanded to whole continents to support these massive new plants (as has happened in the European car industry). Roberto Buaron,[51] of McKinsey & Co., illustrates these various forms of 'economic leverage', which can be applied at various stages through the business system (figure 13.9).

The second and third alternatives, however, rely on using factors other than price to contain competition. Product differentiation, particularly 'branding', is a key device, since it removes the product from some of the most direct elements of competition.

Segmentation and product positioning, which were discussed in chapter 4, are also particularly effective devices for containing competitive pressure. They allow the marketer to concentrate, in Michael Porter's[52] terminology, to focus

[50] Porter, *Competitive Strategy*.
[51] R. Buaron, How to win the market share game? Try changing the rules, *Management Review* (January 1981).
[52] Porter, *Competitive Strategy*.

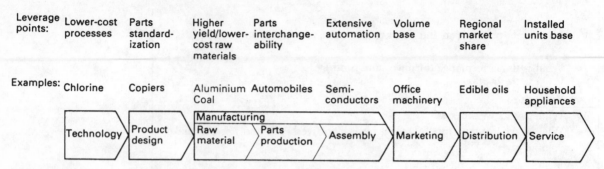

Figure 13.9   Sources of economic leverage in the business system.

his resources to defend his offering within a small segment of the market (where it will have a more dominant position than in the overall market), and to make inroads on the most vulnerable competitive products or services (figure 13.10).

The Power Diamond

Simplifying matters somewhat, but not quite as much as Michael Porter, I would suggest that competitive power can be built on four main fronts – which make up the 'power diamond':

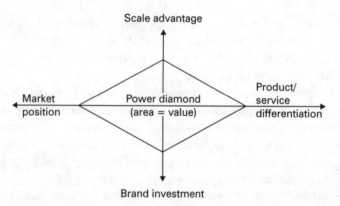

Two of the factors, 'Differentiation' and 'Scale Advantage', are those at the heart of Michael Porter's work, described below. The other two, 'Market Position' and 'Brand Investment' (or, from the other side of the relationship, 'Customer Franchise') are not usually considered in competition theory – though they were explored in considerable detail earlier in this book.

It is the total area between these (which reflects the overall power of the brand), and how the cutting edges (the corners of the diamond) are deployed in practice, which indicate how much competitive leverage the brand may be able to generate.

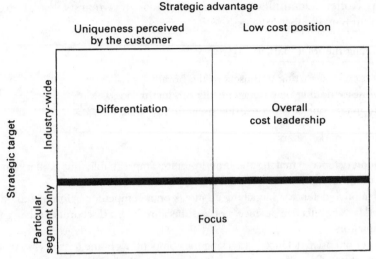

Figure 13.10   Three generic strategies.

Leaders and Followers

As can be seen there is a wide range of competitive techniques. One useful split, however, is that between 'leaders', those products or services that have a substantial market share – typically 50 per cent or more – with a very strong position, and 'followers', those which have minor shares, with marginal positions.

Leaders

In this case, the 'competitive thrust' may not necessarily be the only, or even the main, objective; since leaders stand to gain significantly from market expansion, and their promotional effort will often include elements directed as much to this end as against their competitors. In terms of competitive activity, it is normally expected that companies with major 'brand leaders' will concentrate their effort 'above the line' (on advertising; whereas promotions are shown as 'below the line' on marketing budgets). The reason for this is that, with their large sales, they can easily generate large advertising budgets (a 10 per cent advertising budget on a $20 million brand will produce $2 million of advertising, which will probably dominate advertising in the sector; whereas a comparable 10 per cent cut in price would probably go unnoticed). Their advertising messages may well stress the 'branding' (or strong character) of their offerings, which are likely to be positioned close to the ideal (due to the historical development of the market, where such brands have set the standards); and the messages will probably not be overly competitive.

Philip Kotler[53] identifies two main strategies of a market leader, together with a number of substrategies:

1 Expanding the total market:

- new users – attracting non-users to the brand
- new uses – finding new things for the product to do
- more usage – persuading existing users to buy more

2 Defending market share:

- position defence – making the brand position impregnable (but Kotler also points out that this can lead to 'marketing myopia')
- pre-emptive defence – launching an attack on a competitor before it can be established (a very effective defence, not least because it also discourages other potential competitors)
- counter-offensive defence – attacking the competitor's home territory, so that it has to divert its efforts into protecting its existing products

Expanding market share   As Kotler[54] describes, the Strategic Planning Institute reported (in a study entitled 'Profit Impact of Management Strategies – PIMS') that profitability rises curvilinearly *with market share*; so building market share, even if you are already market leader, can be a very profitable operation (if it can be achieved at an economical cost). It should be noted, however, that other researchers have found other effects (some, indeed, indicating that profit *falls* beyond an optimal level; due to the increased costs of defence).

Conviction marketing   Michael Porter[55] states that: 'Perhaps the single most important concept in planning and executing offensive or defensive competitive moves is the concept of commitment.' He goes on to explain that such commitment can 'deter retaliation', 'deter threatening moves' and 'create trust'. The key element of persuasion is seen to be that the decisions are 'binding and irreversible'.

In other words, by clearly staking out what your position is, you can signal to the opposition exactly what your competitive strategy is; and thus pre-empt moves by them which might destabilize your position or that of the market as a whole.

'Conviction' or 'commitment' marketing, which is described in more detail in chapter 9, is based upon believing in your product or service with such a degree of blinding conviction that the obvious degree of conviction itself becomes the main message. Such conviction marketing, when undertaken by the most powerful marketers, can go much further. It can force the competitors to

---

[53] Kotler, *Marketing Management*.
[54] Kotler, *Marketing Management*.
[55] Porter, *Competitive Strategy*.

fight the battle on ground of your own choosing. At times it may almost seem as if such competitors are mesmerized by the degree of your conviction – if it is strong enough. It is a device normally only available to market leaders; but strong second brands, with aspirations to lead, can also sometimes use it – as Avis has done with its campaigns.

Followers

In these cases, the whole strategy is likely to be fiercely competitive; aiming only to grab the largest share possible of the existing 'cake'. Their main competitive device is likely to be 'below the line' promotion; and, in particular, price competition. The small volume of their business means that they simply cannot generate significant advertising budgets overall, but higher costs (or lower revenue) *per unit* are quite acceptable. Thus a 30 per cent price cut may be seen by the consumer as significant (a similar 30 per cent advertising budget, even on a $1m brand, would generate only $300 000; barely enough for one small, selective national campaign in the press). A more profitable approach, however, is to avoid the main competitors by 'niche marketing' – finding very small segments that are not addressed by the major brands.

On the other hand, Slywotsky and Shapiro[56] suggest that the best approach is to focus on three categories of customer:

1 Customers with low acquisition costs; 'switchables'
2 Customers generating the most return; 'high profit customers'
3 Customers contributing to long-term growth; 'share determiners'

They are less clear, however, as to how these valuable customers can be identified.

Factors affecting 'strong leaders'

Not a few markets are dominated by 'strong leaders'. The Boston Consulting Group[57] claim that, in their experience, 'A stable competitive market never has more than three significant competitors, the largest of which has no more than four times the market share of the smallest.'

Among the strategic implications resulting from this observation, they note:

If there are large numbers of competitors, a shakeout is nearly inevitable . . .

All except the two largest share competitors will be either losers and eventually eliminated or be marginal cash traps . . .

---

[56] Adrian J. Slywotsky and Benson P. Shapiro, Leveraging to beat the odds: the new marketing mind set, *Harvard Business Review* (September–October 1993).
[57] B. D. Henderson, *The Rule of Three and Four* (Perspectives – Boston Consulting Group, 1985).

Anything less than 30 percent of the relevant market or at least half the share of the leader is a high risk position if maintained . . .

The quicker any investment is cashed out or a market position second only to the leader gained, then the lower the risk and the higher the probable return on investment . . .

Our own research[58] shows very much the same pattern, though we have chosen – for the sake of memorability – to encapsulate the relationship in a rather simpler form: **the Rule of 123** – The most competitive markets are typically dominated by 2–3 brands; between them accounting for around 70 per cent of total sales. For maximum stability the "ratio of share should typically be that the **brand leader should hold twice the share of the second and three times that of the third**. The brand leader usually has around 40 per cent of the overall market; and is correspondingly profitable – justifying the investment policies needed to reach this position.

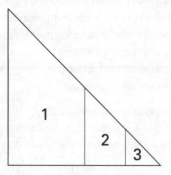

'Followers' beware! The most important message of the Rule of 123 is that brand leaders are heavily entrenched. To dislodge them usually requires a very high level of investment. Hence the great attraction of 'segmentation'; splitting the market into smaller, though viable, pieces where the share can be correspondingly higher, allows a follower in a market to become a leader in the segment.

SELF-TEST QUESTION 13.10

What competitive strategy, or strategies (for different products/services or market segments), does your organization follow?

---

[58] David Mercer, *Death of the product life cycle.*

- Is it a market leader?
- Is it a 'conviction marketer'?
- Is it a follower?
- Is it a niche marketer?
- Does it use price, or differentiation or focus?

Has this strategy been successful? If so, why? If not, why not? Do you think that this is the right strategy? If not, what strategy would you recommend?

SELF-TEST QUESTION 13.11

We now come to your third main piece of work. Using the material you have collected so far (using the desk research techniques described in chapter 3), and the brief analyses you have already undertaken, produce an environmental/competitive report.

At this stage it should only offer a *description* of both the overall environment and, within it, the competitive position (including, in both cases, your organization's own strategies).

The format will depend upon the exact requirements of your organization, but sections that you might like to consider including are:

- The external environment – sociocultural, technological, economic and political
- Summary of the key factors – organizational responses and strategies
- The industry – key characteristics
- Competitive analysis report – for each competitor
- Key competitive strategies – organizational responses and strategies

FURTHER READING

Competitive strategy is a very important aspect of marketing and, in recent years, a considerable amount has been written about it. The two books by Michael Porter (the acknowledged expert), *Competitive Strategy* (The Free Press, 1980) and *Competitive Advantage* (The Free Press, 1985), still offer the best, and most easily understood, coverage of the field. They develop, in considerable depth, the themes which have only been sketched in superficially in this chapter. My only caveat is that you may be so carried away by Porter's enthusiasm for the subject that you too may ignore other aspects of marketing (as did many companies in the 1980s).

In terms of the 'theory' of the environment in general, Gareth Morgan (*Riding the Waves of Change*, Jossey-Bass, 1988) and J. Pfeffer and G. R. Salancik (*The External Control of Organizations*, Harper & Row, 1978) provide stimulating viewpoints; although the latter is considerably more academic, and that much less readable than the former. Igor Ansoff (*Implanting Strategic Management*, Prentice-Hall, 1984) also contributes some interesting comments in the context of corporate strategy.

'Scanning', which is a particularly important topic, was comprehensively covered by Francis Joseph Aguilar (*Scanning the Business Environment*, Macmillan), although the date of publication (1967) may mean that this is more difficult to find. More recently, in 1986, Liam Fahey and V. K. Narayman (*Macroenvironmental Analysis for Strategic Management*, West Publishing) have provided good coverage.

Illustrations of what might be expected to change in the external environment can be found in *Megatrends 2000* by John Naisbitt and Patricia Aburdene (Sidgwik & Jackson, 1990). *The Coming of Post Industrial Society* by Daniel Bell (Heinemann, 1974), although now dated, is also an impressive exploration of the alternatives.

SUMMARY

The wider environment, even that of competitive activity, has only become a feature of marketing theory and teaching within the past decade or so. Although it is an artificial division, and consequently has limitations, the STEP:

| Sociocultural |
| Technological |
| Economic |
| Political |

approach is generally accepted as a framework.

The sociocultural element includes the move to post-industrial society, and within this the major structural changes arising from the IT Revolution. There are, however, changes in social values which may be almost as important – leading to the rise of post-materialism, with less emphasis on consumption. Demographic changes, which are more predictable, are no less significant; for example, the slowing of growth, and consequent ageing, of populations in Western countries.

Technological changes may be particularly important in the areas of information technology, new materials, environmental issues and biotechnology.

The importance of pressure groups, and that of multiple publics (stakeholders), is now slowly being recognized by organizations. Equally, regulation – perhaps driven by consumerism – is a factor of growing importance; although the most immediate threat may come from merger or acquisition activity.

The starting point for dealing with the external environment is environmental analysis (scanning). There is a very wide range of inputs to this process, and a number of modes of dealing with it; including, in theory, those handling weak signals.

Competition is best understood in the context of the industry, and its characteristics, which may include:

Size of market
Number or organizations
Concentration or fragmentation

Product differentiation
Economies of scale
Investment and legislative barriers
Overcapacity

The position relative to other competitors is 'measured' by competitive research, which may include:

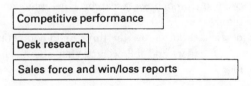

Competitive performance
Desk research
Sales force and win/loss reports

Any competitive strategy needs to take into account the competitors' possible responses:

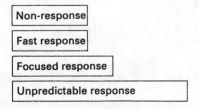

Non-response
Fast response
Focused response
Unpredictable response

Michael Porter identifies three generic strategic approaches; overall cost leadership, differentiation and focus. Others look to another difference:

Philip Kotler suggests a range of military analogies for each of these. For leaders, however, *conviction marketing* may be a significant driver.

REVISION QUESTIONS

1 What are conventionally described as the four main sectors of the external environment? How do these relate to the marketing environment, as well as that of competitors and suppliers?
2 What may be the main technological drivers over the near to medium term? What social changes is the IT Revolution leading to?
3 What may be the major changes in life-style, over the medium term? What demographic changes can already be predicted? What economic drivers may possibly be observed in the shorter term?
4 What are the differences between pressure groups and stakeholders? How may consumerism lead to changes in regulation?
5 Why may mergers and acquisitions be undertaken?
6 What are the modes of, and inputs to, environmental analysis? What are weak signals, and how may they be dealt with?
7 What factors affect an industry's competitive activity? How may economies of scale, and the concentration of business, affect competition?
8 What are the processes of competitive research? How may competitors respond to changes in competition?
9 What, according to Michael Porter, are the three main competitive strategies? How can these be related to leaders and followers? What about military analogies and conviction marketing?

14 Marketing Planning

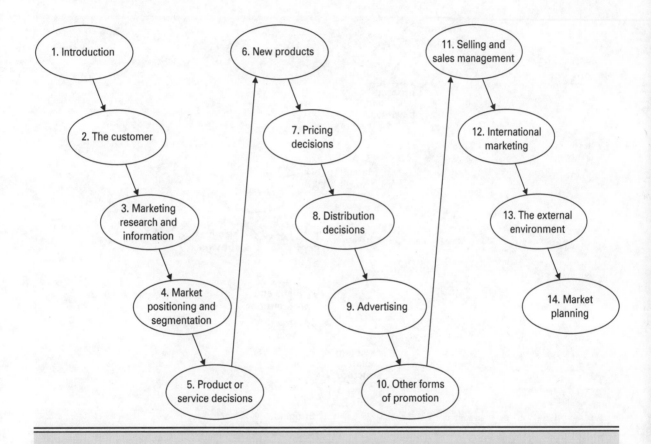

- 1. Introduction
- 2. The customer
- 3. Marketing research and information
- 4. Market positioning and segmentation
- 5. Product or service decisions
- 6. New products
- 7. Pricing decisions
- 8. Distribution decisions
- 9. Advertising
- 10. Other forms of promotion
- 11. Selling and sales management
- 12. International marketing
- 13. The external environment
- 14. Market planning

Introduction

This final chapter brings together the techniques developed in the previous chapters: in theory at least, planning is a central function of marketing.

In the first instance, however, the chapter examines corporate planning, which sets the context for that of marketing. In practice the two are very closely related; and, indeed, much of the theory of corporate strategy is derived from marketing. In truth, the development of the organization's mission and objectives largely determines its marketing strategy. Therefore, the chapter moves from corporate strategic management to strategic marketing, and thence to marketing planning.

Even so, the first formal stage of marketing planning is an extensive audit, to collect all the data needed for the decisions. These are often analysed using the framework of a SWOT (Strengths, Weaknesses, Opportunities, Threats) analysis. Whatever the approach, the outcomes will be the various marketing objectives and strategies. These, in turn, lead to the plans and programmes described in the marketing plan – the structure of which is described. The process of tracking performance against these (targeted) plans is also a final element of the overall planning process.

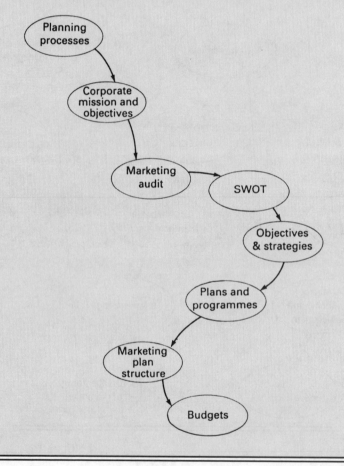

The Marketing Plan

The need for planning is now almost universally accepted by managers.

To the best of your knowledge, which approaches to planning does your organization adopt? How well does it succeed in producing forecasts that turn out to be almost correct?

The use of such plans has a number of benefits, just some of which may be:

> Consistency

> Responsibility

> Communication

> Commitment

- *Consistency.* The individual action plans will, then, be consistent with the overall corporate plan; and with the other departmental/functional plans which should be put in place elsewhere in the organization. They should also be consistent with those of previous years, minimizing the risk of management 'fire-fighting'.
- *Responsibility.* Those who have responsibility for implementing the individual parts of the marketing plan will know what their responsibilities are, and can have their performance monitored against these.
- *Communication.* All those involved in implementing the plans will also know what the overall objectives are, together with the assumptions which lie behind them, and what the context for each of the detailed activities is.
- *Commitment.* Assuming that the plans have been agreed with all those involved in their implementation, as well as with those who will provide the resources, the plans should stimulate a group commitment to their implementation.

On the other hand, Bernard Taylor[1] says:

> Planning is an unnatural process. It is much more fun to *do* something. To quote John Preston of Boston College: The nicest thing about not planning is that failure comes as a complete surprise, and is not preceded by a period of worry and depression.

As Bernard Taylor is one of the leading theorists in this field, he does go on to add an all-important warning:

[1] B. Taylor, Corporate planning for the 1990s: the new frontiers, *Long Range Planning*, vol. 19, no. 6 (1986).

The truth is that planning has failed many times but planning specialists, line managers, consultants and academics have continually modified the process to suit different situations. There is not one system of planning but many systems, not one style but many styles, and a planning process must be tailor-made for a particular firm in a specific set of circumstances.

Plans must be *specific* – to the organization and to its current situation.

This last chapter will, therefore, conclude with an examination of the development of the marketing plan. This brings together all the activities which have been described in the earlier chapters of this book.

SELF-TEST QUESTION 14.2

Does your organization have a formal marketing plan? If not, why not? If so, why? Which of the following reasons – consistency, responsibility, communication and commitment – apply to its use?

The Planning Process

In most organizations 'strategic planning' is an annual process, typically covering just the year ahead. Occasionally, a few organizations may look at a practical plan which stretches three or more years ahead.

To be most effective, the plan has to be formalized, usually in written form, as a formal 'marketing plan'. This is a process which typically follows a number of distinct steps, here illustrated by Malcolm McDonald[2] (figure 14.1). The essence of the process is that it moves from the general to the specific; from the overall objectives of the organization down to the individual action plan for a part of one marketing programme. It is also an iterative process, so that the draft output of each stage is checked to see what impact it has on the earlier stages – and is amended accordingly.

The Corporate Plan

The starting point for the marketing plan, and the context within which it is set, is the corporate plan. In most marketing-oriented organizations the contents of the corporate plan will closely match those of the marketing plan itself; but it

[2] M. H. B. McDonald, *Marketing Plans* (Heinemann, 2nd edn, 1989).

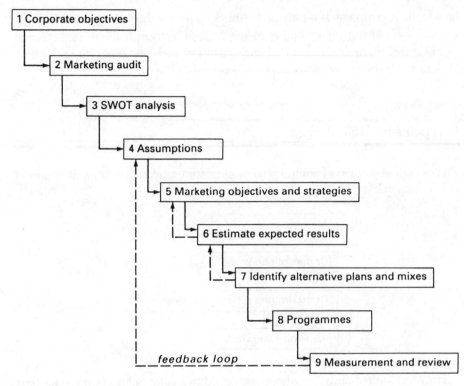

Figure 14.1 The marketing planning process.

will also include the plans for the disposition of the other internal resources of the organization. Thus, the corporate plan is likely to contain three main components:

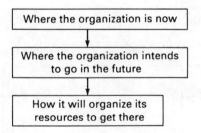

The first category is intimately involved with the customers. In marketing terms, although there are many other factors to take into account, the most important definition of where the company *is* revolves around where it is in the market (and hence where it is with its consumers). The same is largely true of the second stage as well; since, no matter how much its managers may wish otherwise, where the company can realistically expect to go is totally in the hands of its customers. It is only at the third stage that the 4 Ps come into play as vehicles for moving the company to reach its objectives.

There are many recommended approaches to such planning. Philip Kotler,[3] for example, shows the process as in figure 14.2.

Corporate Objectives

The overall objectives of commercial organizations are conventionally supposed to be financial:

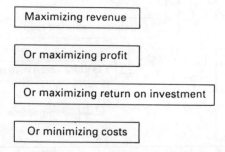

However, other aims are also possible. Many companies choose long-term growth (which may be quite different from revenue maximization in the short term).

Peter Doyle[4] makes a rather different point when he says, 'Earnings per share or ROI measure the *past* performance of the enterprise not its future cash

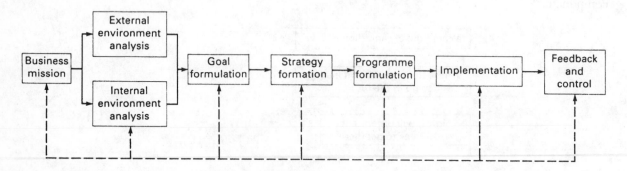

Figure 14.2   The business strategic planning process.

[3] P. Kotler, *Marketing Management* (Prentice-Hall, 7th edn, 1991).
[4] Peter Doyle, Setting business objectives and measuring performance, *Journal of General Management*, vol. 20, no. 2 (Winter 1994).

generating performance. By cutting back on product development and brand support, earnings are boosted for a few years but at the expense of mortgaging the company's future.'

Almost all have an implicit, and very powerful, aim of *survival* (which J. K. Galbraith spelled out so forcefully in his book *The Affluent Society*).[5]

One of the best known 'alternatives', that of 'satisficing' (rather than profit maximization), comes from Herbert Simon:[6]

> In one way or another, they [alternative theories] incorporate the notions of bounded rationality: the need to search for decision alternatives, the replacement of optimization [profit-based objectives] by targets and satisficing [minimal] goals, and mechanisms of learning and adaptation.

Pfeffer and Salancik[7] say, on the basis of considerable research, that:

> We prefer to view organizations as coalitions ... altering their purposes and domains to accommodate new interests, sloughing off parts of themselves to avoid some interests, and when necessary, becoming involved in activities far afield from their stated central purposes. Organizations are social instruments of tremendous power and energy, and the critical issue becomes who will control this energy and for what purpose.

If, however, we accept the traditional assumption, as to the financial basis of the objectives behind the corporate plan, these objectives are ideally meant to be quantified in numerical and, in particular, financial terms.

In the most general terms, though, the 'objectives' behind a strategy address two questions: '*Where* do we want to be?' and '*When* do we expect to be there?'

Objectives for non-profit-making organizations

In the case of non-profit organizations the objectives may be even less clear. Keith Blois[8] suggests five main reasons for the differences from 'commercial' organizations:

1 Ambiguous Goals (more actors and groups of actors are involved)
2 Lack of Agreement in Means–End Relationships (even where there is consensus on the goal there may be disagreement on how to get there)
3 Environmental Turbulence (non-profit organizations seem to be exposed more to turbulence than commercial ones)
4 Unmeasurable Outputs (unfortunately, by definition, non-profit organizations do not have the classically convenient simplicity of 'bottom-line profit')

[5] J. K. Galbraith, *The Affluent Society* (Hamish Hamilton, 1958).
[6] H. A. Simon, Rational decision making in business organizations, *American Economic Review* (September 1979).
[7] J. Pfeffer and G. R. Salancik, *The External Control of Organizations* (Harper & Row, 1978).
[8] K. J. Blois, Managing for non-profit organizations, *The Marketing Book*, ed. M. J. Baker (Heinemann, 1987).

5 The Effects of Management Intervention are Unknown (the lack of precision caused by factors 1–4 is problem enough, but the 'culture' seems to add further barriers to managing these organizations)

Even so, Kotler and Andreasen[9] suggest some possible objectives for such organizations:

Surplus Maximization (equivalent to profit maximization)

Revenue Maximization (as for profit-making organizations)

Usage Maximization (maximizing the numbers of users and their usage)

Usage Targeting (matching the capacity available)

Full Cost Recovery (breaking even)

Partial Cost Recovery (minimizing the subsidy)

Budget Maximization (maximizing what is offered)

Producer Satisfaction Maximization (satisfying the wants of staff)

A final caveat must be that the existence of a clearly defined, and formally stated, 'purpose' may still not explain what the organization's true objectives are. On the basis of his research into US organizations, Charles Warriner[10] makes the generally applicable comment:

> Statements of purpose, thus, must be treated as fictions produced by an organization to account for, explain, or rationalize its existence to particular audiences rather than as valid and reliable indicators of purpose.

It is important that you recognize the complexity which lies behind corporate objectives, and are not seduced by those who would argue that simplicity is the order of the day. Although the problems may have to be artificially simplified, to make them easier to handle, this should not blind you to their true nature. It should also alert you to the fact that, with so many variables which may be periodically in a state of flux, each new situation will be unique; and, despite the fact that rules of thumb will help, *the solutions must be built anew for each problem.*

SELF-TEST QUESTION 14.3

What are the published objectives of your organization? How well do they reflect the real objectives of the management and staff?

---

[9] P. Kotler and A. R. Andreasen, *Strategic Marketing for Nonprofit Organizations* (Prentice-Hall, 1987).

[10] C. K. Warriner, The problem of organizational purpose, *Sociological Quarterly* (1965).

Forecasting

This is the point at which you are likely to enter into the complicated world of forecasting. This can be, these days, a very complex topic. In the next few pages, therefore, I will limit myself just to guiding you through a small number of the most useful, and most practical, techniques. Forecasting can, in general, be roughly divided into two parts:

Short-term forecasting

This is the type of forecasting you will recognize. It is normally based upon a projection of historical trends, usually focused on sales volumes. There are many sophisticated techniques, increasingly using large amounts of computing power, but in essence all of these try to separate out the four main components:

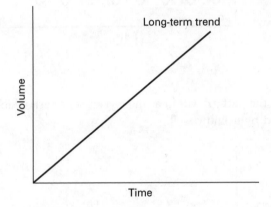

Long-term trends probably represent the most important information you are trying to extract from the mass of data before you.

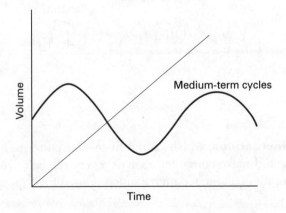

Medium-term cycles are supposed to result from regular economic ups and downs (from boom to bust) which used to be encapsulated in a 5-year 'business cycle', which, unfortunately, became unpredictable in the 1980s. The much quoted 'Kondratieff Cycles' are much longer, if they exist at all, being of the order of 25–50 years; and hence do not normally enter into shorter-term forecasts.

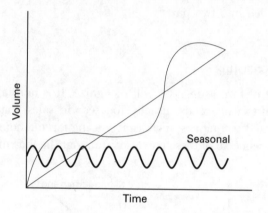

Seasonality is the pattern within a single year, a pattern which most suppliers who are affected by it know well.

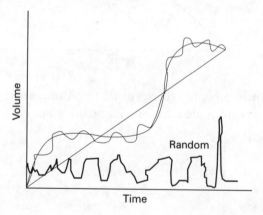

Random fluctuations, which do not fit regular patterns, afflict all products and services, and make computer analysis a very difficult proposition.

The end result of all these patterns superimposed may appear very confusing indeed.

Despite all the sophistication on offer, by far the best advice is to keep it as simple as possible.

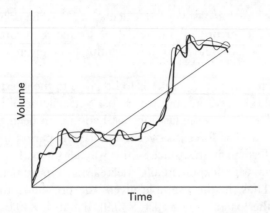

The human eye is much better at resolving the complications shown above than the most powerful computer. Thus, the best approach to forecasting (and certainly the best check on any more sophisticated technique) is 'eyeballing' the sales charts! With some practice you should be able to sort out the main features of what is happening – and that is better than most computer models achieve.

The evidence is that the sophistication adds little or nothing to the accuracy (though it does to the image of the forecasters, and the prices they charge). Worst of all, such unnecessary complexity hinders your understanding of what is going on under the covers of the computer (and hides the fact that most forecasts are really based on human judgement). In any case, even if historical trends are accurately analysed, there is no guarantee that the future will be the same as the past. It is much better that you surface all the assumptions, and make your own judgements in full knowledge of what is involved.

So, I will recommend just two very simple techniques to use (if nothing else but as a check on the forecasts others are trying to sell to you);

EYEBALLING – the technique I mentioned above is the first, and best, method. It merely requires you to plot historical results graphically; and then look for the patterns. Trust your own judgement – until you are proved wrong.

EXPONENTIAL SMOOTHING – this is the mathematical technique which reportedly gives the best results; probably because it is so simple, and consequently easily understood. Indeed, it is a very impressive title for a simple, but useful, mathematical technique; which can quite easily be handled manually. It just allows greater weight to be given to recent periods. Instead of, for example, the average trend over the whole of the last year being calculated, the sales data for each of the months is given a weighting, depending on how recent that month was.

It simply takes the previous forecast, and adds on the latest 'actual' sales figure; except that it does this in a fixed proportion, which is chosen to reflect the weighting to be given to the latest period. The general form is:

$$F_{t+1} = F^t + aE_t$$

where F_{t+1} is the new forecast you are calculating, F_t is the previous one and E_t is the deviation (or 'error') of the actual performance recorded against that previous period forecast; and 'a' is the weighting to be given to the most recent events.

For example, if a weighting of 0.1 is to be given to the latest figure, then the new forecast will be (Previous Forecast) + (0.1 × Deviation of Last Actual from the Forecast). Note that as the last forecast had in turn been produced by the same process (as had the forecasts over the preceding periods), there is no need to subtract any further figures; since in this way all the earlier sales figures are incorporated (but with 'exponentially' decreasing importance as they recede into the past). Thus, in the example given, the preceding three months are represented to the extent of 9% (0.1 × 0.9), 8% (0.1 × 0.9 × 0.9) and 7% (0.1 × 0.9 × 0.9 × 0.9), and so on. Clearly the higher the proportion of the current month (say 0.3 rather than 0.1) the greater the weighting given to recent periods.

Exponential smoothing will not, in this simple form, allow for seasonality; though more sophisticated (but less easily understood) versions can do this.

Long-term forecasting

Thus tends to be qualitative (as compared with the quantitative, numeric, focus of short-term forecasts). It is even more dependent on judgement; and most of the more complicated approaches to it (such as Delphi, or Jury methods) aim to reduce the risks implicit in the judgement by spreading the process over panels of experts. It does not, in the final analysis, absolve the manager from backing his or her own judgement (which is probably better informed, in terms of the specific situation, than that of the 'experts').

Of all the techniques the most useful involves developing complementary scenarios, which allow for the uncertainties involved; as well as expanding the viewpoint of all the managers involved in the process. Unfortunately, in the form most often described it can also be the most complex and sophisticated of these techniques – and in this form perhaps only the very large corporate planning team at Shell have used it really effectively. On the basis of the version which Shell recommend for their line managers who are not part of their corporate planning group, we have developed[11] a form which is more practical for most organizations. The six steps are:

1 Decide the key drivers (forces) for change
2 Bring these drivers together into a viable (meaningful) framework
3 Produce an initial (seven to nine) cluster of similar drivers (mini-scenarios)

[11] David Mercer, Simpler scenarios, *Management Decision* (June 1995).

4 Reduce these to make two or three scenarios
5 Write the final scenarios
6 Identify the issues (for the organization) raised by these

1 Decide the key drivers (forces) for change – *Identify the important variables* – what (in the whole of the external environment, not just the marketing environment) are the most important factors which will determine the future of the organization.
2 Bring these drivers together into a viable (meaningful) framework – *Brainstorm to find the possible outcomes* – work through the different outcomes which different alternatives for these variables may lead to.
3 Produce an initial (seven to nine) cluster of similar drivers (mini-scenarios) – *Link these together in a series of alternative scenarios* – start to build six or seven scenarios ('stories' about the future of the organization, or more importantly its market) which are able to contain these different alternatives.
4 Reduce these to make two or three scenarios – *Refine these scenarios* – then work on the scenarios until they are condensed to two or three meaningful alternative (but complementary) descriptions of the future.
5 Write the final scenarios – *in any form* – usually as a business report, which those using them will find easiest to read.
6 Identify the issues (for the organization) raised by these; *focus* on those issues which will need to be included in corporate strategy.

It should be noted, though, that in terms of the practice observed in many companies, the link between what are thus identified as the key issues in the external environment and what appears as corporate strategy is often tenuous; and the link to actions may be almost non-existent! In our experience,[12] less than a tenth of even those managers trained in the use of scenarios integrated these issues into their final strategies!

The importance of long-range forecasting, overall, is emphasized by Hamel and Prahalad[13] when they suggest that the greatest competitive advantage is a vision of the future.

Corporate Mission

Behind the corporate objectives, which in themselves offer the main context for the marketing plan, will lie the '*corporate mission*'; which in turn provides the context for these corporate objectives. This 'corporate mission' can be thought of as a definition of what the organization is; of what it does: 'Our business is ...'.

This definition should not be too narrow, or it will constrict the development of the organization; a too rigorous concentration on the view that 'We are in

[12] David Mercer, Simpler scenarios, *Long Range Planning*, vol. 28, no.4 (August 1995).
[13] Gary Hamel and C. K. Prahalad, *Competing for the future* (Harvard Business School Press, 1994).

the business of making meat-scales', as IBM was during the early 1900s, might have limited its subsequent development into other areas. On the other hand, it should not be too wide or it will become meaningless; 'We want to make a profit' is not too helpful in developing specific plans.

Abell[14] suggests that the definition should cover three dimensions: *customer groups* to be served, *customer needs* to be served, and *technologies* to be utilized.

Thus, the definition of IBM's 'corporate mission' in the 1940s might well have been: 'We are in the business of handling accounting information [customer need] for the larger US organizations [customer group] by means of punched cards [technology].' Fortunately, as the name itself (International Business Machines) indicates, IBM already had a wider perspective (and its corporate mission was virtually defined by its name).

Ian Wilson[15] suggests that strategic vision, to be effective, should have three characteristics:

Clarity

Coherence

Communications Power

Not surprisingly, these are much the same as those of conviction marketing.

SELF-TEST QUESTION 14.4

What is your organization's corporate mission?

(If your organization has not spelled out its corporate mission, you should make your own judgement as to what this should be. If you have followed the marketing audits through the book, you should by now have a good idea of what this might be.)

Corporate Vision

Perhaps the most important factor in successful marketing is the 'corporate vision'. Surprisingly, it is largely neglected by marketing textbooks – although not by the popular exponents of corporate strategy. Indeed, it was perhaps the main theme of the book by Peters and Waterman,[16] in the form of their

[14] D. Abell, *Defining the Business: The Starting Point of Strategic Planning* (Prentice-Hall, 1980).

[15] Ian Wilson, Realising the power of strategic vision, *Long Range Planning*, vol. 25, no. 5 (1992).

[16] T. J. Peters and R. H. Waterman, *In Search of Excellence* (Harper & Row, 1982).

'Superordinate Goals'. Theodore Levitt[17] says: 'Nothing drives progress like the imagination. The idea precedes the deed.' Even Robert Townsend[18] echoes the statement in his comment that: 'Things get done in our society because of a man or woman with conviction.'

If the organization in general, and its chief executive in particular, has a strong vision of where its future lies, then there is a good chance that the organization will achieve a strong position in its markets (and attain that future). This will be not least because its strategies will be consistent, and will be supported by its staff at all levels. In this context, at the height of its success all of IBM's marketing activities were underpinned by its philosophy of 'customer service' – a vision originally promoted by the charismatic Watson dynasty. Similarly, 'at Matsushita it means never cheating a customer by knowingly producing or selling defective merchandise'.[19]

Henry Mintzberg[20] explains:

> ... in some cases, in addition to the mission there is the 'sense of mission', that is, a feeling that the group has banded together to create something new and exciting. This is common in new organizations.

What a worthwhile vision consists of is, however, usually open to debate; hence the reason why such visions tend to be associated with strong, charismatic leaders. But the vision must be relevant. Robert Townsend,[21] again, adds the very pragmatic footnote:

> Before you commit yourself to a new effort, it's worth asking yourself a couple of questions: Are we really trying to do something worth-while here? Or are we just building another monument to some diseased ego?

The problem for marketers is also that this vision is often unrelated to the markets. IBM and Matsushita were fortunate, in as much as their creeds were of general applicability, of almost religious fervour – though this eventually proved problematic when the former came to abandon it. In other organizations, Alan Sugar's concentration on putting together cheap electronic packages and Clive Sinclair's flair for identifying innovative technologies, for example, had much narrower scope of vision; they may only be successful while they approximate to market needs. The vision will move from being a major advantage to being an overwhelming disadvantage if the market shifts; as did happen to IBM. As Peter Drucker[22] says, 'Every "right" product sooner or later becomes a "wrong" product.' This theme was explored in more detail in the section on 'Conviction marketing' in chapter 9.

---

[17] T. Levitt, *The Marketing Imagination* (Free Press, 1986).

[18] R. Townsend, *Up the Organisation* (Coronet Books, 1971).

[19] R. T. Pascale and A. G. Athos, *The Art of Japanese Management* (Simon & Schuster, 1981).

[20] H. Mintzberg, *Power in and around Organizations* (Prentice-Hall, 1983).

[21] Townsend, *Up the Organisation*.

[22] P. F. Drucker, *Managing in Turbulent Times* (Heinemann, 1980).

The message for the marketer is that, to be most effective, the marketing strategies must be converted into a powerful long-term vision – if such a vision does not already exist. Peter Drucker,[23] once again, says:

> In many markets one prospers only at the extremes: either as one of the few market leaders who set the standard, or as a specialist ... What is not tenable is a strategy in between.

Hickman and Silva[24] put it more simply:

> Visionary executives not only position their organizations to make the most of impending changes, they attempt to influence those changes by causing rather then merely reacting to them.

Such vision, however, demands the extraordinary. As Peter Drucker[25] has said:

> To make the future demands courage. It demands work. But it also demands faith ... the idea on which tomorrow's business is built must be uncertain; no one can really say as yet what it will look like if and when it becomes a reality. It must be risky; it has a probability of success, but also of failure.

Most recently, however, Drucker[26] has also talked in more general terms about the 'theory of the business', listing four specifications for this:

1 The assumptions about environment, mission and core competencies must fit reality.
2 The assumptions in all three areas have to fit one another.
3 The theory of the business must be known and understood throughout the organisations.
4 The theory of the business has to be tested constantly.

Marketing Myopia

In his very influential article,[27] Theodore Levitt stated that:

> The viewpoint that an industry is a customer-satisfying process, not a goods-producing process, is vital for all businessmen to understand. An industry begins with the customer and his needs, not with a patent, a raw material, or a selling skill. Given the customer's needs the industry develops backwards, first concerning itself with the physical *delivery* of customer satisfactions. Then it moves back further to *creating* the things by which these satisfactions are in part achieved. How these materials are created is a matter of indifference to the customer, hence the

[23] Drucker, *Managing in Turbulent Times*.
[24] C. R. Hickman and M. A. Silva, *Creating Excellence* (Unwin, 1985).
[25] Drucker, *Managing in Turbulent Times*.
[26] Peter F. Drucker, The Theory of business, *Harvard Business Review* (September–October, 1994).
[27] T. Levitt, Marketing myopia, *Harvard Business Review* (July–August 1960).

particular form of manufacturing, processing, or what-have-you cannot be considered as a vital aspect of the marketing.

His reason for this emphasis, supported by considerable anecdotal evidence in the rest of the article, was that most organizations defined their business perspectives (now often referred to as 'corporate missions') too narrowly; typically on the basis of the technological processes that they employed (but, at best, upon internal factors). His view, which was enthusiastically seized upon by the more adventurous organizations, was that the link with the consumer, the 'customer franchise', was the most important element.

Adopting a wider perspective has helped many organizations to appreciate better how they could develop. Some organizations, however, have taken the process very literally. Holiday Inns, for example, decided that it was not in the 'hotel business' but in the 'travel industry', and acquired a number of businesses, including a bus company. However, it soon learned that its management skills were not in those areas; it divested itself of them, retrenching to the business it knew best.

Indeed, it is worth noting that such merger and acquisition activities must be considered as viable alternatives to traditional marketing developments. Rowe et al.[28] provide a useful list of the available alternatives (table 14.1).

On the other hand, Levitt[29] himself recognized the danger of the possible over-reactions in his later book, where he added the comment:

> Marketing Myopia was not intended as analysis or even prescription; it was intended as manifesto. It did not pretend to take a balanced position ... My scheme, however, tied marketing more closely to the inner orbit of business policy.

The last sentence seems, at least to me, to be the best comment on the true importance of his contribution. But I will also add Henry Mintzberg's[30] observation that:

> Managing strategy is mostly managing stability, not change. Indeed, most of the time senior managers should not be formulating strategy at all; they should be getting on with making their organizations as effective as possible in pursuing strategies they already have.

Marketing Audit

The first formal step in the marketing planning process is that of conducting the marketing audit. Ideally, at the time of producing the marketing plan, this

[28] A. J. Rowe, R. O. Mason, K. E. Dickel and N. H. Snyder, *Strategic Management: A Methodological Approach* (Addison-Wesley, 3rd edn, 1989).
[29] Levitt, *The Marketing Imagination*.
[30] H. Mintzberg, Crafting strategy, *Harvard Business Review* (July–August 1987).

Table 14.1 Strategic alternatives

Strategic alternative	Focus	External or internal	Purpose or function
0. Status quo	Stability	Internal	Continue in present products/markets temporarily or permanently, depending on product life-cycle
1. Concentration	Single product line	Internal	Do one thing well
2. Horizontal integration	Ownership or control of competitors	External	Gain market power and economies of scale
3. Vertical integration	Transformation of cost centre to profit centre	External	Improve economies of scale; reduce dependence on suppliers or distributors
4. Diversification	Broadening of product line	External or internal	Reduce competitive pressures; gain greater profitability; spread risk
5. Joint ventures	Complementary benefits	External	Spread risk; bring about synergy
6. Retrenchment	Reduction of activity or operations	Internal	Temporarily respond to adversity by permanent phaseout
7. Divestiture	Removal of entity that does not fit	Internal	Realign products/markets or organization
8. Liquidation	Same as item 7	Internal	Same as item 7; situation is usually more severe
9. Innovation	Seizing of leadership position	Internal	Take initiative; gain position early in product life-cycle
10. Restructuring	Cost reduction, growth potential	External	Concentrate on products and divisions with high potential

should only involve bringing together the source material which has already been collected throughout the year – as part of the normal work of the marketing department.

Kotler et al.[31] define it at length:

> A marketing audit is a *comprehensive, systematic, independent* and *periodic* examination of a company's – or business unit's – marketing environment, objectives, strategies, and activities with a view to determining problem areas and opportunities and recommending a plan of action to improve the company's marketing performance.

Indeed, that is exactly what you have been doing as you have worked your way through this book. By now you should have amassed a reasonable amount of data about your organization and its environment. This is the basis of your own 'marketing audit'.

This process should have demonstrated an important truth. While some organizations have successfully employed external consultants to conduct such audits, generally speaking they are best undertaken by the management who 'own' the marketing process. This is partly because they are the best people to understand the subtleties of the information revealed (always assuming that they have managed to cast aside their preconceptions and prejudices). Even more importantly, though, the audit is the best possible learning process for these managers; introducing them to the factors which are most important to their management of marketing. Finally, and most importantly of all, it ensures that those who will have to implement the results of the planning process understand, and are committed to, the assumptions which lie behind it.

As explained in the earlier section on desk research, this material will have been best organized as a *facts book* or 'facts library'. As such, it will have been organized so that facts pertaining to any issue can easily and rapidly be extracted. As part of this process, a degree of analysis may well have already begun, as key elements are highlighted.

The emphasis at this stage is on obtaining a complete and accurate picture. In a single organization, however, it is likely that only a few aspects will be sufficiently important to have any significant impact on the marketing plan; but all may need to be reviewed to determine just which *are* the few.

In this context some factors related to the customer, which should be included in the material collected for the audit, may be:

- Who are the customers?
  - What are their key characteristics?
  - What differentiates them from other members of the population?

---

[31] P. Kotler, W. T. Gregor and W. H. Rodgers III, The marketing audit comes of age, *Sloan Management Review* (1977).

- What are their needs and wants?
  - What do they expect the 'product' to do?
  - What are their special requirements and perceptions?
- What do they think of the organization and its products or services?
  - What are their attitudes?
  - What are their buying intentions?

A 'traditional' – albeit product-based – format for a 'brand reference book' (or, indeed, a 'marketing facts book') is suggested by Godley:[32]

1 Financial data – Facts for this section will come from management accounting, costing and finance sections.
2 Product data – From production, research and development.
3 Sales and distribution data – Sales, packaging, distribution sections.
4 Advertising, sales promotion, merchandising data – Information from these departments.
5 Market data and miscellany – From market research, who would in most cases act as a source for this information.

Godley's sources of data, however, assume the resources of a very large organization. In most organizations they would be obtained from a much smaller set of people (and not a few of them would be generated by the marketing manager alone).

It is apparent that a marketing audit can be a complex process, but the aim is simple: *it is only to identify those existing (external and internal) factors which will have a significant impact on the future plans of the company.*

It is clear that the basic material to be input to the marketing audit should be comprehensive. Accordingly, as suggested earlier, the best approach is to accumulate this material continuously, as and when it becomes available; since this avoids the otherwise heavy workload involved in collecting it as part of the regular, typically annual, planning process itself – when time is usually at a premium. Even so, the first task of this 'annual' process should be to check that the material held in the current 'facts book' or 'facts files' actually *is* comprehensive and accurate, and can form a sound basis for the marketing audit itself.

The structure of the facts book will be designed to match the specific needs of the organization, but one simple format – suggested by Malcolm McDonald – may be applicable in many cases. This splits the material into three groups:

1 *Review of the marketing environment.* A study of the organization's markets, customers, competitors and the overall economic, political, cultural and technical environment; covering developing trends, as well as the current situation.
2 *Review of the detailed marketing activity.* A study of the company's marketing mix; in terms of the 4 Ps – product, price, promotion and place.

[32] C. G. A. Godley, Market research, *Principles and Practice of Management*, ed. E. F. L. Brech (Longman, 1975).

3 *Review of the marketing system.* A study of the marketing organization, marketing research systems and the current marketing objectives and strategies.

The last of these is too frequently ignored. The marketing system itself needs to be regularly questioned, because the validity of the whole marketing plan is reliant upon the accuracy of the input from this system, and 'garbage in, garbage out' applies with a vengeance.

To these, Kotler et al.[33] add two further (more 'bureaucratic', but nevertheless important) audits: a marketing productivity audit, to see where marketing costs could be reduced; and a marketing function audit, to identify weaknesses.

SELF-TEST QUESTION 14.5

At this stage you should, at long last, bring all the previous material (in what has now become your own personal 'facts book') together to produce your formally analysed marketing audit; which answers the various questions listed in the sections above.

Analysis

The analysis of this material will, no doubt, require significant effort. In the first instance it is a matter of selection, of sorting the wheat from the chaff. What is important, and will need to be taken into account in the marketing plan that will eventually emerge from the overall process, will be different for each product or service in each situation. One of the most important skills to be learned in marketing is that of being able to concentrate on just what is important.

In the case of Compaq, it was an awareness of a gap in the market. In the case of Amstrad, it was an appreciation of competitive pricing structures. In the case of IBM, it was an understanding of the overall environmental factors. Each of these companies, with broadly similar products and operating in the same market, probably asked very different questions of their respective marketing audits.

In addition, all the analytical techniques which were described in the earlier chapters can be applied, and should be applied where relevant. It is important to say not just what happened but why. The process of marketing planning

---

[33] Kotler, Gregor and Rodgers, The marketing audit comes of age.

encompasses all of the marketing skills. However, a number of these may be particularly relevant at this stage:

- *Positioning.* As already stated in the earlier chapter, the starting point of the marketing plan must be the consumer. It is a matter of definition that his or her needs should drive the whole marketing process. The techniques of positioning and segmentation therefore usually offer the best starting point for what has to be achieved by the whole planning process.
- *Portfolio planning.* In addition, the co-ordinated planning of the individual products and services can contribute towards the balanced portfolio. Malcolm McDonald[34] suggests a very useful pictorial device which summarizes this information (figure 14.3). The *segments* the organization is operating in are plotted, with the value (to the organization) of each plotted on the *y*-axis and the strength of the organization in that segment along the *x*-axis. In this example the size of the solid circles shows the relative amount of the organization's total turnover that they represent. The dotted circles, on the other hand, show where the organization wants to be (including the volume) in three years' time.
- *80:20 Rule.* To achieve the maximum impact, the marketing plan must be clear, concise and simple. It needs to concentrate on the 20 per cent of products or services, and on the 20 per cent of customers, which will account for 80 per cent of the volume and 80 per cent of the 'profit'.

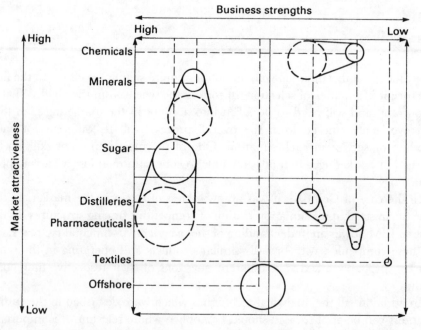

Figure 14.3 Portfolio planning.

[34] McDonald, *Marketing Plans.*

- *4 Ps.* As we have seen, the 4 Ps can son
  but the framework they offer can be very

SWOT Analysis

One technique not previously mentioned, but wh
analysis of the material contained in the marketin
(Strengths, Weaknesses, Opportunities, Threats) a
managers as being the most useful planning tool or
the key pieces of information into two main categori
external factors) and then by their dual positive and nega
and Opportunities, as the former aspects, with Weaknesse.
senting the latter):

- *Internal factors. Strengths* and *weaknesses* internal to the organizatio.
  its position in relation to its competitors.
- *External factors. Opportunities* and *threats* presented by the external en
  the competition.

The internal factors, which may be viewed as strengths or weaknesses
depending upon their impact on the organization's positions (for they may
represent a strength for one organization but a weakness, in relative terms,
for another), may include all of the 4 Ps; as well as personnel, finance and so
on. The external factors, which again may be threats to one organization while
they offer opportunities to another, may include matters such as technological
change, legislation, sociocultural changes and so on, as well as changes in the
marketplace or competitive position.

The technique is often presented in the form of a matrix:

Strengths	Weaknesses
Opportunities	Threats

However, the flowchart of Lusch and Lusch[36] shows the relationships rather
better (figure 14.4). You should note, however, that SWOT is just *one* aid to

---

[35] D. Mercer, research to be published.
[36] R. F. Lusch and V. N. Lusch, *Principles of Marketing* (Kent Publishing, 1987).

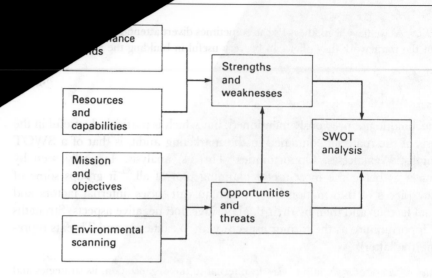

Figure 14.4 SWOT analysis.

categorization. It is not, as many organizations seem to think, the only technique. It also has its own weaknesses. It tends to persuade companies to compile lists rather than think about what is really important to their business. It also presents the resulting lists uncritically, without clear prioritization; so that, for example, weak opportunities may appear to balance strong threats.

The aim of any SWOT analysis should be to isolate the key *issues* that will be important to the future of the organization; and that subsequent marketing planning will address.

Assumptions

It is essential to spell out assumptions. However, most companies do not even realize that they make such assumptions. IBM's key product marketing document was titled 'Forecast Assumptions'; and the agreement on what the assumptions are is often the key to understanding the marketing plan.

You should, however, make as few assumptions as possible; and very carefully explain those you do make.

As an extension to this process, when you estimate the results expected from your strategies, you should also explore a range of alternative assumptions, in the same way that it was earlier suggested that there might be a range of forecasts, each meeting different needs. For example, if you have assumed that the market will grow by x per cent, you might estimate sales from your chosen strategy at £y. However, you should also estimate sales at lower and higher rates of growth in the market ('At rate of growth of $x - 2$ per cent, sales will be £$y - 3$. At a growth rate of $x + 2$ per cent . . .').

The most useful component of this part of the exercise may well be a 'sensitivity analysis'; since this determines which factors have the most influence over the outcomes – and hence which factors should be most carefully managed.

SELF-TEST QUESTION 14.6

Draw up a SWOT analysis for your organization. What assumptions are implicit in this?

Marketing Objectives

Although considerable coverage has, justifiably, been given to the preceding stages of the marketing audit, you should note that (with the results of that audit available) *it is only at this stage (of deciding the marketing objectives) that the active part of the marketing planning process begins.*

This next stage in marketing planning is indeed the key to the whole marketing process. The marketing objectives state just where the company intends to be at some specific time in the future. James Quinn[37] succinctly defines objectives in general as:

> Goals (or objectives) state *what* is to be achieved and *when* results are to be accomplished, but they do not state *how* the results are to be achieved.

They typically relate to what products (or services) will be where in what markets (and must be realistically based on customer behaviour in those markets). They are essentially about the match between those *products* and *markets*. Objectives for pricing, distribution, advertising and so on are at a lower level, and should not be confused with marketing objectives. They are part of the marketing strategy needed to achieve marketing objectives.

To be most effective, objectives should be capable of measurement and therefore *quantifiable*. This measurement may be in terms of sales volume, money value, market share, percentage penetration of distribution outlets and so on. An example of such a measurable marketing objective might be 'to enter the market with product Y and capture 10 per cent of the market by

---

[37] J. B. Quinn, *Strategies for Change: Logical Incrementalism* (Richard D. Irwin, 1980).

value within one year'. As it is quantified it can, within limits, be unequivocally monitored; and corrective action taken as necessary.

The marketing objectives must usually be based, above all, on the organization's financial objectives; converting these financial measurements into the related marketing measurements.

It is conventionally assumed that marketing objectives will be designed to maximize volume or profit (or to optimize the utilization of resources in the non-profit sector), by creating demand or rejuvenating existing demand, say; although the various sub-objectives may indicate many different routes to achieving such optimization. However, as Kotler[38] suggested (in an earlier edition of his book), there may be a number of other objectives:

> Synchromarketing

> Demarketing

> Counter-marketing

Synchromarketing.   The aim may be to 'redistribute' existing sales (which are already at optimum levels) so that they occur at times, or in places, which the supplier prefers. Thus, for example, organizations which have highly seasonal sales (which make inefficient use of resources) may want to increase non-seasonal sales. Walls achieved this by balancing its summer sales of ice-cream with pies and sausages, demand for which peaks in winter. The suppliers of central-heating oil offer special deals for those customers willing to restock their tanks in summer.

Demarketing.   Demand may sometimes exceed supply. In these circumstances the emphasis will be on rationing scarce supplies. Occasionally the supplier, rather than bring on stream expensive new plant, may seek to persuade customers to buy less (or be less dissatisfied with the scarcity). Some suppliers of electrical energy (electricity generators in Europe and the USA) have heavily advertised energy conservation measures to achieve this end (otherwise, the cost of meeting the peak winter loads would be very high – and unprofitable).

Counter-marketing.   In what is usually a public-sector activity (but is occasionally undertaken by the private sector, where some uses of a product are damaging the corporate image), there may be an objective of stopping consumption completely. The anti-tobacco and anti-drug campaigns are the most obvious examples; but McDonald's campaigns to stop its customers dropping litter, or the brewers' campaigns to stop drinking and driving, fall into this category.

---

[38] P. Kotler, *Marketing Management* (Prentice-Hall, 3rd edn, 1976).

More generally, Wong et al.[39] identified three clusters of generic strategies:

'Quality Marketeers' – with strong marketing and R&D skills

'Innovators' – with a desire to innovate and be first to market

'Mature Marketeers' – who are highly profit oriented

> ## SELF-TEST QUESTION 14.7
>
> What are your organization's marketing objectives?
> How do you think they should be changed? What practical effect would these changes have?

Logical Incrementalism

In practice, the setting of objectives – and the subsequent strategies to meet these – is often less tidy. One element of complexity may be introduced by the '*logical incrementalism*' described by Quinn.[40] As described by him, this incremental approach to setting strategy – where it results from a number of smaller decisions throughout the year – has a number of features:

1 SCANNING – since the trigger for the incremental change in strategy is a change in the environment, this approach is very dependent upon sensing the signals which indicate such changes in the environment so a rigorous approach to environmental analysis needed.
2 INFORMATION NETWORKS – a consequent requirement is that managers build the widest possible networks (of human contacts not just computers) to obtain the input which will tell them what is happening in their environment and, more important, to help them sense when change is likely to be needed; the human neural network is a very good analogy for this.
3 GENERATION OF ALTERNATIVES – it might seem that incrementalism would imply instant decisions: 'shooting from the hip'. Yet a key requirement, observed by successful managers, is that they develop a range of alternative solutions which they then think through, often at length, with their colleagues *before* committing themselves to any one approach.
4 BUILDING CREDIBILITY – having taken the personal decision, this may be started – by CEOs for instance – by making symbolic moves (by, say, a very public commitment

[39] Veronica Wong, John Saunders and Peter Doyle, Examining generic marketing strategies and organisations of successful international competitors, in *The Marketing Initiative*, ed. John Saunders (Prentice Hall, 1994).
[40] J. B. Quinn, *Strategies for Change: Logical Incrementalism* (Dow Jones-Irwin, Homewood, Illinois, 1980).

to a new philosophy). It is often accompanied by moves to legitimize new viewpoints – for example by setting up workshops (or retreats) to talk through the issues; preferably off site, so that they are not interrupted (but also so that they are symbolically divorced from the present work).

5 TACTICAL MOVES – even then, the changes may first be introduced as (experimental) tactics rather than strategy, this is where incrementalism can be used to bypass opposition which might otherwise emerge against a formal announcement of the change in strategy.

6 POLITICAL SUPPORT – these new moves will still, though, require the building of political coalitions if they are to be sustained; committees and task forces are favourite devices for developing such support. At the same time opposition will need to be neutralized.

7 CREATING COMMITMENT – when the strategy is finally in place it is necessary to actively build commitment to it throughout the organization.

The importance of this concept emerges in two contexts. The first is that managers moving into the rational phase of the annual planning process need to be aware of the limitations posed by the legacy of incremental decisions which have built up since the last annual exercise. The second is that an understanding of this process helps you put such incremental decision-making in perspective. Most important of all, it alerts you to the fact that it is happening – all the time.

Taking the example of positioning, as and when position drift is detected the wise brand manager will react immediately; he or she will recognize that such response cannot wait for the annual plan. If they understand the implications of logical incrementalism, however, they will inject some of the rational thinking which is supposed to lie at the heart of the annual planning process – for the key to logical incrementalism is, indeed, that it is a *logical* process. In this way it can be just as rational as the traditional process. It is not the same as the random decision-making which infects many organizations. Because it recognizes the reality that decisions are driven by real events rather than a theoretical planning process, it may indeed by rather more effective.

One of the hidden implications of the above processes, which reflects my own experience of much of such decision-making (and is supported by significant amounts of research data), is that making of strategy is a much more diffused process than most managers think. One aspect which is most often stressed in relation to logical incrementalism is that of timing – the decisions take place almost randomly throughout the year rather than tidily during the annual planning process.

A less obvious implication still is that the process is not limited to senior management alone, as traditional theory would suggest. In practice, the process is spread through a number of layers of management – with different degrees of involvement depending upon what particular incremental aspect of strategy is under review. This has major implications for managers throughout the organization, who before probably did not realize just how important was their contribution.

Emergent Strategy

Indeed, incrementalism may go even further. This is most clearly illustrated by a diagram:

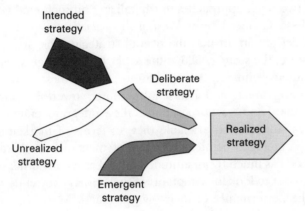

This diagram very clearly shows how the intended strategy, decided upon traditionally or incrementally, is overtaken by events in two main ways. One, which will probably be recognized by the organization, is that of *unrealized strategy*, where it proves impossible to implement the chosen strategy in practice. Johnson and Scholes[41] refer to this form of strategy as 'natural selection'. Thus, following Darwinian principles, the degree to which the organization is successful, or not, depends upon the extent to which it can change to meet these forces.

Less obvious is the *emergent strategy*, which is decided by events in the external environment; and, thus, forced upon the organization. This may not necessarily be recognized, in its totality, by the organization – since many of its implications may be hidden. As markets become more complex, however, such emergent strategies are becoming more common.

Many organizations see both these processes in terms of failure – they have been forced, usually by unpredictable events, to abandon their own strategy. There is, accordingly, a tendency for these unwelcome facts to be ignored until they are so obvious that they cannot be avoided. This is a major error. *Such deviations must be recognized* (probably through one or other form of environmental analysis coupled with networking) as soon as possible, so that the organization can react in good time. Minzberg,[42] as a prime mover of the theory of emergent

[41] Gerry Johnson and Kevan Scholes, *Exploring Corporate Strategy*, 3rd edn, (Prentice-Hall, 1993).
[42] Henry Mizberg, The pitfalls of strategic planning, *California Management Review* (Fall, 1993).

strategy, stresses that one of the major pitfalls of strategic planning is 'its obsession with an illusion of control'.

A much more powerful approach is, though, to be proactive; to seize upon these deviations as the basis for future developments. What needs to be recognized is that emergent strategies are the most powerful of all. They must, by definition, be directly derived from the needs of the market – where even successful deliberate strategies may not ideally match market needs but may achieve their targets by sheer force (especially where conviction marketing lies behind them). Emergent strategies are, thus, likely to be vigorous ones.

There are two main approaches to capitalizing on such emergent strategies. The first of these, favoured in the West, is the *umbrella strategy*. This is a form of very positive delegation, in that the overall strategies, the umbrella, are very general in nature; the strategy allows the lower level managers, who are closest to the external environment, the freedom to react to these changes.

A much more direct, and hence even more powerful, approach is that favoured by the Japanese corporations: they integrate emergent strategies with their own. Indeed it is arguable that, in terms of marketing, to a large extent they use emergent strategies instead of their own deliberate strategies. This is evidenced as much by an attitude of mind as by any other feature. They deliberately go out to look for symptoms of such emergent trends, which can be detected in the performance of their own products. More than that, though, they often deliberately launch a range of products rather than a single one to see which is most successful. It is almost as if they deliberately seek out the emergent strategies by offering the best environment for them to develop – the very reverse of the Western approach, which seeks to avoid them! The Japanese then go on to build on these emergent strategies with a number of very effective tools – most of which are designed to overcome the major problem which accompanies emergent strategies, that they emerge on the scene much later than deliberate ones (and are likely to be visible to all the competitors at the same time) so that *time* is the essence. Thus, time management techniques (including parallel development along with flexible manufacturing and JIT), which have been developed by the Japanese, offer them a significant competitive advantage in handling such emergent strategies.

Marketing Strategies

There are numerous definitions of what strategy is, but again James Quinn[43] gives a succinct general definition:

> A strategy is a *pattern* or *plan* that *integrates* an organization's *major* goals, policies and action sequences into a *cohesive* whole.

[43] Quinn, *Strategies for Change: Logical Incrementalism.*

He goes on to explain his view of the role of 'policies', with which strategy is most often confused:

> Policies are rules or guidelines that express the *limits* within which action should occur.

Even then, his co-editor in another handbook, Henry Minzberg,[44] adds:

> Human nature is such that we tend to insist on a definition for every concept. But perhaps we fool ourselves, pretending that concepts such as strategy can be reduced to a single definition ... Let us, therefore, propose five formal definitions of strategy – as plan, ploy, pattern, position and perspective ...

Simplifying somewhat, therefore, marketing strategies can be seen as the means, or 'game plan', by which marketing objectives will be achieved and, in the framework that we have chosen to use, are generally concerned with the 4 Ps. Examples are:

- product
  - developing new products, repositioning or relaunching existing ones and scrapping old ones
  - adding new features and benefits
  - balancing product portfolios
  - changing the design or packaging
- price
  - setting the price to skim or to penetrate
  - pricing for different market segments
  - deciding how to meet competitive pricing
- promotion
  - specifying the advertising platform and media
  - deciding the public relations brief
  - organizing the salesforce to cover new products and services or markets
- place
  - choosing the channels
  - deciding levels of customer service

In principle, these strategies describe how the objectives will be achieved. The 4 Ps are a useful framework for deciding how the company's resources will be manipulated (strategically) to achieve the objectives. *It should be noted, however, that they are not the only framework, and may divert attention from the real issues. The focus of the strategies must be the objectives to be achieved – not the process of planning itself.* Only if it fits the needs of these objectives should you choose, as we have done, to use the framework of the 4 Ps.

---

[44] H. Minzberg, Opening up the definition of strategy, *The Strategy Process: Concepts, Contexts and Cases*, ed. J. B. Quinn, H. Minzberg and R. M. James (Prentice-Hall, 1988).

The strategy statement can take the form of a purely verbal description of the strategic options which have been chosen. Alternatively, and perhaps more positively, it might include a structured list of the major options chosen.

One aspect of strategy which is often overlooked is that of *timing*. Exactly when it is the best time for each element of the strategy to be implemented is often critical. Taking the right action at the wrong time can sometimes be almost as bad as taking the wrong action at the right time. Timing is, therefore, an essential part of any plan; and should normally appear as a schedule of planned activities.

Having completed this crucial stage of the planning process, you will need to re-check the feasibility of your objectives and strategies in terms of the market share, sales, costs, profits and so on which these demand in practice. As in the rest of the marketing discipline, you will need to employ judgement, experience, market research or anything else which helps you to look at your conclusions from all possible angles.

SELF-TEST QUESTION 14.8

Using the above format, detail your organization's marketing strategies.
   Review them critically. Are they realistic? Do they reflect what really needs to be done?

Detailed Plans and Programmes

At this stage, you will need to develop your overall marketing strategies into detailed plans and programmes. Although these detailed plans may cover each of the 4 Ps, the focus will vary, depending upon your organization's specific strategies. A product-orientated company will focus its plans for the 4 Ps around each of its products. A market or geographically-orientated company will concentrate on each market or geographical area. Each will base its plans upon the detailed needs of its customers, and on the strategies chosen to satisfy these needs.

Again, the most important element is, indeed, that of the detailed plans; they spell out exactly what programmes and individual activities will take place over the period of the plan (usually over the next year). Without these specified – and preferably quantified – activities the plan cannot be monitored, even in terms of success in meeting its objectives.

It is these programmes and activities which will then constitute the 'marketing' of the organization over the period. As a result, these detailed marketing programmes are the most important, practical outcome of the whole planning process. These plans should therefore be:

```
┌──────────────┐
│    Clear     │
└──────────────┘

┌──────────────┐
│  Quantified  │
└──────────────┘

┌──────────────┐
│   Focused    │
└──────────────┘

┌──────────────┐
│   Realistic  │
└──────────────┘

┌──────────────┐
│    Agreed    │
└──────────────┘
```

- *Clear.* They should be an unambiguous statement of *exactly* what is to be done.
- *Quantified.* The predicted outcome of each activity should be, as far as possible, quantified; so that its performance can be monitored.
- *Focused.* The temptation to proliferate activities beyond the numbers which can be realistically controlled should be avoided. The 80:20 Rule applies in this context too. Bonoma and Crittenden,[45] reporting the results of their research into marketing implementation, noted: 'The number of marketing programs in a firm, compared to relevant competitors, will be inversely related to the quality of marketing practices observed.'
- *Realistic.* They should be achievable.
- *Agreed.* Those who are to implement them should be committed to them, and agree that they are achievable.

The resulting plans should become a working document which will guide the campaigns taking place throughout the organization over the period of the plan. If the marketing plan is to work, every exception to it (throughout the year) must be questioned; and the lessons learned, to be incorporated in the next year's plan.

It is at this stage that all the various elements of the plan – from Objectives leading to Strategies leading to Detailed Plans – are finally brought together.

Once again, Malcolm McDonald[46] provides a diagram which very clearly shows the major activities involved in the process (figure 14.5). Although at first glance this looks complex, it is in fact a very functional flowchart of the whole planning process, and nicely illustrates the relationships between the various components.

---

[45] T. V. Bonoma and V. L. Crittenden, Managing marketing implementation, *Sloan Management Review* (Winter 1988).
[46] McDonald, *Marketing Plans*.

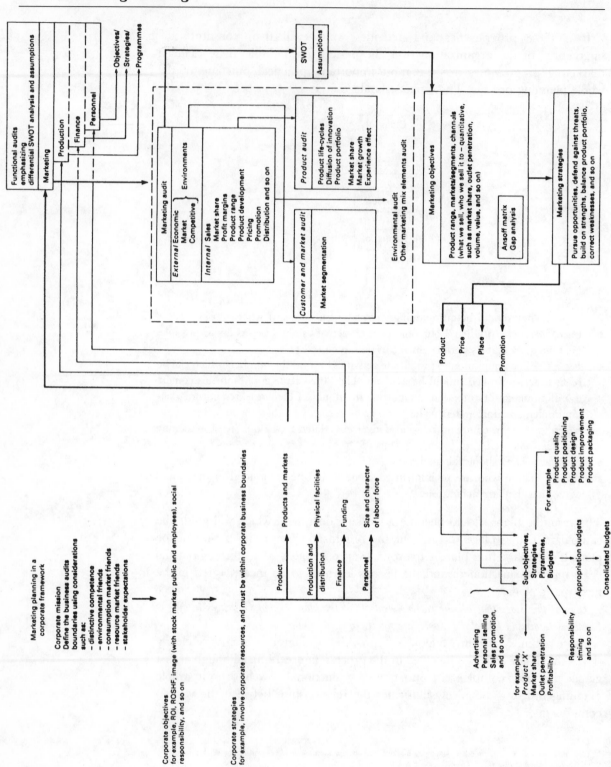

Figure 14.5 Marketing planning processes.

Marketing Plan Structure

The marketing plan itself should, of course, be formalized as a written document; although, in practice, too few companies take this stage seriously enough. The shape that this document takes will depend upon the *exact* requirements of the business, but it might contain the following sections:

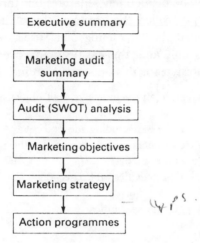

- *Executive summary.* A short summary of the proposed plan, partly to provide the perspective for the rest and partly as a quick reference.
- *Marketing audit summary.* A *brief* summary of the very detailed marketing audit which will have taken place. If it is necessary for management to understand the complexities of the information uncovered in the audit, this should be accomplished in a previous, separate, document.
- *Audit (SWOT) analysis.* Again this must be *brief*, and should concentrate on the few critical *issues* which are addressed by the strategies and plans which come later in the document.
- *Marketing objectives* – in as much detail as is needed.
- *Marketing strategy* – again in as much detail as is necessary to convey this most important element of the plan.
- *Action programmes.* The plans themselves, stating 'what will be done', 'who will do it', 'when it will be done' and 'how much it will cost'.

Malcolm McDonald[47] suggests a rather more specific layout, with rather more emphasis on the analytical elements, which the simple approach recommended above assumes will already have been largely covered by preceding documents:

1 Mission statement
2 Summary of performance (to date, including reasons for good or bad performance)
3 Summary of financial projections (for three years)

[47] McDonald, *Marketing Plans.*

4 Market overview
5 SWOT analyses of major projects/markets
6 Portfolio summary (a summary of SWOTs)
7 Assumptions
8 Setting objectives
9 Financial projections for three years (in detail)

More importantly, he deliberately separates this three-year strategic marketing plan (sometimes just called the 'strategy') from the one-year operating plan (often what is called the 'marketing plan' itself), which is derived from the strategic plan (but only after this has been approved).

His suggested format for this one-year plan includes:

1 Summary of strategic plan (including overall objectives – in numeric terms – and overall strategies)
2 Resulting annual strategies (including sub-objectives – relating to specific products/markets/segments/customers – and strategies – the means by which these will be achieved through actions/tactics)
3 Summary of marketing activities and costs
4 Contingency plans
5 Operating results and financial ratios
6 Key activity planner

It can be seen from this list that the short-term (one-year) plan should concentrate on very specific and quantifiable actions. Indeed, he provides a very useful set of 'forms' which can be filled in to create most of this plan.

Contingency plan

Perhaps Malcolm McDonald's[48] most interesting suggestion, and the one which is least often allowed for, is the 'contingency plan'. Few marketing plans ever are implemented exactly as intended: the marketing environment is a particularly uncertain one, so that it is essential to have full back-up plans to cover for the eventuality that some of the assumptions are proved incorrect. He suggests that the following questions are answered for each assumption, again in the form of a table:

Basis of Assumption

What event would have to happen to make this strategy unattractive?

Risk of such an event occurring (% or high/low etc.)

Impact if event occurs

---

[48] McDonald, *Marketing Plans*.

Trigger point for action

Actual contingency action proposed

SELF-TEST QUESTION 14.9

This is the culmination of all the practical work associated with this book. The instruction is also one of the shortest – *produce the marketing plan.*

(Marketing plans can be quite extensive. In general, however, the longer they are the less effective they will be. The best advice is, therefore, to keep yours as short as possible (preferably fewer than five typed pages of A4). The strength of any marketing plan lies in the strategies and plans it contains; the simpler the concepts that these embody the more likely they are to be carried out.)

Measurement of Progress

The final stage is to establish targets (or standards) against which progress can be monitored. Accordingly, it is important to put both quantities and time-scales into the marketing objectives (for example, to capture 20 per cent by value of the market within two years) and into the corresponding strategies.

As was stated in the section on forecasting, changes in the environment mean that the forecasts often have to be changed. Along with these, the related plans may well also need to be changed. Continuous monitoring of performance, against pre-determined targets, represents a most important aspect of this. However, perhaps even more important is the enforced discipline of a regular formal review. Again, as with forecasts, in many cases the best (most realistic) planning cycle will revolve around a quarterly review. Best of all, at least in terms of the quantifiable aspects of the plans, if not the wealth of backing detail, is probably a quarterly rolling review – planning one full year ahead each new quarter. Of course, this does absorb more planning resource; but it also ensures that the plans embody the latest information, and – with attention focused on them so regularly – forces both the plans and their implementation to be realistic.

Plans only have validity if they are actually used to control the progress of a company: their success lies in their implementation, not in the writing.

Performance analysis

The most important elements of marketing performance, which are normally tracked, are:

Sales analysis Most organizations track their sales results; or, in non-profit organizations for example, the number of clients. The more sophisticated track them in terms of *sales variance* – the deviation from the target figures – which allows a more immediate picture of deviations to become evident. 'Micro-analysis', which is a nicely pseudo-scientific term for the normal management process of investigating detailed problems, then investigates the individual elements (individual products, sales territories, customers and so on) which are failing to meet targets.

Market share analysis Relatively few organizations, however, track their market share. In some circumstances this may well be a much more important measure. Sales may still be increasing, in an expanding market, while share is actually decreasing – boding ill for future sales when the market eventually starts to drop. Where such market share is tracked, there may be a number of aspects which will be followed:

- overall market share
- segment share – that in the specific, targeted segment
- relative share – in relation to the market leaders

Expense analysis The key ratio to watch in this area is usually the 'marketing expense to sales ratio'; although this may be broken down into other elements (advertising to sales, sales administration to sales, and so on).

Financial analysis The 'bottom line' of marketing activities should, at least in theory, be the net profit (for all except non-profit organizations, where the comparable emphasis may be on remaining within budgeted costs). There are a number of separate performance figures and key ratios which need to be tracked:

- gross contribution
- gross profit
- net contribution

- net profit
- return on investment
- profit on sales

There can be considerable benefit in comparing these figures with those achieved by other organizations (especially those in the same industry); using, for instance, the figures which can be obtained (in the UK) from 'The Centre for Interfirm Comparison'. The most sophisticated use of this approach, however, is typically by those making use of PIMS (Profit Impact of Management Strategies), initiated by the General Electric Company and then developed by Harvard Business School, but now run by the Strategic Planning Institute. This covers nearly 3000 Strategic Business Units (SBUs) across North America and Europe.

The above performance analyses concentrate on the quantitative measures which are directly related to short-term performance. But there are a number of indirect measures, essentially tracking customer attitudes, which can also indicate the organization's performance in terms of its longer-term marketing strengths and may accordingly be even more important indicators. Some useful measures are:

- market research – including customer panels (which are used to track changes over time)
- lost business – the orders which were lost because, for example, the stock was not available or the product did not meet the customer's exact requirements
- customer complaints – how many customers complain about the products or services, or the organization itself, and about what

Use of Marketing Plans

As I have stressed, a formal, written marketing plan is essential; it provides an unambiguous reference point for activities throughout the planning period. However, perhaps the most important benefit of these plans is the planning process itself. This typically offers a unique opportunity, a forum, for 'information-rich' and productively focused discussions between the various managers involved. The plan, together with the associated discussions, then provides an agreed context for their subsequent management activities, even for those not described in the plan itself. The length of this whole process is shown by Malcolm McDonald (figure 14.6).

Henry Minzberg[49] makes the pient from the opposite direction: 'Strategy making is a process interwoven with all it takes to manage an organization. Systems do not think, and when they are used for more than facilitation of human thinking, they can prevent thinking.'

[49] H. Minzberg, The fall and rise of strategic planning, *Harvard Business Review* (January–February 1994).

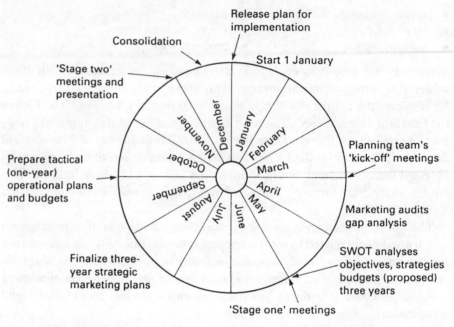

Figure 14.6 Strategic and operational planning cycle

SELF-TEST QUESTION 15.10

What procedures does your organization employ to ensure that its own marketing plan is put into practice? How effective are these procedures?

Budgets as Managerial Tools

The classic quantification of a marketing plan appears in the form of budgets. Because these are so rigorously quantified, they are particularly important. They should, thus, represent an unequivocal projection of actions and expected results. What is more, they should be capable of being monitored accurately; and, indeed, performance against budget is the main (regular) management review process.

The purpose of a marketing budget is, thus, to pull together all the revenues and costs involved in marketing into one comprehensive document. It is a managerial tool that balances what is needed to be spent against what can be afforded, and helps make choices about priorities. It is then used in monitoring performance in practice.

The marketing budget is usually the most powerful tool by which you think through the relationship between desired results and available means. Its starting point should be the marketing strategies and plans, which have already been formulated in the marketing plan itself; although, in practice, the two will run in parallel and will interact. At the very least, the rigorous, highly quantified budgets may cause a rethink of some of the more optimistic elements of the plans.

Approaches to budgeting

As we saw in the earlier section on setting promotional budgets, many budgets are based on history. They are the equivalent of 'time-series' forecasting. It is assumed that next year's budgets should follow some trend that is discernible over recent history. Other alternatives are based on a simple 'percentage of sales' or on 'what the competitors are doing'.

However, there are many other alternatives:

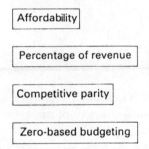

Affordability   This may be the most common approach to budgeting. Someone, typically the managing director on behalf of the board, decides what is a 'reasonable' promotional budget; what can be afforded.

This figure is most often based on historical spending. This approach assumes that promotion is a cost; and sometimes it is seen as an avoidable cost.

Percentage of revenue   This is a variation of 'affordable', but at least it forges a link with sales volume, in that the budget will be set at a certain percentage of revenue, and thus follows trends in sales. However, it does imply that promotion is a result of sales, rather than the other way round.

Both of these methods are seen by many managements to be 'realistic', in that they reflect the reality of the business strategies as those managements see it. On the other hand, neither makes any allowance for change. They do not allow for the development to meet emerging market opportunities and, at the other end of the scale, they continue to pour money into a dying product or service (the 'dog').

Competitive parity   In this case, the organization relates its budgets to what the competitors are doing: for example, it matches their budgets, or beats them, or spends a proportion of what the brand leader is spending. On the other hand, it assumes that the competitors know best; in which case, the service or product can expect to be nothing more than a follower.

Zero-based budgeting   In essence, this approach takes the objectives, as set out in the marketing plan, together with the resulting planned activities, and then costs them out.

SELF-TEST QUESTION 14.11

How does your organization translate its marketing plan into budgets? How effective is this process?

Conclusion

At the end of a lengthy book it is difficult to provide a concise summary. Indeed, it is arguable that the practical strength of marketing comes from its wealth of detailed techniques for handling specific situations.

The one requirement is for the focus to be on the *customer*, and even that rule is, at least in part, broken by conviction marketing. The simplest, but accordingly most powerful, model is that set out below:

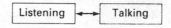

the emphasis very much on listening and on undertaking *marketing research*. A comprehensive knowledge, and understanding, of the *customer – attitudes as well as actions –* is generally at the heart of good marketing.

Defining the *total product or service offering* is the all-important decision, since almost all other decisions will be derived from it. Thus, the techniques, such as *segmentation* and – in particular – *positioning* will probably be the most important for most organizations. On the other hand, the more mechanistic models, such as the product life-cycle and Boston Matrix, may be less widely applicable (and sometimes even misleading).

In the longer term, changes in the wider external environment will probably be critical to the organization's future, and *environmental analysis* may be a skill that needs to be acquired. In the medium term the *competitive strategy* will probably need to be developed.

The delivery systems, for goods (distribution) and messages (promotion), will be very dependent upon the exact nature of the organization's activities; but, again, in-depth knowledge of the exact systems employed will be essential. *Salesforce activities* may well be more relevant to most organizations than those relating to *advertising* (and certainly than sales promotion); but, on the other hand, the *inner market*, and quality in general, are important in almost all sectors.

SELF-TEST QUESTION 14.12

Turn back to your entry for Audit 1.1.

Have you achieved the objectives you set for yourself? If not, what do you need to do to rectify this shortfall?

Has the book helped you to achieve these objectives?

In any case, what more do you need to undertake to continue, and expand, your management education?

The end of one phase of education should always prepare the way for the start of another.

However, above all, it is the ability to continue effectively to meet the *customer's needs* which determines the future of an organization. *As long as you are prepared to talk with your customers, and listen to what they have to say – and want to understand what they are really saying – you cannot fail to be a good marketer.*

FURTHER READING

In terms of overall corporate strategy, a wide range of books have been written, from as many different perspectives; and you may find that one of these most closely addresses your organization's specific problems. For an overall view, however, I find that *Exploring Corporate Strategy*, by Gerry Johnson and Kevan Scholes (3rd edn, Prentice-Hall, 1993), is one of the clearest and easiest to read. *Strategic Management: a Methodological Approach*, 3rd edition, by Alan J. Rowe, Richard O. Mason, Karl E. Dickel and Neil H. Snyder (Addison-Wesley, 1989), also gives a very good insight into the processes involved (particularly those revolving around the work of the Boston Consulting Group). H. Igor Ansoff's *Implementing Strategic Management* (Prentice-Hall, 1984) gives a stimulating (albeit rather academic) overview, whilst the papers in *The Strategy Process*, edited by Henry Minzberg and James Brian Quinn (Prentice Hall, 1991), review some of the more recent developments.

As you might expect, from the number of references to it, to cover the processes of marketing planning I would recommend Malcolm McDonald's book, *Marketing Plans*, 3rd edition (Butterworth-Heinemann, 1994). This is both sensible and readable; it offers a very practical approach (and even provides 'standard forms' for many of the activities).

SUMMARY

In general, the use of plans conveys a number of advantages:

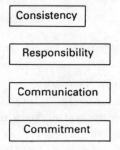

The *corporate plan* should contain three main components:

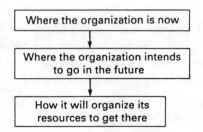

Corporate objectives, which are usually more complex than just financial targets, should reflect the *corporate mission* (including customer groups, customer needs, and technologies), which may reflect a strong corporate vision.

The starting point of the marketing planning process is the marketing audit; the output of which may be one or more facts books, covering a wide range of questions about internal ('product'-related) and external ('environmental', as well as market) factors, and the marketing system itself, as well as the following basic questions:

- Who are the customers?
- What are their needs and wants?
- What do they think of the organization and its products or services?

A SWOT analysis may be used to collate the most important:

Strengths	Weaknesses
Opportunities	Threats

Whatever the form of analysis, the inherent *assumptions* must be spelled out.

This will lead to the production of *marketing objectives* and thence to *marketing strategies* (typically covering all elements of the 4 Ps).

A suggested structure for the marketing plan document itself might be:

All of these detailed plans should be, as far as possible:

- number-based (and 'deadlined')
- briefly described
- practical

These programmes must be controlled, particularly by the use of budgets, for which the overall figures may be derived (as we have seen in earlier chapters) by:

> Affordability

> Percentage of revenue

> Competitive parity

> Zero-based budgeting

REVISION QUESTIONS

1 What advantages accrue to the use of the plans in general? What would be contained in the corporate plan?
2 How may corporate objectives be derived from the corporate mission? What elements may they contain? Where does corporate vision fit in?
3 What may be contained in the marketing audit?
4 How may a SWOT analysis be carried out? How are assumptions dealt with?
5 What are the differences between marketing objectives and marketing strategies? What should marketing strategies cover?
6 What might the structure of a marketing plan look like? What rules might be applied to its content?

Index